T0244487

The Everything War

The Everything War

Amazon's Ruthless Quest to Own the World
and Remake Corporate Power

Dana Mattioli

LITTLE, BROWN AND COMPANY
New York Boston London

Little, Brown and Company
Hachette Book Group
1290 Avenue of the Americas, New York, NY 10104
littlebrown.com

First Edition: April 2024

Little, Brown and Company is a division of Hachette Book Group, Inc. The Little, Brown name and logo are trademarks of Hachette Book Group, Inc.

The publisher is not responsible for websites (or their content) that are not owned by the publisher.

The Hachette Speakers Bureau provides a wide range of authors for speaking events. To find out more, go to hachettespeakersbureau.com or email HachetteSpeakers@hbgusa.com.

Little, Brown and Company books may be purchased in bulk for business, educational, or promotional use. For information, please contact your local bookseller or the Hachette Book Group Special Markets Department at special.markets@hbgusa.com.

ISBN 9780316269773
Library of Congress Control Number: 2024931357

Printing 1, 2024

MRQ

Printed in Canada

For my son, Beckett Walker, and my mother,
Dianne Mattioli, the strongest person I know

Contents

Contents

Author's Note

THIS WORK IS NOT the product of access journalism. While I did a full fact check with Amazon public relations, sharing my reporting to solicit their comments, context, and corrections over the course of several months, the company set up only three interviews for this book. The company-approved interviews were with senior employees, but not members of Amazon's most senior team of executives, the S-Team. The conversations they set up were brief background phone interviews. Jeff Bezos declined requests for an interview, but provided feedback through Amazon representatives.

Despite Amazon's lack of cooperation, my effort to investigate the nature of the story was extensive: I spoke with more than 600 people, including current and former Amazon employees, and the company's competitors, including CEOs, sellers, small business owners, and others who have directly or indirectly been impacted by the company's reach. I interviewed government officials, on background and on the record, which helped shape the nature and scope of the story and the contemporary stakes the company now finds itself in, both in the US and abroad. The book also includes dozens of hours of interviews with seventeen current and former S-Team members at Amazon, all of them conducted without the company's knowledge, and interviews with five current and former board members. In addition to interviews, my sources provided me with hundreds of pages of internal documents, emails, six-pagers, business plans, and strategy memos, which are used throughout this book to underpin some of the reporting.

Parts of the book that are not cited or attributed are the results of certain source interviews, which mostly occurred on background because Amazon makes employees and partners sign binding nondisclosure agreements that can be legally enforced if they speak publicly on sensitive matters.

Given how many industries Amazon is in, and how extensive their power, I also wanted to focus on those who have been harmed by the company, and in so doing, spoke to numerous victims, whose stories and experiences have been essential to the work. I am grateful to all who spoke with me and allowed for their stories to be told.

In 2019 I became the *Wall Street Journal*'s Amazon reporter. It was a beat I sought out after six years of covering mergers and acquisitions at the paper. During that period, Amazon was repeatedly invoked by companies across industries as a source of fear, causing some of them to strike mergers to try to insulate themselves from Amazon's onslaught. While covering Amazon, I focused my coverage on Amazon's business practices, and some of this book builds off of that work. But over the course of my reporting, I realized the story is much more significant and deeper than any article can convey. This book is the result of my efforts to tell that larger story.

Prologue

The Paradox

IN JANUARY 2017, A twenty-seven-year-old law school student published an article in the *Yale Law Journal* about one of the world's most powerful corporations. It led off with a remarkable claim:

> Amazon is the titan of twenty-first century commerce. In addition to being a retailer, it is now a marketing platform, a delivery and logistics network, a payment service, a credit lender, an auction house, a major book publisher, a producer of television and films, a fashion designer, a hardware manufacturer, and a leading host of cloud server space. Although Amazon has clocked staggering growth, it generates meager profits, choosing to price below-cost and expand widely instead. Through this strategy, the company has positioned itself at the center of e-commerce and now serves as essential infrastructure for a host of other businesses that depend upon it. Elements of the firm's structure and conduct pose anticompetitive concerns — yet it has escaped antitrust scrutiny.

Dubbed "Amazon's Antitrust Paradox," the crux of author Lina Khan's argument was that the company had grown to such size and power that the e-commerce giant had "marched toward monopoly."

Like many tech upstarts, Amazon had grown rapidly, but the nature of its reach, and growth, was unparalleled.

Over nearly a quarter century, Amazon progressed from curiosity to dubious growth stock to one of the most celebrated companies in the world. But Khan's manifesto took direct aim at the prevailing sentiment. The nerdy wunderkind argued that either archaic antitrust laws needed to be rewritten, or companies like Amazon needed to be regulated like public utilities. The antitrust framework — first derived and formulated in America's Gilded Age and refined in the twentieth century — could not hope to match a company of the omnipresence, omniscience, and omnipotence of Amazon.

Law review articles are usually confined to a small reader base of academics, but Khan's paper did something unprecedented: it went viral. Politicians such as Massachusetts senator Elizabeth Warren devoured the ninety-six-page report and started looking at the e-commerce giant differently. Was it healthy that a third of all online shopping in the United States occurred on Amazon? Was Amazon abusing its power by running one of the world's biggest marketplaces of online sellers while also competing against those very same sellers? Did its tangled web of businesses spanning retail, cloud computing, advertising, streaming, logistics, and grocery — to name just a few — provide it with data that unfairly helped inform its business decisions?

———

Lina Khan did not stumble into studying Amazon accidentally; instead, she was offered an opportunity. In the spring of 2011, she sat for an interview with the head of the Open Markets Institute, a newly formed DC-based think tank whose work addressed the threats of corporate consolidation and modern-day monopoly power. Open Markets believed that monopolies, or companies using their market power to squash competition, had dangerous effects on democracy and led to lower wages, stifled innovation, and fewer jobs being created. It sought to bring attention to these issues in order to spark a broader anti-monopoly movement.

Khan had recently graduated from Williams College, where she had been the editor of the student newspaper. She had no prior training and hadn't even studied the issues the institute was investigating.

To Open Markets founder Barry Lynn, this was a plus. He didn't mind that she didn't know the issues; he could teach her. But she had something he did like: she could write, and she was intelligent. Her journalism background was a benefit, since the job entailed researching issues around monopolies' power and publishing them in mainstream magazines and newspapers for a mass audience. He offered her the job as employee number 1. Khan's job was to use her journalistic skills to research and analyze topics of corporate power in ways that were digestible to average readers. Lynn wanted her articles to expose the dangers of monopolization.

Her first assignment was to calculate Amazon's impact on the book publishing industry.

"We're going to learn everything we can about the history of the book business, how it's been regulated the last fifty years, and everything about Amazon's business model," Lynn told Khan. He handed her a copy of the 2000 book *The Business of Books: How the International Conglomerates Took Over Publishing and Changed the Way We Read*, by the former editor in chief of Pantheon Books. Thus began Khan's education in antitrust.

She consumed everything she could find: legal documents, antitrust cases, books about publishing. Two months later she delivered an eighty-page paper to her boss that laid out Amazon's business practices in its bookselling business and the history of bookselling in the US dating back to the 1950s.

As Khan educated herself about antitrust policy, she learned that changes in the interpretation of these laws in the late 1970s drastically impacted how the laws were enforced. A movement known as the Chicago school, which espoused less government intervention and had more of a focus on efficiency, built momentum during this period. Robert Bork, one of its acolytes, encapsulated the movement in his 1978 book, titled *The Antitrust Paradox: A Policy at War with Itself*, which made the claim that the way antitrust laws were being enforced was inhibiting competition, not promoting it.

"The only goal that should guide the interpretation of the antitrust laws is the welfare of consumers," he argued. Bork's book was a watershed moment in antitrust circles. The courts started adopting his views, leading to massive changes in the way antitrust would be enforced in the decades to come.

As a result of those changes, big wasn't necessarily bad, and the way companies compete was judged less on their effects on competitors than on their effects on efficiency and prices for customers. Open Markets focused on showing the repercussions of lax antitrust enforcement, highlighting real-world examples and victims of companies consolidating power.

Over the next three years, Khan did monthlong dives into industry after industry, from airlines to metals to chicken farming in order to understand how they were structured and the mass consolidation in corporate America. She published her findings in articles for *Washington Monthly*, *CNN*, and other publications. These articles circled themes she concentrated on: deregulation, consolidation, and a laissez-faire approach to antitrust, and how they generated real harm for average people while enriching the conglomerate class.

While at the think tank, she had read extensively about the business practices of Standard Oil, the Gilded Age monopoly run by oil titan John D. Rockefeller, who was one of the richest Americans to ever live.

Standard Oil was formed in 1870 as an oil refiner and grew during the height of the late nineteenth century when robber barons were feverishly establishing trusts and consolidating power in industries as vast as railroads and sugar. By the late 1880s, Standard Oil controlled 90 percent of America's refining capacity.

In 1890, Congress passed the Sherman Antitrust Act to outlaw monopolistic business practices during a time when the public had grown wary about the power these trusts wielded.

The oil conglomerate was broken up by the Supreme Court in 1911, who ruled that it violated the Sherman Antitrust Act. Rockefeller was accused of bullying competitors into letting Standard Oil acquire them, using predatory pricing, and inking deals with railroad companies to receive lower rates that would make it impossible for his rivals to compete, further cementing Standard Oil's dominance. He was also accused of spying on his competitors.

The more she read about Standard Oil, the more Khan came to believe that there were important similarities between Amazon founder Jeff Bezos and Rockefeller. Amazon's business practices and Standard Oil's had uncanny likenesses, she found. Predatory pricing was one of the focuses of the Standard Oil case, and like the oil titan, Amazon had also been known to price certain goods below cost, bringing competitors to their knees. Amazon's power in so many vertices meant that its rivals often were also its customers, giving the company significant leverage.

Then there was the spying: Standard Oil received detailed reports from the railroads and steamship lines containing information on oil shipped by its competitors. The reports detailed the quantity of oil and kind, names and addresses of the recipients, among other details. Its bribing of rail officials and employees at rival firms for information about shipments, as well as its own ability to spy on competitors, provided the oil giant with powerful intel on the state of the oil industry, allowing it to intervene to steal business and make threats that handicapped rivals.

Once it got these reports, the giant sprang into action. When learning that a rival's order was shipping to a customer, Standard Oil would dispatch its employees to the customer and demand that they turn down the shipment. If they refused, Standard Oil's employees would threaten to discontinue selling its own oil to the merchant or enter a price war that could put them out of business.

Amazon, too, had unparalleled access to data—which was built into how it operated and grew its business. Sellers had accused the company of using their data on Amazon.com to copy their items to better compete with them.

But while Standard Oil was deemed a monopoly, it seemed strange to Khan that more people weren't questioning Amazon's dominance.

Three years after the Standard Oil ruling, the Federal Trade Commission was formed to eliminate unfair competition. More than 100 years later, the antitrust laws were the same, but the change in the interpretation since the 1980s of the vaguely worded laws meant that competitive behavior was viewed through the lens of whether it kept prices low for consumers. By that definition, Amazon was able to grow unscrutinized. Khan argued that the Borkian perversion of antitrust had created its own paradox where antimonopoly laws were not only not stopping monopolies, but actually encouraged people to view them as good for society.

When Khan began noticing the similarities between Standard Oil and Amazon in 2014, Amazon sported a market value around $140 billion. By comparison, that was more than twice the market value for Ford Motor Company. That same year, however, Amazon lost $241 million. More eye-popping was the value Wall Street assigned to the company's meager earnings. Its stock price was disconnected from reality, trading at a 372 forward price-to-earnings ratio when peers such as Walmart and Apple traded at 16 and 14, respectively. Investors had a wholesale disregard for the normal financial metrics used when assigning a company value and made allowances for the Seattle company, which was generally uncommon on Wall Street.

Harvard Business Review ranked Bezos as the best-performing CEO in the world by shareholder returns in 2014. The publication said he'd provided a 15,189 percent total shareholder return for investors since the company's IPO, creating more than $140 billion in market value. From the time of the company's 1997 IPO to 2014, Amazon had only posted just shy of $2 billion in cumulative earnings as profit.

Despite its losses, the valuation paradox lingered, and as Khan dug deeper, she learned that Amazon controlled much of modern e-commerce, which offered clues as to how a meagerly profitable company could be so valuable for analysts. To say it dominated modern e-commerce is beyond dispute. First, Amazon's website is the most powerful platform for online sellers to reach customers, and that includes nearly everything from socks to computers to furniture to drill bits. It is, as journalist Brad Stone called it, "the everything store." Nearly everyone, from book publishers to clothing companies, generate a great deal of business by having their products available on the company's website. Further, it has played a pioneering role in creating the technological infrastructure that underpins millions of companies and government agencies. Its Amazon Web Services (AWS) business is one of its most successful divisions. It also had become one of the country's largest logistics operations — meaning, it had figured out how to efficiently ship, warehouse, and move goods at an unprecedented rate. For customers, this is one aspect that makes Amazon so popular: its ability to deliver a product within days of purchasing. But as Khan began to find, Amazon's dominance, the true nature and scale of it, was singular: in simple terms, the company had positioned itself to be a modern-day utility of sorts, one that no one could ignore. For many consumers, it was one they could not live without.

In phone calls with hedge fund managers, Khan learned that financiers were valuing Amazon's stock as if it was an unstoppable monopoly that would dominate every sector it entered. They were happy to overlook unprofitable and meagerly profitable quarters in pursuit of the company stealing more and more market share. The behavior defied the common laws of finance. Investors traditionally celebrated companies with solid profits. Amazon's stock, however, continued its rise. It was being treated differently.

When speaking to third-party sellers, Khan discovered something troubling. These sellers were a major reason why Amazon was operating at such a massive scale. But Amazon was also selling goods on its website that it made itself, which were competing with the very businesses it had on its platform. Third-party sellers also described being beholden to Amazon. They often felt mistreated by the company, which had squeezed their margins and locked them into costly services. But they were in a catch-22: they felt they had no choice but to sell on the platform because so much of online US commerce occurs on the site. Their bottom lines relied on Amazon, and they could do very little to combat it.

Khan entered law school with six months of recordings, interviews, and notes on Amazon's behavior. During her time at Yale, she drafted her paper. In January 2017, the law review published the incendiary paper attacking prevailing views of antitrust. She argued that Amazon had amassed too much power and that current antitrust laws were unequipped to restrain it.

It had a call to action: the antitrust laws needed to be restored to their original interpretation to better regulate Amazon and companies like it, or companies like Amazon had to be regulated more like utilities. "It is as if Bezos charted the company's growth by first drawing a map of antitrust laws, and then devising routes to smoothly bypass them. With its missionary zeal for consumers, Amazon has marched toward monopoly by singing the tune of contemporary antitrust," she wrote.

Once the paper went viral, Khan's life, in a matter of years, changed dramatically. In 2021, at just thirty-two years old, she became the youngest FTC chair in the institution's history. She was included in "40 Under 40" lists and made *Time* magazine's Time100 Next, which profiled "emerging leaders who are shaping the future," alongside the singer Dua Lipa and the actress Florence Pugh. The *New York Times* wrote a glowing profile of this wunderkind who was taking on the antitrust establishment.

With her ideas spreading like wildfire, she would become one of the leading faces of the modern antitrust movement. But the most important thing was she spotted something in Amazon — and Amazon specifically — that few had seen. On September 26, 2023, as chair of the FTC, Khan's agency sued Amazon for maintaining an illegal monopoly.

But the truth is, none of this was by accident. Bezos, and Amazon, did not appear out of thin air or accidentally stumble into dominance. From the beginning, Bezos saw things and had a rapacious hunger to win. He had created a company and a culture in his own image and programmed it to succeed at all costs. Under the battle cry of "customer obsession" — the company's guiding principle — there was a Machiavellian pursuit of growth. It meant using Amazon's size, leverage, and access to data across industries to choke competition, big and small.

But in order to understand how we arrived at this moment, we must begin earlier, to see how Bezos's killer instinct took shape and how Amazon developed a pattern of behavior that would become inseparable from his way of doing business. This book unveils a side of Amazon, and its leader, that has never been told before: its ruthless quest, by any means necessary, to tactically — and strategically — take control of not just a single industry, but as many as it could corner. As its tentacles spread into ever more industries, Amazon synthesized its power, giving it the type of leverage rarely achieved by modern corporations and leaving a trail of its rivals' corpses in its wake. Bezos and Amazon were fundamentally driven by a competitive edge that would stop at nothing—if it could own the world, and be in your home, and be everywhere, it would. The only way to understand it is to see it, and, in doing so, understand just how perfect a lens Amazon is into what befell the American economy and its business climate from the 1990s to the present.

PART I

Building the Juggernaut

CHAPTER 1

What Main Street Didn't See Coming

THE YEAR WAS 1994. Ace of Base's single "The Sign" was at the top of the charts and *Home Improvement* was the number one show in the ratings. Every weekend, families across America descended upon their local malls, the one-stop shop for birthday presents at KB Toys, a gift bag to go with it at the Hallmark store, and a book for the class reading assignment from Waldenbooks, one of the country's largest bookstore chains. Teenagers congregated at the mall, too, for different reasons. Aside from spending their babysitting money on earrings from Claire's and posters from Spencer Gifts, it was a key backdrop for their social life, so much so that they earned the nickname "mall rats."

The first indoor mall in the United States opened in 1956. The creation of an interstate highway system allowed Americans to move farther away from city centers and to the suburbs. Retail followed them, with developers setting up large, indoor malls with dozens of stores to cater to the burgeoning population.

Anthony Cafaro Jr., the co-president of Cafaro Company, is from a family that helped pioneer the proliferation of malls throughout the country. His grandfather started Cafaro Company in 1949, creating strip malls and shopping centers in the downtown areas of a number of

Midwestern cities. The strip centers had a formula. Cafaro would build a store for a grocer and then add spaces for a pharmacy, a shoe store, and a dry cleaner. The spaces would be rented. As the American middle class moved to the suburbs, Cafaro broke ground on its malls.

The malls also had a formula. They provided one-stop shopping, parking, and restaurants, and were anchored by large department stores such as Sears and JCPenney. The department stores leased 100,000-square-foot spaces in the mall under market value. Department stores attracted so many shoppers, who would spend their money at the food court and smaller stores in the rest of the mall, that the developers gave them a major break on their rents. Anthony Cafaro Jr. was the third generation of the family in the mall business. At twelve years old, he began working summers for the company, painting yellow parking spaces in the lots and maintaining the fountains at the center of the mall. He fondly recalls the days of the malls being a community meeting center, where babies took their first photos with Santa and moms brought their children for back-to-school shopping.

The 1980s and 1990s were the glory days for this corner of retail. Cafaro recalls that whenever they'd open a new mall, retailers would compete to be accepted as tenants. "We would have retailers basically bidding to get into a mall space. It wasn't difficult to lease these stores; people lined up," he said.

At the time there was such a frenzy to open malls that the developers were in a bitter race against each other to plant their flags. Because a suburb could typically only support one big mall, Cafaro recalls his grandfather telling him stories of developers breaking ground on their lots without even first lining up anchor tenants just to prevent another developer from entering the market. "They would start digging to claim their territory," he says. Between 1970 and 2000, the number of malls in America grew from 276 to 1,017, according to the International Council of Shopping Centers.

The malls had a symbiotic relationship with the towns they occupied. They were a big employer, with their tenants hiring clerks and shopkeepers and vendors. They also generated sales taxes that funded public schools, roads, and other infrastructure projects.

In 1994, not only were the malls thriving, but so was much of retail. Main Street was full of local toy stores, boutiques, and specialty shops that neighbors popped into for daily needs. A whole host of big box stores filled strip malls in suburbia in those years: Circuit City, Borders, Toys "R" Us, and Linens 'n Things — all now defunct or bankrupt — had giant footprints.

And the number of stores sprawling across America was as eye-popping as the size of the stores themselves. It was the age of the super-store. In the late 1980s and through the 1990s, retail chains shifted to this format, opening up giant boxes exceeding 40,000 square feet to offer unlimited selection. The name of the game was expansion, with the nation's top retailers announcing newer, bigger stores seemingly every week in order to get closer to where their customers lived and bolster their sales.

"Every time something would open up, like a Bed Bath & Beyond, a Linens 'n Things would follow," recalls Peter Schaeffer, a retail analyst in the 1990s. "Almost for every business, there was a duplicate of it to compete with, which was great for consumers."

"In the 1990s we were like a rocket," says Mickey Drexler, a retail legend nicknamed the "merchant prince" for his ability to spot trends and understand his customer. During the 1990s Drexler was CEO of Gap Inc., and in 1994 he launched the company's Old Navy concept to rave reviews. Old Navy catered to a more price-conscious crowd and allowed parent company Gap to capture more sales from new customers. He later became the CEO of J.Crew. During the 1990s, Gap, like everyone else, was focused on expansion.

Wall Street rewarded the growth of retail companies. "In the 1980s and 1990s, the stocks were flying," recalls Richard Baum, a Goldman Sachs retail analyst during the period. "There was still a lot of growth left."

The act of shopping in person created a community in local towns. Main Street store owners knew their regular customers by name; they sponsored local Little League teams and holiday events and employed members of their communities. Healthy traffic and revenue to these stores buttressed local real estate developers and landlords. The money recirculated within the towns and cities through the local merchants, and they also generated sales taxes for local projects and school systems. The relationship was symbiotic.

Kathy McCauslin-Cadieux's story was a common one. She opened the doors to her first boutique in Strasburg, Pennsylvania, in 1989. She paid $500 a month in rent for a historic building in the heart of town that was a fixer-upper. She and her husband at the time patched the roof and cleaned out the cobwebs, and she merchandised it with women's clothing and accessories. Creative Elegance, as she named it, became a fixture in the suburban town.

Each day, McCauslin-Cadieux greeted her customers with the same welcome: "How can I spoil you?" she would shout, often running across the boutique to hug her loyal shoppers. McCauslin-Cadieux delighted in helping her "ladies," as she called them, pick out designer blazers, dresses, and accessories. "I knew their closets better than they did," she says. "I loved making the women who came in feel beautiful."

McCauslin-Cadieux's Creative Elegance boutique took off, allowing her to open two more locations in Pennsylvania. Her success enabled her to employ two dozen women, and the store grossed more than $1.5 million in sales.

Between her loyal following and foot traffic from the bustling downtown, she was able to exceed her financial goals.

These were simpler times. Customers didn't carry cell phones everywhere they went. Fewer than 23 percent of Americans owned computers in 1993. Most didn't readily access the internet or understand the potential for what it would soon disrupt. The notion that a computer could stop customers from shopping at their local JCPenney or displace the experience of a wide-eyed child running through the doors of a Toys "R" Us was more fantasy than possibility during these days.

Little did McCauslin-Cadieux know in 1994 that a former hedge fund employee in Seattle was planning to use computers to gun for her business—and all of Main Street.

———

That summer, a thirty-year-old Jeff Bezos and his wife, MacKenzie, left their cushy jobs on Wall Street and gambled it on a risky idea: the internet, they believed, offered an undeniable opportunity. They wanted to figure out how to commercialize it.

Both of them had been employed at D. E. Shaw, a quantitative hedge fund known for revolutionizing trading by using computer-generated models to make investment decisions. Bezos had been in his fourth year at the hedge fund when his boss, legendary investor David Shaw, tasked his rising star to research the opportunities of a nascent technology: the internet. The internet had been limited to a small group of scientists, academics, and an always-prescient David Shaw, who used the technology at his hedge fund, where many of his employees were not cut of traditional hedge fund cloth but were computer scientists. Bezos, too, fit the mold. He had majored in computer science and electrical engineering at Princeton University and before joining Shaw had worked at a telecommunications startup and Bankers Trust.

Shaw was bullish on the internet's potential beyond the small circles it had been used in. He had applied algorithms to trading to outperform the broader stock market, helping to pioneer the use of computing power for such uses. But there were certainly more opportunities.

Internet usage had begun to expand beyond the early adopters of computer scientists and academics like Shaw and was on the brink of adoption by ordinary people. There was a major opportunity as it became more mainstream, he told Bezos and other D. E. Shaw employees.

The hedge fund embarked on a fact-finding mission to research ways the internet could disrupt ordinary tasks. Shaw gave Bezos the assignment to explore selling things on the internet. He tasked colleague David Siegel with researching the financial services use cases of the web and told Charles Ardai, another employee, to look into other areas where this new technology could be applied.

If any of the areas had legs, the idea was for D. E. Shaw to be at the forefront of commercializing them.

Shaw was especially keen on the potential of being a first mover on e-commerce. In talks with his staff, Shaw described a hypothetical scenario of customers using the internet to buy a garden hose, having it delivered to their homes, and then leaving feedback on the product for other shoppers. It was the first spitballing session regarding what would later become online product reviews, employees at the time recall.

For months, Bezos researched the project. The projections for internet usage growth were staggering. The more Bezos looked into the possibilities, the more excited he got.

In researching the possibility of online commerce for Shaw, Bezos came across extraordinary statistics about the growth in the number of bytes being transmitted over the web. "Anything growing that fast, even if its baseline usage was tiny, it's going to be big. I looked at that, and I was like, 'I should come up with a business idea on the internet and let the internet grow around this,'" he later told private-equity executive David Rubenstein in an interview. He decided that he'd be the one to commercialize it.

Bezos studied reams of mail-order catalogs to understand what sorts of items the companies stocked and shipped to customers. Books seemed like an opening. There were too many titles to fit into a single catalog, and they were small enough to ship inexpensively. Of the twenty products he had been researching, books presented the best initial opportunity.

He and MacKenzie decided to give it a go. But first, Bezos broke the news to Shaw.

"Jeff, this is a really good idea. I think you're onto a good idea here, but this would be a better idea for somebody who didn't already have a good job," Shaw told Bezos during a two-hour walk in New York's Central Park.

Shaw tried to dissuade him. He also told Bezos that D. E. Shaw could enter the space as a competitor. The idea, after all, had originally been Shaw's, and the research Bezos had done was on Shaw's dime.

"The idea was always that someone would be allowed to make a profit as an intermediary. The key question is, who will get to be that middleman?" Shaw said in an interview with the *New York Times*. He intended for his company to be that middleman.

In the summer of 1994, Bezos left his job at D. E. Shaw and ventured off on his own.

Shaw was generous about Bezos leaving to found what would become Amazon. "Nobody knew quite how generous he was at the time," says a former employee who worked at D. E. Shaw during Bezos's tenure. Shaw's instincts in each space materialized. The other two ideas Shaw seeded turned out to be successes, but in those cases, D. E. Shaw benefited from the upside. The project Ardai worked on became the email service Juno, which went public and later merged with NetZero. Shaw sold Siegel's project, an online brokerage technology unit, to Merrill Lynch. Shaw was shrewd and his instincts were good. Though he wouldn't know it at the time, letting Bezos walk away would change the course of American business.

After resigning, the newlyweds left their cushy life in Manhattan. They packed up their Upper West Side apartment, abandoned a combined salary approaching $1 million a year (mostly Jeff's salary), and bet it all on an idea that that was far from a sure thing. Bezos self-funded the early days, helped by an initial $100,000 investment from his parents' life savings (later bumped up to $245,000). He warned them there was a 70 percent chance they'd lose their investment. It was all risk, and there was no guarantee it would work.

After flying to Texas to pick up an old Chevy Blazer, they drove west without a specific destination in mind. While MacKenzie drove, Bezos typed the first version of his thirty-page business plan on his laptop and narrowed the location of their new home down to Portland, Oregon, or Seattle, Washington.

Bezos was shrewd from the start. His Wall Street mind was in motion. In addition to finding a city with hiring potential to staff the startup, the financial whiz kid also wanted to leverage the system. In the cutthroat world of hedge funds, employees are always looking for what they refer to as "arbitrage strategies," and Bezos was no different. His new company would have a spate of advantages over physical retailers, one of the most important being its tax treatment. Washington state had a small enough population, and because of the way tax laws were enforced at the time, his new company could ship books to customers across the rest of the country tax-free, with only customers where the company was physically located paying sales tax. It also had an ample supply of techies working at Microsoft and was located near a major book distributor. They headed toward Seattle.

Given what the retail and Main Street environment looked like at the time, the odds were stacked against Bezos and his startup. What's more, the internet represented something of an Oregon Trail for stalwart pioneers smart enough to navigate it and, more importantly, monetize it.

In 1994, only 3 percent of Americans had ever signed onto the World Wide Web, yet Bezos was creating an entire business predicated on the belief that they would come in droves.

The majority of Americans didn't own computers. The ones that did had a steep learning curve and dial-up modems. They sure as hell didn't trust them enough to type their credit card numbers into the abyss to buy goods they could easily get at the mall. Most average Americans were confused by the nomenclature of the new technology. Newspapers spoke of the "information superhighway" or "I-Way" and defined the internet as a "global computer network." While adoption was rapidly expanding, Americans were still grappling with a very steep learning curve.

A *Wall Street Journal* profile of Bezos in 1996 describes e-commerce as "one of the iffiest business propositions of modern times: retailing on the Internet."

But that wouldn't intimidate Bezos. Since childhood, he had been a consummate inventor and tinkerer. Problem solving came innately to him, and he achieved much of what he set his mind to despite humble beginnings.

He was born to Jacklyn Gise, a seventeen-year-old high school student in Albuquerque, New Mexico, and nineteen-year-old Ted Jorgensen. While his biological father was not around to raise him, Bezos's maternal grandfather's influence on him was indelible, helping to shape who Bezos would become. His mother later married a Cuban immigrant with a Horatio Alger–like success story who adopted Jeff as his son and whose last name Jeff would come to adopt.

Bezos learned by doing. He was schooled in the Montessori method and exhibited precociousness from his earliest days. Into his adolescence, Bezos kept inventing. He made an automatic gate closer out of cement-filled tires. He built a device made of baking pans to trap his siblings. These proclivities started early. As a toddler, he even used a screwdriver to dismantle his crib, his mother later told an audience, saying it reinforced her notion that he was wired differently.

He approached his studies with the same tenacity he did his inventing, graduating valedictorian from Miami Palmetto Senior High School in Florida. At Princeton University he graduated summa cum laude from the school's honors program.

Problem solving and self-reliance always stuck with Bezos. As the thirty-year-old settled into his modest ranch-style home and began to map out the start of his new company, figuring out how to get customers to shop online in 1994 seemed like one of the biggest, juiciest problems to solve.

———

Bezos started in the stereotypical fashion of many technology entrepreneurs. He began working out of his garage, in his case in the city of Bellevue, just a short drive from Seattle, and hired employees to staff his online bookselling business.

He initially called the company Cadabra, short for the magic word "abracadabra," in order to convey the mystique of making a book appear on someone's doorstep after ordering it on the internet. But "Cadabra" sounded too similar to "cadaver," so in early 1995, Bezos incorporated the company under the name Amazon. He was drawn to Amazon because it was one of the world's largest rivers and conveyed size. An added bonus: being at the beginning of the alphabet ensured it would be near the front of directories.

The business was anything but a guaranteed success. Nick Hanauer, a Seattleite who worked for his family's pillow and duvet manufacturing business, met Bezos earlier in Jeff's days at D. E. Shaw when Bezos was dating Anne Dinning, a D. E. Shaw employee who was old friends with Hanauer. (Dinning would go on to join D. E. Shaw's executive committee and is currently one of Wall Street's highest-ranking women.) Hanauer and Bezos stayed in touch even after Dinning and Bezos broke up, bonding over the opportunities the nascent internet could present. "He and I both, for different reasons, had an incredibly early interest in e-commerce," recalls Hanauer.

Hanauer begged to invest in Amazon and became one of the first investors, handing over $45,000. "It was literally every dollar of free cash I had," recalls Hanauer. His enthusiasm to invest in Amazon and his understanding of Bezos's vision for Amazon's business model was not the norm.

In meetings with other potential investors, the most common question Bezos fielded was "What's the internet?" Hanauer's own father and brother passed on investing in Amazon during its initial round. "My dad said, 'Why would I ever go to an online bookstore when I enjoy going to physical bookstores so much? I get so much pleasure out of that. Why would anyone ever want to shop online because it's fun to go shopping?'" Hanauer remembers.

Tom Alberg, a Seattle-based technology executive who cofounded venture capital firm Madrona Venture Group, was one of Bezos's first meetings. He was impressed by Bezos and his business plan, but needed some time to think about whether he wanted to invest. In August 1995, he told Bezos that he would invest only when the entrepreneur had secured the rest of the $1 million he was seeking. It took sixty meetings, most of them rejections, for Bezos to net his first $1 million in fundraising. Most angel investors committed just $50,000 each. (Just a few years later, the internet frenzy he was partly responsible for creating would result in entrepreneurs collecting $10-million checks with the ease of a phone call. Investors would throw more money at internet entrepreneurs than the entrepreneurs even knew what to do with.) In November, Bezos called Alberg to say he had $1 million in commitments, and Alberg forked over his $50,000 investment. Alberg would serve as an Amazon board member for two decades and become a close confidant of the CEO.

Charles Katz, a partner at Seattle law firm Perkins Coie LLP, met Bezos during his early days of working out of the garage. When he arrived, Bezos was sitting behind a desk made of a door laid on top of four pieces of wood — a scrappy and cheap alternative to buying a desk. Bezos needed a corporate lawyer, and he filled Katz in on his business plan. Katz was impressed by the young entrepreneur's energy and industrious nature. And even though his idea sounded far-fetched to the lawyer, Bezos seemed confident.

"I remember Jeff saying to me, 'You know this isn't about books,' " recalls Katz. Books were the easiest category to begin with, the entrepreneur explained to the lawyer, "But we are definitely going to move into other areas," he said.

CHAPTER 2

Growth over Profits

EACH MORNING, AMAZON'S EMPLOYEES filed into a dumpy Seattle office with stained carpets on the same block as a heroin needle exchange. Employees at the time describe working well into the evening and then leaving the office to find perpetrators bent over the back of a police car getting frisked.

The offices were so cramped that even the kitchen where workers warmed their lunches and made tea doubled as someone's office. Another employee worked out of a broom closet, and several employees set up their desks in hallways.

But the atmosphere and the seventy-hour workweeks were acceptable for many of Amazon's first employees, who made up a merry band of misfits who believed they were changing the world.

Shel Kaphan, Amazon's first employee, who would be responsible for creating the original technology behind Amazon.com, joined the company from Kaleida Labs, a joint venture between Apple and IBM. He didn't have a classic résumé—he graduated from college over the course of a decade, working at an MIT spinoff in between—but was by all accounts a brilliant engineer.

Kaphan started at Amazon when the company was still operating out of Bezos's garage, alongside a British programmer named Paul

Davis, who joined the company in 1994 after holding a job at the University of Washington.

Many of the early employees were from the Seattle area, and in the early 1990s the vibe was grunge, with the area having birthed acts like Nirvana and Pearl Jam. Flannels, ripped jeans, and body piercings were de rigueur.

Amazon's earliest employees had a bohemian sensibility. Some were hippies by nature with interests in music and the arts. Many had worked in academia. One had a background researching climate change. Another had a creative writing MFA. One had been a carpenter before being hired to a senior position running Amazon's warehouse. On nights they weren't working until all hours, many frequented the Crocodile, Seattle's famous rock nightclub where acts such as R.E.M. would play.

There was a common mission among many of the early employees to democratize reading. "People like myself were like, 'Oh, isn't the internet wonderful for education? This will be great for making any book available to anyone in the world.' A lot of us early Amazonians were not at all financially driven," recalls Jonathan Kochmer, one of Amazon's earliest employees. Though he conceded that Bezos "was absolutely certain it could be monetized tremendously."

On July 16, 1995, Amazon.com went live. The website wasn't much to look at. It was gray and blue with lots of clunky hyperlinks and strange fonts. It touted itself as having "One million titles, consistently low prices."

The strategy at first was crude. Amazon listed titles from two of the biggest book distributors in the US: Ingram and Baker & Taylor. When customers placed an order for one of their titles, Amazon would order it from the distributor, then repackage the books from its own warehouse and ship it to the customer. It was an asset-light strategy that allowed the upstart to test its concept without holding tons of expensive inventory. The only items Amazon kept continually in stock were bestsellers that had high demand. At the end of the day, Bezos, MacKenzie, and other senior executives would often come into the warehouse to help employees clear the day's books and get them out the door to the post office.

By not having the overhead of stores and employees to staff them, Amazon was able to price its books lower than physical bookstores could. The savings from not having to pay for physical real estate and hundreds of employees to staff them meant they could sell books to their customers at cheaper prices.

Bezos's instincts about e-commerce — however unlikely they seemed at the time — proved correct beyond his wildest dreams.

Within its first week of launching, Amazon had $12,438 in sales. By the end of 1995, Amazon sales hit $511,000. "In the early days, we had three scenarios: low case, medium case, and high case," remembers Hanauer, who served as an adviser to Amazon's board for five years. "Within months of launch, we were beyond the high-case scenario. No matter how ambitious the forecasts were in our planning and our selling documents, we went way beyond."

One occurrence the company had underestimated in its initial business plan was the number of calls to its phone number. This was the early days of e-commerce, and people hadn't developed the habit of typing their credit cards into their computer and trusting that the item would arrive at their doorstep days later. Customers called the customer service line at the end of their online checkout and said, "I see I have to give my credit card. I'm really not comfortable doing that. Can I give it to you over the phone?" recalls Todd Tarbert, the lawyer who incorporated Amazon and advised it in those first few years. After they were instructed on how to enter their credit card information, they'd call the customer service line back, this time to check if Amazon received their order, he said. Subsequent calls were fielded from customers asking when the order would arrive.

Amazon's first employees tended to the business like a needy infant. After working long days, they'd log in at night to check on the website and make sure it was fully functioning. If they spotted an issue, they'd drive to the office in the middle of the night to fix it. One former employee described the early years of the website launching as holding on to the side of a rocket ship by his fingernails.

It was all hands on deck, and everyone needed to be a jack of all trades to keep up. Bezos was a constant presence, working alongside his staff. The atmosphere, for a time, was collegial: at the company picnic, Bezos even sat in a dunk tank as employees pelted balls at a target to try to submerge him.

But Bezos didn't seem to have the same long-term goals as the people he had hired to help prove his concept, and even the sense of a collegiate atmosphere would soon prove fleeting. One afternoon at Amazon's offices, Kaphan and a handful of other employees were chatting with Bezos when the founder piped up: "The problem with you guys is you don't have killer instinct," Bezos said derisively. It was a glimmer into the former Wall Street executive's aspirations, and a distinct break with the more idealistic mindsets of many of his earliest staffers. (Amazon disputed that Bezos said this.)

For example, when Bezos was looking for a domain name for the company, he registered Relentless.com (a website Amazon still owns that redirects you to Amazon.com) before settling on Amazon. Friends pointed out that "relentless" has a certain sinister connotation to it, according to journalist Brad Stone. He ditched naming his company Relentless, but a drive to win at all costs was second nature to him and apparent from the start.

"We definitely did not have a killer mentality," said Davis, employee number 2 at Amazon, of some of the company's early mission-based employees. Davis had also joined Amazon during the garage days, programming Amazon's website alongside Kaphan. He says both he and Kaphan were a bit idealistic about the company they worked for and what purpose it was serving for its customers.

In those early days after the site launched, emails flooded in from customers throughout the country thanking Amazon. "It's so great that you're doing this because going to bookstores for me is a 200-mile round-trip drive," people would write. Davis loved reading them.

Pre-launch, there was no guarantee that what they were creating would amount to any measure of success. But after it launched and so quickly took off, it raised existential questions for some of Amazon's earliest employees.

Orders came in from every state in just a month's time. Davis pulled Bezos aside. The Englishman was a big book lover and frequented a beloved Seattle independent bookstore called Elliott Bay, which had been an institution in the city since 1973.

"What happens if what we're doing shuts down Elliott Bay?" Davis asked Bezos.

"I love Elliott Bay. We could never shut down places like Elliott Bay," Bezos replied. Davis would later recall that it's hard to know whether Bezos believed what he said, but suspected that Bezos did mean it. "I think that the success of the company, to some extent, even took him by surprise," Davis said. (In a testament to how cherished the bookstore is in Seattle, Elliott Bay does still exist.)

In fact, prior to launch, Bezos was skeptical that shoppers would show up. "We had very low expectations for starting off, and thought it would take a long, long time for consumer habits to adopt to buying online at all," he said. In those days, the mall was considered one-stop shopping for most Americans. The closest well-known comparisons to what Bezos was trying to achieve in the long run — the ability to buy anything from home without leaving your couch — was the Sears catalog or the Home Shopping Network. eBay launched in 1995, but its whole business was person-to-person sales and more akin to an online flea market.

Davis ended up leaving the company in 1996. "One of the main reasons I left was that I could already sense after a year what the corporate culture was that Jeff wanted to build. The only way we were going to succeed was by being some combination of incredibly smart and ruthless." (Amazon disputes that the culture is ruthless.)

That same year, Scott Lipsky joined Amazon to be the company's vice president of business expansion. He spent a lot of time with Bezos, and the two often went to lunch together, where they would discuss work and their personal lives. Lipsky identified as an empath, someone who is able to read the emotions of other people. He recalls Bezos being very fascinated by that ability.

"Jeff knew he was not empathic. He was a very driven, vision-focused CEO," said Lipsky. "I got a constant sense that he had this real, deep personal obsession with the idea of people understanding other people in a deep way."

Hanauer also saw signs of Bezos's lack of empathy. The pace was as frenetic as ever inside the startup. Walking around headquarters, it was common to see sleeping bags stuffed under employees' desks. Kochmer recalls a stretch where he didn't leave the office for an entire month. He slept under his desk. Kay Dangaard, one of Amazon's earliest spokespeople, said the building was abuzz and programmers often spent the night. "The odor was horrendous," she said.

At an early company offsite meeting, engineers explained that they were constantly working into the early morning, often sleeping under their desks in order to handle the workload. As Hanauer recalled, they complained that the company wouldn't cover the cost of a pizza order delivered to the office at midnight to help them power through their work. Bezos heard these complaints and refused the request. Yes, Bezos had instituted a culture of extreme frugality, only opting to spend money on things that benefited the customer. But this felt different from that sort of penny-pinching. "It was 'You're hungry, you pay for it,' " Hanauer said, which showed just how unempathetic Bezos was to their situation. "I was flabbergasted, so was everybody."

The lack of empathy would persist for years, revealing itself in the dressing down of employees in meetings whom he deemed unprepared or not up to the task. "In the first cycle of Amazon, he didn't view it as chewing people out. It's worse to a degree for the person because in their mind it's like, 'I just was clearly exposed as being a fucking moron,' " an S-Team member said. But to Bezos it was all business. "Jeff, I don't think ever thought he was being mean to anybody," the person added. "He had a very low tolerance of stupidity."

———————

Bezos's ambition would soon reveal itself in a big way.

In 1996, Amazon's sales exploded. Amazon started the year with around a dozen employees but bulked up to 150 by year's end to process the orders.

With Amazon's sales taking off like a rocket ship, Bezos was excited to take Amazon public. Raising money in a public offering would provide a cash infusion to fund its expansion plans and help Bezos preserve his lead over booksellers while raising awareness about the company's website. Barnes & Noble was readying its own website to sell books online, and Wall Street saw no reason other booksellers like Borders couldn't follow suit.

An IPO would also provide funding to pursue similar disruption in categories beyond books.

Amazon hired advisers such as investment bank Deutsche Morgan Grenfell and law firms Perkins Coie LLP and Wilson Sonsini Goodrich & Rosati to work on the IPO. The advisers holed up in Silicon Valley, pulling all-nighters to draft Amazon's IPO prospectus. "We worked around the clock on it," recalls Charles Katz, who was the lead lawyer at Perkins Coie for Amazon on the IPO. Bezos micromanaged the entire affair, poring over every detail in the prospectus.

Initially, the company said that it wanted to raise about $37 million in an IPO selling 2.5 million shares of Amazon's stock for $13 each, giving it a $300 million valuation. A *Wired* article at the time called the valuation "a pretty penny for a firm that lost about $6 million last year. And Amazon.com's prospectus suggests those losses could grow larger."

Amazon's lack of profits wasn't new for a company going public at the time. Software maker Netscape's public offering two years prior was one of the biggest frenzies on Wall Street. The unprofitable company's shares surged more than 150 percent in its debut, with investors clamoring to get a piece of the internet. But the vast majority of companies going public had solid earnings.

As part of an IPO process, management teams meet with potential investors to tell their story and defend the company's business model. Bezos and his CFO at the time, Joy Covey, went on an investor roadshow, meeting with possible shareholders. Bezos went into the meetings optimistic. He had proven his business model and was well on his way to creating an entirely new industry. But investors were skeptical.

In private meetings, prospective investors pummeled the two executives. Amazon was bleeding money, and there wasn't a standard way to assign a value to a company with no profits in sight that had lost nearly $6 million the previous year. What's more, Amazon was one of the earliest e-commerce IPO offerings, so there weren't many companies to compare it to. The investors warned of competition from retail's biggest giants, who could launch their own websites, and pressed a cagey Bezos for more details of his business plan.

Other IPOs that year ran the gamut. Semiconductor company Rambus went public the day before Amazon, and its share price nearly doubled the day it started trading. Rambus had become profitable merely two quarters prior to going public.

In a sign of the times, one of the year's largest IPOs was from a traditional clothing company. Ralph Lauren had $117.3 million in profits for the year leading up to its IPO and raised a whopping $767 million.

The thinking inside Amazon was "It doesn't matter if we're losing money; let's own the space," recalls Katz. "Amazon was about to be challenged by Barnes & Noble."

What Amazon lacked in profits, it made up for in revenue growth. By that measure, Amazon's figures were eye-popping, recalls Mark Bertelsen, one of Amazon's lawyers from Wilson Sonsini. Amazon's revenues doubled in each of the most recent four quarters in the company's IPO prospectus.

The roadshow didn't rattle Bezos. A day before going public, Amazon's underwriters held a pricing call with investors. This all-important temperature check happens before every company goes public and is a delicate dance. Bankers sound out investors on the demand for a company's shares and, like the tale of Goldilocks, try to price the shares not too high and not too low, but just right. Pricing a stock too high runs the risk of the company trading below where it's priced, a black eye on Wall Street that could spook future investors. Underpricing it means the company doesn't raise as much as it could and leaves money on the table. It's part art, part science, and Wall Street's top bankers pride themselves in getting as close as humanly possible to the highest range of pricing.

Despite the questions about Amazon's profitability, investors eventually bought into Bezos's vision at the roadshow. Underwriters on the deal fielded strong demand from investors, and the preliminary orders for Amazon's stock exceeded the number of shares the company planned to sell.

Frank Quattrone — the lead banker on Deutsche Morgan Grenfell's team — was a legend on Wall Street. The mustachioed dealmaker had a reputation for obtaining every possible cent for his clients on his deals. Quattrone told Bezos that Amazon should be priced at $16 per share, the high end of what Amazon had identified as its trading range.

Bezos wanted more, former Amazon director John Doerr recounted to CNBC. Bezos was intent on eking out every last bit of value out of the IPO. He questioned the banker. Why not $17, he asked. He went a step further and asked, would an attempt at $18 per share be a failure? Quattrone couldn't say definitively that it would be a failure, but he tried to explain the delicate pricing process, which was based on the demand the underwriters had from investors. In the end, Bezos won. Amazon would price at $18 per share.

When the lawyers came downstairs to tell Dangaard the price, she sat in her office alone for a moment. Soon she heard the office erupt as the opening price became public. "The doors opened and all these kids were running around yelling and screaming, '$18! $18!'" she recalled. On May 15, 1997, Amazon went public at $18 per share. Employees were glued to their screens watching Amazon's stock rise. Some were giddy with excitement, bragging about how many millions of dollars they were now worth.

The company raised $54 million. The stock rose to $23.50 by the end of the day, giving Amazon a valuation exceeding $560 million on its first day of trading and making Bezos — whose family owned more than 50 percent of Amazon's equity — a multimillionaire many times over on paper.

As Bezos was about to hop on some investor calls, Dangaard pulled Bezos aside and offered an unsolicited piece of advice: "One of the things I would really like to tell you is as you're getting more and more wealthy: be humble."

As they walked into the conference room for the start of the investor calls, scribbled across Bezos's notes in large letters were the words "HUMBLE. HUMBLE. HUMBLE."

Bezos and his company hit the big leagues with its IPO just two years after launching its website and without showing a cent of profit.

————

Once Bezos had a taste of success, he was dead set on preserving it. Amazon's IPO attracted the attention of the world, but it also put a target on its back.

Just days before Amazon's IPO, Barnes & Noble launched its own website. Bezos and Barnes & Noble CEO Leonard Riggio had a bit of a rivalry. Bezos caught wind of the announcement of Barnes & Noble's new e-commerce site and tried to front-run it. A few months before Barnes & Noble's big reveal, Amazon announced that it would begin selling bestsellers at a 40 percent discount and double its selection to 2.5 million titles. "Selection and price are important. We just doubled one and slashed the other," Bezos said in a statement.

In fact, Amazon employees were so concerned about Barnes & Noble's online entry that Bezos gathered all of his employees into a room to calm them down. "It was so scary for all of us, this idea that now we finally had a big competitor. That literally everybody's parents were calling and saying, 'Are you OK?,'" he said in an interview years later with Axel Springer.

By the end of its first year as a public company, Amazon's market value had rocketed to $1.3 billion. Sales reached nearly $148 million, and customers grew from 180,000 to more than 1.5 million. Meanwhile, the company lost $27.6 million.

Amazon employees say the losses were by design. "He was very belligerent about the fact that the company should not and would not be turning a profit for a very long time. He saw the only path to success there being continued expansion and reinvestment," says Davis. (Amazon denied that Bezos was "belligerent.") Erich Ringewald, who joined Amazon in 1999, said that Bezos was adamant about reinvesting any free cash flow from established businesses, like books, back into the company. "He did not want to show a profit. He was managing the company to at best break even."

———

In his effort to stay ahead and preserve his first-mover advantage, people who knew him at the time said Bezos's Machiavellian streak would often show.

Amazon had in a very short time disrupted the bookselling space, and Bezos and his team took note of how scared the established booksellers were of the upstart. But as he had told Katz, this was never about books. Could he replicate this dynamic across retail, writ large?

Amazon picked 1,000 of its customers to email with a simple question: what else would they like Amazon to sell? The responses were overwhelming, showing that people were willing to outsource anything they needed at that very moment to the website. One of the responses that stuck with Bezos was a request for Amazon to sell windshield wiper blades.

At a 1998 off-site meeting of Amazon's management team at a Seattle hotel's conference room, the leadership team plotted a methodical push into future categories, recalls Eugene Wei, who was a strategic analyst at Amazon at the time and attended the meeting.

Each vice president presented a report on a certain vertical, going through the competitive analysis for the product, margins, and total market size, and what Amazon's share could look like. One pitched music and compact discs. Another pitched VHS tapes and DVDs. They discussed getting into selling computer software and magazine subscriptions, and even moving outside the US and tapping into consumers abroad. Later that year, Amazon began expanding its offerings to include music and movies. Just as it turned to Ingram and Baker & Taylor for books, it partnered with a distributor called Valley Media for access to new inventory.

The methodical push into each new category impressed Amazon's early employees. It seemed like everything Bezos touched turned to gold. First, he created an online bookstore that went up against entrenched booksellers like Barnes & Noble, as well as the independents. It was a success. Then, he went after record stores by selling music in June 1998. Success.

Meanwhile, the engineering teams were hanging on by a thread just to meet Amazon's book demand. "We could barely keep the wheels on the bus," recalls Greg Linden, who started as a software engineer at Amazon in 1997. "There were so many customers. So many orders. And now Jeff wants to sell music, movies, and, what is this, hardware tools? Are you kidding? And he wants, what? To do it in Japanese and German? It was all hands on deck. Suddenly all the code had to sell things other than books. Suddenly all the code had to handle languages other than English."

Even while expanding into new categories, Bezos worked to maintain the lead he had in books. In November 1998, Barnes & Noble announced a deal to buy book distributor Ingram. The acquisition would give Barnes & Noble ready access to a distribution center full of books that could jump-start its still-fledgling e-commerce efforts. Ingram also happened to be Amazon's single largest supplier, accounting for about 40 percent of the company's inventory in 1998.

Amazon released a statement on the planned acquisition that was meant to get the attention of antitrust regulators, saying that the deal "undoubtedly will raise industry-wide concerns." It was the closing line, however, that raised eyebrows. "Worry not...Goliath is always in range of a good slingshot," Bezos wrote. The founder characterized Amazon as David going up against Goliath and threatened that Amazon was coming for Barnes & Noble. It was highly unusual and cutting for corporate speak, but had Bezos's signature micromanagerial style all over it: a press release punctuated with pithy quotes that assured it would be picked up by the media.

It was also tone deaf. Just a few years since launching its website, Amazon had already become the Goliath of bookselling based on its stock market valuation. While its sales were still smaller than Barnes & Noble's in 1998, it was closing the gap. Since the prior year, its revenues more than quadrupled to $610 million, compared to Barnes & Noble's $3 billion. Such speed of growth was unprecedented. Thus, while still smaller than Barnes & Noble by sales, the company was being valued on its meteoric growth by Wall Street. Barnes & Noble, in fact, responded by pointing this out: "Well, Mr. Bezos, what with a market

capitalization of some $6 billion and more than four million custom-
ers, we suppose you know a Goliath when you see one. Your company
is now worth more than Barnes & Noble, Borders, and all of the independent bookstores combined. Might we suggest that slingshots and
pot shots should not be part of your arsenal."

The Federal Trade Commission later recommended that Barnes &
Noble's deal to buy Ingram be blocked. Barnes & Noble walked away
from the deal, slowing down its ability to catch up to Amazon online.
(In this case, the FTC provided some relief to Amazon, and perhaps the
idea of it being a David stuck. Yet, the company would go on to become
an irrefutable Goliath, and not just in books. Decades later, the FTC
would be faced with a far greater threat as they took on Amazon, a
Goliath of unparalleled proportions.)

By 1998, Amazon had become bigger than all of its bookselling
competitors combined by market cap alone. Bezos's wealth would also
enter the stratosphere. He was valued at $1.6 billion and made the
Forbes list of richest Americans. However, Amazon was still bleeding
money—it lost $124 million that year—and still had no profits in
sight. As the company grew its top line, it continued to focus intensely
on funding that growth. Amazon continued to add to its workforce and
invested in building more warehouses to broaden its offerings. To
entice shoppers, it priced its inventory at a discount, meaning Amazon's margins were pretty low. This all came at a cost. It was a gambit
that made Amazon continuously unprofitable, but it paid off, for Wall
Street didn't seem to care. Its stock continued to climb.

Bezos and CFO Covey had upended how shareholders judged the
worth of retailers, causing them to suspend normal metrics like profit.
The effect of this would reverberate across Wall Street and Main Street
in the decades to come.

In Bezos's first annual letter to shareholders, he acknowledged that
they shouldn't expect quarterly profits, and if they do, then maybe this
isn't the right company for them to invest in. There would be no short-
term management to Wall Street for this CEO. "We believe that a fundamental measure of our success will be the shareholder value we
create over the *long term*. This value will be a direct result of our ability

to extend and solidify our current market leadership position," he wrote.

He then shared a bulleted list of his approach to managing. It included: "We will continue to make investment decisions in light of long-term market leadership considerations rather than short-term profitability considerations or short-term Wall Street reactions."

Investors ate up the pitch. With the exception of the tech bubble bursting in the early 2000s, which wiped out a large number of dot-com companies and made a major dent in the stock market valuations of technology companies, Amazon's included (the company's stock price fell by more than 90 percent), investors showed extraordinary patience with them nonetheless. They allowed Amazon to post losses in pursuit of growth.

Investors would not be so generous with Amazon's competition.

––––––––––

Reporters and analysts scrambled to figure out what industry Amazon would disrupt next as it built out its warehouses to carry more and more goods to ship to customers. In a March 1999 meeting with analysts in San Francisco, CFO Covey was asked if there was anything Amazon wouldn't sell. "Cement," she said. "It costs too much to ship," according to a report from tech journalist Kara Swisher.

Just a few months later, Amazon expanded into categories such as toys and electronics, and the offices inside Amazon were aflutter. The breakneck pace at which Amazon was expanding was unheard of. "It would take three years to start a toy store from the ground up. We were opening up new businesses every four to six months," recalls Paul Capelli, one of Amazon's first public relations officials.

It was the same pattern over and over. Capelli would write the press release announcing Amazon's new area of expansion. He'd send a draft of it to officials at Nasdaq ahead of time because of the surge in trading that inevitably hit once the press release crossed the newswire. "Every time we put out a press release, I knew the stock was going to jump hundreds of points," he said.

On July 13, 1999, after Capelli sent his press release announcing that Amazon would expand into selling toys and electronics, the phones began ringing off the hook. Wall Street loved Amazon's expansion "rinse and repeat" approach. With each new category it expanded in, Amazon chose growth over profits. Those gains often came at the expense of its rivals. It was seen as a zero-sum game. For every item that Amazon sold in the new categories it entered, it meant a loss from a physical store that merchandised that item.

"We were really competing against physical retail," says Capelli. "There was nothing like us out there at the time." Amazon's disruption of entire categories revealed its more ambitious vision. "We spoke back then about how we were going to conquer Walmart."

Without such leeway from the investment community, some early employees doubt Amazon could have become the behemoth it became. "As I look back, the thing I was most impressed about is the ability of Joy [Covey] and Jeff to manage Wall Street and to continue to convince them of the broader, long-term vision that every dollar we spent has to go back into the company," says Capelli. He says that if Wall Street demanded that Amazon show profits, they would have fallen behind. "We were in a race," he says.

The company's ability to upend entire retail verticals sent early warning shots throughout corporate America. Retailers in the categories where Amazon had not yet methodically expanded started bracing themselves for potential entry and threw money into their own websites and distribution centers.

But the problem for many of them was that Amazon's rise came just as brick-and-mortar retailers had invested in massive superstores. These costly 40,000- to 100,000-square-foot structures were expensive to build, stock, and staff, but this was retail's way of offering unmatched selection, said Norman Axelrod, CEO of Linens 'n Things from 1988 to 2006. Then along came Amazon, with nearly limitless selection because it wasn't constrained by the limitations of shelf space. Instead of hundreds of stores dotted across the country to reach consumers, Amazon just needed a few well-placed warehouses. The economics of scale were vastly different.

Axelrod, like many other retail CEOs, launched a website for Linens 'n Things. But the costs were challenging. In addition to funding the website and distribution centers, he had to also face the overhead costs of hundreds of stores. He also had less-forgiving shareholders, who, unlike Amazon's, wouldn't welcome losses as part of his strategy. Amazon's competitors were beholden to Wall Street and weren't given the same leeway. The idea of a publicly traded retailer reporting an earnings loss and being celebrated by its investors was unthinkable. This forced them to be cautious about how and where they spent their resources.

"For public companies, it was really challenging to make an all-in investment on e-commerce," Axelrod said. He chose to invest less than $25 million in online operations for Linens 'n Things rather than the $100 million plus that the company would likely need to invest to be competitive. "It would have destroyed earnings in the short term," he said of a major investment.

This scenario played out across the retail landscape. In the late 1990s, Jerry Storch, a senior executive at Target, spent $10,000 buying the domain name for Target.com and got into a bit of an argument with colleagues about the cost. "They were like, 'Why are you wasting money on that? We own Targetstores.com,'" recalls Storch, who later went on to run Toys "R" Us.

"How do you compete with someone who spends a billion dollars on technology and can lose whatever they want and Wall Street still treats them like the hero?" Storch questioned. At Target, he said there was pressure to invest in and grow e-commerce revenues while not denting profits. "Investors had no patience for losses. You had to deliver on your quarters."

As for what would have happened to publicly traded retail companies posting quarter after quarter after quarter of losses? "They would be out of business," says Baum, the Goldman Sachs retail analyst. "Wall Street would never put up with it." But the truth was more complicated: Wall Street was changing how they were evaluating companies, and they were far more forgiving to the ones becoming first movers taking advantage of the web. While other companies were beginning to develop an online presence, they weren't internet companies. They were trying to use the web, however awkwardly, as a way to broaden their core brick-and-mortar businesses.

Amazon was already ahead of the competition when it came to online selling, and the pass from Wall Street would ensure it extended its lead against profit-bound competitors.

As Amazon expanded into more and more categories, sales grew. In 1999, the company added nearly 11 million new customers and Amazon's market capitalization crossed $30 billion. Bezos was even named *Time* magazine's Person of the Year for 1999. His profile in *Time* encapsulates how far online shopping had come in such a short period and how Bezos had helped to pioneer e-commerce long before anyone believed in its viability.

Bezos's background of home run after home run made what happened next for Amazon a rare miss.

In 1999, Amazon employees began hearing murmurs of a top secret project in the works. Management had selected a group of a dozen engineers to create an auction site from scratch, going head-to-head with eBay.

Retail had been slow to embrace online sales, but eBay was an early adopter, launching its business in 1995. When it launched, "It scared the crap out of Jeff," says Davis. "When they came online, I remember Jeff basically saying, 'Well that's over.'" In the four years since, eBay had cornered the market of online auctions, and Wall Street rewarded them, too, for their ingenuity. Bezos felt threatened by eBay and how they were operating, employees from the time said.

Bezos became fixated on eBay, which, unlike Amazon, was regularly profitable. The online flea market had a very lean operation — it hosted a platform for buyers and sellers to connect, and took a cut of each sale. Buyers bid on items for a predetermined period of time, and the seller shipped the item to the customer with the highest bid. It had no warehouses and no inventory, resulting in high margins. eBay went public a year after Amazon with a frenzied reception. Its shares nearly tripled on the first day of trading. "There is no hype here. This is a solid company that is profitable, and that is atypical for virtually every other Internet company out there," an expert told CNET at the time of the IPO.

Word started to spread throughout Amazon's offices that the company was going to "kill eBay," recalls Steve Yegge, an Amazon technical program manager at the time. The small team of engineers worked in secret to copy eBay's model feature for feature in just three months.

For all the innovation that Amazon later became known for, it also did a fair amount of copying along the way (a habit that it would not abandon as it continued to grow). In 1999, Amazon launched an online auction site on Amazon.com. Investors cheered the move, sending Amazon's stock up 8 percent after the announcement of the initiative.

The service immediately flopped. "It was an engineering marvel and a business failure," said Vijay Ravindran, one of the engineers on the team to build the technology. Despite replicating much of eBay's functionality, customers didn't come.

Auctions were a rare public failure for Amazon, but it would prove important for another reason. It set the stage for one of the company's most important businesses, which would reshape Amazon for decades to come: Amazon Marketplace. The team would eventually pivot to creating something entirely new. In 2000, the company opened up its doors to individual sellers around the world on its third-party Marketplace, creating a business that would go on to transform Amazon into one of the country's largest retailers.

In launching Marketplace, Amazon allowed stores, individuals, authors, and others to list new and used items on Amazon's website to sell.

Internally, the move was fiercely debated. Amazon had a team of employees who were responsible for the sales of the items they merchandised. In other words, the team in charge of Amazon's music business, which shipped CDs from its inventory, would now have to compete with not only shoppers going to a Tower Records store, but also third-party sellers listing the same CD on Amazon.com when customers entered a search query. If a customer ordered the CD from the third-party seller, Amazon collected a small fee, but that meant a missed sale for the employee overseeing music sales on Amazon's first-party side of the business. It also meant a missed sale for Tower Records.

With the addition of Marketplace, Amazon's retail business now had two competing teams: first-party (which were managed by Amazon employees from Amazon's inventory) and third-party, or Marketplace (which gave outside retailers an online presence). This created a dynamic inside the company that would harden over time: in addition to competing with other retailers, Amazon's own employees were also vying internally for the same customers.

Despite the concerns, Bezos directed his team to move forward. It was the quickest way for Amazon to have the unlimited selection he dreamed of, even if it did ruffle some feathers internally. The year Bezos founded the company, he told employee number 2, Paul Davis, that he wanted it to be the "Sears of the 21st century." This was his shot.

The decision to compete with eBay—however initially flawed the execution—would ultimately lead to one of Amazon's greatest innovations, become the backbone of its success, and become the muse for future businesses within Amazon.

As it turned out, Marketplace was a win-win for Amazon, both for its sellers and customers. Amazon collected a fee on every item a merchant sold, as well as a listing fee. The merchant got their products in front of millions of customers, and customers were able to find loads of different products all in one place. Expanding selection led customers to shop more frequently, shifting the website into a one-stop shop, an online destination that only years prior would have sounded completely unrealistic.

It was also an early example of what Bezos would later call a "flywheel," a self-reinforcing loop that speeds up as it's fed. With Marketplace, adding more selection meant customers would shop more, and if customers shopped more, more sellers would sign up, and if sellers wanted to reach Amazon's customers, they might feel pressure to offer competitive prices in order to win the sale. The low prices would cause customers to return again and again.

By the turn of the century, Amazon was selling toys, electronics, and consumable products, and they started dabbling in mergers and acquisitions. The company's Marketplace blew open the door and had begun changing the psychology of selling anything.

Even back in 1999, before the birth of Marketplace, and when he was profiled by *Time*, you could feel where Bezos's mind was headed. When visitors walked into Amazon's corporate headquarters, which was once an art deco hospital for US Marines, they'd see the CEO's face placed on a bookshelf and surrounded by packaging peanuts. A framed copy of the issue hung on the wall. Inside the pages, the young CEO gives a glimmer of the world domination he was setting out to achieve:

"You name it, Amazon will sell it. 'Anything,' says Bezos, 'with a capital A.' And that's the point: Jeffrey Preston Bezos is trying to assemble nothing less than Earth's biggest selection of goods, then put them on his website for people to find and buy. Not just physical things that you can touch, but services too, such as banking, insurance, travel," the profile said.

CHAPTER 3

"The Invasion of the MBAs"

IN THE YEARS FOLLOWING Amazon's IPO, the company feverishly recruited new employees, expanding from around 600 in late 1997 to 7,600 just two years later.

Unlike the bohemians and idealists of the early days, many of the new hires were Ivy League grads and MBAs, full of competitive nerve and ambition, who ushered in a new level of intensity. The misfits were being replaced by a group that was more aligned with the values Bezos cherished.

"We hired them by the dozens. They came in with the same uniform: khaki pants crisply pressed with a blue oxford shirt. They all dressed like Jeff," recalls Tod Nelson, one of Amazon's earliest employees. It was a stark contrast to the T-shirts, jeans, and body piercings of Amazon's earliest employees.

"It was like the invasion of the MBAs after the IPO. It was disorienting and depressing and stressful," laments another one of Amazon's first employees. Worse yet, he says, the new hires had Bezos's ear. "I think [Bezos] was putting up with the quirky, nerdy culture as long as he had to." Amazon disputed the characterization and said that Bezos "celebrated and worked to maintain a quirky, peculiar culture."

With Amazon's sales taking off and the company expanding rapidly into selling virtually everything, Bezos recognized a need to bring in the type of team that would take the company to the next level. He became more obsessed with two things during interviews: a candidate's SAT score and an Ivy League degree—even better if it was from his alma mater, Princeton.

"It was clear that we were headed in a direction that was kind of like Mao Tse-tung, like we're going to capture the wisdom of Jeff and everyone is going to be inculcated with the wisdom of Jeff," said an early employee.

The true roots of Amazon's culture started to take shape. The people with the killer instinct Bezos had long coveted were arriving in droves. Success was enabling Bezos to finally create a company in his own image.

———

Years earlier, at a 1997 off-site retreat, Bezos took the stage and proclaimed that Amazon should have a "culture of metrics," according to former employee James Marcus's book *Amazonia*. He urged attendees to think about what all of the data Amazon collected even back then— sales, items added to carts, minutes spent on the site, books clicked on but not purchased—could reveal about customers and how Amazon could leverage that.

The MBAs clung to such metrics as they filtered in. They talked about getting "eyeballs" and "share of wallet" and produced endless spreadsheets. Early employees resisted the urge to roll their eyes in meetings as they listened to the MBAs spew off business school jargon. Many of the new hires were poached from other companies, ones that fit the mold of what Bezos was trying to institute culture-wise, and these new employees brought the ethos of those firms to Amazon.

When Bezos wanted to expand beyond books, it was these MBAs who were tasked with researching and presenting the options for CDs, international expansion, and other products. They drove major decisions at the company.

Unlike the early employees who were motivated by democratizing reading, many of the new hires were motivated by wealth. "After the IPO, Amazon was viewed to be one of the most successful companies of the internet. So certainly there were a lot of people at that point that joined explicitly in anticipation of financial gains," says employee number 11, Jonathan Kochmer. Whether they came from cutthroat industries, like Wall Street, where sharp elbows are the norm, or from other firms with harsh cultures and autocratic leaders, such as Apple, they shared the qualities Bezos wanted and could relate to the boss's intense drive to win.

Jeff Blackburn was emblematic of the types of hires Amazon made during this period. After working on Amazon's IPO while at Deutsche Morgan Grenfell, Blackburn traded in his Silicon Valley digs at the height of the dot-com boom for life in Seattle at the fledgling company.

The contrast was a stark one. The square-jawed investment banker left a sleek Menlo Park office and a world of pressed shirts, mahogany conference rooms, and titans of industry for jam-packed, low-budget offices and a giant pay cut.

He had worked under legendary banker Frank Quattrone and brought to Amazon the intensity and money-making ethos synonymous with Wall Street. Blackburn had always been known for his competitive drive. The six-foot, four-inch jock thrived on winning.

In high school in Concord, Massachusetts, he earned ten varsity letters in football, basketball, and tennis. In the winter, he was the star forward on his basketball team, known for his rebounding skills. Come spring, he was one half of a two-Jeff tennis duo dubbed the "Twin Towers" because of their height. In 1987, they won the state title. In the fall, he captained the football team and was named a county all-star twice.

Blackburn wasn't merely athletic. He went to Dartmouth College for undergrad, a leafy Ivy League school known for drawing WASP-y types. There, he majored in economics and public policy while playing outside linebacker for Dartmouth's football team. He started every single game during his time on the team.

"Ever since I was a little boy, I've loved to compete and been energized by the team aspect of sports," Blackburn would later say. That uber-competitive drive would fuel a career in the most competitive of spaces: After Dartmouth, Blackburn went to work at Bridgewater Associates. The hard-charging hedge fund run by eccentric visionary Ray

Dalio is known for its cultish culture. Dalio espouses "radical transparency," where employees are encouraged to openly fight and criticize each other in daily reviews of coworker strengths and weaknesses. Underlings live by a publication called "Principles." One of them reads: "Don't 'pick your battles.' Fight them all."

After Bridgewater, he received an MBA from Stanford University and worked at Morgan Stanley and then Deutsche Bank at the peak of its technology dominance at the height of the Silicon Valley tech boom.

After working on Amazon's IPO, Blackburn was hired to work on business development at Amazon.

Jeff Wilke, a Princeton alumnus with an MBA and master of science degree in chemical engineering from the Massachusetts Institute of Technology, joined to be Amazon's vice president and general manager for operations. The thirty-two-year-old was a devotee to Six Sigma manufacturing practices. Steve Kessel, an alumnus of Stanford's MBA program, joined to work on the books business. Amazon poached Delta Air Lines CFO Warren Jenson to head up finance and Apple executive Diego Piacentini to run international retail. Steve Jobs, the sharp-tongued CEO, tried to convince Piacentini to stay. "Well then, I thought you were smart but I was wrong. Indeed you are stupid. Only someone stupid could decide to join a money-losing retailer," Jobs told him when he decided to leave Apple for Amazon. Andy Jassy, a native New Yorker, got both his undergraduate and business degrees at Harvard. The detail-obsessed graduate started at Amazon to work in marketing the Monday after getting his MBA, sneaking in right before the IPO.

Dave Clark, who joined Amazon in 1999, was the first business school graduate to join Amazon's logistics arm. In meetings, Amazon's human resources director referred to him as "The MBA" because she was so excited to have him on board and upgrade Amazon's talent.

As the culture shifted with the alpha types arriving in droves, some of Amazon's earliest executives left. Employee number 1, Shel Kaphan, resigned in 1999 after years of being disintermediated at the company he helped build. He felt misused by Bezos.

With these new hires coming in and taking control of key business divisions that were part of Amazon's expansion, in the late 1990s, Bezos formed his leadership team, which he started calling the S-Team in 2001. This team would become the most powerful group within the company, operating as Bezos's consiglieres, and would be composed of executives who would steer the company forward. One former S-Team member called the group Amazon's "nerve center."

The S-Team spent a ton of time together in those early days, eating breakfast together every Monday. Every Tuesday, they met for hours to discuss various issues and different business units.

A few times each year, Bezos assigned the group a book to read. These included Walter Isaacson's *Leonardo da Vinci* and Eliyahu M. Goldratt's *The Goal*, a novel about a small factory at risk of being shut down because of operational inefficiencies. Many explored cautionary tales, such as Jacquie McNish and Sean Silcoff's *Losing the Signal*, about the demise of the smartphone maker BlackBerry, a market leader that fell from grace by underestimating the competition and consumer habits. BlackBerry had been the go-to device for powerbrokers in Washington, DC, and the C-suite (it was even given the nickname "CrackBerry"). But the mobile leader failed to evolve, ceding market share to rivals Apple and Google, and never recovered from its precipitous fall.

That particular choice is worth flagging because, at his core, Bezos is driven by a preoccupation that permeates the culture of the S-Team.

Bezos often said that big companies have a horrible track record of remaining relevant, and that it could be possible that his company could succumb to the same fate, like the great behemoths of years past. So, he fostered a philosophy called "Day 1," which encourages his workforce, no matter how big it gets, to always think like a flexible, nimble startup. That is, it's always Day 1. Day 2 is death.

He's drilled this mantra verging on paranoia into his employees. "He is right that if you look at history, so many companies become big and complacent, and then they die. And, you know, it's probably going to happen to Amazon one day," said former S-Team member Nadia Shouraboura, who worked at the company between 2004 and 2012.

Specific words and phrases were often repeated when discussing leadership at Amazon. In late 2001, Wilke and a few other executives began drafting the company's first set of principles based on some values that came up frequently in meetings.

When they presented them to Bezos, the ever-exacting boss said that they weren't "Amazonian enough," so, with his input, they revised them. They would eventually land on ten, and some of them were inspired by ideas drawn from companies where these executives had previously worked.

"They are not just a poster on the wall," Wilke said. In fact, they became embedded deeply into the cutthroat culture: the principles would drive hiring and firing decisions and provided the guiding tenets for how Amazonians should work. (They were evoked so often that they took on an almost biblical power, so much so that even executives who left the company could be heard reciting them at new employers or even at home.)

They included things like "Think Big" and "Deliver Results." But the most important one, the North Star for the company—invoked by Bezos in countless interviews, speeches, and keynotes—is "Customer Obsession."

In its purest sense, customer obsession is a good thing. It prompts Amazonians to always innovate on behalf of the customer and to intuit what the customer wants, from low prices to fast shipping—indeed, it would permeate nearly everything they would do, veering on zealotry.

But it would also provide cover for unethical behavior as Amazon grew and became more and more powerful. "I think the characterization of Amazon as being a ruthless competitor is true," Kaphan said, years after leaving Amazon, in a *Frontline* documentary. "Under the flag of customer obsession, they can do a lot of things which might not be good for people who aren't their customers."

Beyond customer obsession, other principles encouraged blunt communication, incredibly high standards, and open discord. In many ways, these mirrored Bezos's traits. "He doesn't know how to say 'thank you,'" said Marc Onetto, an S-Team member until 2013, of Bezos. "He knows how to challenge you and kick your butt. I used to work for [General Electric CEO] Jack Welch, so I told [Bezos] 'I have so much leather down there it doesn't hurt anymore when you kick my butt,'" Onetto jokes.

Other early employees say the boss didn't mince words. He'd regularly tell employees their ideas were "flat-out dumb" or chide them for not anticipating a question.

The culture the company was creating, coupled with some of Amazon's practices around compensation and performance reviews, made the workplace a pressure cooker. Around the time of the leadership principles, Amazon introduced other mechanisms meant to align the workforce to be more efficient and better at what it did, but they also laid the groundwork for an often toxic culture.

Amazon's employee review process was overhauled in this spirit, but employees say it had unintended consequences. In the late 1990s, Bezos became interested in chip-maker Intel's performance review system. Since the 1980s, Intel had used "stack rankings," where employees were graded on a bell curve each year against their colleagues. At the end of the rankings, Intel put the bottom 5 percent of employees on a performance improvement plan, and those who failed to meet the plan's targets were fired.

General Electric, too, had an employee review plan under legendary CEO Jack Welch that was even more draconian. Every year, General Electric fired the bottom 10 percent of its workforce.

Bezos adopted stack ranking. He told his senior team that Amazon, too, had underperformers, and that he didn't trust managers to fire them when they had so much work to get done. The thinking was "I'm under pressure with work to do. I have 200 people on my team, and I can't get rid of twenty people even if they are the bottom performers because they are still performing," said a person in the meeting who later became an S-Team member. Bezos recognized this and made it mandatory to eliminate the poor performers each year. (Amazon's spokesman disputed that Amazon does stack ranking, while confirming that it currently has a percentage goal for unregretted attrition in place. Internal documents, my interviews with S-Team members, and public reporting show years of Amazon's use of stack ranking.)

Amazon began cutting the bottom 10 percent of its workforce annually. Most years, managers were able to refill the positions with new hires, with the aim to recruit people better than those let go, thus elevating the workforce. (Today, Amazon aims to eliminate the bottom 6 percent of its workforce each year.)

With the company attracting MBAs from the top business schools, the talent was already performing at a high level. Even still, they'd have to audition every day to keep their jobs over their peers.

Tod Nelson remembers when the company first started stack ranking. All of a sudden, he had to justify his existence, answering questions about what numbers he hit, ranking himself against his peers, and quantifying his sales conversions. "It was horrible. Jeff had told us again and again not to optimize for optics, meaning don't do something to look good," he recalls. "But after that review process, everyone started to optimize for optics. You performed for your boss. You had to deliver."

The culture became less forgiving and more metrics oriented. "Sometimes really good, talented people got jammed in there," recalls Vijay Ravindran. Employees who suffered a loss in their family or were dealing with personal issues that caused them to be distracted at work could find themselves on the chopping block, he said.

Faisal Masud, who left the company in 2011, echoes this. "You're only as good as your last three months at Amazon," he says. Masud thrived in the environment, but said it was utterly devoid of any empathy. Moving fast, driving hard, and getting stuff done vastly outweighed collegiality and relationship building. "Empathy was fundamentally missing," he said.

As Amazon became bigger and bigger, employees of this competitive workforce, nearly all of them used to academic and professional success, would come to weaponize the leadership principles to justify any business rationale that could get them ahead of each other. In interviews, countless brilliant employees said that the pressure to succeed at Amazon caused them to seek therapy for the first time in their lives. Despite having prestigious résumés and working long hours at Amazon, many employees describe an atmosphere where they felt undervalued.

"A lot of people have imposter syndrome when they're working there and don't feel adequate," said Suresh Dhandapani, who worked at Amazon for thirteen years before leaving in 2020. "There was this constant feeling that you can't take your foot off the gas. Everybody else around you is working very hard, and you either fall behind or you don't want to let those people down," he said.

What's more, Amazon structured employee compensation in a way that stock options are backloaded. In those early days, most employees received 60 percent of their options after year 2. In 2002, employees began receiving just 5 percent and 15 percent of their restricted stock units in years 1 and 2, and 40 percent in year 3 and 40 percent in year 4 on the job — if they lasted that long — which some employees say creates a succeed-at-all-costs atmosphere at the company. That system lasts today. If you were in that bottom of the bell curve before year 4, you could leave hundreds of thousands in compensation (if not millions) on the floor.

The new employee review system based on individual metrics compared to your coworkers' rankled many of the original Amazonians, but even they had to step in line if they wanted to keep their jobs.

———

As the ruthless culture inside took shape, the "customer obsession" rule also drove how ruthlessly it would operate with any company or organization that worked with Amazon. "Customer obsession" gave cover to a win-at-all-costs ethos, which rewarded customers while squeezing partners to acquiesce. This meant that the company was unfazed by the impact of its decisions on its partners, who were foundational to its business model, and in its view, for good reason: only the customer mattered. And from the outside, it was working. By the early aughts, the company was considered a leader of online commerce, and in 2000, despite being bruised by the dot-com crash, Amazon notched $2.8 billion in sales.

When Amazon came out the other side of the dot-com bust, it doubled down on processes. Metrics and efficiencies became even more important to its operations. While many companies were gun-shy after the bust and slowed down expansion plans, Amazon kept sprawling into ever more businesses.

Sometimes, even employees failed to understand the scale of what Bezos set out to achieve. At a town hall with employees following the bust, one of them asked Bezos when Amazon would begin reinvesting in its core businesses of books, CDs, and movies. Bezos became irate. Amazon didn't have a core business, he declared. He had moved well beyond the company being defined by the products it sold — in other words, he was always looking ahead, not satisfied with where they were, but where they were going next.

At a leadership team off-site meeting that year, Bezos emphasized to his team that Amazon needed to expand, and quickly. "We need to branch out. We have to be able to ship a live elephant through our distribution centers," he told them, showing the scale of what Amazon needed to become in terms of selection.

Even still, Amazon had done what much of retail couldn't do, which was spend heavily on building out its own e-commerce business. But there was a growing recognition in the retail sector that every retailer needed to have an online presence. It was costlier and trickier than most anticipated. So, Amazon took advantage and helped rival retailers develop their e-commerce operations. While still much smaller than traditional retailers by revenues, Amazon had amassed so much power and expertise in powering online shopping that it could operate as a feudal overlord in the sector. And as is customary with feudal overlords, Amazon charged a fee to its tenants.

Inside the company, the S-Team talked about Amazon's "total addressable market" (finance speak for a company's top revenue potential) as "everybody else's operating margin," recalls Warren Jenson, Amazon's former CFO and an S-Team member. Put another way, if your company made money, Amazon viewed you as the competition and was coming for your business. While ambitious, the company would make good on that.

In 2000, Amazon struck a deal to host Toys "R" Us's website and fulfillment. In the case of Toys "R" Us, the company had its own website and logistics network, but stumbled badly at operating it. The prior Christmas, Toys "R" Us didn't deliver online orders in time and was fined by the FTC. For Toys "R" Us, outsourcing this side of their operation to Amazon was a potential solution, and the latter was more than willing to comply. Amazon, for its part, had struggled with knowing which toy merchandise to stock during that Christmas and had difficulty getting the alchemy right. Amazon began hosting Toys "R" Us and Babies "R" Us and later signed up Target and the bookseller Borders.

Toys "R" Us's contract provides an example of what rivals handed over. In exchange for ten years of exclusivity selling toys on Amazon .com, Toys "R" Us agreed to pay Amazon $50 million per year, a payment to Amazon for every toy Amazon shipped for them, and a percentage of the price for each toy sold. Amazon was given the option to acquire 5 percent of Toysrus.com, and Toys "R" Us agreed to redirect its website to Amazon.com. Amazon executives scoured the annual reports of the retailers it partnered with before hammering out the terms of the agreement, according to former executives. When speaking with Toys "R" Us, Amazon saw that the toy retailer's e-commerce operations had an $86 million earnings loss the year prior. This meant that Amazon could use its leverage to demand a very large yearly fee from Toys "R" Us as long as it still amounted to less than the losses the company was already accruing. Essentially, the worse shape the partner's e-commerce operations were in, the more Amazon could charge.

Looking back now, it is incredible that any retailer—let alone several—would agree to so many concessions to partner with a company that would become its largest rival (though, to be fair, they wouldn't know it at the time). But they did know that Amazon was essentially becoming a major utility for online commerce. Toys "R" Us's CEO called Amazon "the gold standard in online retailing" when announcing the partnership. Amazon fulfilled a need. Retailers didn't feel confident enough to set up their own online shops, and if they did, they didn't feel like they could get enough traffic. Their shareholders often wouldn't justify the expense of building out massive logistics networks to get online orders to their customers. Instead, many opted to partner with Amazon, but partnering with Amazon came at a cost. It was a devil's bargain, but what choice did they have?

"We weren't capable of doing what we needed to do in 2000 by ourselves," explains John Eyler, Toys "R" Us's CEO at the time.

In the Toys "R" Us deal, Toys "R" Us selected and bought the merchandise to sell through Amazon. Amazon stored it, shipped it, and handled customer service.

In those early years, with e-commerce being the Wild West, Amazon got a number of lucky breaks that it deftly exploited. Wall Street allowed them losses because of their new business model. They would bypass having to charge sales tax in most states. And competitors underestimated Amazon's potential, which meant they made decisions that would later harm them. In the early aughts, few companies understood the potential of harnessing data. But Bezos, even years earlier, had impressed upon his employees just how powerful the troves of information the online business collected was. Information about what people ordered and what they clicked on but didn't order, and a relationship with the consumer via their email inboxes were all a part of a new digital currency emerging on the internet. For traditional retailers just hoping to get a website up and running, these weren't considerations. But they were things Amazon wouldn't ignore.

In 2001, book chain Borders also turned to Amazon to host its website. The company had launched a website and warehouse on its own, but for years it generated small sales and lost a significant sum of money for the bookseller, said Greg Josefowicz, the CEO of Borders at the time. In the press release for the partnership, he called Amazon "the world's recognized e-commerce leader." Instead of suffering years of losses as it built up its own e-commerce capability and fine-tuned it, he sold off the warehouse and turned to Amazon to run Borders .com.

Mike Edwards, who took over as CEO of the bookstore chain in 2009 and eventually led it through its bankruptcy, said the deal was a major misstep. The deals came with another nonmonetary cost. Partnering with Amazon provided it with customer data and directional information about their businesses. Borders learned that the hard way.

"We were literally walking into the enemy and saying 'Here's our plans.' It was an extremely poor idea," said Edwards. The partnership gave Amazon customer data, contact information, and more. "Amazon was literally growing on the backs of their competitors and funding themselves through their competitors," he said. When Borders—the country's second-largest bookseller—shuttered, more than 11,000 people lost their jobs and 400 stores closed, he said. "I can't think of a harder day," Edwards said.

This was an example of the feudal arrangement in action. Amazon was the lord with all the leverage, which would only grow more powerful over time.

In the case of Toys "R" Us, the ten-year contract became too onerous for the toy seller to carry out. Toys "R" Us claimed that Amazon breached the exclusivity terms of their partnership by allowing other toys to be sold on Amazon.com. Toys "R" Us flagged 4,000 toys being sold on Amazon through other merchants on Amazon's website. It was another example of Amazon's competing interests. Employees on the Marketplace side of the business wanted as many sellers hawking as many items as possible through the website, collecting fees each step of the way, even if it violated partnerships like the one the company had with Toys "R" Us.

During the years of the partnership with Amazon, Toys "R" Us did not turn a profit on e-commerce, says Eyler. In 2004, Toys "R" Us sued to break the contract and would become one of the first of many Amazon partners who would allege wrongdoing by the giant. Toys "R" Us won the lawsuit, but it would be far from the last time that Amazon was a thorn in the retailer's side.

"We are at a point in the relationship with Amazon where we have no trust whatsoever in dealing with this organization," said Eyler, then Toys "R" Us's chief executive, in testimony as part of the company's lawsuit to exit its contract. That sentiment would be echoed by countless partners.

CHAPTER 4

Spreading Its Tentacles

DURING A BRAINSTORMING SESSION at Bezos's house in the summer of 2003, Amazon's leadership team discussed the company's strengths. Amazon had mastered shipping vast arrays of items for itself and even fulfilling orders for other retailers. It had opened its doors to merchants around the world, creating an online bazaar. It had mastered endless selection and low prices. It had disrupted retail and had finally become the online "Sears catalog" Bezos had once envisioned.

But beyond the nuts and bolts of taking and fulfilling orders, Amazon was also skilled at computing infrastructure and at running data centers that powered all of this activity. Amazon's website, order processing, and logistics network required storing massive amounts of data and computing capacity. This meant keeping records on customer information, inventory, transactions on the website, and loads of other information that, while invisible to the customer, was important to the shopping experience.

"The first realization we had was that we actually had a real core competence in running infrastructure," recalls Andy Jassy, who attended the meeting in Bezos's living room, in a chat at Harvard.

In 2001, Jassy became Bezos's technical adviser. In the now-coveted role akin to a chief of staff, an up-and-coming Amazonian is picked to be Bezos's shadow. They attend his meetings, follow up on his behalf, and travel the world with the CEO.

In order to support their retail business, the company had hired loads of engineers with the goal of making changes to their site more effective and quickly implementing new features that senior leaders wanted added. But software projects were taking longer than anticipated. Bezos tasked Jassy to find out why.

Jassy set up meetings with a bunch of product development leaders to learn more. "Look, I know you guys think these projects should take two to three months end to end, but I'm spending two to three months just on the storage solution or just on the database solution or just on the compute solution," they told him. Before they could jump into their core work, such as personalizing Amazon's website for customers or recommending items, they all had to address the basic fundamentals of how to make it work on the back end.

Allan Vermeulen, the company's chief technology officer during this period, describes the problem this way: "If you're building a house nowadays, you buy a furnace that's all built and you buy PVC pipe for your plumbing and all that stuff. And at the time, you couldn't buy those pieces. You have to build them for each individual project," he recalls. "So, if the first thing engineers do is spend six months figuring out how to build a furnace, [it] takes a long time to build a house."

Before setting about making the improvements to Amazon.com and adding features, each team had to first procure the servers, set up the data centers, and do all of the back-end work for each project, and teams working on other features on the website were doing that in parallel. It slowed down the projects they were working on.

"What they were building didn't scale beyond their own project," Jassy said of the revelation in the Harvard fireside chat. This was playing out throughout the company, with engineers constantly reinventing the wheel for their projects, spending 70 percent of their time coming up with storage solutions and computing infrastructure. "That was a big realization for us, because Amazon is a very strong technology company. We figured if we had that problem, probably lots of other companies did, too," Jassy recounted to journalist Kara Swisher.

During this period, before an entrepreneur could launch a company that relied on digital technology, they had to first invest, at minimum, hundreds of thousands of dollars in hardware that included servers for data centers (in simple terms, a data center is a physical location where a network of computers processes large amounts of data for storage, distribution, and processing). There were then additional costs to support it, such as electricity to power the servers, staff to maintain them, and licensing the appropriate software. It was a high barrier to entry for companies.

Jassy put together a presentation called a "vision document" for Bezos and his S-Team on this potential new business line of providing the building blocks of such web infrastructure that Amazon, but also other companies, could then build on top of. It was clear to Jassy that the company needed to build this business for Amazon's use in order to speed along its own projects. But if Amazon was going to make an investment to get up to speed, it might as well try commercializing the new business by selling it to others, freeing them from the same drudgery Amazon was experiencing and enabling them to focus instead on their core businesses. They could outsource this problem to Amazon, for a fee.

The vision document didn't have a financial model. Jassy told the team that depending on how the company would execute it, it could be a million-dollar business or a $10 billion–dollar business, but it was impossible to project. What's more, the business would be capital intensive at the forefront, with Amazon having to invest in servers, data centers, networking gear, and a team. Jassy asked the S-Team for fifty-seven employees for what amounted to, as he put it, "really just an idea on a piece of paper." He was nervous, but Bezos was all in. Jassy would head up the project.

For three years, Jassy's team worked on creating the business that would eventually transform the internet. They were working to allow companies and programmers the ability to get computing power and data storage on demand by essentially renting out these capabilities.

The companies or programmers who used the service could then access the resource online, paying fees according to usage, akin to the internet version of using a utility, like gas or electricity. Customers wouldn't have to buy or maintain their own data centers, which was far more costly. Amazon would handle all of that, as a service provider.

In 2003, as Jassy's team got to work building what would become Amazon Web Services (AWS), they second-guessed themselves about whether any clients would come. "There were lots of times afterward where we would question ourselves and say, 'I don't know. Will people buy storage from us? Will people buy compute from us? Will people buy database services from us? Or should we just focus on developing the e-commerce tech we know people will use?'" Jassy told a reporter at *Intelligencer.*

While Jassy's team built AWS, Amazon had its first profitable year in 2003. It was a combination of multiple factors. For one, its Marketplace business, where sellers from around the world sold their items, was much more profitable than its first-party retail business. Hosting the e-commerce operations of Toys "R" Us, Borders, and other retailers also padded earnings (the Toys "R" Us lawsuit wouldn't happen for another year). And an efficiency push driven because of the dot-com bust led to cost cutting at the company. All of these measures began paying off around this time, even if the earnings Amazon reported were modest.

In March 2006, AWS officially launched with its first product: Simple Storage Service. It allowed users to get data storage for a fee of fifteen cents per gigabyte. Later that year, it launched Elastic Compute Cloud. Both were successes. As it turned out, Jassy's instincts were correct: online storage was a problem hardly anyone else had solved.

Once it scaled, it turbocharged the company's profits. Ironically, the very conditions that enabled Amazon to remain unprofitable for years gave it the leeway to build the business that would not only accelerate its growth, but provide the majority of the company's profits, all without compromising its low-margin retail business. AWS contributed roughly three-quarters of the company's overall profits in 2021. Jassy earned a place on the S-Team in 2003.

AWS pioneered cloud computing, allowing companies to sign up for their service seamlessly with a credit card and pay as they go. Anyone, from government entities like the Central Intelligence Agency to corporations as varied as Apple and Goldman Sachs, would realize the benefit and sign up. (In a sign of how powerful AWS would become, Apple, which has competed against Amazon over the years in selling phones, streaming devices, and tablets, pays more than $2 billion to AWS every year for its services, according to an AWS executive.) More important, AWS would provide Amazon with another service — this time not for consumers, but for businesses and organizations. These profits would fuel future departures outside of retail and subsidize the low prices (and losses) that helped Amazon disrupt retail for good (brilliant, indeed, that this new venture enabled them to keep prices low and keep their edge in retail, as the majority of the profits came flowing in elsewhere). Amazon was beginning to break into new sectors, and AWS was the first step in that direction.

———

With the launch of AWS marking Amazon's first major expansion outside of retail, the company was beginning to grow its empire. Bezos was building Amazon into a conglomerate, a large corporation composed of disparate businesses. Ironically, as Amazon began this process, the very idea of a conglomerate as a good business model had grown increasingly out of fashion with Wall Street. But that wasn't always the case.

In the 1960s, low interest rates made financing deals cheap, and a focus on using mergers to buy growth spurred a boom across industries, giving birth to the modern conglomerate. In addition to horizontal mergers, where two competitors in the same industry join forces to better compete, often bringing together direct competitors to increase market share, CEOs started acquiring companies outside of their sector. Diversification became the name of the game and resulted in sprawling companies with disparate business lines in unrelated industries. For example, at its height, ITT Corporation showed just how far this diversification could go. Originally founded in 1920 as a communication business known as International Telephone & Telegraph, in its early years it invested in or bought similar companies in the communications sector. But between 1960 and 1977, the midsize telecommunications firm acquired more than 350 companies, creating a universe of 150 affiliates, including holdings such as Sheraton hotels, Avis car rentals, and Continental Baking, the maker of Wonder Bread.

The rationale behind the conglomerate structure was simple: being in a number of unrelated businesses was a natural way for CEOs to hedge their bets. For instance, if one business unit, such as insurance, suffered a downturn, the company could offset those losses with other areas that were experiencing a surge in demand. Companies deliberately built disparate empires in order to insulate themselves from cyclical declines.

In its heyday, General Electric, which was cofounded in 1892 by Thomas Edison with the help of J. P. Morgan, was the gold standard. The company was born from a merger between Edison's venture and another company that made generators and electric lights. Through the decades, the blue-chip company manufactured unrelated products ranging from light bulbs to plane turbines to curling irons. It had a bank division, GE Capital, which was once a massive lending operation that at its peak had more than $600 billion in assets ranging from commercial real estate to Thai auto loans and accounted for around half the company's profits. It was a leader in healthcare, innovating the MRI machine. In insurance, it had mortgage, life, and reinsurance businesses. The company had even owned NBCUniversal. Jack Welch, the company's late CEO, who was at the helm from 1981 to 2001, made nearly 1,000 acquisitions and other deals during his tenure. And for decades, the company was untouchable.

Into the 1990s, companies continued the trend of conglomerate building. Industrial company Tyco International, for instance, made more than 700 acquisitions that turned itself into a business hawking everything from undersea fiber-optic cables to adult diapers and clothes hangers. CEOs used their growing stock prices as currency to gobble up more companies through acquisitions. In addition to diversifying, it had the result of padding CEOs' wallets. All of these acquisitions created bigger companies with bigger market valuations and bigger compensation packages for those in charge.

For a period, the stock market had rewarded titans of industry that built up massive companies of unrelated or loosely related businesses. This kind of growth often drove up their stock, making their shareholders quite happy. During the 1990s, GE was one of the most valuable companies in the US by market value. Other conglomerates also made the list of the top ten most valuable companies during the decade.

Conglomerates often centralized back-office operations across the different businesses to bring down costs, creating efficiencies. Being a conglomerate also allowed for cross-selling the company's other products. In the case of General Electric, an aviation customer could also be sold insurance or banking. This is how conglomerates achieved economies of scale.

But by the twenty-first century, the sentiment around these massive corporations began to sour. The rise of corporate raiders—many of which were powerful hedge funds—came for the conglomerates and inserted themselves deliberately into how and what the companies should be doing. A hedge fund, in simple terms, is a group of private investors who strategically invest in the market in order to make money. During the 2008 financial crisis, some of these funds targeted conglomerates, buying up enough stock in ones they believed were underperforming to the point where they held enough leverage to make strategic decisions that they believed were in the company's best interest. One of their favorite demands: making companies streamline their businesses and focus on their one core competency. They were essentially conglomerate killers, ushering in a new era.

Famed activist investor Carl Icahn was particularly feared in America's boardrooms. The billionaire, who inspired the Gordon Gekko character in Oliver Stone's *Wall Street*, made a habit of forcing companies to make divestitures and break up. The brash activist, who was known for his sharp tongue, publicly called for a break up of media conglomerate Time Warner Inc. in 2006 and harangued the company's management. He demanded that Time Warner spin off its AOL business into a separate public company and spin off its publishing and cable units as well. Streamlining business operations became a major twenty-first-century trend in corporate America — but not one that Amazon would follow.

In the demerging and breakups, the activists argued that the sum of the parts equaled more than the whole, and that everything other than the main business line was merely a distraction to management. Since conglomerates owned multiple businesses, if any of them were underperforming, it would often drive down the stock of the conglomerate itself, something often referred to as a "conglomerate discount." For example, in 2018, the activist hedge fund Third Point, founded in 1995 by Daniel Loeb, urged industrial conglomerate United Technologies to break itself into three pieces. The industrial giant made elevators, jet engines, and air conditioners, but Third Point argued that the company's stock price lagged that of its competitors because of the conglomerate model. "To reverse its years of underperformance and realize the full potential of its franchise assets, we believe UTC should split into three focused, stand-alone businesses," Third Point wrote in a letter to the company's board. In 2020, United Technologies followed the activist's plans.

In the case of one of the most famous breakups of all time, the sum was indeed worth more than the whole. Standard Oil fiercely fought against lawsuits to break up the company, but the truth of the matter is that as a result of the 1911 breakup, John D. Rockefeller's wealth hit the stratosphere. Within a year of the breakup, the shares of the subsequent companies had doubled in most instances.

In an unintended consequence, some conglomerates became too big to manage, opening themselves up to corporate scandals like the ones experienced by General Electric, Samsung Electronics, and Toshiba. While CEOs argued that they had a managerial or strategic solution that would make their portfolio of businesses operate more efficiently, the activists felt otherwise, arguing that their businesses were simply too large and bloated to manage effectively, and, in some cases, even questioned the capabilities of the leadership teams. Both General Electric and Toshiba were involved in accounting scandals. The heir to Samsung was arrested for bribing a former South Korean president.

The empires of Honeywell, DowDuPont, Tyco, ITT, and even General Electric were dismantled as they sold off divisions, spun off units, and broke up their companies. The breakups weren't mandated by regulators; instead, the companies either realized that the structure was no longer tenable or activist investors pushed for them to break up. In both cases, the sentiment was the same: the model was no longer as profitable as before, and a change was required. In 2021, General Electric announced it would spin off three distinct businesses: GE HealthCare Technologies, GE Aerospace, and GE Vernova, the latter focused on renewable energy. "A healthcare investor wants to invest in healthcare," GE's CEO, who led the breakup, told the *Wall Street Journal*, explaining that investors who avoided GE because of its hodgepodge of businesses would be more inclined to invest in sector-specific pieces of it once they were spun off. "We know we are under-owned in each of those three sectors, in part because of our structure."

"The notion of plugging financial services and industrial companies together, maybe it was a good idea at a point in time, but it is a uniquely bad idea now," said Jeff Immelt, a former CEO of General Electric, in 2018.

For Bezos, all this breaking apart that was becoming the norm in corporate America as AWS launched would not deter his own ambitions to be everywhere. If other companies felt like breaking up their conglomerates to make them more profitable, Bezos was focused on something that required his company to be as expansive as possible. And to be everywhere, Amazon's empire building was essential since the emerging and disparate divisions were all serving a much grander goal.

———

In meetings with senior leaders, Bezos would describe a world where customers didn't just visit Amazon.com once a month for various items like paper towels and batteries. Instead, Amazon would become embedded in the customer's lifestyle. Bezos would come to call this the "daily habit," which would make Amazon an essential part of people's lives in both implicit and explicit ways.

The company dissected habits that people formed, such as watching videos or listening to music, and decided that whatever those categories were, Amazon needed to be in them.

"Jeff was talking about making Amazon a 'daily habit' at a bunch of meetings," recalls Roy Price, who headed up Amazon Studios until October 2017. "When you think about music and video, that puts you in touch with the brand on a daily basis, so if you want to increase [the] frequency of touchpoints, transform the brand from someplace I occasionally go to get a book to something I am in touch with every day. The change for Amazon was moving from a retailer that you went to when you needed to buy something to a service provider who was just part of your lifestyle," Price said.

Just as Amazon had fully disrupted retail, it would now methodically spread its tentacles into other areas of industry — creating a bigger and bigger flywheel — with a focus on integrating itself into everyday life.

Bezos set in motion an army of hypercompetitive employees charged with finding every conceivable way the company could extend its reach beyond its retail core to touch customers more frequently. "They do it out of fear. If they stop innovating, someone will take their place," explained a longtime board member.

There was a relentless push to build new businesses and to actively find areas where they weren't present but needed to be. Even if the conglomerate model had grown out of fashion, the company's push into new sectors and industries gave it similar advantages that conglomerates of the past benefited from: for example, the cloud computing service was able to offset the low-margin retail business. And keeping prices low for customers was essential, for it continued to enable them to work at margins that other retailers simply couldn't deliver and steal market share. It also meant that Amazon's foothold in retail would remain singularly appealing to customers. And while this was in service of the customer, it was also in service of the company's flywheel.

Amazon would start to increase all of its advantages in an exponential way in the 2000s. Unlike his predecessors who merged their way to conglomerate status, Bezos began building an empire largely from scratch, spinning up new business units inside Amazon in far-flung industries like he had with AWS. As Amazon moved into different sectors, it remained tethered to Bezos's directive of integrating itself into people's daily lives. Its components reinforced one another so that the sum was greater than its parts, unlike other companies whose parts proved ineffective and drove the raiders — or the companies themselves — to spin them off. Amazon, meanwhile, had an imperial mindset, capturing areas it needed to be in and focusing on gaining leverage where it could as it grew.

In 2006, the same year it launched AWS, it also launched Amazon Unbox, allowing customers to download movies and TV shows, giving it a foothold in the entertainment sector. It was a precursor to Amazon Studios, Amazon's movie- and television-making arm, which launched in 2010. In 2007, Amazon started its push into groceries, launching the beta version that eventually led to Amazon Fresh. In 2007, Amazon launched its Kindle e-reader, on which customers could read ebooks, newspapers, and other digital media. The device would enable the company to establish itself as a market leader in the space, as traditional media like books were becoming available both in digital and physical form. It enabled Amazon to capture the customer on both ends: buy physical books through their website, and if they wanted to read ebooks, they could buy the Kindle device. Amazon also launched a publishing platform for authors, which challenged the traditional publishing industry. They had already disrupted the retail side of the book business, but this push enabled them to become content creators, too. In 2008, Amazon acquired audiobook company Audible.

"He's a genius. And I define genius in the fact that he would think about things two years ahead of a normal person," says former S-Team member Marc Onetto. "Sometimes he would say things, and I'd say 'He is crazy.' And then two years later, I'd say 'he was right.'" Onetto says Bezos's vision for what AWS would become was one of those moments.

Many of Amazon's newer business lines would follow the model of AWS, where Amazon's retail business served as its muse. Some of them would start small but soon scale into something bigger. For example, in 2008, Amazon started an advertising division that originally served up advertisements in search and on Amazon's web pages, where shoppers could click on links leading to websites outside of Amazon.com. This later morphed into sellers buying ad space to get better featured on product searches on Amazon.com. Like AWS, advertising has turned into a massive profit center for the company. Similarly, Amazon Logistics built the infrastructure to deliver items to customers, and then decided to turn around and sell that service to other companies and merchants. All the while, it innovated its retail business. In 2005, Amazon launched a membership program called Amazon Prime, which gave members free two-day shipping on Amazon.com orders in exchange for a yearly fee.

It kept fine-tuning its logistics network to be able to ship the volume of products it was selling through its warehouses. When Amazon first started, even its warehouses were initially staffed with white-collar professionals packing and shipping books. Tod Nelson recalls that one colleague in the warehouse in the late 1990s was a rocket scientist. Another was a computer programmer. But as Amazon scaled, it would hire warehouse workers en masse.

Amazon's flywheel was taking shape in pragmatic ways: As the company added more third-party sellers to Amazon.com, the selection increased. When selection increased, it added more convenience to the site, attracting more customers. As more customers shopped, more sellers would sign up to sell on Amazon.com in order to get in front of those shoppers. In order to get them to pick their products, they had to be competitive on pricing, often lowering their prices to get the sale. The low prices attracted even more shoppers, and more shoppers attracted more sellers, and so on. Feed any piece of that flywheel, and the entire flywheel spins faster and faster, entrenching Amazon further and further into a retail powerhouse.

As the company added more businesses outside of retail, the flywheel would begin to spin at dizzying speeds. It's what made their expansion plan cohesive. Not only did the individual businesses have their own flywheels, but they fed into a larger Amazon flywheel. As more customers came flocking, more sellers showed up. See the divisions through the flywheel, and the cohesion comes into focus: In order to show up among a sea of other merchants, sellers would buy ad space from Amazon to appear at the top of search results. This gave Amazon another fee it could pull from a seller, and it made the ad business another service they could sell. The more advertising profits Amazon had, the more it could reinvest those profits into future inventions. The more video content the company provided as a perk of its Prime membership program, the more shoppers would sign up for Amazon Prime and spend more money on Amazon.com. As more shoppers came to Amazon.com, more sellers would sign up to reach them, and they would join Amazon's Fulfillment by Amazon shipping network to reach customers quickly and be eligible for the powerful Prime program, and so on. Feeding each piece of Amazon's conglomerate spun the overall flywheel faster, created more power and efficiencies, and made the company indispensable to shoppers, sellers, vendors, and even competitors, who would have no choice but to work with Amazon. This would eventually give Amazon the type of leveraging power not often achievable in corporate circles.

But the new businesses would require patience. Bezos opened his 2006 shareholder letter, the year that Amazon launched AWS, with this: "At Amazon's current scale, planting seeds that will grow into meaningful new businesses takes some discipline, a bit of patience, and a nurturing culture." The seeds he was referring to were the new businesses Amazon would launch. "In our experience, if a new business enjoys runaway success, it can only *begin* to be meaningful to the overall company economics in something like three to seven years. We've seen those time frames with our international businesses, our earlier non-media businesses, and our third party seller businesses." As the company launched more and more businesses in those ensuing years, the seed metaphor was apt: it would enable them to grow different businesses with the flywheel mindset driving its underlying vision. It would take years for those seeds to grow into trees and for the roots to spread, eventually creating a chokehold on much that it touched. But Bezos was disciplined and would not rush the process.

By the end of the decade, Amazon had planted the seeds that would allow it to later grow into one of the world's biggest logistics companies, one of the US's largest digital advertisers, a major Hollywood studio, the most dominant cloud computing company in the world, and a disruptor of food retail. The astonishing range of commercial activities the company entered would put it head-to-head with juggernauts such as FedEx, Google, Netflix, Microsoft, and Kroger.

While the aforementioned companies are market leaders in one or two industries, Amazon, uniquely, through its inside-out expansion model, had inserted itself into all these industries (and soon would become a dominant player in many of them).

———

The incredibly efficient and massive flywheel across industries would be the key to Amazon's success. Each entity could amass significant data that could then be leveraged and exploited by another division within the company. In other words, Amazon could use its dominance in one area to exert leverage in another.

It was becoming a conglomerate, but its diversification of businesses was enabling it to tip the balance in its direction, in large and small ways, whether that meant cheap goods for customers or data storage for countless organizations, including competitors. Individual merchants were caught between needing Amazon's growing customer base and the fees being levied on them to reach those customers eating into their margins. But whatever service they provided, it was becoming clear that Amazon was beginning to hold all the cards, and as they grew, the terms of any deal would favor Amazon at anyone else's expense.

Once the Amazon conglomerate was in motion, it would achieve a state of unprecedented reach. Its diverse offerings, whether in cloud computing or advertising, coupled with the powerful customer base from Amazon Marketplace, forced everyone to pay Amazon in some capacity

for their own self-preservation. All roads, whether they came as customers, competitors, or partners, began leading to Amazon. By design,
Amazon had created a conglomerate of significant size and reach. It
would, in many ways, become essential, as everyone would come to
need it for their own purposes. Avoiding Amazon, in a way, became
impossible.

Amazon, of course, would exploit these arrangements in the best
possible way, reaching a position of unassailable leverage. Its imperial
mindset, unbeknownst to the customer, was a brilliant bait-and-switch:
you needed Amazon, and as it spread its tentacles, it would become
better and better at ensuring that such needs would accelerate. (It's not
a coincidence that another name for the trustbusters of the Gilded Age
was "octopus hunter.")

As Amazon entered new business lines, the company also expo-
nentially began amassing large amounts of data. Its operations across
industries provided the giant with more data than most companies
anywhere in the world. In an economy where data is now ascribed a
higher value than oil, the sheer amount of information Amazon collected seemed to justify its often lofty market valuation.

All this data was king, and it was foundational — because at Amazon, data tells you things, and the more data it had, the more ways that
it could be used. And use it they did. In the cutthroat win-at-all culture
inside Amazon, employees looking for an edge couldn't resist using
Amazon's vast trove of data in whatever way they could, even if it bordered on the unethical. The culture was about winning, and anyone
who has to win will often do whatever it takes to stay on top.

———

Around the turn of the decade, Amazon began to convert much of its
system's potential energy into kinetic power. It had turned itself into an
e-commerce giant, selling goods from countless sellers, from brand
names to smaller companies. But much of that, it was learning, it could
do all by itself. Efficiency — for the sake of the customer, always — compelled Amazon to vertically integrate some operations with maximum
aggression.

What if Amazon began making its own products, leveraging its own platform to sell them, which would put it in competition with the very sellers who were paying to sell on their site? What started out as a small experiment inside Amazon would turn into a big business line and a major source of scrutiny. But first, it had to start.

In 2009 Amazon launched Amazon Basics, a private label brand that started with a few electronics products, such as blank DVDs and A/V cables. The strategy was simple and well worn throughout traditional retail. Amazon identified national brand items popular with customers, found factories abroad to manufacture its own versions, and priced them lower than the brands selling similar items. One of the key factors that determined whether Amazon would create a private label item is that Amazon must collect a higher margin on the product it creates than it collects from the one it is selling on Amazon.com from other brands. So, if an Amazon third-party merchant sold iPhone chargers that Amazon collected a fee on, Amazon would only make an Amazon Basics version of that charger if Amazon's margin would be higher than what it collected in the category.

The press release at the time had little fanfare. Buried in it was the understatement of the decade: "We will continue to gather input from customers and evaluate opportunities for new products under the Amazon Basics brand. We aim to offer our customers as wide a selection as possible…"

In the early days, Amazon's approach to coming up with items for its private label lines was pretty rudimentary. It simply tested what it could sell under its own brand name. It didn't have a data-driven approach that it would later harness (and get in trouble for). Instead, employees looked at industry trend reports and went to trade shows. Private label executives flew to Guangdong, China, and walked massive convention halls at the Canton Fair, where Chinese factories that manufactured products for big brands sent their salespeople to show off their creations, from computer keyboards to speakers. Canton is China's largest trade show, where brands and retailers flock to find suppliers for their products.

"There were like 5,000 vendors, and it took us three days to go through the whole thing," recalls Tony Chvala, an Amazon private label executive until 2012. Chvala and his team stopped at each of the stalls to peruse the wares on display. This gave them a sense for cutting-edge technology on the horizon, such as different USB drives and mice, and also helped them come up with ideas for which items to add to their Amazon Basics line of products. They returned to Seattle with suitcases of samples from the manufacturers, as well as factory information, so that they could choose which factory to partner with and slap their Amazon Basics brand on.

Amazon Basics was an experiment that didn't have a coherent strategy to start. Internally, there were a lot of skeptics, which reflected the amount of resources they invested in the division: five people, recalls Faisal Masud, the director of Amazon Basics until 2011.

For the first few years, Amazon Basics consistently missed its numbers. "I would get blasted in those meetings," said Masud.

Their approach, in part, reflected a miscalculation: the brand was focused on offering too many products, across categories, but Amazon wasn't primarily known as a maker of goods, not like Microsoft or Apple. Why would anyone want an Amazon-made product when reputable brands had built themselves up as leaders in certain sectors (and were being sold on their Marketplace)? For example, Amazon Basics sold computer ink, which was a total disaster. So, too, were other products they released. So they started fine-tuning.

They began to find success by looking at areas of demand from customers where Amazon could offer as high a quality product at a much lower price.

"One of the very first products was the HDMI cable, which was exceptionally disruptive at that time," said Chvala. Monster, the premiere HDMI cable maker, priced its cables at around $79 to $119. Best Buy's own brand was priced lower, at around $30, which made it an appealing alternative. Then Amazon Basics launched its version and sold it for around $6 to $8, recalls Masud. This cut-rate pricing caused an explosion of sales for Amazon Basics. "We were just annihilating the market," said Masud.

It was one thing to price below Monster's cables. They had marketing costs, a retail markup, and other fees they had to bake into their price. But how did Amazon Basics undercut Best Buy's house brand so steeply? "They have stores to consider, they have a lot of other overhead that we just didn't have at that time," said Chvala. Amazon was once again able to do what traditional retail simply couldn't: operate at margins that no one else could execute at without going out of business. HDMI cables became Amazon's first private label item to sell more than 1 million units. "Everybody was happy, including Jeff Bezos," recalls Chvala. "He really wanted private brands to be a success."

At the time, as they perused Amazon's sales data, one thing was made clear. The troves of information from Amazon's exploding number of third-party sellers were off-limits. Amazon executives told its new private label team that they were forbidden from using data unfairly against individual sellers on Amazon Marketplace.

––––––––

Most of Amazon's early growth came by building its own businesses, but it began branching out into sizable acquisitions around 2008. While it had bought small companies here and there during the early years, that year it spent around $280 million on acquiring Audible. The next year it spent nearly $850 million snapping up online shoe seller Zappos. The Zappos deal was the biggest in the company's history at the time, and while only a decade old, it had already become one of the leading online shoe sellers in the country. At the time, Amazon hadn't been able to make much headway in shoe sales, or apparel in general. With Zappos, which had an avid fan base, Amazon could now add those customers with the acquisition. Internally, the group tasked with mergers was impressive: Blackburn, the former banker turned Amazon employee, was now luring a team of heavy hitters from Wall Street's top firms, such as Barclays, Credit Suisse, and even white-shoe law firms like Skadden to Amazon. This group would grow into a large and formidable internal deal-making team.

Amazon emails dating back to its early days and anecdotes from former employees show an intense focus on specific companies Amazon wanted to handicap. And the tragic story of Quidsi would reveal just how forceful their tactics could be.

In 2009, Amazon set its sights on a small, innovative company based in New Jersey. Run by Marc Lore and co-founder Vinit Bharara, this early e-commerce player was revolutionizing the way new parents shopped for diapers and baby goods.

Born in 1971 and growing up in Staten Island, New York, Marc Lore initially wanted to be a farmer. He was intrigued by the idea of planting a seed and growing it into something. He liked starting things from scratch and had an entrepreneurial mind. When he was a boy, he set up lemonade stands for spending money, and he started tracking stocks by the time he was ten. He was an autodidact, soaking up information wherever he went, later becoming the first college graduate in his family.

After graduation, Lore went into banking. He had a lucrative job at Sanwa Bank in London, but the burgeoning tech startup scene in the 1990s excited him. He quit his job to be a technology entrepreneur, without having a specific business idea in mind. His boss at the time thought he was crazy, but seeded him his first investment anyway.

Lore found success starting an online sports card trading company called ThePit.com, which he sold to Topps for $5.7 million in 2001 before delving into online diaper sales with his elementary school friend. In 2005, he and Bharara started Quidsi, the parent company of Diapers. com. Baby products, including diapers, turned out to be a big business opportunity. In 2010, Quidsi planned to ship more than 500 million diapers, but the company also sold an array of items new parents needed, including formula, car seats, strollers, and baby wipes. In 2010, Quidsi also expanded into selling cosmetics and drugstore products.

As Lore and Bharara were ramping up their business, Amazon was studying their success. For months, Amazon had been trying to figure out how the New Jersey–based e-commerce player was able to deliver bulky packages of diapers within twenty-four hours during a time when shipping typically took days. Diapers.com had garnered a rabid following among moms — a coveted demographic in retail — who were shoppers with continuous needs as their babies grew. Amazon wanted that demographic, too. When mothers bought diapers, they would often remain loyal, continuing to purchase other goods their babies needed, especially higher-margin products.

An internal Amazon document from August 2010 explains why Amazon was so laser-focused on moms:

> Moms are one of the most important customer segments for Amazon: they control the vast majority of household purchases, shop online regularly, and will see their income and expenditures grow throughout their life. Women control or influence 85% of all consumer purchases in the US, and that number grows even higher when looking only at consumable household expenditures, such as food at 93%. When women become mothers, 85% report that having a baby 'changed their purchasing habits,' and the average cost of a baby's first year is more than $10k. According to Proctor *[sic]* and Gamble, women report using 5–7 retailers regularly before becoming a Mom and narrow down to 2–3 after becoming a mom. By attracting new Moms to Amazon and exposing them to a convenient and addictive shopping experience, we have the opportunity to immediately increase incremental revenue and drive repeat visits to the site-but most importantly, we can solidify Amazon as a choice for a lifelong shopping destination.
>
> The Amazon Mom program will focus on serving the needs of Moms in the 'prenatal' through toddler' (17M Moms) stage. These early years are a pivotal point when Mom's free time decreases dramatically and yet she faces enormous new purchasing challenges. By introducing Mom to the convenience of Amazon, and offering meaningful benefits relevant to her needs, our goal is to grow a loyal, high-spend membership base to more than (redacted number of) Moms, reaching (redacted percent) of the target population by 2015.

Like Quidsi, Amazon could have tried to develop its own way to attract mothers, but instead, it decided to face down a business that was already doing it successfully. A team of Amazon executives researched the startup. Doug Booms, one of Amazon's chief dealmakers, sent an email in February 2009 with the subject line "Diapers.com — looked at them ever?" He was flagging Quidsi's explosive growth and floated the idea of buying them.

Another executive responded to the email suggesting a casual take-over chat. "We can approach them through the 'we would be willing to explore a range of relationships' angle," he wrote. Bezos's underlings ordered up an in-depth competitive analysis on Quidsi.

The team manually clicked through Quidsi's website and made a list of every single brand the company offered, comparing that to Amazon's offerings to identify gaps. An employee even called up Quidsi's customer service hotline to pump the operator for information that could be valuable to Amazon. He bragged about this in an email: "You'd be surprised as to how much competitive intelligence I've gather [*sic*] just by calling various competitors and asking." He included a transcript of his call where he didn't even identify himself as an Amazon employee.

Amazon developed a twelve-step plan to beat Quidsi. In emails detailing the plan, action items included "Beat or meet Diapers.com's delivery speed," "Beat or meet Diapers.com's 6PM order time cutoff," and a range of other ideas around accepting coupons, personalization, and refunds to make Amazon a more attractive destination than Quidsi for baby products.

"More evidence these guys are our 1 competitor," a February email from Doug Herrington, then vice president of consumables, read. "I think we need to match pricing on these guys no matter the cost." Amazon would go a step further than just match Quidsi's prices.

Over the course of the next year, with Bezos's direct involvement, Amazon implemented a ruthless "plan to win" against Quidsi.

In an email chain Bezos was part of in June 2010, Herrington lays out some of the ways Amazon could set about destroying the startup. He says that he's initiated a "more aggressive 'plan to win'" against Quidsi that included doubling its discounts on diapers and baby wipes to 30 percent and a free Prime program for new moms. The team brought in its legal department to discuss the discount to make sure it wouldn't be considered "predatory pricing" and introduce an antitrust risk, according to a person involved. Predatory pricing occurs when a company lowers their price of a good or service below cost in order to drive away a competitor. After the competitor has been beaten or obliterated, the company raises its prices back up. Standard Oil was known for the practice, which helped it gain dominance. Amazon's legal team determined that because Amazon had so small a share of the diaper market at the time, it wasn't going to raise any regulatory attention.

On the day that Amazon slashed its price of all diapers on its site by 30 percent, Jeff Blackburn approached a Quidsi board member with a message: Quidsi should sell itself to Amazon. It sounded like a threat, the board member recalls. At that point, Quidsi wasn't for sale, and it had big growth plans.

Once Amazon slashed its price of diapers, though, Quidsi started to unravel, says Leonard Lodish, another Quidsi board member. The Quidsi management team did the math and realized that Amazon was losing $12 for every box of diapers it sold. Internal documents show that Amazon lost $200 million selling diapers in just one month at its discounted price. For the first time since 2005, Quidsi missed its internal monthly projections. The company's investors were unnerved by Amazon's assault on the startup. While Quidsi was trying to raise $100 million in funding from venture capital firms, some turned them down, spooked by Amazon's onslaught.

"What Amazon did was against the law. They were selling diapers for below cost," said Lodish. "But what were we going to do? Sue Amazon for antitrust? It would take years and tens of millions of dollars, and we'd be bankrupt by then."

While all companies pay attention to the competition — after all, they must be good stewards of their shareholders' money — what Amazon did here was different. Amazon was willing to sustain losses for a long enough time to either put Quidsi out of business or make them capitulate. The ability — and patience — to bleed a competitor went beyond the pain most companies inflicted on their rivals.

Boxed in and losing money, Quidsi felt forced to sell and began speaking to Amazon and Walmart about a deal. While Quidsi executives hated Amazon for undercutting them, they took the meeting anyway, and Amazon very quickly presented a $545 million offer.

Then, during a dinner among Amazon senior executives and Lore and Bharara, an email popped up on the entrepreneurs' phones. It was from Walmart and contained a fully baked $650 million offer. Thrilled, they made an excuse to step into the hallway to discuss what to do. The offer was for much more than what Amazon was offering and had the added bonus of not coming from their nemesis. When they entered the dining room with the Amazon executives, they shared that Walmart had just made a superior offer that they intended to pursue. Amazon relayed a message: if Quidsi chose to be bought by anyone other than Amazon, then Amazon would slash its price of diapers to zero. The Quidsi co-founders were shaken by the threat. Amazon was willing to essentially give away free diapers in order to put them out of business. It was an extreme example of predatory pricing, with Amazon being able to raise prices again once their competitor was eliminated.

Walmart's mergers and acquisitions (M&A) contract included a clause that stated if there were any material changes to Quidsi's business in the months between the time they agreed on a deal and the time the deal closed, Walmart could walk away from the deal. Such deal clauses, sometimes called MAC clauses, are standard in takeovers. MAC clauses protect a buyer in an acquisition from getting stuck buying a company whose business suddenly declines before the deal closes.

This put Lore and Bharara in an impossible spot. Knowing that Amazon could destroy their business by cutting its price of diapers to zero if it took the Walmart deal, which would have triggered the MAC clause and thus allowed Walmart to walk away, Lore and Bharara tried to amend the contract with Walmart to remove the clause. If Walmart removed the clause, it would have locked them into completing the Quidsi acquisition, or possibly paying a breakup fee if they decided to walk away, which they would have done if Amazon made good on its threat to essentially give away diapers for free. Walmart declined to remove the clause. Lore and Bharara had no choice but to sell their company to Amazon, under the exact same terms as its initial offer. With no negotiating power, Quidsi had to accept the reality that they either sold to Amazon or would be put out of business.

In November 2010, Amazon announced that it was aquiring Quidsi for $545 million. "When we bought Quidsi part of the thesis was to keep it away from Walmart. [We were] worried it would accelerate their e-commerce," recalls an Amazon executive who worked on the Quidsi deal. "Keeping it away from competitors and extending our lead was part of the equation. It created a bigger moat."

Lore and Bharara became instant multimillionaires from the sale to Amazon. Both grew up in modest surroundings, and now they had generational wealth. But neither of them felt like celebrating. They would now be reluctant Amazon employees.

"I remember being pretty depressed the next day in the way the whole sale happened," Lore said in a podcast interview. "We had a vision for what we wanted to accomplish, and we had built an incredible company and had amazing people working there, and I felt like we had sold out because the vision we had set out to achieve was no longer possible because Amazon was just going to consume it, push it on the side."

A month after Amazon announced its Quidsi acquisition, it stopped letting new members join its Amazon Mom program, which offered even bigger discounts on diapers. The FTC was in the process of reviewing the acquisition, so Amazon reopened the membership, but with smaller discounts, journalist Brad Stone wrote.

Lore always regretted the deal with Amazon, but it wouldn't deter his entrepreneurial spirit—and he even got a second chance with Walmart. He left Amazon in 2013 and a year later founded Jet.com, an online marketplace similar to Amazon's third-party Marketplace that touted low prices. In 2016 he sold Jet to Walmart for $3.3 billion, the largest e-commerce deal ever at the time. He stayed on with Walmart several years after the deal, becoming Walmart's e-commerce chief and leading the retailer's own competitive battle against Amazon.

Amazon closed down Quidsi in 2017, saying it was unprofitable. Yet, shutting down Quidsi did not mean it lost market share for baby goods; on the contrary, Amazon remains one of the leading e-commerce retailers for baby goods. It absorbed Quidsi, forced it into a corner, took its customers, and then eventually put it out of business anyway. In the end, Amazon still came out the winner.

————

As it grew, Amazon was becoming better and better at figuring out how to leverage its power. It could come in different forms: merchants felt the need to buy ad space in order to vie for their customers' attention, and then Amazon turned around and began selling their own select products at prices that annihilated the competition. Like with Quidsi, they wouldn't simply compete, but could also destroy the competition, forcing your hand, making you either kneel to their demands or force you out of business entirely. Their cloud computing service was essential to running the cloud, which made all those companies and organizations who relied on the service amplify its flywheel, which further entrenched its footprint. And yet it never stopped growing or looking for opportunities, given its "Day 1" mindset. But how they would capture their edge, in any given direction, was never clear — until you came out on the other side of it. As Amazon continued to integrate into everyday life, it continued to meet with partners and entrepreneurs from different industries. For some, those meetings turned into cautionary tales.

In 2012 Leor Grebler created a voice-activated device called Ubi that would be a first-to-market of its kind of device: it listened to voice commands and effected actions through digital or computing means. Creating Ubi during this time period was itself a technological marvel. At the time, the concept of speaking to a device and commanding it to perform tasks, like turning the lights on and off and sending emails, was not mainstream.

And yet they had done it. The accomplishment was all the more impressive because Grebler and his two cofounders had managed to create this while simultaneously holding down demanding day jobs. Grebler spent most days selling education technology on the road, traveling throughout the US and Canada and pitching his company's products. So, all he had was his evenings and the weekends, and he spent all that time developing and working on the device.

In November 2012, Grebler decided to sound out Bezos on his revolutionary device. He had no access to Bezos, so he guessed a handful of email configurations that could potentially be the CEO's. In his email, he requested a meeting to discuss, as he put it, his "Android-based voice-operated always-on computer that's been compared to the Star Trek computer." Miraculously, it worked, and Bezos assigned one of his deputies, Greg Hart, to follow up.

Grebler was ecstatic. Maybe his small company would develop a partnership with Amazon or even license their technology to the giant. Even more exciting was the possibility that Amazon was big enough that they could even acquire Ubi. Both he and Bezos were Star Trek fans — something they bonded over in their initial email exchange — and so there seemed to be some goodwill. The potential of an Amazon partnership could, if it all worked out, change Grebler's life.

"Jeff passed along your email to me. I'm a VP in our Kindle organization and am interested in taking you up on your offer to connect," wrote Hart in an email to Grebler. Interestingly, while he identified himself as a vice president on the Kindle team, Hart had recently been tapped to head up a secret project at Amazon creating what would years later become its Echo device and Alexa voice assistant (this information was not disclosed to Grebler). Hart eagerly offered to fly to the Bay area, where Grebler would be for work the next week, for a meeting.

Early on, Grebler and his two cofounders signed a nondisclosure agreement with Amazon. Such an agreement is standard in deal talks and when companies explore partnerships; it prevents the companies from sharing what they learned as a result of the talks. Grebler discussed his device and technology with the tech giant and held five meetings bound by that nondisclosure agreement.

In early 2013, a team of Amazon executives, including Hart and another team principal, Al Lindsay, flew to Toronto to meet with Ubi's team to see a demonstration of the technology and how it worked. Prior to the meeting, Amazon called and said that it would be terminating its NDA. It was strange to suddenly void confidentiality in the middle of talks, but Grebler was new to all of this and agreed. Being green, he thought it was possible that companies voided NDAs before making an acquisition offer.

The letter from an Amazon executive stated the following: "any Information we receive from you on or after December 6, 2012 (including without limitation your email dated December 6, 2012 inviting us to review potential product proposals) will not be considered confidential information of UCIC (Ubi's parent company) and is not subject to the NDA. This is true even if the material is marked or otherwise designated as confidential."

During the demonstration, Ubi told the participants the weather in the area after receiving voice-activated instructions; it turned the lights in the room on and off; it checked flight statuses and sent emails. The demonstration worked perfectly.

But after that final meeting, Amazon's contact started to fade. Despite a chummy rapport with Hart and Lindsay during the meetings, Grebler's emails and phone calls now went unanswered and unreturned.

On November 6, 2014, Grebler received an email from his brother with the subject line "uh oh." It contained a link to an article about Amazon's new Echo device. He was gutted.

The Echo was a command-answering digital device. It had been nearly two years since he gave Amazon the demonstration of his Ubi. In the interim, Grebler had sold more than 3,000 Ubis through Kickstarter and his website. In the summer of 2014, he even began selling them on Amazon.com.

Grebler held meetings with a law firm to consider legal repercussions, but determined he didn't have the funding to sue the technology giant. Inexhaustible resources are yet another advantage that shields giant corporations like Amazon from the exposure of predatory and potentially illegal practices. The median cost to litigate a patent through appeal where between $10 million and $25 million is at stake in the US is $3 million, according to the American Intellectual Property Law Association. It's a sum most startups simply can't spend.

The Echo launched to the public on June 23, 2015.

"It was a really difficult time after that," Grebler says. In the six months that followed, "we ended up burning through our cash and ended up having to downsize most of the company. We moved out of our offices. I worked out of a Regis lobby for most of the time without pay." Grebler had just become a new dad, and his wife was recently out of work. Grebler, with his bubbly personality, dorky laugh, and stereotypical Canadian politeness, felt defeated.

Six months after the Echo started selling, Ubi discontinued its product and tried to pivot to becoming a voice-enabled services provider. That folded in 2019. Grebler now works as a product manager for a tech company and moved his family to Israel.

During the course of their six meetings, Grebler says he provided Amazon with a trove of proprietary information. "They saw all the things we wanted to do with the device [like] music and shopping. It was almost a road map for the product." A former Amazon executive who worked on the Alexa team early in its creation said work on Alexa began in the fall of 2011. Bezos, referring to Echo as "the *Star Trek* computer," has said that the company began working on it in 2012. While Amazon had begun on the project around this time, it took years for Amazon to hire a team to work on it, create the brains for Alexa, and figure out the speech technology and all of the other components that go into making such a device. It met with Ubi as it was still figuring out how to make such a product viable. While it can't be definitively confirmed that Amazon copied Ubi, the timing and what Ubi handed over can't be seen as inconsequential. Ubi would be the first in a long trail of startups that would claim that Amazon unfairly used intelligence gained from proprietary deal and partnership talks to create its technology in-house.

An insidious theme was emerging: Amazon was a black hole, sucking in any and all opportunities, but doing so on its own terms, racking up victims, large and small, along the way.

CHAPTER 5

Inside Your Home

THE UBI AND ECHO episode was a piece of a larger sector assault that was becoming emblematic of how Amazon could maximize its ecosystem dominance — from customer access to logistics to its Marketplace to information.

Indeed, Amazon's aggressive entry into the personal device space was a case study in the kind of omnipotence it would achieve in countless categories.

It all started on November 19, 2007, with the launch of its Kindle e-reader device. Like Apple's iPod before it, which allowed thousands of songs to fit into your pocket, the Kindle was equally revolutionary. Avid readers could download hundreds of books and read them on one small device.

Gregg Zehr, a senior executive who worked on the original Kindle device, said Bezos realized two things at the time that the company was developing the e-reader. One was that Amazon needed to expand selection on Amazon.com, where around 80 percent of the products sold at the time were books, CDs, and movies. The company partly needed to do that because of Bezos's second revelation: soon books, CDs, and videos would move to digital downloads instead of physical purchases. Bezos wanted to be well positioned for that shift by having devices to sell those digital products while also expanding the selection of physical items moving through Amazon's warehouses when those items inevitably became digitized. "We saw this as existential. We needed to solve this, or we would be disrupted," Zehr said. They decided they would start with a device for digital books first.

In October 2004, Amazon started a secret team dubbed Lab126 to begin work on the hardware side of Kindle. Zehr headed it up. The small team worked in a shared space in a law library in Sunnyvale, California so that it could attract top engineers from Silicon Valley. They would become an essential part of Amazon's hardware ambitions, poaching employees from Apple and other consumer electronics companies.

Lab126 spent three years developing the product, and it was a gamble. The hardware business is notoriously difficult, and at the time, Amazon had no experience building physical goods internally (Amazon Basics wouldn't launch until years later, and at this point much of what Amazon focused on was selling other vendors' items).

Bezos was committed to the project, even if it wound up being a dud. But the team needn't fear: Kindle sold out within five and a half hours of its release. Amazon had a blockbuster on its hands.

The Kindle device was a game-changer for Amazon in many ways. In addition to having an Amazon-branded device in its customers' homes, it was now further ingrained in a daily habit: reading. And with every book a customer paid to download to its Kindle, Amazon took a cut of the price. The Kindle was and remains a book-selling machine — it has sold more than 487 million books as of November 2022, and Amazon sells 83 percent of ebooks in the US. Its immediate success spawned a thirst for the company to expand into more devices.

"The origin story of the (devices) organization is Kindle," said Dave Limp, whom Amazon hired to run the devices organization in 2010, in an interview. "It was about building a flywheel that was a device. [It] got people to get more convenience to buy and read books. The reading experience was better, you could read in sunlight, you didn't have to think about battery life, so you read more," said Limp. That flywheel eventually extended to a self-publishing platform for authors that Amazon launched.

Prior to Amazon, Limp had worked at Apple for more than eight years, where he was director of its PowerBook laptop division in North and South America. After Apple, he worked as chief strategy officer of Palm Computing, which made small computers that fit into the palm of your hand called personal digital assistants. He had a lot of experience at companies developing hardware.

Devices were another foothold—a massive one—in the customer's daily habit.

Amazon doubled down on developing devices that, like the Kindle, could offer customers consumer electronics that they could interact with on a daily basis. Lab126 and other Amazon teams furiously worked on prototypes for different devices: smartphones, streaming devices, and voice assistants.

In the spring of 2014, Amazon launched the Fire TV set-top box, allowing customers to stream television and movies. It was a big hit. The announcement would put Amazon in head-to-head competition with Roku, which had a yearslong head start in streaming, and Google's Chromecast.

But while some took off, others failed. Amazon was late to the device game, and sometimes it showed. Its summer 2014 launch of a mobile phone called the Fire Phone was an abject failure, with Amazon having to take a $170 million write-down.

The devices team became a pet project for Bezos, who dedicated a significant amount of his time and energy to the group. He weighed in on what to name the devices and was actively involved when the company acquired other device makers. In the case of Ring, the maker of internet-connected doorbells with video cameras, internal Amazon emails show that the company was worried that it was late to the segment "by years" and decided it was best to acquire Ring rather than trying to build a competing version itself.

Bezos viewed devices as core to Amazon's broader ambitions and flywheel. Devices were beacons in his customers' homes, delivering back the most invaluable information and data that informed Amazon. They also served as conduits to connect Amazon's various tentacles, which had continued to spread. On the Fire TV stick, customers streamed content from Amazon Studios and got served up advertising from its advertising arm. On Kindle, customers downloaded books from Amazon's Audible to listen to, bought books from Amazon's online catalog, and downloaded from authors that are part of Kindle Direct Publishing, Amazon's publishing arm. This fed Amazon's flywheel, begetting more interactions with customers throughout its growing empire.

This is by design. The Kindle "fundamentally defined how we think about our business model as an organization," said Limp in the interview. "It is not about making just another piece of consumer electronics," he said, emphasizing that Amazon already sells tons of consumer electronics on its website from other companies. "But it's not what we want to be doing. What we try to do is build a...certainly a piece of consumer electronics, a piece of hardware, that is deeply integrated to a service."

Because of these services and the data these devices provide to Amazon, it often sells its devices below or at cost just to get a foothold. "We don't have to make money when we sell you the device," explained Limp. "Instead, we make money when people actually use the device."

John Depew, who worked for five years at Lab126 creating hardware for Amazon, remembers being confused by Amazon's device ambitions when he first joined in 2010 from Apple. At Apple, Depew's entire mandate was to simply make great products. As such, Apple's business model around products was more traditional: sell their products at a markup — priced higher than it cost to make it — so that they can make money off of the sale.

While Amazon was entering the hardware space much later than companies like Apple, Microsoft, and Roku, it had a different goal and business model than the competition. "I didn't realize this at the time I was hired, but the whole idea behind all these electronics [at Amazon] was to sell stuff from the store," Depew recalls. "These were all Trojan horses to get to your pocketbook. I'm going to give you electronics, and you're going to buy from the store and not realize what's happening." (To show how far it would go to try to hawk ebooks, Lab126 even made a prototype of a surfboard with a Kindle embedded into it. Alas, it didn't go into production.)

That fundamental difference in their business model meant that Amazon often undercut the competition. Device makers would cry foul about Amazon's pricing strategy, saying that it made it tough to compete. They called it predatory pricing. Patrick Spence, CEO of the speaker company Sonos, became an outspoken critic of Amazon's pricing strategy. He called Amazon's pricing of certain devices "illegal." "They just take money from their monopoly business, they just subsidize, subsidize, subsidize," he told a reporter at *Protocol*. But in modern interpretations of antitrust law, where low prices benefiting the consumer reigned king, they had little recourse.

––––––

In late 2014, Amazon introduced the world to its Echo smart speaker devices, which had a voice-activated assistant called Alexa that would respond to commands such as playing a song, setting a timer, or giving you the day's weather forecast. The voice-activated speaker would soon change the consumer lexicon, with "Alexa" being uttered millions of times a day in homes worldwide. It brought Amazon firmly into the living room, bedroom, and bathroom of millions of customers, and, given its range of capabilities, seamlessly became integral to their lifestyles.

Amazon was a bit gun-shy on the heels of the catastrophic failure of its Fire Phone. Instead of making hundreds of thousands of smart speakers to ship to customers, Amazon only started with 80,000 Echos. Instead of a big rollout, Echo soft launched in November 2014 to Prime members who could join a waitlist for the product. That list quickly surpassed Amazon's most ambitious predictions, with more than 109,000 customers signing up, according to Brad Stone's *Amazon Unbound*. Like the Kindle, Amazon seemed to have a hit on its hands.

It turned out that people liked talking to their Echo speakers—a lot. While Apple's Siri had launched years earlier, many consumers preferred using their Echo speakers. Consumers quickly adopted the technology, and there was an appetite to use their voices to control other items in their homes, too.

By 2017, Amazon was the biggest voice-enabled speaker on the market. The name *Alexa* became synonymous with speaking to a computer (much to the chagrin of women named Alexa around the world). As of June 2022, there were more than 87 million Echo devices in US homes, representing 28 percent of Amazon shopper households. The company holds the top position globally in the smart speaker market, according to research firm Canalys.

Because Amazon became synonymous with voice-activated speakers, being that it was the number one maker of such devices, device makers offering voice assistants felt like they had no choice but to partner with Alexa. In 2015, Amazon launched Alexa Voice Service for this very purpose. Alexa Voice Service offered an authorization process for companies to enable their devices like Philips smart light bulbs or Bose soundbars to be compatible with Alexa's functionality.

This gave Amazon more access to the technology of hundreds of its competitors and would help it gather data emerging from users' homes, on their bodies, and even in their cars, whether it was from their own devices or that of their partners. (As of early 2023, more than 500 million Alexa-enabled devices both from Amazon's brands and other device makers sit in customers' homes around the world.)

The Alexa authentication process required a lot from its participants, especially for companies doing custom implementations of Alexa into their hardware. Partnering companies, such as another speaker company, would have to apply for Alexa authentication every time it released a new product. They could go down one of two paths: for smart products without a microphone, they could apply for a "Works with Alexa" badge, where a customer would use their own Echo device to control a product. Or, they could have Alexa built into their own hardware. In order to qualify for either, device makers had to send their products to either Amazon or a third-party lab for testing. To have Alexa built into the hardware, many partners had to share their newest proprietary product with Amazon well before it hit the market if they wanted to launch with the Alexa capability.

Engineers on the Alexa Voice Service team said that in the first few years of the business, it took more than eighteen months to certify the products, meaning that if a device maker wanted to launch with Alexa embedded into it, they would have to send their prototypes well ahead of time. They say that more recently, the lead times have shortened to two to three months (in the best-case scenario).

Even so, that's an eternity for electronics makers who keep their newest products closely guarded secrets from just about everyone. Inside these companies, the latest hardware typically is given a code name and worked on in satellite offices with blacked-out windows to prevent leaks. It's even more daunting considering who was on the receiving end of these corporate secrets. The price of entry is such that Sonos, Dell, and many others share their technology with one of their biggest competitors.

Amazon said that "certification requirements vary based on the type of integration and device" and that partners could choose to send preproduction devices to a verified independent lab for testing instead of Amazon. Amazon only started offering third-party lab testing in 2020.

Amazon's Alexa Voice Service website lays out how the company partners with other device makers. "We've consulted with commercial device manufacturers through concept definition, design review, integration, feature development, testing and certification, marketing, launch, and post-launch." In other words, Amazon often has the privilege of embedding its engineers with device competitors early on in their product development, giving them a peek under the hood of their newest technology, which made guarding their proprietary products harder to keep as an exclusive, in-house secret.

The Alexa Voice Service lab is like a candy shop for technologists. Here, engineers and other Amazon employees experiment with the newest technology from the world's biggest developers, conducting strength tests and audio-acoustic testing to make sure that the Alexa voice experience is as good as it would be on Amazon's own Echo devices.

Devices, from voice-enabled subwoofers to smart locks and ceiling fans, fill cubicles at Alexa Voice Service's offices in Amazon's Day 1 building, where the Alexa team works. Amazon said that prototypes are stored and handled in secure device labs with access limited to only those who need to know about them to do their job.

The group reported to devices head Dave Limp, whose office was also in the Day 1 building.

At Amazon, Limp's remit was expansive. As the company introduced more and more devices, his universe encompassed Alexa, Fire TV, Kindle, Fire Tablets, and a host of other areas.

Each week, Alexa Voice Service sent Limp a weekly business review chronicling which companies it was integrating and which products they had. Limp's main goal was to create products that would fly off the shelves and get embedded in more and more customer's homes. These reports were like delivering sheep to a wolf.

Companies didn't pay Amazon to build Alexa into their hardware. "No one paid a cent to get Alexa on their devices," said a longtime engineer for Alexa Voice Service of the built-in service. (Partners pay a small fee if they go the other route, to get a "Works with Alexa" badge.) Instead, Amazon had to pay a team of expensive engineers and sound technicians to do all of the heavy lifting.

This was strange for the notoriously frugal company. To boot, Amazon's devices business is a giant money loser for Amazon. The company lost more than $5 billion a year for a number of years since 2018, according to internal documents.

But while Amazon wasn't charging consumer electronics companies to embed Alexa into their hardware, it was collecting something arguably more valuable. "When you enable a device to integrate with Amazon, you're letting Amazon into the home of our customer to get their information. The channel to the customer is what's valuable," said the former Alexa Voice Service engineer.

It soon became clear that getting Alexa-compatible was hardly "free." There was another cost. As a number of companies felt bound by the reality that they needed the Alexa voice technology, it also, for some, became a deal with the devil. Especially since there was no alternative.

———

In 2000, a group of friends and colleagues in Santa Barbara merged their company Software.com with Phone.com and needed to figure out their next move. John MacFarlane, the leader of the pack, pitched his three friends some ideas. The first was around aviation and providing LAN connections. The friends vetoed it.

However, they all had a love for music, but found that storing their CDs and navigating the tangled cables and wiring issues to get a home up and running was a major frustration.

In 2002, they launched Sonos with the mission "Filling your home with music." This was an ambitious target at the time. Americans filled their homes with CD players with wires sticking out from behind clunky entertainment centers.

Sonos's range of high-end speakers would pipe music and audio content throughout a customer's home, using internet-connected multiroom audio components that delivered music throughout the entire house. This eliminated the yards of cables and transformed the home entertainment space. The company took off, steadily gaining market share over the years.

A Sonos board member was an early adopter of Amazon's Echo device, and MacFarlane, Sonos's CEO at the time, noticed a few Sonos employees also using Echo speakers. "There was a cacophony of voices about it," MacFarlane recalled years later.

During the Christmas season of 2015, Sonos devices sold slower than the company anticipated. Echo had been out for a year and was eating into Sonos's sales, even if its sound quality was inferior to Sonos's products. That holiday season, Amazon sold more than a million Echo devices. While the industry had discussed voice commands for years, no one had broken into the space in a meaningful enough way, including Sonos. Then along came Amazon.

MacFarlane decided Sonos was moving too slowly to change. On the heels of investment bank Allen & Company's big CEO conference where he spoke to other corporate titans about technological change, he decided Sonos had to go all-in on voice commands. Around this time, Amazon contacted the company to partner on voice.

Sonos had already been selling its speakers on Amazon.com for years, providing Amazon with directional information on sales and customer demand. But now it had to partner with them in a different way. It decided to get certified for Alexa.

More than six months before launching their newest speakers, Sonos sent a prototype to Amazon's Alexa Voice Service team in Seattle.

"They get a very early look at what we are intending to do," said a senior Sonos executive of Amazon. Sonos executives found the process intrusive. They questioned the lead time that Amazon wanted on their products and the level of detail the company requested.

"It's disconcerting, but you don't really have a choice," said Craig Shelburne, a Sonos cofounder who served as chief legal officer until late 2018.

An Amazon spokesman said that in the early days of Alexa Voice Service, implementations were "bespoke and took time." The spokesman confirmed that Sonos shared prototypes with Amazon. "Sonos was new to building for voice and requested use of our Echo Spatial Perception (ESP) technology and wake word engine, which we provided for free. They were the first-ever third party to use these technologies. We conducted extensive testing to make sure they worked for customers."

The Sonos team was aware that Amazon touted firewalls between its disparate divisions in order to protect certain data, but had heard of the rumors that those firewalls were not very strong. For years, there had been persistent allegations from Amazon's third-party sellers that Amazon's private label team was using their data to copy their items. Amazon had always denied the allegations, pointing to an internal policy that prevented such behavior. But many partners worried about Amazon's size and reach and that the firewalls were either not being enforced or were weak. If the rumors were true, the Sonos management team worried that Amazon could copy their technology through its partnership with Alexa Voice Service. Their paranoia was not unfounded.

In 2015, Google, another of Sonos's close partners, infringed Sonos's patents, according to Sonos executives. Sonos claimed that the tech giant violated more than 100 patents in products such as its Google Home and Chromecast Audio devices. MacFarlane, who was CEO of Sonos until 2017, was angry and began contemplating legal action against Google. He called Amazon's device head Dave Limp to tell him what Google had done and warned him that Amazon better not go down the same route. Limp assured MacFarlane that Amazon wouldn't violate Sonos's patents.

But Amazon wasn't true to its word, according to Sonos executives. On reviewing Amazon's products, Sonos believed that Amazon also went on to infringe 100 Sonos patents. MacFarlane says he doesn't know if Amazon used the Alexa Voice Service process to copy Sonos's patents, but acknowledges the access they had as a result of it. "They certainly had access to units so they could reverse engineer. Certainly had access to a large number of Sonos engineers that they could question as a result of the Alexa Voice Service process," he said.

While Sonos executives claimed that Amazon and Google both infringed on its patents, given its size, the company had the resources to sue only one of the tech giants. They chose Google. Amazon's power as an online retailer created a tricky high-wire act for partners to navigate. Many relied on Amazon as a sales channel and couldn't risk confronting the company for its transgressions out of fear that Amazon would kick them off of the site, which was a major platform they relied on to reach customers. Sonos was no exception. One Sonos executive said part of the reason for suing Google over Amazon was fear of retaliation from Amazon on the retail side. If Amazon were to cut Sonos off from selling its products on its website, it could have an immediate negative impact on the company's sales. The need for competitors to sell on Amazon's vast e-commerce platform, where nearly 40 percent of all online shopping occurs, has insulated the technology giant from many lawsuits. (In 2021 Sonos would stop selling on Amazon.com because of the company's business practices.)

As Sonos moved forward with a lawsuit against Google, Amazon was insulated from scrutiny in this case. Meanwhile, in 2018, Amazon launched what Sonos executives viewed as a copycat version of their subwoofer, a high-margin product for their brand.

An Amazon spokesman said the company strongly refutes that Sonos technology was used in its subwoofer.

Sonos was hardly alone; other consumer electronics makers also became wary of partnering with Alexa Voice Service after feeling they had been burned.

Belkin International, a Los Angeles–based electronics maker, was another case. It, too, felt like it had been taken advantage of by its partnership with the Alexa Voice Service team.

Belkin was founded by Chet Pipkin, an against-all-odds CEO who was the son of working-class parents who didn't attend high school. His mother was the illegitimate daughter of a North Dakota farmer, and his father traveled by horse and wagon from Texas to Oklahoma in the 1920s, residing in abandoned homes along the route. The two met after World War II. It's believed that his great-aunt was the inspiration for Ma Joad in Steinbeck's *The Grapes of Wrath*, which was published to great acclaim in 1939. Pipkin grew up in humble surroundings but had a drive that set him apart.

After dropping out of college, Pipkin went looking for work at the electronics shops where he lived in the South Bay of California. He had a hunch that computers were the next big disruptor, and went shop to shop, asking if he could hang out and observe. The owners allowed him to as long as he did odd jobs along the way. He started to notice a disconnect between the sales agents at the stores looking to make a sale and the customers confused about how to connect their products together. Connecting a printer to a computer was a particularly common pain point for customers, he realized. Pipkin started fashioning easier-to-use cables on his parents' dining room table and returned to the shops to sell them. In 1983 he formally launched Belkin. The company is now a major manufacturer of screen protectors, phone chargers, and headphones, among other products.

In 2015, Belkin partnered with Amazon to make its Wemo smart plug compatible with the voice assistant. The partnership allowed users to tell their Echo devices to make Wemo's smart plug do tasks such as turn lights on and off with a simple voice command.

In order to get the Alexa certification, Belkin sent prototypes of its Wemo smart plugs to Amazon, Pipkin says.

The partnership with Amazon started off really strong between the two companies, but about two years in, Belkin started seeing its technology show up in Amazon's smart plugs.

"There have been occasions where from our view—they would

have a different view—the ideas and the tech, I don't know what the right word is...stolen, utilized, advanced, put into Amazon private label items. Our experience with them is that they're not a trustworthy partner, but they're extremely predictable," said Pipkin, who was CEO of the company during this period.

Belkin no longer sends its newest technology to Amazon for Alexa certification. "Our next generations of Wemo innovations, they don't go to Amazon first, or they don't go to Amazon at all, or [we] send a very limited basis to Amazon," said Pipkin.

———

As Amazon grew into disparate businesses, partnering with companies while also competing with them, it assured its partners that they followed protocols to prevent Amazon from learning proprietary information. In 2014, for instance, Amazon introduced their Seller Data Protection Policy, which private label employees were to abide by. The policy forbade private label employees from accessing sales data from individual third-party sellers on Amazon's Marketplace. This was meant to protect Amazon's sellers from being copied by Amazon's own brands.

But the rapid growth across businesses, each with its own troves of data, could be tempting for those looking to get ahead. And Amazon's internal systems to safeguard data were lacking.

In 2015, members of Amazon's S-Team were presented with the results of an internal audit of employee access to data across Amazon. The report showed that nearly 4,700 Amazon employees had unauthorized access to third-party seller data on Amazon, according to *Politico*.

"Permissions are not adequately restricted, making it possible for unauthorized users to view Seller-specific information such as performance history and authentication keys, edit inventory levels and pricing, and manage returns," the internal report read, according to *Politico*. It mentions similar findings from a 2010 internal audit. The report shows that Amazon's general counsel David Zapolsky was aware of the findings, as was Jeff Wilke, a senior executive on the retail side of Amazon's business at the time.

The report identified an Amazon employee who spied on seller data in order to goose the chances of winning Amazon's coveted "Buy Box" placement on Amazon.com, which leads to more orders.

The S-Team discussed the audit and identified Amazon's information security — or the process of protecting information from unauthorized access — as a weakness. "It was another example of where Amazon needed more segmented access controls for lots of reasons," said a former S-Team member who was briefed on the report. Amazon declined to comment on the results of the audit, which they say are privileged.

But the lax controls would persist for years. "The company still operated in this really startuppy way, meaning you often had access to data that for your job you didn't need access to," says Kristi Coulter, who left Amazon in 2018 after eleven years at the company. "When you're moving fast, you're not really thinking as clearly about 'well, how do we make sure that only the right people have access to this data set.' The internal infrastructure of the company is basically Popsicle sticks and like duct tape, often."

And because the refinements of the evolutionary forces of Amazon were so key, because your success at the company largely depended on how inevitable you could make those forces, data was king at Amazon. It was the measure of any Amazonian's ability to play God in their sector.

———

In addition to the risk of the intrusive Alexa Voice Service process, once device makers get approved for Alexa Voice Service and equip their devices with the functionality, they often find Amazon using that continued relationship as a way to gain leverage with their partners. It wasn't as clean-cut as adding Alexa to your device. Instead, Amazon had an ongoing relationship with many of their voice partners and demanded more and more data over time.

Vivint Smart Home, a maker of doorbell cameras, garage door openers, and other connected-home devices, first integrated with Alexa in 2016.

In late 2017, Amazon was launching an update to its Echo speakers and told Vivint that it would allow the company to remain functional on the Echo device only if Vivint agreed to give it not only the data from its Vivint function on Echo, but from every Vivint device in those customers' homes at all times, people involved told me.

Vivint executives were shocked by the request. Their customers typically have about fifteen Vivint devices in their homes, and the company has more than 1.5 billion pieces of data coming in daily from customers that the company monitors for home security issues. It was already abiding by Amazon's initial terms of sharing data with the company when Vivint customers used the Alexa function in its interactions, but this request to share data (called "current state") from customers' homes around the clock was going too far. Vivint declined to hand over the data, which was a bold move. There was a chance that if Amazon discontinued Echo's ability to function with Vivint, customers would defect to a different device.

A Vivint executive sent the following email to an Amazon vice president, laying out what he viewed as bullying:

> A few months ago, your team informed us there was a new version of the Alexa Smart Home API coming that would require us to provide our device's current state in real time to your platform. We spent billions of dollars to place tens of millions of devices in our customer homes, and the insight we generate on home activity through these devices is perhaps our most valuable asset. We have been straightforward from the beginning that we weren't going to implement the new APIs to share all our customers' private and valuable home activity data because there is no apparent value to us or our customers. We have a lot of respect for Amazon and value our partnership, but the recent strong arm tactics used to get us to adopt the new API are concerning. If I understand correctly, you have communicated to our team that our Echo supply, existing smart home skill and camera API integration are all in jeopardy unless we adopt the new API. If this is your stance, it will be very difficult for us to continue to rely on Amazon as our primary voice assistant partner.

Despite refusing to share the data with Amazon, Vivint remained functional on Echo devices.

Ecobee, a Canadian-based maker of smart thermostats, was put into a similar position with Amazon. The device maker was Alexa enabled, allowing customers to control temperatures in their homes by using the Alexa command, and shared that data with Amazon when customers invoked the Alexa wake word.

But in 2020, the company received a brazen demand: Amazon requested that Ecobee also provide the tech giant data from its voice-enabled devices even when customers weren't using them. It wanted millions of data points from those customers' homes: what the temperature was throughout the day and other details, even when the customers weren't home. The Canadian company said no, fearing that complying would violate the trust and privacy of its customers.

Ecobee also worried that Amazon would glean insights from its users that it could use in competing products.

Amazon responded that if Ecobee didn't serve up its data, the refusal could affect Ecobee's ability to sell on Amazon's retail platform. Amazon knew that for Ecobee and many other partners, Amazon.com is their biggest sales channel. Veiled threats to suppress their products, remove them from promotions such as Prime Day, or fully kick them off of the biggest e-commerce platform in America are the type of arm-twisting Amazon sometimes invokes to force concessions from partners, say former Amazon executives, as well as CEOs who have been opposite them.

Amazon's power to compel other companies to align with its interests is on full display in the devices sector, and this behavior was replicated across Amazon's various arms. Its ability to shift from facilitator or partner to mobster can occur in the blink of an eye.

———

One of the most pervasive ways Amazon wins against competitors is by using its platform as leverage. In these cases, Amazon has the upper hand, using a practice called "self-preferencing" in antitrust circles. Because Amazon competes against the very device makers that sell on

Amazon.com through its own device brands, it often promotes its own products and suppresses those of competing brands. For those brands, which rely on Amazon as a major selling channel, that sort of suppression can be costly.

A common theme started to emerge for Amazon's top device sellers once they became competitors. After years of successfully selling their gadgets on Amazon.com, suddenly their ability to promote their goods on Amazon's website through Amazon ads was cut off. The change in ability to advertise always aligned with Amazon launching a competing product or acquiring one of their competitors.

This was not a coincidence. Behind the scenes, Amazon's device executives were doing everything in their power to make sure that their own devices were successful, and that included suppressing competition on its website.

One of the tools at their disposal was control of advertising placements on Amazon.com. With 2 million sellers hawking their goods on the platform worldwide, the most efficient way to make sure that your wares show up in search results is by buying keywords that people are searching for. So, if you sell slow cookers, you might buy ads for the search terms "pressure cooker" and "crock pot" to outbid the hundreds of sellers with similar items and land on page 1 of the search results.

The first page of Amazon search results is the holy grail. Seventy percent of shoppers don't scroll beyond the first page, making buying keywords all but required for most sellers. These ad placements are so powerful that Amazon's advertising business grew from just $8.3 billion in 2018 to more than $31 billion by 2021, according to internal documents. Their digital advertising business is now a bona fide juggernaut, ranking only behind Facebook and Google's advertising arms in the US. While Amazon sells lots of different types of advertisements across its properties, its search advertisements, like sponsored product advertisements, make up the lion's share of revenues because of how integral they are to a seller's success. If you buy a sponsored product placement for a certain keyword, your item could show up on page 1 when someone searches for that term. Ideally, if the platform was neutral, ad spends would dictate search result rankings between competitors. But through its devices and private brands businesses, Amazon is also a competitor. This made things far more complicated.

In addition to buying generic keywords, another popular tactic is to buy the keywords of competitors to try to siphon off traffic from their product to yours. So, if you sell Adidas sneakers, you might bid on the keywords for "Reebok" or "Reebok Classic."

In meetings, Amazon's device team strategized on how to prevent rival device sellers from picking off shoppers looking for Amazon's Fire TV streaming devices, Echo speakers, and Ring doorbells. While Amazon's own products almost always were at the very top of the search results for keywords for rival device companies—a giant advantage—Amazon didn't want to allow the same for its competitors. So, for instance, a shopper searching for a Roku streaming device will often be bombarded with competing Fire TV sponsored product placements on the very top of the page. For products that largely provide the same functionality—like a streaming device—customers could be swayed by what appeared at the top of the search results, especially if it offered a lower price.

The devices teams wrote down a list of what they called tier 1 competitors, or the biggest threats to its device business. The list included Roku and Arlo smart doorbells. Amazon then suppressed the advertising abilities of the competitors on this list—and in some cases, entirely cut off their ability to advertise.

Roku is Fire TV's most fierce competitor, and for years the company jockeyed with Amazon for the top spot in streaming devices in the US. Roku had a slightly higher number of users than the Fire TV, but Amazon was steadily closing that gap with its own range of devices. (In late 2022, adoption of Fire TV sticks began exceeding that of Roku, with Fire TV accounting for 40 percent of streaming media players in US consumers' homes, according to Parks Associates.)

Like many companies, Roku considers Amazon its most dangerous competitor, yet sells its products on Amazon.com. In 2022, Amazon was Roku's second-largest retail channel. Given the amount of sales Amazon commands, not selling on its platform wasn't an option for

Roku. Like many big brands, Roku bought keywords on Amazon to ensure its devices showed up in search results. Until, one day, it couldn't.

For Roku, their advertising problems started with the company's inability to buy keywords pegged to Amazon's Fire TV. Roku would submit a list of twenty or so variations of the keyword "Fire TV," which are able to be bought by other brands, only to receive an error message on the ad-buying platform that the keywords were unavailable. This eliminated Roku's ability to pick off shoppers looking for Fire TV streaming devices and direct them to their own devices, but searches for "Roku" on Amazon often appeared with giant banners at the top of the page advertising Amazon's Fire TV products. It felt like an uneven playing field.

Soon, Roku's advertising abilities became even more limited. The company was no longer permitted to even buy its own keywords on Amazon.com. So, when shoppers searched for Roku devices on Amazon, oftentimes resellers of their products — frequently listed at higher prices than their own — showed up at the top of the search results. Amazon declined to comment on how showing customers higher-priced goods reconciled with its "customer obsession" policy.

The *Wall Street Journal* ran its own tests on the keywords. In a search on Amazon for "Roku Streaming Stick," Amazon featured its Fire TV products four times under "Featured from our brands" on the first page of search results, which generally show about twenty to twenty-five results. The Fire TV products showed up twice more on the first page of results.

By comparison, a search for "Fire TV" in the *Journal*'s tests showed an Amazon "Fire TV" banner across the site's search results, with the Amazon logo followed by three Amazon products sold by Amazon. There were no sponsored results in that search, meaning that Amazon didn't allow anyone else to buy their keyword for the search.

When you own the ad exchange, you also get to use it in ways that advantage your own goods. The *Journal* found that "Amazon limits competitors' advertisements by using up to five of the 12 spaces typically sold as advertisements to highlight its own offerings, according to a *Journal* analysis of search results. For six days, the *Journal* downloaded search results for 67 keywords describing Amazon products and those by competing brands including Google, Roku and Arlo."

When Amazon's devices team launches a new product, part of its strategy for bringing it to market is to determine which keywords to suppress in advertising, people on the team told me. Employees are told to mark any discussion of this practice internally at Amazon with "privileged and confidential" in the subject line of emails so that regulators cannot access them. Roku had been flagged. For years, Roku couldn't participate in the powerful sponsored search advertising marketplace on Amazon. That sort of blackballing is consequential. More than 50 percent of product searches in the US start on Amazon.

Interestingly, preventing sellers from buying such keywords goes against Amazon's own stated policies. According to Amazon's advertising website, any seller is eligible to buy keywords for its sponsored search advertisements. Some types of products are prohibited from being advertised in sponsored products, such as sex toys. Amazon's own products aren't on the list of keywords or categories restricted for sponsored product advertisements.

Arlo Technologies, a smaller manufacturer of smart security products and doorbells, was the market leader for smart security devices for years. The company's success put it on Amazon's executive team's radar. Emails in 2017 among Amazon's management team discussing a potential acquisition of Ring referenced Arlo's top position at the time. Ring held the second sales position, followed by Google Nest and startup Blink, according to the internal emails.

"To be clear, my view here is that we're buying market position — not technology," Bezos wrote on December 15. "And that market position and momentum is very valuable." (An Amazon spokesman said, "Buying market position is very normal.")

Since Amazon bought smart camera and doorbell startup Blink in late 2017 and Ring in early 2018, Arlo has been unable to buy keywords on Amazon's sponsored product advertisements for Ring products, said Arlo executives. Amazon's Ring devices, though, have appeared at the top of the search results for "Arlo" in banner placements touting "Featured from our brands," showing a suite of Ring doorbell devices.

Arlo's team raised this issue with Amazon's advertising team. Arlo was concerned that it could buy keywords for competitors like Eufy and Wyze, but not for Ring or Blink, Arlo executives told me. The advertising team apologized to Arlo executives but said that there was nothing they could do about the issue.

The pattern played out across the devices space. Once Amazon bought Wi-Fi networking router company eero in 2019, Netgear was cut off from buying any advertisements pegged to the "eero" keyword. Facebook was cut off from buying ads tied to Amazon's Echo Show device, a smart speaker with a screen that competes with Facebook's Portal device. For more than a year starting in 2017, Amazon had also blocked Google from selling its Chromecast streaming devices, some Nest smart thermostat devices, and Google Home products on Amazon.com. All of the Google devices Amazon banned compete with Amazon. In retaliation, Google said in December 2017 that it was pulling its YouTube online video service from some Amazon devices. In 2019, Google reversed course.

The practice of blocking advertising from competitors at Amazon was a long-standing one. Internal Amazon emails from 2010 show top executives, including Blackburn, creating a framework to keep daily deals website Groupon from advertising on Amazon.com. Amazon was in the process of signing a big advertising deal with the daily deal site in Japan when Amazon executives weighed in to nix it. "Groupon is blocked + let's keep a clear line on this. No deal site e-commerce competitors allowed to advertise on amazon.x sites," wrote Blackburn in the email, creating a precedent to keep Amazon's competitors from advertising on its website.

When we published a story outlining this anticompetitive behavior for the *Wall Street Journal*, it struck a nerve inside Amazon. Their typically uncooperative public relations team went a step further, turning outright hostile about the story.

Instead of addressing the facts we presented in the story, Bezos's personal public relations chief sent a statement that read: "News flash: retailers promote their own products and often don't sell products of competitors. Walmart refuses to sell [Amazon brands] Kindle, Fire TV, and Echo. Shocker. In the Journal's next story they will uncover gambling in Las Vegas." A quick search on Walmart.com shows that Walmart does sell Amazon Echo, Ring, and Kindle tablet devices on its website through third-party sellers.

It turns out that Bezos personally wrote Amazon's comment himself, a theme that would emerge whenever Amazon made brash public-facing comments. (For this book, Amazon toned down its response, admitting that "for some keywords related to Amazon devices, we may offer more limited advertising inventory.") Amazon's aggressive strategy tended to backfire for the company, yet over the years they doubled down on it, with public relations executives afraid to push back against their billionaire boss. In the comments for the story and on Twitter, people latched on to the comment, calling it "arrogant" and "wild." One commenter wrote: "Their 'newsflash' guy could use some class." Little did he know he was referring to the world's richest man.

CHAPTER 6

Venture Capital or Corporate Espionage?

IN 2015, A DIRECTOR on Amazon's corporate development team, where the company did mergers and acquisitions, had an idea to spread Amazon's tentacles even further into the world of dealmaking. Paul Bernard had joined the corporate development team two years prior, after holding a similar position at Nokia and working at investment bank Goldman Sachs, and saw an opportunity for the company to leverage its access and dealmaking chops in a new way.

Bernard wrote a six-pager, Amazon's internal mechanism for making pitches on business ideas, about creating a new program that straddled corporate development, where deals were done, and its new hit product: the Echo smart speaker. The idea was to create an internal venture capital arm to find the world's most promising technology companies that were excited about voice technology and invest in them at the earliest stages. The fund would also help build out Amazon's Alexa ecosystem, helping these companies integrate with Alexa.

Bezos liked the pitch, and in June 2015, the Alexa Fund launched with an initial $100 million to invest in startups. "So I was turned into a venture investor, trying to figure that out in real time," Bernard told *TechCrunch*. Alexa Voice Service was launched the same day.

The Alexa Fund was "open to anyone with an innovative idea for how voice technology can improve customers' lives," according to its press release. On its website, entrepreneurs could apply for the chance to meet with Alexa Fund executives for funding. All they had to do was hand over their number of customers, annual revenue, and other information into a portal that the Fund's team would evaluate.

The traditional goal of venture capital firms is to find promising, young startups to invest in at their earliest stages. These venture capital firms use their investors' money to take a stake in these technology companies, essentially making a bet that they will become big successes. The startups, in turn, use the venture capital funds as a way to finance their businesses and grow. Once the company reaches a size where it can sell itself or go public, the venture capital fund cashes out at a multiple of its original investment. For example, Sequoia Capital turned a roughly $60 million investment in messaging app WhatsApp into a $3 billion windfall when Facebook bought it in 2014. But there is, of course, the other path: investing in startups that don't achieve their targets and shut down, causing the venture capital firm to lose its investment. Traditional venture capital firms are ranked based on their returns for investors. Not every investment is a hit, but the big wins offset the duds and create ample returns for the firm's investors.

Amazon's venture capital fund had different goals. An exit, such as the sale or IPO of the companies it invested in, was not a priority. Neither was it driven primarily by financial gain. "It really was positioned as an idea of getting more people to build on Alexa. It was really about funding the developer community," said a former Alexa Fund employee. Instead of making money through exits, Amazon was seeding the most innovative companies in a space it had helped popularize — voice assistant technology. Companies that weighed investments from the Alexa Fund often skeptically wondered what was in it for Amazon if they weren't after financial returns.

Amazon declined to comment about whether the Alexa Fund has profit targets and would not provide the rate of the Alexa Fund's returns.

"There's a certain amount of healthy skepticism or fear with any product you have that you introduce to their ecosystem. We are all aware of the fact that Amazon can destroy your business overnight if they want to do that," said venture capitalist Jeff Morris about entrepreneurs meeting with Amazon's Alexa Fund.

Even so, droves of founders contacted the fund for a meeting and a chance to secure financial backing.

———————

On the corporate development side of the business, where acquisitions were struck, Amazon had assembled a top-notch army of lawyers and former bankers to meet with hundreds of companies that could help Amazon expand further beyond its retail roots. Their job was to find the next big ideas, the ones the company couldn't develop from within.

It was a long-odds business. For every company they would acquire, like a Quidsi or Whole Foods, there were dozens more they would meet with and inspect, only to pass.

But it turns out even the passes weren't always a loss.

Few passed up a meeting with Amazon, even skeptics. This gave the company unfettered access to the world's most interesting and innovative companies. Under the auspices of potentially buying or investing in these companies, Amazon had detailed access to them, in the process scooping up proprietary information on their customers, financial reports, engineering, and underlying technology.

While the corporate development team snapped up companies like Zappos and video game company Twitch, and the Alexa Fund made investments in Ring doorbells, it also left a trail of burned entrepreneurs in its wake.

These companies were sometimes strung along for months, giving Amazon a wealth of information and road maps to their product and strategy. And then it happened again and again: Amazon would suddenly lose interest, only to turn up later with a competing product. Numerous founders described a pattern to me: they would meet with Amazon's team for months and share proprietary information with the understanding that Amazon would possibly invest in them or buy them, only to experience the business world's equivalent of ghosting a love interest on Tinder. Later, Amazon would issue a press release touting something eerily similar to what the founder shared with Amazon. And while founders have their own gripes about traditional venture capitalists, traditional VCs don't launch their own companies and compete with startups.

These entrepreneurs felt that both the Alexa Fund and Amazon's massive corporate business development arm operated less in the fashion of typical dealmaking and more like a corporate espionage unit.

The founders caught in this trap said they felt like they had been exploited by the tech giant. Over the phone with me, some even cried when recollecting their experiences. When I cold-called a prominent venture capitalist to get his take about Amazon's behavior, he was short with me until he realized the purpose of my call. "Thank God you are covering this," he said. "Amazon is the devil."

———

Jonathan Frankel was one of the founders wooed by the Alexa Fund. Frankel did not fit the profile of most technology entrepreneurs. He wasn't a hoodie-sporting bro who had dropped out of Stanford to create the next hot tech startup in his garage.

Frankel was a Philadelphia-based rabbi and family man with a degree from Harvard Law School. People who interacted with him often describe him as one of the nicest people they've ever met.

Frankel was having trouble keeping track of his three young sons throughout his three-story Philadelphia home. He wanted to be able to check in on where they were throughout the house when he heard the inevitable tussle between them or needed to reach them on different floors. After consulting with a contractor on an intercom with camera functions, he was quoted $3,500 for a clunky intercom system that was as advanced as the ones his own parents used in his childhood. He then went online to find a cheaper alternative, but also struck out. Identifying a gap in the market, Frankel decided to create a wireless intercom system with screens himself at a reasonable price point:

$250. He and two cofounders researched the market, found a product-engineering laboratory to make a prototype, and worked tirelessly to bring the product to fruition.

In 2016, their company, Nucleus, launched and quickly gained traction. Home improvement store chain Lowe's carried the product in hundreds of its locations. Nucleus was also selling through Amazon.com.

Later that year, the trio engaged the Alexa Fund and other venture capitalist firms simultaneously. They were thrilled to receive a seed investment from venture capitalists, including BoxGroup and Greylock Partners. The $5.6 million investment was led by Amazon's Alexa Fund. The Alexa Fund wrote a check for more than $1.5 million, making it one of its biggest investments at the time of the deal.

Behind the scenes, the other co-investors had reservations about letting Amazon into the deal. They worried that it would be like letting a fox into a henhouse. They were concerned that Amazon, with its sprawling empire and giant push into voice technology, would glean information from the startup as a result of its investment. While there hadn't yet been Alexa Fund recipients that raised the alarm about working with the venture arm, there was an acknowledgment that Amazon had become a true conglomerate and was rapidly expanding into any area of opportunity it found. Nothing was too off target for Amazon, which in this period operated in areas as diverse as air cargo, was working on developing delivery drones, and had a number of its own devices, including a Dash button that customers could push to repurchase consumer goods like detergent.

"Our biggest concern at the time that we invested was that Amazon could come up with a competing product," one of the investors said. Again, Amazon relied on touting the firewall that the company had to assuage concerns. In this case, Alexa Fund representatives told co-investors there is a firewall between the Alexa Fund and Amazon itself, the investor said.

Nucleus's co-founders had similar concerns about Amazon copying them and raised this to Alexa Fund leader Paul Bernard. He calmed the cofounders' concerns about some troubling legalese they found in their contract for the deal. He told them it was just boilerplate language used in every Amazon contract and that Amazon wasn't working on, nor did they plan to work on, anything similar to Nucleus's product. He was persuasive enough, and Nucleus's cofounders signed on the dotted line.

As a result of its investment, an Alexa Fund executive earned a board observer seat at the company and got access to Nucleus's financials, strategic plans, and other proprietary information. It is not uncommon for venture capitalists to get board seats at firms they invest in, depending on the size of their investments.

Just as Amazon had grown a giant internal team of dealmakers from some of Wall Street's top investment banks, its legal team had also swelled. Lawyers from top white-shoe firms such as Skadden Arps and Cravath, Swaine & Moore made up the ranks of a truly formidable legal team.

This team was essential not only in dealing with the day-to-day legal matters, but also in drafting contracts that protected Amazon in its meetings with companies it considered buying or investing in.

When entrepreneurs met with Amazon for a meeting, many didn't know that by signing its nondisclosure agreements, they were potentially allowing Amazon to use their ideas and intellectual property.

Buried in these NDAs was a clause that many founders glossed over or missed. But the founders who read their NDAs closely enough before rushing to meet with Amazon were taken aback by the language. The clause stated that nothing in Amazon's agreement with the other company prevents Amazon from "using, for any purpose and without compensating the Disclosing Party, information retained in the memory of the Receiving party's Personnel who have had access to Confidential Information." This so-called residuals clause, in essence, prevents the tech giant from being sued or held liable if any of its employees who attended meetings with deal targets remembered details from those meetings and later used them in an Amazon product. And because the Alexa Fund often brought in executives from Amazon's devices team to meetings with entrepreneurs, it meant that any information retained by the people in the room might be used in Amazon's devices with impunity.

While Amazon repeatedly assured founders about firewalls the company had in place to protect their trade secrets, mechanisms like residuals clauses and the fact that Amazon often looped other executives across the company into the deal to do due diligence tended to undermine those assurances.

A lawyer at Amazon said the clause was akin to a "get-out-of-jail-free card" for the technology giant. The lawyer acknowledged that it was hard to "unsee" what they learned in due diligence with these companies, when buyers or investors get very detailed access to a company's proprietary information for the purpose of making an investment decision.

These residuals clauses sometimes appeared in the deal contracts of other technology companies' transactions, but Amazon *always* included them.

One entrepreneur who took more than a dozen meetings with venture capital firms in Silicon Valley as part of his Series A funding was startled when he received his NDA from Amazon. He spotted the clause and was concerned. None of the other firms he had met with used a similar clause in their paperwork. A former lawyer in the Amazon devices unit said some entrepreneurs spent months trying to negotiate taking the clause out of Amazon's contracts because they were so startled by it.

At investment banks, which broker mergers and acquisitions day in and day out, there is an internal group called a conflicts committee whose purpose is to prevent the bank from becoming involved in deals that could present a potential conflict for themselves or their clients. Before an investment bank engages with a corporate client that may want to explore a sale or buy another company, the lead banker explains the client to an internal committee, which is often composed of lawyers, compliance officers, the head of investment banking, and, in certain situations, the bank CEO. This group discusses whether there is any reason not to work with the client. For instance, if Coca-Cola wanted to explore an acquisition and contacted JPMorgan to represent them, but JPMorgan had in the past advised Pepsi, the conflicts committee would rule against the investment bank taking on Coca-Cola as a client. The rationale here is that JPMorgan would have been privy to nonpublic, proprietary information about Pepsi through its work with them in the past, and working with its rival might compromise that trusted information.

Amazon declined to outline the internal conflict checks that it does before engaging with deal targets or founders through the Alexa Fund. A spokeswoman said, "We have careful controls to keep confidential information secure and shared with a limited number of people." Reporting from sources indicates that target company data often made its way into other Amazon departments beyond the ones the founder shared the information with.

With its sprawling empire of disparate businesses where employees frequently moved between divisions, many former Amazon employees and companies who had met with Amazon say that the company lacked the proper internal governance tools to safeguard the information it learned in dealmaking meetings. For one, it had the residuals clause to protect it in such scenarios, but it often brought executives and engineers from other business units to deal talks, sometimes unannounced. During a conference call with the Alexa Fund during the height of the pandemic, one founder was startled to see several Amazon employees on the screen who had not been on the original meeting invite. They did not introduce themselves until the entrepreneur pressed them for their names and titles. They were not from the Alexa Fund, but from other parts of Amazon.

"The diligence process is where everything goes horribly wrong," said a former senior Alexa Fund employee. "Part of the mandate was to bring in internal experts from either inside of Alexa or inside AWS to do the diligence on a product, and the people that were doing that work were not part of the Alexa Fund. There was no reason for them to not use the info that they got. We're bringing in people who have no incentive but to take your good ideas and use it on their teams and build their things."

In one scenario, a so-called data room was set up for an Alexa Fund meeting between Amazon and a startup called Hello Alfred. Data rooms are normal parts of M&A transactions. This portal is where target companies provide confidential information and documents to a buyer to access on a limited basis in order to evaluate the target company in a secure setting. Only certain key executives are given access to the data.

New York–based startup Hello Alfred had created software for property managers in charge of big apartment complexes to provide services like rent payment and maintenance requests and perks like dry cleaning delivery to their residents. Hello Alfred's co-founder Marcela Sapone had worked in private equity prior to launching the company and was familiar with tracking mechanisms used in data rooms to ensure that only the approved executives were accessing them. Her team tagged its documents to make sure that they were not accessed by employees beyond the agreed upon set. Soon after, she started noticing something alarming. "The folks that were accessing the documents had nothing to do with the Alexa Fund and were product managers on other initiatives," Sapone recalls. She looked their names up on LinkedIn to see what parts of Amazon's sprawling empire they worked on. One former Amazon employee involved admits that "it was very shoddily done," in reference to not properly safeguarding access to the documents.

Sapone called her lawyers to say it seemed that Amazon had breached the terms of their NDA, but was told there wasn't much recourse. In the middle of all of this, a very senior executive from Amazon's dealmaking group showed up at Hello Alfred's Manhattan offices unannounced and asked where the engineering team sat. He began counting the company's engineers before Sapone found him in the office. The number of engineers a startup has is a proxy for how advanced the company's technology is and also part of how startups were valued. While Amazon did not go on to create a Hello Alfred competitor, the way the situation unfolded showed the lack of firewalls at the company.

In 2016, Doppler Labs, a consumer electronics startup that made inner ear headphones, got an introduction to Bezos. Doppler had recently been valued at $250 million and was on the verge of launching its "hero product," wireless earbuds that also let users adjust the volume of real-life sounds around them. But being a smaller player in the cutthroat consumer electronics market is tough to go it alone. Many companies in the space either find an exit, like Oculus did when it sold its virtual reality gaming technology to Facebook a couple of years earlier, or end up running out of money because of the costs associated with developing the products and bringing them to market in a competitive space.

Bezos was enthusiastic during that initial email, according to Doppler cofounder Noah Kraft. He was quickly put in touch with Amazon's devices head Dave Limp. Kraft and his cofounder flew to Seattle where they had this "big kumbaya meeting" where Kraft says that Limp told him that he wanted to either buy the company or make a big investment in Doppler. Doppler had been talking about a deal in the $500 million to $1 billion range, Kraft says.

Kraft was ecstatic. Soon, he was in talks with Apple, Google, Microsoft and others because of how quickly Amazon said they wanted to move. He hired investment bankers from Morgan Stanley to manage the process in order to get the best deal for his investors. The night before Amazon's deal team was flying out to meet for expanded deal talks, Kraft's bankers called him. Amazon was saying he had to sign a contract that said that whatever Amazon's team retained in its memory from the meeting could be used without penalty. None of the other suitors requested this, Kraft recalls, and he pushed back. They had the meeting, but Doppler got feedback from all of the potential investors that they wanted to revisit the talks once Doppler's new product launched.

Six months later, following the launch, Doppler reached back out to Amazon to say that it was either going to sell itself or do a Series C fundraising round. The Amazon team told Kraft they were happy he'd reached back out and they were ready to move forward, Kraft says.

In June 2017, after two days of due diligence looking into Doppler's technology alongside senior engineering and devices executives, Amazon's team reserved a private dining room at the restaurant at the Four Seasons in San Francisco. They popped champagne and referenced an impending partnership. Amazon's team gave Kraft homework: Write a business plan of how Doppler could fit into Amazon's suite of hardware. He turned it in, dubbed "Amazon Ears" with the understanding that Amazon would be soon making an offer to acquire his company.

The talks went on, and Amazon indicated they would soon be making Doppler their offer, Kraft says. But the summer slipped by and Doppler, which had delayed its Series C, began running out of cash. "They go dark and we start scrambling and spend the whole summer trying to raise money," recalls Kraft. "By October, we are running out of money."

Only then did Amazon come back with its offer: $10 million. A far cry from the $500-million-plus offer Doppler had been expecting. Kraft and his team were crestfallen. He said that Amazon's executives kept telling him to take the offer to save face. A deal would allow him to say he'd been acquired by Amazon, they said.

He turned them down and sold his intellectual property to Dolby. In 2017, he shut Doppler down.

In 2019, Amazon launched its Amazon Echo Buds wireless earbuds. "Look at what we sent them and what Amazon released; it's nearly identical," Kraft says.

Amazon denied copying Doppler's product or using its technology. "Our experience is that the vast majority of companies that Amazon has interacted with in the course of business have had positive experiences," Amazon's spokesman said.

In acquisition scenarios, Amazon's corporate development team often left companies with a feeling that it was more interested in fishing for information that gave itself a competitive advantage than in actually buying or investing in them.

Andy Dunn was about to take his men's fashion company to the big leagues. His startup, Bonobos, had straddled a unique place in retail.

Instead of loads of storefronts, Dunn used his MBA from Stanford to think outside the box. In 2007, he cofounded the company with a direct-to-consumer model where men logged on to his website, filled out a questionnaire, and were shown clothing tailored to their preferences.

Bonobos had a few retail stores where men could experience the brand, but the items were not for sale, only for show. It was the tailored approach that made the brand unique. And it worked. Their line of khaki pants in a range of colors was a bestseller and became a staple in the closets of young men working in finance in Manhattan.

In 2016, Bonobos sounded out offers from some of the top private equity firms and retailers in the country. Dunn and his team flew out to Seattle to meet with the biggest fish of them all.

At a meeting at Amazon headquarters, company executives asked very pointed questions about Bonobos's business despite lacking the traditional enthusiasm potential buyers typically display.

A senior executive from corporate development sat with his arms crossed in the back of the room throughout the entire meeting. Dunn noticed the body language and was struck by how indifferent the Amazon representatives seemed to be. They didn't seem all that interested in buying his startup. "It definitely felt like the probability of a transaction here was 0.0 percent," Dunn recalls.

After the meeting, the retail behemoth went quiet. "They had people in the room who would have been in a really good position to learn everything they could from us and then apply that to their own private label brands," said Dunn. Alongside Amazon's corporate development team sat a senior Amazon Fashion executive, he said, who had oversight of its private label clothing lines.

Months later, Amazon launched new private label khaki pants, making their motive for the meeting, from the Bonobos team's perspective, all the more glaring. In luring them with a potential offer, was it simply a bait and switch? After all, Bonobos signature product was khakis. "It felt dirty," one of Bonobos's bankers recalls.

The Amazon Essentials slim-fit khakis and flat-front chinos sell for less than $25 (Bonobos chinos sell for closer to $100).

Bonobos was later acquired by Walmart for around $300 million. "I think meeting entrepreneurs who worked really hard to build something for the express purpose of extracting info to run your business better if you have no purchase intent is just a shitty way to be," said Dunn in an interview. He said Walmart had a "no fishing expedition" philosophy during due diligence meetings, and he appreciated that. Their view was "We don't take meetings just to learn."

Dunn thinks Amazon is a monopoly. "It's not a monopoly through market share, because they're very good at saying 'we're 1 percent of total retail.' It's a monopoly through the fact that they're in eight businesses, and the collective impact that that has on the ecosystem is monopolistic. It's like a very clever way to do monopoly, because probably none of those eight businesses could be identified as such. But look at the aggregate impact on the ecosystem," says Dunn.

———

Over and over again, Amazon made promises about firewalls between its disparate divisions, but founders said that it was hardly the case in practice.

Limp, the head of Amazon's devices, was a popular guest at Alexa Fund meetings with the entrepreneurs. Top executives and engineers from Lab126, the team responsible for making Amazon's device hardware, frequently attended as well. In its firewalls speech to founders, Fund representatives said that data wouldn't be shared with other parts of Amazon, but in practice, employees from other groups were often in these meetings.

After Nucleus signed its legal documents with the Alexa Fund, having turned over proprietary information as part of the deal, the company once again did exactly what it said it wouldn't do.

Eight months after starting their partnership, Amazon announced its Echo Show device, an Alexa-enabled video-chat device that did many of the same things as Nucleus's product. The night before the announcement, an Amazon Alexa executive called one of the Nucleus cofounders with a heads up about the impending product announcement and ended with a contrite apology.

Nucleus's founders and their investors were furious. One of the founders held a conference call with some investors to seek advice. He said there was no way his small company could compete against Amazon in the consumer space, according to people on the call, and began brainstorming ways to pivot Nucleus's product.

An Amazon spokeswoman said that the Alexa Fund told Nucleus about its plans for an Echo with a screen before taking a stake in the company. Several people on the Nucleus side of the deal disputed that claim. In fact, Nucleus had even spotted the clause in the contract before signing, and Amazon had told them not to worry, some of the people said; Amazon had no interest in building products that would compete with Nucleus, they were told.

Before Amazon created its copycat, the Nucleus device was sold at major retailers such as Home Depot, Lowe's, and Best Buy. Once the Echo Show hit the market, those sales declined sharply and retailers stopped placing orders. Amazon was somehow selling its Echo Show for less than it even cost Nucleus to make theirs, making it impossible to compete. A few months after the Echo Show launched, Nucleus laid off half of its employees.

Nucleus threatened to sue Amazon. At a meeting with Amazon's lawyers, Nucleus was given two options. "They said 'If you sue, we will put the full weight of Amazon behind this, or you could settle,'" said a person familiar with the meeting. Nucleus chose to settle, with Amazon agreeing to pay Nucleus $5 million (a fraction of the $38 million valuation it once was worth) without admitting wrongdoing.

Nucleus reoriented its product to the healthcare market, where it has struggled to gain traction. "There was $15 million invested into it, but it will never be worth $15 million," said one of the people.

The story played out time and time again. And even before the formation of the Alexa Fund, Amazon had a fraught history with companies it had taken stakes in.

In 2010, Amazon invested in daily deals website LivingSocial, gaining a 30 percent stake and representation on the startup's board. Former LivingSocial executives said Amazon began requesting data.

"They asked for our customer list, merchant list, sales data. They had a competitive product, and they demanded all of this," said one. LivingSocial declined to hand over the data.

LivingSocial executives began hearing from clients that Amazon was contacting them directly and offering them better terms. Amazon also began hiring away LivingSocial employees. Groupon bought LivingSocial, including Amazon's stake, in 2016.

"We may have been naive in believing they weren't competitive with us, and we ran into conflicts over employees, merchants, customer lists, and vendors," said John Bax, LivingSocial's chief financial officer until 2014.

In 2016, Daniela Braga accepted an investment from the Alexa Fund into her Seattle-based startup DefinedCrowd. The CEO's technology company built training data for artificial intelligence, a hot arena in the sector that would become more and more coveted as time went on.

As part of the Alexa Fund investment, Amazon gained access to the technology startup's finances and other confidential information. Because of its board observer role, an Alexa Fund representative was able to sit in on certain parts of DefinedCrowd's board meetings.

But in the spring of 2020, Amazon's cloud computing unit launched an artificial-intelligence product that does almost exactly what DefinedCrowd does, Braga told me later that year.

The product from Amazon Web Services, called A2I, competes directly "with one of our bread-and-butter foundational products" that collects and labels data, said Braga. After seeing the A2I announcement, she limited the Amazon Fund's access to her company's data and diluted its stake by 90 percent by raising more capital elsewhere. She stopped filling them in on new clients, deal sizes, and key hires.

In one case, a founder had the last laugh. Whoop, a Boston-based company that makes wearable fitness trackers, met with the Alexa Fund in 2018. At the time, the company was running out of money, and according to its CEO, Will Ahmed, Amazon took "lots of info about our technology and never invested." Ahmed learned that during due diligence, Alexa Fund employees consulted Amazon employees in different parts of the empire. For all of its talk about firewalls, information seemed to frequently move between Amazon divisions during deal talks.

In 2020, Amazon launched its Halo device, a wearable fitness tracker that Whoop's CEO called "a direct knockoff of the Whoop," in a post on LinkedIn. During its launch, an Amazon product manager even tweeted "Whoop, there it is" about the Halo, in what Whoop executives interpreted as Amazon arrogantly rubbing the copycat in their face. "It made me feel stupid for spending that much time with them, and a little naive," Ahmed said. He considered legal action, but the expenses of pursuing a lawsuit against a company like Amazon were daunting. Instead, he decided to go head-to-head with Amazon. After the Halo announcement, Whoop's investors reached out with their condolences, but to his credit, Ahmed persisted. In the 2021 version of the Whoop, he even inscribed a message meant specifically for Amazon on the device's circuit board: "Don't bother copying us. We will win." The only people who would have seen that message were companies trying to crack into the Whoop hardware to copy its features. It turned out to be prescient.

Despite all the pressure and leverage Amazon placed on so many companies, in this case, David did manage to beat Goliath. In 2023, Amazon shut down its Halo division. In a tweet with a link to the news about the shut down, Ahmed posted a peace sign emoji, as to say "good riddance." In the end, he did win, as Whoop is still in business.

————

But Ahmed's story was not the norm. Amazon had gotten so big, and so smart about using the vast amounts of data it collected from its various arms, that it could predict and anticipate consumer needs; identify, create, or clone solutions to those needs; and destroy the very "partners"-turned-competition whose own work and labors supplied the consumer insights it needed to displace them—all under the guise of supporting them through what appeared to be a traditional venture capital firm.

"They are using market forces in a really Machiavellian way," said Jeremy Levine, a partner at venture capital firm Bessemer Venture

Partners. "It's like they are not in any way, shape, or form the proverbial wolf in sheep's clothing. They are a wolf in wolf's clothing."

Amazon was a flat, horizontal-looking platform with the capability of going vertical to disrupt entire categories with the flip of a switch. It was an evolutionary leap — a technological mutation — of the nineteenth- and twentieth-century monoliths that the twenty-first-century American legal system was not designed to combat.

And at least a few regulators were alarmed.

PART II

War Games

CHAPTER 7

Loopholes, Power Plays, and a Billionaire's Media Gamble

IN 2000, AMAZON HIRED Paul Misener, a lawyer who was advising the company as outside counsel, to start the company's public policy operations. Misener was hired during the wave of MBAs, and he had the right credentials: he was a Princeton alum (a year ahead of Bezos) with a degree in electrical engineering and computer science and had a law degree from George Mason University. Misener understood the regulatory world. Earlier in his career, he served as chief of staff to a commissioner at the Federal Communications Commission, the regulator for radio, television, and cable communications. Prior to that, he had worked at Intel on policy issues.

Misener bootstrapped the public policy team's efforts, which was, in its early years, operating very differently from the growth and hectic energy of the Seattle headquarters. For one, he found a rundown nineteenth-century row house on C Street in Washington, DC, to set up shop. The building was notorious for spotty internet service, and the team often walked to the sidewalk to take phone calls because of poor reception. Worse, the air-conditioning was nonfunctioning, making muggy DC summers nearly unbearable, especially in the cramped quarters, where employees hardly had any space of their own. But the building, with all of its flaws, was cheap. Other corporate offices in the vicinity cost up to seven times more than Amazon's DC office, and at Amazon, where frugality had long been one of the company's guiding principles, this earned management brownie points back in Seattle.

At first, Amazon's public policy team only occupied the third floor of the building because a plaintiff's lawyer and the government affairs office for the Cherokee Nation worked on the other floors. But when those tenants moved out, the division co-opted the entire four-floor building.

In the early days, Amazon was a growing business, and Misener kept his team small. His strategy was to focus on only a few areas of policy that affected Amazon because of how scrappy his team was. In situations where other companies or think tanks could take the lead on policy that also affected Amazon, he deferred to them, glad to take work off of his team's plate. For years, Misener and his small team handled all of Amazon's public policy work.

Misener was mild mannered and well respected by his employees. He collected antique books, with more than 1,000 volumes lining the walls of his library, including the first publication of George Washington's papers in 1820, a prized possession for the bibliophile. Some of his colleagues describe him as "too nice" for DC.

For more than a decade, Amazon's public policy team would operate in this manner: undermanned, underfunded, and focused on just a few issues that had big consequences for the company's business. The most important issue for Amazon, where Misener dedicated the bulk of his attention, was sales taxes.

Tax avoidance is a critical part of Amazon's origin story and was a part of Bezos's calculations early on when he was developing his business plan. As the CEO set across the country in his Chevy Blazer, he had purposely picked cities located in tax-friendly states or with small populations for his headquarters. Bezos was familiar with the ins and outs of the US tax code and keen to exploit it.

He wanted as many potential customers as possible to enjoy low prices, and removing sales taxes from the overall price of goods would help him do just that. "I even investigated whether we could set up

Amazon.com on an Indian reservation near San Francisco. This way we could have access to talent without all the tax consequences. Unfortunately, the government thought of that first," Bezos admitted in a 1996 interview with *Fast Company*. (Federal Indian reservations are typically exempt from taxation.)

Misener was the man to execute on the plan to exploit any and all tax loopholes. And he and his team succeeded. For most of its history, Amazon.com enjoyed a sales tax benefit that it fought tooth and nail to preserve. For years after the website launched in 1995, Amazon didn't collect sales tax in most states across the US. How? Amazon was ruthlessly judicious in where it located its employees. It also took advantage of the tax code in how it designated its warehouses.

As a result of a 1992 Supreme Court decision regarding mail-order catalogs, the US tax code was written in a way that retailers only had to collect sales taxes in places where they had employees and operations, such as stores. When the Supreme Court ruled on the decision, the internet was by no means ubiquitous and Amazon didn't exist. The Supreme Court could not have anticipated the ripple effects its decision — which was tailored around mail-order catalogs — would have for years to come. The decision was made during the heyday of brick-and-mortar businesses, which did collect sales taxes, yet would set a precedent that would be deftly exploited by a major disruptor that would use it to avoid them. Bezos, a master of arbitrage, was clued in to the outcome of the case, and it influenced some of his earliest decisions.

Amazon was shrewd in where and how it located its various properties. The company had warehouses in some states that delivered to the rest of the country and limited hiring to a few states, such as Washington. The state had a relatively small population compared to states like California, so charging sales taxes to customers there as a result of its headquarters being located there wouldn't alienate a ton of shoppers.

Amazon engaged in "entity isolation" for its warehouses, a way to designate its growing number of warehouses in different states as *subsidiaries* of Amazon rather than Amazon operations. This made them exempt from collecting sales taxes in those states, a move that some tax experts viewed as a very aggressive strategy that bordered on tax evasion. These Amazon "subsidiaries" had Amazon employees who were working on Amazon's core business, yet the company classified them differently in order to dodge taxes. And as we know, Amazon didn't have stores, so this saved them from having to pay taxes in most states, unlike nearly every other retailer.

The result was substantial. Some called the tax benefit Amazon's secret sauce, allowing it to keep prices lower than its competitors, stealing share from big box stores and small businesses that collected taxes and therefore sold their goods at higher prices for the same items sold on Amazon. "It was absolutely a massive competitive advantage for us," said an Amazon employee who worked on the tax issue. Shaving off the cost of sales tax from an item provided a big advantage in the age of savvy shoppers who used price comparison tools.

A 2011 report by Credit Suisse estimated that if Amazon was forced to collect sales taxes in all states it operated in that year, it would have lost more than $650 million in sales. Between 1995 and early 2012, Amazon collected state sales tax in only five states, despite increasing calls by its critics to end this tax advantage.

State sales taxes took off in the 1930s during the Great Depression as a way for states to fill their coffers. In fact, taxes make up the lion's share of state revenue, with more than 70 percent of revenues derived from taxes. Sales taxes are of particular importance, making up nearly half of all state tax revenues. These taxes helped fund fire departments, schools, and road work. By avoiding collecting sales tax, Amazon deprived many states of an important revenue source. When states started calculating what they were missing out on, it was staggering. California, for instance, estimated that Amazon owed it $83 million in sales taxes for 2011 alone. Texas sent Amazon a tax bill for $269 million in uncollected sales taxes for the years 2005 to 2009. Those sums could have helped states fund projects from roads to public safety to school funding, which would have benefited residents.

It's also tough to underscore exactly how big a competitive advantage this was for Amazon compared to other retailers. The Seattle-based company prided itself on its low prices, and this gave it another way to shave off up to 9 percent off of its prices, plucking customers from the competition at a crucial phase of Amazon's history.

Amazon's tax advantage reverberated through the retail landscape and exacted real consequences on its competitors, as well as state and local budgets.

———

Sears was founded in 1893 and had survived recessions, wars, pandemics, and shifting consumer habits throughout its history. The historic department store was the original everything store, selling items as vast as toolboxes and washing machines to assemble-it-yourself Craftsman-style homes that dotted the suburbs.

In the late 1960s, Sears's annual sales were nearly 1 percent of the nation's gross domestic product. The company at one point had a rich history of innovation; it was responsible for starting Allstate Insurance, Discover credit cards, and residential real estate company Coldwell Banker. Sears had even owned Dean Witter Discover & Co., a massive brokerage house that it later spun out. Dean Witter later acquired investment bank Morgan Stanley, creating the prestige investment bank it is known as today. "The idea was for Sears to be a one-stop shop for your whole life," a Sears historian said. The company had at one time held such an important place in the American psyche that Bezos had even aspired for Amazon to be its digital equivalent when he started out.

But despite its storied past, by the 2010s, the landscape had massively changed. Online shopping altered the playing field, and one competitor in particular had deftly exploited a tax loophole that struck Sears particularly hard. Every week the executive management team at Sears filed into a conference room at its Hoffman Estates, Illinois, headquarters for a pricing strategy meeting. There, the company's executives discussed the Seattle-based competitor that threatened to bring about the department store's demise. Sears was under assault from Amazon and needed to address customer dollars shifting from their storefronts in malls to the online retailer.

"The biggest threat from Amazon as they started to get into other categories is customers knew they could buy from Amazon and pay no taxes," says Ron Boire, Sears's president from 2012 to 2015, who attended these pricing meetings. Because consumers were savvy and compared pricing, Sears executives had to make tough decisions about how it priced its items. This often meant wiping out their margins.

Let's say Amazon and Sears carried the same Sony television for $500. Yet, Sears would collect an additional $42 in sales tax. In order to not lose the sale, Sears would lower its price to around $468 to stay competitive, recalls Boire. That same calculus was applied to category after category, product after product, creating a race to the bottom in an industry already operating on low margins. In many cases, this caused Sears to sell items at a loss.

"Consumer electronics is a great example of where margins got so compressed because of Amazon it basically drove the industry to near-zero margins," Boire told me in an interview.

On top of the tax loophole, Amazon also had the luxury of not having Wall Street analysts pounding them on their profits. The rest of retail did not. Shrinking margins meant shrinking profits. Shrinking profits created angry shareholders and, if they shrunk too steeply, eventually led to bankruptcy filings. After more than 100 years of business, Sears filed for bankruptcy in 2018.

Boire has gone head-to-head with Amazon repeatedly throughout his retail career. He was CEO of Barnes & Noble and specialty retailer Brookstone. (Barnes & Noble suffered a steep decline in its market value. Brookstone filed for bankruptcy in 2018, after he had left.) He was also president at Toys "R" Us, which later filed for bankruptcy. Amazon's fingerprints are on a lot of these bankruptcy filings, CEOs say.

"I don't think Amazon would have become Amazon without that tax advantage for as long as they had it," Boire said.

At the New Jersey headquarters of Toys "R" Us, CEO Jerry Storch would complain relentlessly to politicians about Amazon's tax break. The two companies had had years of tension since the blow-up of its e-commerce contract and subsequent lawsuit, and Amazon's sales tax advantage was a thorn in the CEO's side.

During his first week on the job in 2006, Storch got a phone call from Jeff Bezos, whom he considered a friend. "How's it feel to work with poor performing people?" Bezos asked, much to the new CEO's surprise. Storch figured that Bezos might have still felt bitter about Toys "R" Us's lawsuit against Amazon to prematurely end its e-commerce partnership. Since that conversation, Storch had been navigating how to compete against Amazon and all its advantages over traditional retailers.

One day over lunch, Storch's boss, financial titan Henry Kravis, who cofounded private equity firm KKR, relayed a message from his wife to Storch. KKR had taken Toys "R" Us private in a leveraged buyout and placed Storch at its helm to oversee the turnaround. "Toys "R" Us's website isn't as good as Amazon's," Kravis told Storch. At the time, Amazon was spending more than a billion dollars a year on technology, recalls Storch. His own budget didn't even approach a fraction of that. "I can't have a site as good as Amazon's," replied Storch. "You couldn't stay solvent and do that." But the uneven playing field from investors wasn't Storch's only worry.

The iconic toy retailer was the original so-called category killer. Since 1957, Toys "R" Us had attracted generations of children to its hundreds of stores around the country, where it had unmatched selection. But online shopping meant that customers were able to compare prices. If Amazon and Toys "R" Us had the same Barbie doll on their websites, even if they sold it for the same price, it was cheaper on Amazon because they didn't collect sales tax.

"It was just so wrong," said Storch. "Amazon knew exactly what they were doing." Storch knew firsthand how significant not having to charge sales taxes was. Whenever states had a "sales tax holiday" before back-to-school shopping or other major shopping events, his sales in those states would explode. Amazon had that sort of advantage year-round.

In 2011, Storch met with Chris Christie, who at the time was New Jersey's governor, to make his plea to tax Amazon. Toys "R" Us employed thousands of people in New Jersey at its forty-plus stores and at its Wayne, New Jersey, headquarters. It was one of the top private employers in the state and generated tens of millions of dollars in sales tax revenues for New Jersey, Storch said. Meanwhile, Amazon wasn't collecting sales tax in New Jersey.

"You're going to put me out of business; you are going to have vacant downtowns. Every small business is going to be shuttered by this. What are you doing?" Storch said he told Christie. The warning fell on deaf ears.

A year later, New Jersey vied for Amazon warehouses, offering rich tax incentives to the company. In 2012, Christie announced that Amazon would be building two new massive warehouses in New Jersey. At the press conference next to him stood none other than Paul Misener.

One of those warehouses would be in Robbinsville, New Jersey. The icing on the cake: New Jersey was allowing Amazon to have a tax break called a payment in lieu of taxes (PILOT). Amazon would pay a set fee to the city, amounting to $22 million total over the course of twenty years. According to local media at the time, "Such deals generally result in lower tax revenues for a town, but serve to attract development because of the amount of money businesses can save initially." Amazon would start collecting sales taxes in New Jersey in mid-2013. At the time, Christie said sales tax could add between $30 million and $40 million to the state treasury.

"Politicians are often very short-term focused so they were able to say, 'well, we brought jobs to Robbinsville, New Jersey,'" said Storch.

Indeed, in the press release, Christie crowed about all of the jobs he created. "Amazon's multi-million dollar investment in this one facility alone is expected to result in the creation of hundreds of full-time jobs in addition to temporary, seasonal and construction jobs," the governor said in the release. At its height, Toys "R" Us employed more than 10,000 people in New Jersey, said Storch. Just a few years later, as a result of filing for bankruptcy, it would employ none. (Amazon currently employs 46,000 full- and part-time employees in the state, the majority working in its warehouses. Between 2010 and 2021, New Jersey experienced a significant drop in employment in certain parts of the retail sector. The number of people employed by sporting goods, hobby, book, and music stores dropped by nearly 33 percent. The number of people employed by clothing stores dropped by 32 percent. The number of people employed by electronics and appliances stores fell 27 percent).

Amazon declined to answer questions on how much it has paid as a result of its PILOT in Robbinsville and declined to provide details on how much it has collected in sales tax in New Jersey.

———————

Misener and his team had been dead set on protecting Amazon's sales tax advantage for as long as humanly possible. By 2008, Amazon had physical locations in seventeen states that charged sales taxes, but collected sales taxes in only four of them.

In 2011 Amazon began negotiating state sales taxes with individual states. A public policy employee said Amazon began to change its stance toward sales tax when there was a realization that it would have a physical presence in every state and would have to collect sales tax anyway. By this time, the states where Amazon had warehouses had begun pushing Amazon to collect sales taxes, no longer allowing them to claim that warehouses didn't count as a physical footprint. It took years to negotiate with the states, with Amazon only starting to collect sales tax in some states as late as 2017.

Once the states had stopped permitting Amazon to claim its warehouses were non-taxable subsidiaries, Amazon changed its strategy. Instead of fighting for the ability to not collect sales tax, it began pushing for other sorts of subsidies in exchange for Amazon growing its operations in those cities and states. Amazon secured years-long tax breaks and subsidies from the towns and cities where it built, as it had done in Robbinsville. These took the form of property tax exemptions, sales tax abatements, and other subsidies. According to Good Jobs First, a research organization that tracks corporate subsidies, US communities have awarded Amazon more than $6.3 billion in economic development subsidies, including tax abatements, across its businesses. Amazon is not alone in getting subsidies to expand in different states. States offer these incentives to attract economic development and create jobs. Internally at Amazon, however, even this metric would be tracked. The public policy team was given goals to get certain dollar amounts of incentives each year across states since 2015. In some years, that goal was as much as $1 billion, and in other years, Amazon secured hundreds of millions of dollars in subsidies and other incentives.

For over a decade, Amazon was able to exploit these tax loopholes—alongside other factors—that gave the company an edge in gaining critical market share. It now collects sales taxes in every state that charges them, but the decades-long pass was yet another foundational piece to Amazon's rise.

"Gaming public policy was part of Jeff Bezos's strategy from the beginning," said Stacy Mitchell, co-executive director of the Institute for Local Self-Reliance, an anti-monopoly group. "He very cleverly used the sales tax advantage and later public subsidies. You can't overstate how much that drove Amazon's growth."

———

Beyond his knack for exploiting tax loopholes and tasking his public policy team to push forward to find any avenue of opportunity that benefited the company in the space, Bezos himself was not very political. Most people close to him and who worked beside him for years say they don't know which way he votes. He didn't talk about presidential elections at work and identified as a Libertarian.

Libertarians tend to advocate for individual liberties and limited government interference. They are fans of free markets. In Bezos's case, the billionaire supported Libertarian causes such as gay marriage, marijuana legalization, and a more liberal view of immigration. Though on the surface more liberal-leaning, Bezos was pragmatic, less politically inclined than business savvy.

While some CEOs thrive on hobnobbing with policymakers and government officials in order to share their company's narrative or influence bills, Bezos avoided it at all costs. As hokey as it sounds, the CEO wanted to spend his time devoted to Amazon's moonshots and customers. He felt his time was better spent elsewhere, and to him, meetings on Capitol Hill seemed like a lot of time and effort without much payoff. (In this vein, Bezos also didn't spend much time networking with other CEOs. He's only attended the World Economic Forum in Davos twice—in 1998 and 1999. The conference is regularly attended by the world's CEOs and power players.)

Seattle was a well-worn path for visiting dignitaries and US government officials. A short trip to the Pacific Northwest could yield a very productive group of meetings. Presidential hopefuls and members of Congress flew into Seattle-Tacoma International Airport and packed their trip with visits to the CEOs of Starbucks, Microsoft, Boeing, the Nordstrom family of the famed department store chain, and other corporate titans. There, they could fundraise with the large corporations or network as a way to work on future deals and investments that required political capital.

These CEOs would graciously accompany the lawmakers on a campus tour, pointing out all of the innovation their respective companies did and all the good for society they created. Requests for the same treatment from Bezos were regularly declined.

When Vice President Al Gore visited Seattle during his term, public relations chief Kay Dangaard shuttled him around Amazon's office, not Bezos. Same with the speaker of the house, says Dangaard. Bezos behaved the same if asked to take meetings in Washington, DC, as well.

"Hey, if I wanted to come to Washington, DC, to do this, I wouldn't have hired you," Bezos once told Misener after a request for him to meet with legislators, according to several people Misener relayed this to. (Amazon denies that Bezos said this.)

And even as Amazon grew, it didn't spend the amount of money in the capital that most companies of its size spent. Amazon was a tiny player in Washington, DC, where companies fund think tanks and hire expensive lobbyists to make cases that serve their respective interests. In 2010, Amazon spent just over $2 million on its lobbying efforts, a small sum for a company that had achieved startling growth, clout, and recognition in the retail space. (For context, Microsoft spent nearly $7 million that year and Walmart spent more than $6 million, according to the Center for Responsive Politics.)

When it was a nascent book retailer, Amazon didn't need much lobbying power. What was most important during that phase was preserving its sales tax advantage. But as Amazon expanded into other categories and other industries, spreading more and more tentacles, it would soon recognize that it would require much more of them on the lobbying front than the narrow scope it had focused on.

Bezos always knew that as Amazon expanded into more businesses, the company would inevitably come under scrutiny. But at this phase, he was more comfortable outsourcing that to his deputies.

As the 2000s turned into the 2010s, Amazon had shifted from upstart to existential threat for many observers, rivals, and erstwhile partners. Competitors started to curse Amazon more and call on Washington to look into the growing company.

The slings and arrows started to pepper the company, from big box and Main Street stores to book publishers. Much as Walmart was the bogeyman of the 1990s, with towns and mom and pops fighting to keep them from opening in their neighborhoods, much of that ire began turning to Amazon in the 2010s.

With clouds on the horizon, Amazon began to methodically arm itself for future skirmishes with competitors and eventually with Washington itself. That would mean more aggressively expanding the scope, and nature, of its public policy division in DC.

In 2012, Misener hired Brian Huseman, a young and aggressive up-and-comer who had spent seven years at the Federal Trade Commission as a lawyer and had worked for chip maker Intel. Huseman wasn't interviewed at Amazon's DC office, and so after he joined, he was surprised to arrive at a townhouse erected in 1890 with just a few employees on his first day. But that would soon change. Amazon later made another key hire that would further their ambition in Washington. The team and its power would broaden. They would soon go on the offensive and combat the critics that were now making noise about Amazon's dominance and whether it was growing in good faith.

Meanwhile, Bezos was about to make a decision that would prove consequential in ways that even he could not foresee.

———

A decade into the twenty-first century, the newspaper business was, like retail, in the middle of its own reckoning. Newspapers for too long had clung to their print editions, relying on revenue that came from the numerous advertisements that dotted their pages, tossed to their many subscribers' homes, to fund their operations. Their online versions were treated as second class, and many at first didn't have paywalls in place, so monetizing their content online was challenging. They, too, were late to understand what the internet would disrupt.

As customers spent more and more time online, the newspapers too slowly followed them. And that hurt their coffers.

In 2012, print advertising revenue dropped by $1.5 billion, dipping below $20 billion for the first time since 1982. It was the seventh consecutive year of print advertising declines. National advertising dropped by 10 percent in 2012. The industry was shrinking, with lay-offs at newspapers happening at a steady clip, and local newspapers shuttering, creating news deserts across the country. Since 2005, more than 25 percent of newspapers in the US have shut down.

Even the storied *Washington Post* wasn't immune from the secular trends. Since 1933, the *Washington Post* had been owned by the well-regarded Graham family. Katharine Graham, the matriarch, was a well-known mainstay of political power brokers in the nation's capital. There was a long-standing joke that you couldn't run for president without first having dinner at Katharine's home and receiving her blessing. Her reporters blew the lid off of political scandals, famously breaking the Watergate investigation that led to President Nixon's resignation. They also famously were involved, along with the *New York Times*, in the release of the Pentagon Papers, which uncovered covert actions by the US government during the Vietnam War.

But as the digital age took hold, the Graham family was having trouble navigating the advertising environment and the shift from print to online, and it began shedding subscribers as a result. Don Graham—Katharine Graham's son—began secretly meeting with potential suitors to save the company and better position it for the digital age.

Unsurprisingly, billionaires had been known to swoop in to snatch up the nation's ailing newspapers. Media mogul Rupert Murdoch bought the *Wall Street Journal* in 2007, adding to his conservative media empire. When Murdoch bought the paper, it caused the newsroom to revolt at the idea of a partisan owner trying to sway its reporters to write articles that had a conservative agenda. (At the *Journal*, the news side operates independently from the editorial, or opinions, side, which is more aligned with that agenda.) In 2012, Warren Buffett's Berkshire Hathaway bought sixty-three newspapers from Media General and admitted it wasn't a great investment at the time of the deal (more so, he cared about the papers staying in business, an act of benevolence over prudent business decision-making). Casino magnate and conservative political donor Sheldon Adelson in 2015 bought the *Las Vegas Review-Journal*.

Billionaires flocked to the thin-margin business in decline because it provided something that wouldn't necessarily make them richer but offered another type of value: influence. There were some who bought the papers out of civic responsibility, like Buffett, who, when he announced his deal, said, "The newspaper business is a declining business, and we will pay a price to be in that. That is not where we will make real money at Berkshire." But by and large, these were vanity purchases, and skeptics looked at the acquisitions as power plays.

In 2013, the *Washington Post*'s Don Graham reached out to an old friend, Bezos, whom he had met years earlier.

In the 1990s, on the heels of Amazon's IPO, Bezos was invited to lunch with Katharine Graham and her son Don at their private dining room at her Georgetown mansion. There were about a dozen guests in total, and Katharine fell asleep mid-conversation at the family's George III dining table during the lunch, recalls Dangaard, who attended with Bezos. The matriarch was awoken by the booming sound of Bezos's laugh as the tech entrepreneur and her son were deep in discussion.

Don tested the now billionaire's interest in his family newspaper.

Bezos initially turned Don down, only to later email him: "If you're interested, I am," the *Wall Street Journal* reported. It moved quickly from there, and Don found a savior for his family's crown jewel.

On the morning of August 5, 2013, Bezos announced a deal to buy the *Washington Post* for $250 million. The announcement took the media world by surprise, since it wasn't a particularly savvy business move, given the business climate for newspapers. It wasn't the billionaire's first departure outside of Amazon. In 2000, he founded space exploration company Blue Origin. But at this point, the bulk of Bezos's attention was focused on growing Amazon. Buying the *Washington Post* wasn't an Amazon acquisition, but a personal gamble on Bezos's part.

This would ingratiate Bezos to the Grahams. As one Washington insider put it: "If you wanted a friend in DC, you couldn't have a better friend than Don Graham." From the outside, his decision could have been seen as part of Amazon's own reckoning with how to rethink their Washington strategy, but that was not the case.

Bezos had long been a disruptor of industries — the perfect person to help the paper navigate what lay ahead. "The internet is transforming almost every element of the news business," wrote Bezos to *Washington Post* employees in an email the day the deal was announced. He even used some of Amazon's "customer obsession" language, but substituted in readers instead of consumers. "We will need to invent, which means we will need to experiment. Our touchstone will be readers, understanding what they care about."

Ironically, while Bezos was becoming more attuned to the fact that *his* crown jewel — Amazon — would soon be in Washington's crosshairs, those around him say he was, with this acquisition, more like Buffett, compelled to save the historic paper. He didn't envision using it to sway the paper's coverage or exploit it for Amazon's policy battles. (Unlike Buffett, however, he wasn't resigned to the paper being a money loser.)

It was an interesting act of goodwill for the billionaire, who up to this point hadn't been known for his philanthropy. For example, Bezos hasn't signed the Giving Pledge, started by Bill Gates, Melinda French Gates, and Buffett in 2010 as a way for billionaires to promise to donate the majority of their fortunes to philanthropic causes during their lifetimes or when they die. Bezos didn't appear on the Philanthropy 50, which tracks the top donors in the US, until 2018.

As the saying goes, no good deed goes unpunished. Ironically, buying the *Post* would later become a bit of an Achilles heel for the billionaire and Amazon.

————

There was more irony to Bezos buying a newspaper: his own company rarely talked to the press. Up until that point, it had operated in near-total secrecy. Journalists' calls and emails to its public relations team often went unanswered. Reporters could typically expect a "no comment" if they reached someone to address their stories. Any negative stories about the company could sway public opinion and lawmakers, especially without Amazon weighing in and trying to shape the narrative. Yet, inside the company's public relations division, requests for comments on negative stories, especially ones related to the company's sales tax issues, would be emailed between employees, often with "LIG" written at the top, meaning "let it go," according to employees.

Around the same time that Bezos bought the *Washington Post*, Amazon's board of directors had started to make the case that Amazon's media and Washington strategy needed to change.

There was a steady drumbeat of more critical press aimed at the company, and it had been getting louder as of late. Competitors had begun beating up on Amazon more and calling on Washington to look into the growing company. They complained about Amazon's sales tax advantage and that the company was hurting Main Street and big box stores. The earliest drumbeats of antitrust allegations also started to be levied from book publishers, who alleged that Amazon was pressuring them to price their ebooks a certain way and faced retaliation on Amazon's website if they refused to comply.

Amazon no longer could have the luxury of ignoring the bad press.

CHAPTER 8

Crafting the Message

AMAZON'S BOARD HAD BEEN pressing Bezos to take Amazon's public image more seriously for quite some time. But inside Amazon, there was a tendency to behave with the ethos of an upstart, which was reinforced by Bezos's rallying cry of "It's always Day 1." But the types of battles and behaviors that a true upstart engages in don't befit a company with a $150 billion market value. Instead, it could make them look like an aggressive bully.

Amazon's public image had far outpaced its internal one, and the company was facing a bit of a reckoning in 2014. "This is what happens — you think you're small until well after you're large, and so you end up with a kind of right sizing to the reality," said an Amazon board member. A senior public relations official during this period put it this way: "Amazon was in an identity crisis. It hadn't yet realized the responsibility it held in the world, or the fact that you made it and now you were a big, established company."

Around this time, Amazon was in a public dispute with publisher Hachette Book Group over pricing terms for its ebooks and had used its muscle as the country's largest bookseller to apply pressure in order to try to get the concessions it wanted. First, Amazon slowed the delivery of some Hachette books to weeks-long waits, deterring customers from buying them, Hachette claimed. Amazon also removed the preorder button on certain Hachette titles, hurting both the publisher and its authors.

Amazon's ability to inflict pain on partners and their earnings by leveraging Amazon.com is a tactic many had experienced, but when it was made public, competitors began to notice a pattern emerging. For example, the blowback from its Hachette tactics became lead stories at the world's top newspapers, and adding to the fire were famous authors like Malcolm Gladwell publicly decrying Amazon's retaliatory actions. This caused CEOs across industries Amazon hadn't yet entered to take note. (Years earlier, Amazon completely pulled books from Macmillan, another big publisher, from Amazon.com when it was in a dispute with the company.)

Amazon's treatment of its warehouse workers had also become a focus for national and local newspapers. A dispatch from the Pennsylvania news outlet *Morning Call* was particularly damning. In 2011, the paper revealed that Amazon had stationed ambulances outside of sweltering warehouses in the summer to treat employees (including pregnant workers) with heat-related illnesses rather than investing in air-conditioning in the warehouses. In some cases, the temperatures inside the warehouses exceeded 110 degrees Fahrenheit. Amazon PR didn't answer questions for the story, instead emailing a generic statement on behalf of the manager at the warehouse. It was a brutal look inside the working conditions these warehouse workers faced and caused a backlash for the company. Scrutiny of Amazon's poor treatment of its lowest-rung workers would only intensify, both from the press and from the public, in the years to come.

The board and Bezos felt that the outside world was misunderstanding how Amazon was creating the tools that helped consumers and small businesses. The world didn't understand that AWS, for instance, underpinned the technology for thousands of startups, and Amazon was being maligned as a result, they thought. They needed someone to change the narrative and focus on positive attributes, like all of the jobs created by the company's technology and platform.

The board had been urging Bezos to upgrade Amazon's presence in DC and rework its media strategy. Eventually, Bezos relented and gave the okay to make a big hire in the space, and Amazon began a search for someone to head up all of public policy and media relations.

Up until this point, public relations was almost entirely focused on product PR and the consumer. This kept in line with Bezos's customer-obsessed mission but meant the company was late to doing the normal corporate and crisis public relations common for most companies of its size. Amazon was also woefully behind its peers in DC, and as the company was pushing into new areas, its old approach would no longer work.

The hire had to be a hitter with connections in DC for the public policy side of the job and an ability to recast Amazon's image in the media. But even though Bezos agreed to the hire, he pushed back on the seniority of the role. The board had a "big argument" with Bezos about whom the new hire should report to, recalls one board member. Jamie Gorelick, an Amazon board member with Washington bona fides and who had served as a former United States deputy attorney general and general counsel for the Department of Defense, stepped in and told Bezos that whoever took this new role needed to report directly to Bezos himself. (Amazon disputed that Bezos didn't want the new hire to report to him.)

Amazon had a very nontraditional reporting structure for its public policy and public relations teams. Public relations reported to Diego Piacentini, Amazon's head of international retail, who was in charge of the vast network of operations in thirty-one countries around the world. Misener's public policy team reported to Amazon general counsel David Zapolsky. The idea would be to merge both groups and have the new leader report directly to Bezos. "Jeff didn't see that it was important to have public relations at the highest-level position," said the board member, but the CEO trusted Gorelick's judgment and relented. Gorelick also told Bezos that he needed to spend more time in DC and take government relations more seriously. Other CEOs like him were making the rounds, and while Hill visits weren't his favorite activity, Bezos did commit to coming to DC more frequently.

The search for the right person for the combined public policy and public relations role was a particularly long one. The ideal person would have to have knowledge of how the press worked but also be able to navigate the intricacies of Capitol Hill.

Jay Carney had recently come off a three-and-a-half-year stint as President Barack Obama's press secretary and was looking for his next gig. The forty-nine-year-old was a creature of the Capitol and looked good on paper. He grew up in Northern Virginia, just outside of Washington, and moved in the right social circles. His kids went to Sidwell Friends School, a ritzy private school responsible for educating the children of presidents and diplomats. (Malia and Sasha Obama both attended, as did Chelsea Clinton.) After Obama's first press secretary left the job in 2011, Vice President Joe Biden enthusiastically recommended Carney to Obama after Carney served as communications director for Biden during his term. Carney got the job and, over time, became close with the president. To wit, his dog Flash is cousins with the Obama family's dog Sunny. He also had a deep understanding of the press, as he had spent nearly two decades as a journalist for *Time* magazine, eventually becoming its Washington bureau chief.

"The press secretar[ies] for presidents are usually in great demand, because they know what it's like to be under pressure, they know how to manage the press in a thorough and thoughtful manner and are usually unflappable in time of crisis," said Nels Olson, a senior leader at executive recruitment firm Korn Ferry, which places applicable candidates in board, CEO, and government affairs positions. With technology companies under fire after the 2016 election in what became known as "techlash," Olson says many turned to high-ranking DC insiders to join their companies and boards, bringing along their connections.

In fact, there had become a bit of a revolving door between the government and technology companies. Uber hired David Plouffe, a top Obama political strategist, to become its senior vice president of policy and strategy in 2014. Facebook hired a former Clinton press secretary in a senior communications role before later hiring Nick Clegg, the former UK deputy prime minister, to head up global affairs and communications in 2018.

Similarly, Carney was busy taking meetings all over Silicon Valley after leaving the White House in 2014. Tech was still belle of the ball, and opportunities abounded. He considered heading up communications and policy at a bunch of different tech companies or going in-house at a venture capital firm. He even entertained the idea of writing a book.

Given his background, Carney was a hot commodity. While he was biding his time on the speaking circuit, being paid to make speeches regaling audiences about his trips aboard Air Force One and what it was like working with a president, corporate America was wooing him. Apple, Uber, and Salesforce were all courting him to head up communications.

In the midst of his meetings, he got a phone call from a headhunter for Amazon. Despite the Obama administration being notoriously chummy with Big Tech, Carney had never met with anyone from Amazon during his time at the White House. While Google and Facebook executives frequently met with White House staffers, Amazon executives did not. Even on fundraising visits to Seattle, Carney had never encountered anyone from the company, which was yet another sign of how absent Amazon was from standard corporate behavior.

Nonetheless, Carney took the meeting. On a trip out to Seattle in September 2014, Carney met with a whirlwind of Amazon's S-Team members, including Bezos himself. He had prepared very little for the visit, scanning some media clips during his flight. And while he enjoyed learning more about the company, he was keeping his options open. But it appeared as though he left the right impression.

Later that year, Bezos emailed Carney saying he was excited about potentially working together. He invited Carney and Carney's then wife for dinner with him and MacKenzie at an upscale restaurant in Seattle. The two flew in for the meeting. Over Italian food and wine, the couples enjoyed an intimate evening, talking about casual things, like raising children. Amazon never came up, and Bezos didn't talk shop, which was refreshing for Carney. The dinner sealed the deal for him. It was also a welcome change in Bezos's thinking. "One of the reasons we brought in Jay Carney was because Jeff was terrible in seeing any value in public relations," said an Amazon board member.

In February 2015 Amazon announced that Carney was joining the company as senior vice president for global corporate affairs. He would report directly to Bezos. In addition to heading up all of Amazon's public relations, the company would restructure Amazon's DC operations and have the lobbying and public policy teams report to Carney. At the time, both divisions had a total head count of fewer than 200 people.

It was an inflection point for Amazon's public policy team and public relations teams. For years they had operated under the ethos espoused by Bezos of "we don't talk about ourselves," but Carney's hiring signaled change and that Bezos was finally listening to his own team. Amazon could no longer get away with hiding in the shadows. It took a while, but once it decided to pivot, it did so in a big way.

————

The process of currying influence in Washington is big business. Lobbying firms consisting of former congressmen, chiefs of staff, campaign managers, and high-powered lawyers litter the District of Columbia, charging more than $1,000 per hour to convince lawmakers to make decisions that would benefit their clients' businesses.

Corporations had different approaches at their disposal. This could take the shape of influencing policy, advocating for officials to vote a certain way, securing spending earmarks, or joining expensive trade associations to do the dirty work on their behalf. For the companies that lobbied well — from the pharmaceutical giants to oil companies — lobbying was not just a necessary evil, but potentially profitable. These companies deftly deployed their teams of lobbyists to influence politicians to roll back regulations on their behalf, delay legislation that could impede their own interests, and advocate for bills that would usher more spending their way. In the case of the oil lobby, it has for years banded together to try to strike down climate change regulations that would hurt their bottom line.

Amazon's spending on these hired guns would explode. In 2012, Amazon paid $2.5 million to lobbyists. By 2019, Amazon would spend a record $16.1 million on lobbyists, becoming the second-largest company by lobbying spend. Amazon went from having little lobbying power in Washington, DC, to spending more money than almost any other company in the country.

Early on, Amazon's small team of hired influencers tried to push the company's agenda on dozens of initiatives, from drone delivery of customer orders to government contracts and trade policy. As the businesses Amazon started years earlier grew bigger, the company went on a hiring spree led by Carney, who was able to procure a budget to grow commensurate to the size of the many different industries Amazon operated in. The team brought on former staffers from the Department of Defense and Federal Trade Commission, ballooning Amazon's internal policy staff in DC to hundreds of people. These groups contracted work out to external lobbyists to supplement their work on areas as diverse as SNAP benefits for its grocery business, Federal Aviation Administration policy for its logistics network, and privacy-related matters for the devices business.

Right before Carney joined, Amazon upgraded its digs, moving out of the townhouse and into splashy offices on Capitol Hill complete with a rooftop terrace and fitness center. Misener lobbied to stay in the shabby townhouse and rent a neighboring one to add more space, but the staff nearly mutinied. Frugality was no longer a priority.

Carney's appointment was good news for Brian Huseman. For three years, Huseman had toiled under Misener without the power he thought he should be able to exert. Misener was slow and steady and methodical. Huseman was extremely ambitious and wanted to make a splash.

With the addition of Carney, Huseman saw an opportunity to move into the big leagues. He cozied up to the new boss and was promoted to vice president of public policy, reporting straight to Carney. Misener would be shunted aside.

Amazon juiced up its political action committee, an internal fund dedicated to making contributions to elected officials. "The fundamental 'business model' of members of Congress is to get elected so they can do good (according to their views); yet to get elected, they must raise money. We have significantly increased the size and reach of our PAC. Contributions to the PAC have increased 63 percent from 2013. We anticipate we will collect over $400,000 in contributions in 2015 and hope to increase that figure next year, resulting in $1 million in receipts for this election cycle," according to a slide in Carney's presentation to Amazon's board members in 2015.

Carney would latch on to an internal campaign called "Watering the Flowers." The goal would be to get in front of as many decision makers — senators, governors, and politicians — to tell Amazon's new story. The "flowers" are elected officials. Watering meant nurturing their views with Amazon's messaging. A software system tracked each member's meetings and influence with officials, which meant ensuring they were taking the appropriate number of meetings annually to properly grease the wheels. They categorized them into categories: VIP (very important policymakers without Amazon employees in their districts) and ACE (Amazon constituent engagement).

Carney put a strategy in place to try to demystify Amazon, refashioning it for policymakers in the best possible light. That included arranging for them to walk the company's warehouse outside of Washington, DC. "Virtually unanimously, policymakers emerge from an FC [fulfillment center] visit with a much better view of Amazon as a whole, as well as Amazon's impact within their particular community," a slide in a deck Carney presented to Amazon's board in late 2015 read. Even Elizabeth Warren, the Democratic senator from Massachusetts who later became one of Amazon's most outspoken critics, visited an Amazon warehouse in Fall River, Massachusetts, in 2017 as part of the program. "I'm here to celebrate because Amazon has discovered a local treasure," the senator said, highlighting the people they had hired in the area.

Carney's team created a tool for all public policy team members to have data about how many employees Amazon had in a certain city, state, or district nearly instantly. In other words, an Amazon employee could pull up the company's head count and investments in a congressional district in real time during a meeting. "The only bargaining chip Amazon had was the number of jobs we were creating in districts," said a member of Amazon's public policy team. "The implication is like 'you owe us.'"

As retailers were vacating Main Street after being destroyed by Amazon, Carney was flipping the script. *Look how many people we employ in your state, Mr. Governor,* his staff were saying. *Amazon creates more jobs than Main Street is losing, Mr. Senator.*

―――――

In addition to revamping Amazon's DC strategy, Carney shook things up in a major way at its press office.

In Amazon, Carney saw a unique opportunity. The company had shrouded itself in mystery—unmarked warehouses, speaking very little about itself—all so that customers could be delighted by the magic of a box showing up on their doorstep. But by 2015, online shopping wasn't new, and there was no need to try to keep its operations so covert. What's more, Carney thought that the very things that Amazon was trying to be secretive about were things he could leverage. Amazon had a massive, growing workforce, especially at its warehouses. There were all of these people behind every Amazon order, moving actual objects around the world. He thought the company should celebrate and humanize their impact and role.

In keeping with his new approach, five months into his role, he found himself responding to press in a different way than Amazon typically engaged with the media. In August 2015, the *New York Times* published a scathing article that painted a picture of Amazon employees crying at their desks and toiling through the night and colleagues openly fighting over the company's guiding principles. The *Times*'s reporters Jodi Kantor and David Streitfeld interviewed more than 100 current and former Amazonians for its piece, which depicted a grueling and unforgiving work environment, even for corporate employees.

Amazon's culture is a very touchy subject with senior management. The story had an immediate impact, and to this day, employees reference it. Many say it mirrors their own experiences, even though Amazon temporarily adopted a softer, gentler side following the story—even temporarily moving away from stack ranking—as a form of damage control.

In prior years, Amazon would have not participated in the story and wouldn't have addressed it publicly once it ran. But with Carney now at the helm of PR, the company took a different approach.

Two months after the story ran, the executive took to blog-publishing site Medium to publish a post titled, "What the New York Times Didn't Tell You." Carney was only at Amazon for about eight months, yet here was an opportunity to unveil his proactive media strategy. In his post, he picked apart the few sources the *New York Times* was able to get to speak on the record in an effort to discredit the entire story.

A former Amazon employee, Bo Olson, told *Times* reporters that he had witnessed many of his colleagues cry at their desks. Carney punched back. "Here's what the story didn't tell you about Mr. Olson: his brief tenure at Amazon ended after an investigation revealed he had attempted to defraud vendors and conceal it by falsifying business records."

Carney did a point-by-point takedown of the named sources and the report's authors in an attack that was not only unprecedented at Amazon, but at most companies. He called into question the "journalistic standards" of the *Times* and its reporters (Streitfeld had a Pulitzer; Kantor would become a Pulitzer recipient a few years later). Some top Amazon PR chiefs acknowledged that the response was certainly aggressive. But Bezos backed the idea to publicly criticize the reporting in the blog post, and complained to friends about how unfair the article was. As for Carney's rebuttal, the tone was more in keeping with his style than one would think.

In his former role as White House press secretary, Carney could sometimes become testy with reporters. "He clashed with reporters," recalls ABC News's Jonathan Karl, who was in Carney's briefings during the Obama administration. "In those briefings he would not just answer questions, but he would sometimes be harshly critical of the reporters for what they were asking. You know, shooting down the premises of questions and questioning the motivations."

In a podcast interview, Carney discussed his urge to put reporters down when he was White House press secretary: "If I didn't internally take a breath and just roll with it and I let my emotions get the better of me, I could win the exchange, it would feel great, right? I would put that reporter back in his place. Then I would go back and see Fox was playing the loop all day long because it looked terrible on TV. It looked like I was being a jerk."

This type of combativeness became a hallmark of Amazon's press shop under his leadership. The tactics would become so aggressive that *Mother Jones* wrote an entire investigation into Amazon's PR practices titled, "How Amazon Bullies, Manipulates, and Lies to Reporters." According to the article, "Amazon's comms team readily employs these rarer, bare-knuckle PR tactics. The ultimate result isn't just that reporters have a harder time writing stories. Some may be deterred from writing on the company at all. And if those that do are deceived and unduly influenced, then by extension the public is as well."

A month after publicly tearing into the *New York Times*, Carney presented his vision to Amazon's board for the combined teams he oversaw. The strategy document from November 2015 outlined the new direction the teams would take under Carney. "The marriage of the two functions reinforces a flywheel: when PR is effectively communicating about Amazon to key audiences, we are able to influence the decisions government entities make that affect our businesses. And when policymakers speak favorably about us or make decisions that positively affect our businesses, the result is an even stronger story for PR to tell."

It details the "Watering the Flowers" system and says that the pass that Amazon largely got from media and government officials for most of its history no longer held up as the company grew and disrupted ever more industries. A key focus of the team's efforts: present Amazon as a benefactor of small businesses. "In the U.S., eBay has long held itself out, with much reputational success, as the protector of small businesses. One of our goals is for policymakers to think first of Amazon, not eBay, when they think of a company that enables small business. We have begun our program in this space by bringing our first small business success story to DC and to Brussels," Carney's memo to the board said.

From here on out, in an effort to reframe the narrative, Amazon's messaging with politicians would focus on a few strategic areas: all of the hiring it does; the small businesses it supports, such as its millions of sellers, authors, and developers; and its investments in local areas when it opened warehouses and other offices.

In typical Amazon fashion, Carney quantified the work his public policy team had done under his direction: "This year in the U.S., we have conducted 316 policymaker meetings, 275 meetings with policymaker staff, 23 policymaker visits to Seattle headquarters, and 52 visits to FCs or other corporate offices."

Interestingly, a note in a draft version of the presentation by Drew Herdener, one of Amazon's top public relations chiefs, summed up the company's new strategy more succinctly: "We want policymakers and press to fear us," he wrote, describing that as a mantra for both teams. The comment, which wasn't meant to go public but was obtained by Reuters, revealed the company's new direction. And it showed how a new pugnacious corporate stance would start to form, both with the press and with DC.

———

As Carney and his team were combating negative coverage of Amazon and trying to discredit news reports as biased, what was happening within the company was far worse than what the media was reporting at the time. The unforgiving, hard-charging corporate culture and stack-ranking policy instituted during Amazon's early years weighed heavily on employees, causing some to crack.

One November morning in 2016, an Amazon engineer sat at his desk at Amazon's Apollo office building in the South Lake Union area of Seattle and typed out a suicide note. Shortly after, he walked into the hallway and pressed the elevator button to take him to the building's roof.

The engineer had reported to the Apollo building nearly every day for the last four months. This morning was different, though. He was ready to end his life.

The engineer thought Amazon would be his dream job. But the first few months turned out not to be ideal. He worked late into the night most nights — sometimes until four a.m. — and through the weekend. The construct of work-life balance didn't exist at Amazon, but that was okay for him. He funneled all of his energy into his work.

After asking his boss for a transfer to a different team, he began experiencing retaliatory behavior. Even though the boss had given the engineer high marks during his performance review, he began to openly criticize him, according to the suicide note.

Weeks later, the engineer's boss put him on a performance improvement plan, or PIP. PIPs are dreaded at Amazon, as they are usually a precursor to being terminated. It's Amazon's way of managing an employee out of the company.

The engineer was crushed. He had done his work and spent countless hours trying to please his boss. It felt like the ultimate insult.

On the morning of November 28, he sat at his desk in the twelve-story glass Apollo building, opened up a new email, and began typing.

Hi Everyone,

This will be my last email in this world.

I don't want you to mourn for me. I want you to learn something from my experience.

He went on: "I can't leave [*sic*] with such an insult which should not be given to me, so I will end my life now," referring to the performance improvement plan. In the note, he even called his boss a murderer.

Then, the engineer walked into the elevator and pressed the button for floor 12. At 11:44 a.m., his email with the subject line "I WILL JUMP OFF APOLLO AND GIVE MY DEATH TO THE MURDERERS ARE [*sic*] THANKSGIVING PRESENT" hit the inboxes of his colleagues. Jeff Bezos, Jeff Wilke, Doug Herrington, and other senior executives were all copied.

The final line of the email ended with "Now, if you have time, look out of the window, watch me fall."

His body came smashing into the floor of the third-floor deck. In 911 calls from that morning, frantic Amazon employees asked the dispatcher to quickly send help. The engineer could be heard screaming in pain and writhing around in the background of the calls. He was injured, but survived.

None of Amazon's senior management addressed the event to employees. Bezos was silent on it. Worse yet, the company made its IT team delete the suicide email from employee inboxes. Amazon said they deleted the email because it contained "aggressive and inflammatory language" about other people on the team.

It exposed a rift between the PR message Amazon was trying to show and the reality inside the company. While months earlier Carney had disputed the accuracy of the harsh work culture described in the *New York Times* story, many employees said they recognized themselves in the anecdotes of the piece. The engineer's story, while extreme, is indicative of how Amazon's exacting standards and draconian employee review system can take its toll.

Many employees have recounted having to take leaves of absences to address mental health issues developed while at Amazon or slogging through work in what they deemed an unhealthy environment in order to get to their last vesting period and payout. One called the stock payments a "golden straitjacket" rather than a "golden parachute."

"Most AWS employees hate working at AWS," said Jason Napieralski, a former cloud computing employee at Amazon. "They see it as a sentence they are getting through to get to have a better life," he said.

Much has been written about the substandard work conditions of Amazon's warehouse workers, and for good reason. They made up the bulk of Amazon's workforce and had much different backgrounds from the employees who would sit in corporate offices around the world. The warehouse workers tended to have lower incomes and be less educated. They did manual labor and often suffered injuries on the job from repeated motion. Many lived off of government subsidies despite their work for the tech giant. But at Amazon's corporate offices, employees faced their own struggles and were under different sorts of pressures.

———

On November 9, 2016, Donald Trump—to the shock and surprise of most political observers—was declared the winner of the presidential election. Amazon officials panicked. They, like much of corporate America, had been preparing for a Hillary Clinton administration, which was perceived as much more Amazon friendly. The team hadn't workshopped what a Trump White House would mean for Amazon because the polls strongly showed a Clinton win, and the sentiment in DC and coastal cities was that Clinton was a shoo-in. Election night left

Amazon executives flat-footed when it came to their strategy, which they were shoring up aggressively, with the incoming administration.

After all, they had made a big bet on hiring a Democratic political operative to guide the company's strategy in DC. Carney would have no clout in a Trump White House, rendering his connections useless.

Amazon knew Trump would be a big problem, that he was a critic, but didn't imagine he could win. During his presidential campaign, Trump blasted the technology giant and Bezos's control of the *Washington Post*. He called Amazon a monopoly and signaled that he would go after it for antitrust violations if he were elected.

In one exchange with Sean Hannity at Fox News during the spring ahead of the fall election, Hannity brought up that the *Washington Post* had twenty reporters dedicated to investigating Trump. In response, Trump said that Amazon "has a huge antitrust problem" because of how many areas it controls. He also said that Amazon "is getting away with murder, tax-wise," and that Bezos was using the newspaper as a tool for political power. Trump claimed that Bezos believed the presidential candidate thought Amazon was a monopoly, "and he wants to make sure I don't get in."

On the campaign trail, Trump's team scheduled roundtables with small mom-and-pop businesses in the dozens of cities he visited in order to gin up support for his campaign. In city after city, town after town, he heard the same thing from beleaguered family businesses: they were being squeezed out by Amazon. Their decades-old businesses were at risk of closing because of the giant, recall two Trump officials who attended such meetings.

"It was a frequent conversation. You go out and speak to people and people wanted to know about this: the small shop owners, the small business owners," says Jay Sekulow, a former personal lawyer to Trump. "Even the [big] box retailers were having a problem, and then you went down to the local retailer that had like the men's store, forget it."

The Trump officials said those stories stuck with the candidate, who saw the decimation of many Main Streets as he campaigned across the country.

Even if Trump wanted to defend the small business owners he met with on his campaign stops, one of his aides pointed to the hypocrisy of that stance. Trump himself had stiffed small businesses he worked with as a real estate executive. Defending small businesses made for a great stump speech, but there was also no denying that Trump also had a personal grudge with Bezos. In fact, most of Trump's top aides attribute most of his vitriol to Bezos's ownership of the *Washington Post*. The newspaper's coverage of the presidential candidate had been critical throughout the campaign season. The irony, of course, being that the *Washington Post* was bought by Bezos, not Amazon, yet it gave Trump an opening to criticize both Bezos and Amazon anyway.

Despite his social standing, Trump had very thin skin. His top White House aides said he felt betrayed by the media, who, prior to his presidential run, had doted on him. "Trump was obsessed with how the media covered him. He read the *Washington Post*, the *New York Times*, and the *Wall Street Journal* cover to cover every morning, always looking for mentions of himself," said one former close confidant.

Just weeks before the election, Bezos took direct aim at the presidential candidate at a *Vanity Fair* conference, reiterating his desire to boot Trump off the planet. Months earlier, Bezos had tweeted "Finally trashed by @realDonaldTrump. Will still reserve him a seat on the Blue Origin rocket. #sendDonaldtospace." At the conference, he reiterated his view. "I have a rocket company, so the capability is there," he said, continuing his spat with Trump.

Carney and others tried to convince Bezos not to engage with Trump, saying he would use Twitter to return fire, but Bezos ignored their advice. And in this case, Trump didn't engage, as he was too busy fighting fires because of a bombshell scoop by none other than the *Washington Post*, which had obtained video footage from a 2005 *Access Hollywood* interview Trump had done where he said the infamous line about women: "When you're a star, they let you do it. You can do anything…Grab them by the pussy. You can do anything." The story, so close to the election, and so shocking, created a PR fiasco for Trump, with many critics publicly claiming that it would sink his campaign. And Trump, ever sensitive to how he's portrayed, would not forget it. It was yet another blow from Bezos's newspaper, and this one had the potential to be deadly.

But the story did not sink his campaign. The night of the election, Amazon's public policy team watched with horror as polling numbers began indicating that Trump, however improbable it once had seemed, would become president.

At six a.m. on that Wednesday morning, emails began flooding into Amazon's public policy staff from Huseman. They needed a strategy, and quick.

At a nine a.m. meeting in the Bo conference room (all of the DC conference rooms are named after presidential dogs, with half from Republican presidents and half from Democratic presidents), Huseman and his team started sketching out their plan.

They had spent weeks plotting who they would know in a Clinton White House, but that was now useless. On a big whiteboard in the conference room, they mapped out the next steps: who they knew in Trump's office, who might be appointed to different Cabinet positions, and who on Amazon's public policy team already had those connections. They brainstormed on Republican lobbyists and consultants they could work with and secure before competitors claimed them. For instance, someone on the team who knew New Jersey Republican Chris Christie put out some feelers with his team since it was believed he could get a position in the Trump administration.

Across the country in Seattle, Amazon's S-Team was also trying to digest the news and its repercussions. Later that week, while Carney was in China on a scheduled business trip, the company's board was meeting. Legal messaged Huseman without much notice asking him to present the company's Trump strategy to the board of directors.

Amazon's board of directors was worried that Amazon hadn't laid the groundwork for Trump's transition team, said a person at the meeting. "What the board was really concerned about was Trump's bias against Bezos and Amazon, and no matter how prepared we were for the transition, none of that would change," the person said. The board was also worried about what a regulatory environment would look like under Trump and wanted to know how Amazon planned on navigating it.

When Huseman briefed the board, he discussed where Amazon and Trump had common ground and shared priorities: job creation, economic investment, and infrastructure. These would be the areas Amazon focused on with the new administration.

After returning from China, Carney reiterated the plan to the board. "Carney after the Trump election just thought we needed to get the facts to as many policymakers as possible. He said, 'Let's get politicians to go see the fulfillment centers,'" said an Amazon board member. "Watering the Flowers" went into overdrive, and the company hired a full-time staffer dedicated entirely to "Conservative outreach."

Carney also told the board that Amazon needed to "neutralize" the animus of the incoming president. He began a strategy of touting Amazon's job creation and positioning Amazon as supporting the economy. "Jobs is the number one currency in Washington," the board member said.

Being blindsided by the election caused Amazon's public policy team to drastically change its approach to future elections. "We didn't plan for a Trump victory like we should have," admitted an Amazon senior public policy official. The company stopped putting too much stock in pundits and polls, said senior Amazon public policy officials. Instead, Amazon would game out how they were positioned in the event of either candidate winning, mapping out potential connections, analyzing if they have the right lobbyists in place regardless of which party won.

———

As Trump was preparing for his transition to the White House, he scheduled a forum at Trump Tower on Fifth Avenue in New York with some of tech's biggest CEOs. Surprisingly, Bezos was invited to the December meeting. Amazon's team worried he would be walking into the lion's den, but it seemed improper to refuse a personal invite from an incoming president.

During his campaign, Trump had been critical of Big Tech. Bezos was singled out more than his peers, but Apple was criticized by Trump for manufacturing iPhones abroad, and there was a sense that the incoming president could have a contentious relationship with Big

Tech, given its reputation as a liberal bastion. This meeting was scheduled to assuage some of those concerns.

Amazon's public policy team covered their bases, prepping talking points and answers to questions that Bezos might receive at the meeting. "There was a *lot* of prep and sleepless nights that went into preparing Jeff for Trump Tower," recalls one of Amazon's public policy employees. Bezos was told to highlight Amazon's investments in the economy and the number of employees the company had, recalls another executive who helped prep Bezos.

That Wednesday in December, Bezos, Carney, and Huseman drove down Manhattan's Fifth Avenue. Since Carney was too prominently linked to the Obama administration, he wouldn't accompany Bezos into the meeting but instead hung back across the street with other staffers from the companies meeting with Trump so as not to be a distraction. This would become a theme.

Bezos walked through the grand lobby of Trump Tower as cameras flashed around him. He stepped into the golden elevator alongside Huseman and headed up to a conference room alongside other peers, such as Facebook's Sheryl Sandberg, Microsoft's Satya Nadella, Tesla's Elon Musk, and tech investor Peter Thiel. Also there were Trump's adult children Ivanka, Donald Jr., and Eric. Bezos looked nervous as he entered the conference room, according to a Trump aide, but to be fair, all of the CEOs looked slightly on edge.

In his opening remarks, Trump bragged about the "hundreds" of companies that had asked to come to the meeting before saying, "I am here to help you folks do well." The thirteen tech executives went around the table introducing themselves. When it came time for Bezos, he said: "Jeff Bezos, Amazon.com. I'm super excited about the possibility that this could be the innovations administration."

The meeting was a polite one. As Bezos left the meeting, he asked a Trump aide if he could use a conference room to make a phone call. Once inside the room, Bezos's booming laugh could be heard by everyone outside the door. He was excited about how the meeting had gone, and Bezos briefed Carney and Huseman to give his download: Trump asked good questions, and on balance it was a positive meeting. The team left Trump Tower feeling like they had just had the best-case scenario with the mercurial president-elect, who seemed to have the most issues, out of everyone in the room, with Bezos.

Huseman and Carney crafted a statement on Bezos's behalf saying the CEO "shared the view that the administration should make innovation one of its key pillars, which would create a huge number of jobs across the whole country, in all sectors, not just tech — agriculture, infrastructure, manufacturing — everywhere."

While the initial meeting went better than expected, it wouldn't foreshadow the ongoing relationship with the Trump White House and Bezos.

————

After Trump won, lobbyists with Trump connections came out of the woodwork to pitch themselves to stumped corporations that had anticipated a Clinton win. One of the best-positioned lobbying firms for the Trump era was Ballard Partners, a lobbying firm run by a Trump confidant with the ear of the mercurial president. To the extent that there was a cottage industry that sprouted up around the president, Ballard cornered it.

Brian Ballard read Trump's *The Art of the Deal* while serving as chief of staff to Florida governor Bob Martinez. Ballard wrote Trump a letter offering the businessman his help, if he ever wanted it. Trump wrote back, and this sparked a decades-long friendship. Ballard was instrumental in getting Trump elected as president and served as the "Chairman of Trump Victory" in Florida. He led the campaign's finance efforts in the state in 2016.

In 2017, Ballard took out office space in Washington, DC, and parlayed his close ties to Trump into a full-time federal business. For years, he had run a smaller state lobbying firm in Florida, where Amazon had been a client for state matters since 2008. In 2017, Amazon became one of his first federal clients.

Ballard's services became so in demand that in 2019, his firm generated $1.7 million per lobbyist, compared to the industry standard of $300,000, the *Wall Street Journal* found.

Working with Ballard had its perks for Amazon and opened doors at an openly hostile White House. Just a few days after the Trump Tower visit alongside Bezos, Huseman boarded a plane to Orlando. Trump was in the midst of his USA Thank You Tour 2016, where he held rallies in a few cities with his supporters to thank them for their votes. That week, he was holding one in Orlando at the Central Florida Fairgrounds. Prior to the big rally, Ballard had arranged a $5,000-per-head Transition Finance Committee meet-and-greet with the president-elect. Ballard invited Huseman as a guest.

Huseman, who is openly gay, was involved with Amazon's LGBTQ affinity group, Glamazon, but had voted for both parties over the years. Those close to him describe him as opportunistic above all else, deftly holding his nose and kissing rings to get things done, even if it meant courting Trump officials who held views he diametrically opposed. That, after all, was part of the job for public policy executives.

When Huseman got to the front of the reception line to greet the president-elect, he shook Trump's hand and conveyed how much Bezos enjoyed the Trump Tower meeting. While he didn't personally agree with Trump's rhetoric, the most important thing at the time for Amazon's public policy team was trying to forge a productive relationship with the incoming president, people familiar with the meeting said.

Employees bristled at Huseman kissing up to Trump. Like much of the technology sector, the majority of Amazon corporate employees were liberal. Back in Seattle, where the local government leans more progressive, any move that could be deemed as pro-Trump could incense employees. "People in the office were outraged," said one DC employee. Soon enough, a framed photo of Huseman with Donald Trump appeared in Huseman's office, prominently placed, inducing eye rolls from the staff. Huseman also kept a framed paparazzi photo of himself and Bezos in the gold Trump Tower elevator in his office.

While Amazon's DC office was more measured — employing a mix of Democrats and Republicans to do its work on the Hill—they generally weren't Trump fans. Even a number of the Republicans in the office couldn't bring themselves to vote for the brash real estate tycoon. Shortly after Trump was elected, the office began a quarterly tradition called the Think Big Award, where an employee was honored for their service. The trophy for the ceremony was a copy of Trump's book *Think Big: Make It Happen in Business and Life*. Each quarter the book was given to a new employee who picked a passage to read in Trump's voice. It was signed by colleagues with notes of encouragement to the winner.

Notes written by employees in the book read: "The HQ2 project isn't just big, it's YUGE" (referring to Amazon's search for a second headquarters and to Trump's idiosyncratic style). One note carried a Trumpism from the book: "Always remember what DJT says: 'You have to think big and be creative to solve problems that scare the crap out of most people.'" After a few quarters, the awards were abandoned because Huseman worried that the optics of mocking a current US president didn't set the right tone.

But while some employees in Seattle and DC ridiculed the new president, Amazon's lobbyists were trying to do their best to court him. Because of his friendship with the president, working for Jeff Bezos was a tricky high-wire act for Brian Ballard. Trump would erupt into tirades any time he brought up Amazon and was fixated on finding ways to hurt Amazon's business. The president would often forget that Ballard was working for Amazon and would call his old friend, saying he was pissed off at Bezos and the tech giant and that he wanted to find ways to "screw them," a Ballard employee told me.

With Trump himself being a dead end, Ballard's team back-channeled other members of the White House, like White House economic adviser Larry Kudlow and the President's son-in-law Jared Kushner, who was a senior adviser to Trump. Kushner at one point told Amazon board member Jamie Gorelick, who had represented him and his wife Ivanka on legal issues, that he admired Bezos and Amazon. Kushner became so fond of Bezos personally that he became an important ally for Amazon within the Trump White House. "Whenever we needed some sort of deflector, Jared was willing," said a person involved in Amazon's White House efforts.

Amazon employees and their handlers would file into Kudlow's office in the White House to talk economic policy. The Trump adviser would crack jokes about how much he used Amazon as a shopper, despite his boss's hatred of the company.

Kellyanne Conway, a senior counselor to President Trump, was also a prolific Amazon shopper. At a black-tie Washington event in 2018, she joked with a tuxedo-clad Bezos about her teenage daughter, Claudia, who was a big spender on the site.

"Do you have a blacklist where you're adding the drug kingpins, narcotics traffickers, and the terrorists and the murderers?" she asked the billionaire.

Bezos leaned in conspiratorially. "We do. Do you have some names to add?" he asked.

"Claudia Marie Conway," the president's senior adviser cracked. Bezos's laugh filled the air. Despite her boss's venom, Conway had a soft spot for Bezos.

And the truth was, Amazon public policy officials spent a decent amount of time at the White House, trying to ingratiate themselves to Trump's administration, unbeknownst to Trump. Conway worked closely with members of Amazon's team on veterans' issues, being that Amazon is a big employer of former veterans. And despite Trump's vitriol, the US government remained a large client of Amazon's, with the CIA and NASA storing its sensitive data in Amazon's cloud.

But not everyone in Trump's White House had warm feelings toward Amazon. "Amazon needs to be broken up. It can't be this conglomerate," Trump's trade adviser Peter Navarro said to me in an interview. He claims that if Trump had been reelected, the administration would have forcefully gone after the tech giant (why they didn't go after Amazon in Trump's first term, however, remains a mystery).

———

One June evening in 2017, Jeff Bezos had an unlikely dinner date: Donald Trump. Bezos had agreed to dinner at the White House alongside *Washington Post* publisher Fred Ryan, executive editor Marty Baron, and op-ed editor Fred Hiatt for dinner with the president and his wife,

Melania, and Jared Kushner and Ivanka. (At the last minute, Ivanka pulled out of the dinner, angering the first lady.)

Trump's rhetoric about Bezos and the "Amazon *Washington Post*," which he claimed should be registered as a lobbyist for Amazon, had not subsided. In fact, that's why the president was willing to meet. He was incensed about the newspaper's coverage of his White House and wanted to talk to its top decision makers about his concerns.

Bezos for years had known that owning the newspaper was a "complexifier," as he called it, for Amazon. But the *Washington Post* was an independent newspaper that had reporters engaging in news-gathering processes with sources inside major agencies, including the White House. It was the reporters' job to report about national politics and backroom dealings and expose the tensions within the White House, even if the sitting president found it uncomfortable.

Sitting at a dinner table inside the Blue Room, a state parlor which is usually reserved for important guests, the men tried to explain this reporting process to the president. It didn't seem to compute. Trump at this point was a frequent guest on Fox News, which had different news-gathering processes and standards, and was usually favorable to the president. He made comments that if he owned the newspaper, he would just make the sort of coverage he disliked stop. In other words, he wanted to know why the men couldn't simply call off the hounds. The men politely explained that's not how things worked. The *Washington Post* would cover the Trump White House fairly, just like it would with any White House. They were stalwart about protecting the journalistic integrity of the paper and the freedom of the press.

At his core, the president couldn't believe that an owner of a newspaper wouldn't use it to attack his enemies and wouldn't influence coverage, according to senior White House aides. Even though Trump couldn't get them to capitulate, the dinner was mostly congenial. Bezos was given a White House tour, and throughout the night the group discussed politics and other topics.

Trump was persistent. The next morning, Bezos's mobile phone rang with a call from the president, Marty Baron wrote in his book *Collision of Power: Trump, Bezos, and the Washington Post*. He had one request of the billionaire: make the *Washington Post*'s coverage of the president more fair.

———

One person that was conspicuously missing from such meetings was Jay Carney. When Carney joined Amazon's public policy team, senior members expected him to spend a lot of time on the Hill, broker relationships, and open doors for the company. "Jay said he wouldn't add value in Republican meetings, and we stopped asking," said a senior public policy executive at Amazon. Trump White House aides say they never saw Carney at the White House.

In fact, Carney did not attend any meetings at the White House during Trump's four years in office. Before taking the job at Amazon, the executive made the choice that he wouldn't be a phony. He wasn't going to be like the other public policy executives who cut checks to both Republicans and Democrats, and he wasn't going to glad-hand politicians with whom he had diametrically different values. He found that wasn't credible.

Once Trump became president and Trump's team espoused more extreme views, Carney knew he didn't feel comfortable engaging with them. Had it been a more moderate Republican in the White House, there would not have been resistance. Carney had been friendly with John McCain earlier in his career, with the Arizona senator even attending his engagement party. He had cultivated good relationships with people like former Republican speaker of the house John Boehner. But the Trump White House was no typical Republican administration.

Some in the DC office became frustrated that Carney didn't make any attempts to be bipartisan. Yes, he had been hired right before a Republican ascended to the White House, but he should still be involved in senior White House meetings, they thought. Carney didn't even ask for detailed briefings following his staff's meetings with the White House, some of the people said.

Instead, through the Trump administration, Carney made some high-profile flubs that actually worked against his team's efforts.

Speaking at a conference for tech news site *GeekWire*, Carney contrasted his experience at the Obama administration and reporting on prior administrations to what he was seeing in the Trump administration: "Virtually with no exception, everyone I dealt with in those administrations, whether I personally agreed or disagreed with what they thought were the right policy decisions or the right way to approach things, I never doubted that they were patriots. I never doubted that they believed they were doing things that were in the best interest of the country. I don't feel that way now, and I worry."

Carney also said that he never lied during his time as White House press secretary. "When you can't answer something or you don't have a good answer to give, you say, 'I'll take that question' or 'I don't have an answer for you.' You don't lie. And there doesn't seem to be that standard today."

The comments caught the attention of the president's inner circle and irked his son. "Hey @amazon So is it your companies [sic] official corporate position that the the [sic] thousands of Americans who work in the Trump Administration aren't 'patriots' because that's what your top spokesman (and former Obama hack) @JayCarney just said???" tweeted Donald Trump Jr. (The typos were in his original tweet).

Carney had to respond by saying that his comments were his personal views, not the official position of the company. The DC office viewed it as yet another unnecessary misstep from Amazon's leadership. As the DC team tried to forge relationships, Amazon's executive team continually found ways to damage them.

CHAPTER 9

Techlash

IN JANUARY 2017, TWENTY-SEVEN-YEAR-OLD law school student Lina Khan's article was published in the *Yale Law Journal*. It would become a watershed moment in antitrust circles and transform Khan's life. Every word of the article would also be pored over by Amazon's top brass.

Khan argued that the unprecedented size of Amazon, and other companies like it, was the result of how antitrust laws were being interpreted, which for decades had enabled corporations to grow as long as they were benefiting consumers. Her paper provoked a question: were we approaching antitrust all wrong? It would bring a great deal of attention to Big Tech and whether their size and influence were actually causing more harm than good. Ironically, it took aim at a former Yale Law School professor who had a pioneering role in reframing the very conditions Khan was objecting to in her paper.

The fact that Amazon was able to exist in its current form, she argued, is the work of a movement, which began in the 1950s and was personified by one man: Robert Bork, a former federal judge, Yale professor, and conservative firebrand who had transformed how modern antitrust thinking was applied. In essence, Khan thought that Bork's reinterpretation of antitrust laws created monopolies like Amazon, which the legal consensus had deemed acceptable. She believed that for

Amazon to be stopped, Bork's interpretations would have to be undone, and that a return to the original intent of antitrust laws would be essential. Amazon, she argued, was a malignant consequence of Bork's view, whose influence indelibly made their staggering growth and power possible.

Bork was an acolyte of a movement formed at the University of Chicago, where he received both undergraduate and law degrees, known as The Chicago School of economics. The Chicago School was instrumental in shaping conservative policies and most closely associated politically with the rise of Reagan. His time at the university in the 1940s would prove transformational for the budding lawyer, who sported a beard and disheveled, frizzy hair.

Bork was surrounded by a group of economists and legal minds who argued specifically for a laissez-faire approach to policymaking. They felt that there was too much focus on the power of corporations and not enough concern about the role of government overreach. This movement espoused a hands-off approach to government regulation, putting faith in markets. (Coincidentally, John D. Rockefeller founded the university with the American Baptist Education Society.)

The economist Aaron Director, considered a godfather of the movement, was particularly influential on Bork's thinking. (Director was the brother-in-law of Milton Friedman, the Nobel Memorial Prize–winning economist.) Bork was one of Director's students at the University of Chicago Law School, and later described his teaching of economic analysis on antitrust law as "what can only [be] called a religious conversion. It changed our entire view of the world." Bork's beliefs, shaped by these scholars, would morph to more vociferously criticize government intervention and regulation. He and his peers advocated applying an economic analysis to antitrust law, but the Chicago school of thinking would move to other areas of the law as well.

Antitrust laws had been first drafted in the late nineteenth century as the Gilded Age ushered in new types of corporate structures called trusts. These trusts organized a number of businesses in the same industry in order to control the production and distribution of a product or service. As a result, railroad and oil titans came to control key rail, refining, and pipeline infrastructure, which Progressives believed often resulted in higher prices for customers. While their companies helped to spur the Industrial Revolution and transformed the American economy, these barons were also publicly criticized for exploiting their workers and engaging in unethical business practices in pursuit of profits. Further, they were actively using their size and power to prevent other firms from competing with them. "The reason that nineteenth-century Americans hated monopolies was not so much because they are large," said historian Richard White, who wrote a book on nineteenth-century railways called *Railroaded: The Transcontinentals and the Making of Modern America*. "They hated them because nobody else could go into business against them. And if they wanted to take your business away from you, they could." Congress reacted by passing the Sherman Antitrust Act on July 2, 1890, which for the first time allowed the federal government to dissolve trusts. In other words, it was the first federal act to outlaw monopolistic business practices.

At the time of its passage, new technological advances were facilitating a shift in America from an agrarian to industrial society. Railroad, steel, and other industrial companies were on hiring sprees to fuel their growing businesses, and the nation's farmers became frustrated by the pricing of the rail owners, who could gouge local farmers.

The immense changes underway were making headlines, and the press at the time reflected both the excitement and anxieties of the period. The same week the Sherman Act passed, the front page of the *New York Times* had articles marveling at the ability to make "artificial ice." An advertisement on the front page boasted the headline "Five Hours to Washington," reading, "The fastest trains in America are in service between New York, Philadelphia, Baltimore and Washington via Jersey Central."

Another dispatch chronicled the formation of the Farmers' League movement, which grew out of the desperate situation the country's farmers were experiencing, not least the pressure of taxation and other factors that were making their way of life untenable. "Political evils and business depression that now afflict the country are due to unequal and excessive taxation and corrupt political methods," its author wrote, paraphrasing the sentiments of the president of the Farmers' League. It went on: "Professional politicians and boodlers and monopolists shape legislation for their own gain." In other words, tensions were forming between those who made a living under pre-industrial conditions and the arrival of the new industrial titans whose power and influence was becoming unparalleled in American life.

It was reflected in the distribution of wealth, as the gap between the poor and rich started to change dramatically. In 1850, prior to the Civil War, there were just nineteen millionaires in the US. By the end of the 1890s, that number had swelled to about 4,000.

In 1901, Theodore Roosevelt became president, and his presidency hailed the dawn of a new age, as a new progressive sentiment swept the nation, whereby the government would play a more active role in reforming big business to protect the general welfare of the American working class. He would become the first US leader to directly go after trusts. Roosevelt, using the Sherman Antitrust Act, ordered his Department of Justice to sue Northern Securities Company, a railroad trust, which Roosevelt believed was a monopoly, in 1902. Financier J. P. Morgan, one of Wall Street's most powerful bankers, who had helped create the trust, had a compelling interest to ensure it remained intact. Tim Wu, a progressive legal scholar, calls Morgan "history's greatest monopolizer" in his book, *The Curse of Bigness: Antitrust in the New Gilded Age*. He provides a look at the scope of the financier's reach: "Morgan merged hundreds of steel firms into US Steel, built railroad monopolies in the West and the Northeast, created an Atlantic shipping giant called the International Mercantile Marine Co., and served as the real force behind AT&T's conquest of the telecommunications industry." With Roosevelt threatening his railroad profits, Morgan rushed to the White House to try to see if anything could be done to salvage the Northern Securities situation. It wouldn't work. The case went to the Supreme Court, as Northern Securities sued to appeal the decision, but the court sided with the federal government. The railroad trust would be broken up.

The case earned Roosevelt the title of "trust buster," and during his presidency, his administration filed more than forty antitrust lawsuits.

In 1906, the US government sued Standard Oil for restraining trade and monopolizing commerce. Standard Oil was investigated for a number of its business tactics, from exclusionary cartels to predatory pricing and the practice of obtaining rebates from the railroad. Rockefeller also deployed a tactic in his dealings that caused competitors to capitulate, aware that they had few options to compete with the giant if they spurned its advances. Standard Oil's employees would give smaller companies the option to partner with the oil giant. But if you spurned that offer, watch out. "Unless you resist Rockefeller, you can survive," explains White. Wu put it more bluntly, comparing Rockefeller's operations to Mongolian conqueror Genghis Khan: "Join the empire, or face complete destruction."

The company's thirst for growth was inexhaustible and indiscriminate. As investigative journalist Ida Tarbell wrote: "And nothing was too small: the corner grocery in Browntown, the humble refining still on Oil Creek, the shortest private pipe line. Nothing, for little things grow." The results were such that in a decade's time, Standard Oil's market share grew from 10 percent to over 90 percent.

The sheer size of the company was staggering. "The company transported more than four-fifths of all oil produced in Pennsylvania, Ohio, and Indiana. It refined more than three-fourths of all United States crude oil; it owned more than half of all tank cars; it marketed more than four-fifths of all domestic kerosene and was responsible for more than four-fifths of all kerosene exported; it sold to the railroads more than nine-tenths of all their lubricating oils," wrote economic historian Daniel Yergin in *The Prize: The Epic Quest for Oil, Money, and Power.* In 1911, the Supreme Court determined that Standard Oil had violated the Sherman Antitrust Act and ordered that the company be broken up and forced to divest its major holdings.

In 1914, the Wilson administration would become even more aggressive in addressing monopolistic behavior. Wilson formed the Federal Trade Commission, which expanded government oversight, and signed the antimerger statute known as the Clayton Antitrust Act.

Mergers were often shot down to ensure that smaller businesses could compete, and the courts often upheld these decisions, seeing corporate expansion as a byproduct of unfair behavior rather than managerial competence.

For decades, antitrust law was enforced in the style of the trust busters. But over time, critics asserted that such interference actually caused more harm than good and inhibited competition. The Chicago school and Bork led this charge. He and his colleagues saw the meddling as too intrusive. They argued that the free market would sort itself out and did not require expansive government oversight, and believed that antitrust laws should be more narrowly interpreted in order to spur economic efficiency.

———

In his attic office in his New Haven home, sitting at a desk made out of an old door by his wife, Bork set about putting his ideas to paper while puffing on Kent cigarettes. Bork even taught himself calculus to better conduct an economic analysis on the state of competition and monopoly power. The lawyer started putting pen to paper — or, in his case, Scripto pencils to yellow legal pads — in the 1960s, recalls his son, Robert Bork Jr., who fondly remembers disrupting his father's work in the smoke-filled room with a rattling window air conditioner when he was a child.

Different work engagements and a family illness caused Bork to pause work on the book for periods of time. But in 1978, Bork published his magnum opus, *The Antitrust Paradox: A Policy at War with Itself.* In it, he picked apart cases in which the government challenged mergers and debated how prevalent tactics, such as predatory pricing, were. Predatory pricing, or pricing below cost to acquire market power, had been deemed key to Standard Oil's growth, but Bork contested that this was the path to the company's dominance. "It seems unwise, therefore, to construct rules about a phenomenon that probably does not exist or which, should it exist in very rare cases, the courts would have grave difficulty distinguishing from competitive price behavior," he wrote.

The way antitrust was being interpreted and enforced "significantly impair[ed] both competition and the ability of the economy to produce goods and service efficiently." He bemoaned the "populist hostility to big business" and the difficulty of businesses to conduct mergers. In Bork's view, big businesses weren't necessarily bad. They could provide efficiencies for businesses and customers by lowering the costs of goods or services. But the Supreme Court at the time had been too focused on the "survival and comfort of small businesses."

Our interpretation of antitrust, Bork argued, needed to be drastically changed. Regulators should stop focusing on how many rivals were in a market, or the size and scale of corporate power, and instead on what he called "consumer welfare." The laws needed to protect consumers, which wasn't how the law was being handled during the progressive era. His framework in many cases would allow companies to get bigger so that they could become more efficient, achieve economies of scale, and be able to provide lower prices to customers. "Business efficiency necessarily benefits consumers by lowering the costs of goods and services or by increasing the value of the product or service offered; this is true whether the business unit is a competitor or a monopolist," Bork wrote.

Part of the problem with antitrust laws is that they are infamously vague in nature and could be interpreted in different ways. Up until the adoption of the Chicago school of thinking, it was common for antitrust laws to be enforced to keep large companies from dominating smaller rivals and to prevent behavior like predatory pricing and tying arrangements, which is when a company with one product or service requires a buyer to buy another of its products or services.

In the 1960s, there were a number of antitrust cases that made their way to the Supreme Court that prompted this group to question what the purpose of antitrust laws was. Even centrists unrelated to the Chicago school thought some of the decisions went too far. "In the 1960s it did a very abrupt flip and became extremely aggressive to the point that it broke up firms, at least in merger cases, increased prices and was quite harmful for consumers," says Herbert Hovenkamp, an antitrust law professor at the University of Pennsylvania Law School.

"There were decisions that condemned mergers simply because

they enabled firms to produce better products. The theory behind the 1960s movement was that we need to do more to protect small businesses, and in order to do that, we need to make bigger firms more expensive or less innovative. In striking down the merger of a shoe manufacturer and shoe retailer, the Supreme Court even acknowledged that its decision would result in higher shoe prices," said Hovenkamp. (Bork wrote that the decision was in contention as one of the worst opinions in history.)

The Chicago school was responding to cases like these. In one case, *Utah Pie Co. v. Continental Baking Co.*, a Utah-based frozen pie maker sued Continental Baking and two other national frozen pie makers selling in the Utah market. Once Utah Pie entered the market, given its regional proximity to customers and vendors, it had lower costs of business and therefore could cut its prices and offer cheaper alternatives to the national brands. Continental and the other national brands countered in order to remain competitive. In its first full year of business, Utah Pie acquired 66.5 percent of the Salt Lake City market, according to Bork. Nonetheless, the regional company sued the national brands for countering with a price cut of their own specifically in Utah, while selling at a higher price point in other states where the competition wasn't nearly as steep. Utah Pie maintained its dominant regional position in the market during the period and had been the reason for the price war. But the Supreme Court sided with Utah Pie. This rankled members of the Chicago school, who felt like the courts were protecting small competitors, not competition. In their view, the competition worked: customers benefited from it because it enabled them to pay less for the product. As Bork put it in his book, "Defendants were convicted not of injuring competition, but, quite simply, of competing."

The publication of Bork's book was a watershed moment in policy circles and introduced the American public to a new economic vernacular that had previously been limited to academic circles. The book encapsulated decades of work done by the Chicago school, presenting the movement's arguments in a way that attacked the previous era's establishment ideas. The idea of "consumer welfare" came into fashion. The school and Bork's arguments were so influential that his consumer welfare standard came to be interpreted as conduct that enabled companies to provide consumers lower prices or better-quality goods and services. This became the most important variable in determining competition issues. Size, as it were, was no longer the be-all and end-all. What mattered instead was the consumer and what was in the consumer's best interest.

Bork's book and his focus on efficiency resonated with economists and conservative antitrust theorists in the inflation-ridden 1970s. It filtered down to the courts, where judges ultimately decide how antitrust laws are interpreted. "I don't know how many people write a book and then have the Supreme Court adopt your thinking the next year, while the ink is still wet," his son told me in an interview. Bork succeeded in changing the way that the laws were interpreted, with corporate behavior evaluated through the lens of the consumer welfare standard. Since then, the courts and even policymakers have adopted a more free-market approach, ending an era of regulatory oversight that defined the first half of the twentieth century.

The repercussions reshaped corporate America and the nature of competition. "There was clearly a big change in government enforcement beginning with the Reagan administration. A lot of the 'big is bad' sentiment was dropped," said Doug Melamed, a former acting assistant attorney general in charge of the antitrust division at the Justice Department. The effect of corporations on small business, or what is popularly known as mom-and-pop businesses, became largely irrelevant. If a company could create more efficient markets and deliver better pricing, the government was less likely to interfere.

This gave rise to a more narrowly focused approach to regulating mergers and acquisitions, which allowed mergers in markets that were already pretty concentrated. "Since the antitrust revolution — ushered in by the Reagan administration — the line of illegality moved to be much more receptive to big mergers — and as well to exclusionary conduct," says Eleanor Fox, professor emerita, New York University School of Law. "Markets have been allowed to get more and more concentrated."

An article Khan co-wrote years later titled "Terminal Sickness" chronicled how deregulation from this period in the airline industry and a nonstop wave of mergers affected consumers. The article detailed US cities no longer having adequate local airline service or having higher prices to travel from these smaller hubs. It showed how Pittsburgh, St. Louis, and Memphis suffered following a 1978 decision to deregulate the airline industry in order to spur price competition. The new policy led to more mergers, with acquirers downscaling the hubs of the companies they bought. It resulted in Cincinnati/Northern Kentucky International Airport having two-thirds fewer flights through it between 2004 and 2012, jacking up prices for consumers in that area and also leaving them with fewer options to fly directly to other parts of the country.

In 1987, President Ronald Reagan announced that he was nominating Bork to the Supreme Court. Bork's economic thinking was widely admired by mainstream conservatives of that era (he was the solicitor general under Nixon), and his position on social issues was radically conservative as well and so drove liberal opposition. Bork's opposition to abortion and contraceptives, among other issues, caused a backlash; after the civil rights revolution, and after the court had passed landmark decisions such as *Roe v. Wade* and *Brown v. Board of Education*, Bork was cast as an extremist who could potentially undo these civil rights gains.

Within an hour of the announcement, Massachusetts senator Edward M. Kennedy said, "Robert Bork's America is a land in which women would be forced into back-alley abortions, blacks would sit at segregated lunch counters, rogue police could break down citizens' doors in midnight raids, schoolchildren could not be taught about evolution, writers and artists could be censored at the whim of government, and the doors of the federal courts would be shut on the fingers of millions of citizens for whom the judiciary is — and is often the only — protector of the individual rights that are the heart of our democracy."

Civil rights groups and members of the Democratic Party sought to discredit the judge. The committee voted to reject his nomination.

But Bork's legacy in antitrust loomed large, and his impact on policy cannot be understated. During his lifetime and beyond — Bork would pass away in 2012 — his influence at Yale Law School would resonate through the years that Khan attended. One of Bork's good friends taught the law school's principal antitrust class. He'd wistfully recount anecdotes about his friend and suggested that students read Bork's opus prior to the start of classes.

Now Khan was arguing to unwind his legacy on the way companies compete. The consumer welfare standard no longer worked in the age of Amazon, she argued.

Just as Rockefeller had forced competitors to partner with Standard Oil or risk obliteration, a similar dynamic was playing out at Amazon. And like Standard Oil, where Tarbell described no competitor as being too small to target, Amazon also could be rapacious in its thirst for winning, making no competitor too small to be immune from its onslaught.

"Standard Oil reduced competition, while Amazon has increased the many retail options consumers and suppliers already have, including by giving small- and medium-sized businesses additional ways to reach consumers (these sellers are thriving). Standard Oil drove oil prices higher, while Amazon has a well-deserved reputation for low, competitive prices. By any objective measure, Amazon has been an incredibly innovative company and procompetitive influence in retail," an Amazon spokeswoman said in response.

More broadly, the Bork worldview had enabled companies such as Amazon and other contemporary behemoths (in the twenty-first century, these would be Big Tech) to dominate certain areas and crowd out competitors as long as prices remained low (or free) for consumers, people in Khan's camp alleged.

Robert Bork Jr. says it's impossible to know whether Amazon would exist in its current form if not for his father's book. "I would think certainly my father's ideas in antitrust and other ideas about regulation and things that the Reagan administration did and others have done to free markets as much as possible makes Amazon possible," he said. But he adds: "Being big is not illegal."

Khan's law review paper took direct aim at Bork and his consumer welfare standard, exposing it as entirely unequipped to deal with present business conditions and the unfettered growth of the largest and most influential companies.

————

Khan was an unlikely person to take on Jeff Bezos, one of the richest people in the world. She spent much of her time in the library; she didn't even have an Amazon Prime account. She was more comfortable among stacks of books than being in the spotlight.

Khan had always been different from her peers. She spent the first eleven years of her life living in London with her Pakistani parents, who met when they were college students in the city. The family later immigrated to the United States. Her dad worked as a management consultant and her mom worked in the information services space. Driven by her work ethic and insatiable curiosity, Khan was initially drawn to journalism.

While in high school in Westchester, she wrote a story for the school's newspaper exposing the discriminatory practices of a local Starbucks that refused to seat students. Her reporting even got mentioned by the *New York Times*.

While studying political theory at Williams College in Massachusetts, she became an editor of the college paper. She graduated magna cum laude, having written her senior thesis on the political philosopher Hannah Arendt. Afterward, she would find herself at the Open Markets Institute, where she discovered an innate interest in antitrust, before heading to Yale for law school.

Who knows if she would have become famous if not for her paper, which took on a life of its own after publication. Just as Bork's book had an outsized impact in the 1970s, Khan's Yale rebuttal started to circulate among lawyers and antitrust experts. She began to hear from general counsels within major companies, who were fascinated by her arguments. Then her thesis did something remarkable: it went mainstream.

In short order, following the publication of Khan's article, Amazon managed the impossible. It became the target of bipartisan common ground between Democrats and Republicans in a fraught political landscape. They couldn't agree that the sky was blue, but the danger posed by Amazon, brought to light, drew the interest of both parties.

Amazon as a target of President Donald Trump's ire would become well known. "I have stated my concerns with Amazon long before the Election. Unlike others, they pay little or no taxes to state & local governments, use our Postal System as their Delivery Boy (causing tremendous loss to the US), and are putting many thousands of retailers out of business!" he tweeted in March 2018. But he wasn't alone in his thinking.

———

Khan's paper published in the middle of a broader reckoning gripping Silicon Valley and the country's tech giants. Following the 2016 presidential election, a zeitgeist had begun to take hold in the US. Politicians started attacking the big four technology companies — Facebook, Google, Apple, and Amazon — as well as some of their peers. The animosity was coined "techlash." While the sentiment was turning on social media giants like Facebook, Amazon would get caught in the same net, even if its own behavior — and the criticisms — were different from what was being levied against other companies in the Valley.

The election was a turning point for Democrats. A number of prominent tech executives endorsed Hillary Clinton. Among them were Facebook COO Sheryl Sandberg, Salesforce CEO Marc Benioff, and Box CEO Aaron Levie. Apple's CEO Tim Cook even held a fundraiser for the candidate. While Sandberg was cozy with the likes of Hillary Clinton, her company, and other social media juggernauts, were aiding irreparable damage to the former first lady's 2016 presidential bid.

Fake news littered Facebook's newsfeed, causing preposterous stories to go viral. News articles from unverified sources spread like wildfire on Facebook, Twitter, and YouTube. Suspected Russian operators flocked to both Facebook and Twitter to spread disinformation about the Democratic nominee, along with anti-Clinton content in general. Between the two social media platforms, there were thousands of fake accounts and bots deluging feeds with polarizing messaging that engulfed the political discourse, and it became difficult to tell a truth from a lie as content went viral on shock value, however absurd the claims. The bots worked to energize conservative voters around issues like gun rights and immigration, driving them to the polls. At the same time, a Russian fake news campaign worked to keep Black Americans from voting for Clinton, or voting at all, a Senate report later revealed.

In addition to the divisive posts and groups that they created, they were funneling money into Facebook's powerful advertising arm to take out ads to promote their views. Facebook's profile-targeting features allowed them to reach specific types of audiences. Facebook wasn't only allowing disinformation on its website; it was profiting from it.

After the election, the Federal Bureau of Investigation, the Central Intelligence Agency, and the National Security Agency determined "with high confidence" that Russian president Vladimir Putin had ordered an influence campaign to damage Clinton "and harm her electability and potential presidency." They also determined that this was done to help Donald Trump's chances of winning. Russia's tool of choice? US social media companies. More than 126 million Americans came in contact with incendiary political ads bought by a Kremlin-linked company around the time of the election on Facebook.

Clinton acknowledged the damage the proliferation of these fake accounts and stories on social media did to her campaign. "The epidemic of malicious fake news and fake propaganda that flooded social media over the past year, it's now clear that so-called fake news can have real-world consequences," she said a month after the election. Years later, Clinton was still focused on Facebook's role in the election. "Mark Zuckerberg should pay a price for what he is doing to our democracy," she said in 2019. "Part of our problem, those of us who are appalled by this war on truth and this fake news which is truly surrounding us these days, is we're not very good at combating it. It's hard because you're up against algorithms, plus all these other powerful forces, it's really hard."

Democrats were infuriated and saw firsthand the power of unregulated misinformation on social media to damage an election. Years later, Senator Elizabeth Warren, then pursuing her own presidential run, would jokingly say Facebook endorsed Trump during the 2016 presidential election while calling for the technology "monopolists" to be broken up.

The Republicans, for their part, needn't be reminded of technology's ills. They shared a long-standing derision toward technology companies and the elites running them. Republicans viewed the Silicon Valley firms as left-leaning organizations and big donors to Democratic causes and campaigns. Trump, who in so many ways benefited from social media exposure, was also critical of Big Tech.

The techlash would only amplify in 2018, when the world learned of Cambridge Analytica. As the *New York Times* wrote, "The firm harvested private information from the Facebook profiles of more than 50 million users without their permission, according to former Cambridge employees, associates and documents, making it one of the largest data leaks in the social network's history. The breach allowed the company to exploit the private social media activity of a huge swath of the American electorate, developing techniques that underpinned its work on President Trump's campaign in 2016." The political data firm had ties to Trump. Robert Mercer, a billionaire computer scientist turned hedge fund manager who was a big-time Republican donor, was a major financial backer of the firm. Steve Bannon, who ran Conservative news organization Breitbart before joining the Trump campaign as campaign chief, sat on the company's board.

Democrats called for investigations, and Facebook was accused of being complicit in enabling bad actors to play dirty on their platform. Chris Hughes, who cofounded Facebook, even said later that the company should be broken up.

The idealism that drove Big Tech's early success was replaced by a far more intensive examination of their power. The companies that had feel-good messages of "connecting" us and "obsessing" over its customers were now being questioned in a new light. How were they using the massive amounts of data they collected? Were their market shares in advertising, search, and online commerce too high? Were their technologies and automations innovating people out of jobs and replacing them with robots? Were their social media products designed to be addictive? Was it healthy for users to be connected all the time, or did it raise mental health concerns? Should they be responsible for policing content on their platforms to prohibit misinformation? All of these questions were being asked. Just years prior, many of these same technology companies had been courted by the Obama administration, which cozied up to Big Tech and allowed these companies to explode in size through mergers. Obama held these companies up as bastions of innovation.

Tech companies began collectively being referred to as "Big Tech" in the same derisive manner that shared the nefarious echoes of "Big Oil" or "Big Pharma" from years past. These were no longer idealistic upstarts with ping-pong tables in the office and kombucha on tap. Instead, they were being seen as monoliths with size, power, clout, and influence.

Other industries with such power — the automotive industry, banking, pharmaceutical companies — were regulated. Why not tech? The backlash and frustration would drive interest to look deeper, and more deliberately, at whether Big Tech needed to be reined in, too powerful to continue unscrutinized.

And it wasn't just the politicians taking note. The public was reckoning with this new reality as well. "Facebook was a company that was incredibly popular among the public writ large, and particularly liberals, prior to 2016. It now ranks with tobacco companies, oil companies and the NRA in driving Democratic anger," Dan Pfeiffer, a White House communications director under President Obama, told the *Washington Post* in 2019.

———

After Khan's manifesto took off, she became a hot commodity in Washington. Different politicians jockeyed to have her come work with them. "It's probably the most important law review article written in our lifetimes," said Matt Stoller, a former colleague of Khan's at Open Markets, who is now director of research at the American Economic Liberties Project, a nonprofit that advocates for more aggressive enforcement of antitrust laws.

Khan had initially planned to clerk for federal judge Stephen Reinhardt on the US Court of Appeals for the 9th Circuit in California after graduating from Yale, but the judge suddenly passed away. So she changed course and returned to DC to work with Barry Lynn at Open Markets again.

Amazon now had a problem and knew it. When the paper was published, Amazon's legal and public policy teams read it and took it seriously. They debated what their public response should be. But despite the paper making the rounds, Khan herself was a nobody. What if their response made them look like a bully? What if it drew even more attention to Khan's work? So, they decided to do nothing, which in hindsight nearly everyone at Amazon now agrees was a mistake. "We should have done more to discredit it," said someone with knowledge of what went on inside the company at the time.

In early June, while Khan was at Open Markets, Amazon general counsel David Zapolsky contacted her. He would be in town in mid-June and would love to meet. It sounded casual.

So, Khan and Lynn were surprised when they arrived and were greeted by eight senior-level Amazon executives and lawyers. All had clearly done their homework. There was nothing casual about it. They referenced articles Khan and Lynn had written prior to the manifesto and panels where Khan had spoken. They proceeded to attempt to poke holes in her argument. The executives told Khan that she didn't understand Amazon; they didn't engage in the business practices she described in her article. That week, Amazon announced its acquisition of Whole Foods. The Khan meeting was just another item. The real reason Zapolsky and his team were in DC: to alert regulators of their acquisition.

And it was then, when Amazon bought Whole Foods, that traffic to Khan's article exploded. Everyday consumers started to use "Amazon" and "monopoly" in the same sentence.

Back at headquarters, some of Amazon's top brass remained dismissive of Khan's arguments. They viewed the points as amateur, with little chance of ever being adopted. As long as the consumer welfare standard was in place, Amazon's leaders felt like they were protected, say former executives.

But in DC, antitrust became a regular talking point at Amazon's offices. Huseman had identified it as an under-the-surface threat as early as late 2015, but Khan's paper firmly kicked it into high gear. The company set out to hire its first public policy employee tasked exclusively to deal with antitrust and how it would impact the company's business.

———

In the eyes of Khan and the antimonopoly movement, Borkian standards for antitrust had significantly neutered the FTC and DOJ. They criticized antitrust regulators for rarely bringing forward big monopoly cases, and for not for holding Big Tech accountable. They argued that the last major monopoly case against a technology giant was the Department of Justice's lawsuit against another Washington state technology giant: Microsoft. In 1998, the Department of Justice and twenty state attorneys general sued Microsoft for violating antitrust laws by unlawfully "tying" its Internet Explorer web browser to its Windows operating system software. The press release from the time said, "Microsoft unlawfully required PC manufacturers to agree to license and install its browser, Internet Explorer, as a condition of obtaining licenses for the Windows 95 operating system."

In 2000, a federal judge ruled that Microsoft used its monopoly power over operating systems for personal computers, siding with the government. In a shocking move, the judge ordered a breakup of the technology giant into two companies: one for its Windows operating system and one for everything else. This was a monumental ruling. Breaking up a company that had grown mostly organically because of its business practices (rather than trying to block a merger that would allow it to get bigger) was uncommon as an antitrust remedy. But a year later, the US appeals court affirmed the basic finding that Microsoft engaged in a course of anticompetitive conduct that violated antitrust laws, it remanded the remedy question to the trial court, and the parties then agreed on a remedy that did not include breaking up the company.

Few monopoly cases had been brought forward against technology companies since, and in general the number of cases brought forward have dropped precipitously since the Chicago school's argument had become the standard approach. "Between 1970 and 1999, the United States brought about 15 monopoly cases each year; between 2000 and 2014 that number went down to just three," Tim Wu noted in a *New York Times* op-ed.

Acolytes of the Borkian view started derisively referring to Khan's arguments as "Hipster antitrust" because it clung to a 1960s standard of how antirust should be enforced. Critics derided the movement as using antitrust to try to cure societal ills and misguidedly viewing big as bad.

But Khan was not alone. Efforts to question Amazon's business practices were gathering steam abroad as well. In 2014, Danish politician Margrethe Vestager became EU competition commissioner. It would make her one of the most powerful politicians in Europe. During her tenure, Vestager aggressively took on big US technology firms. She hit them with billions of dollars in fines and was skeptical of how these companies, which had grown to hold dominant positions beyond the US, used the troves of data they collected. She ordered Apple to repay €13 billion to Ireland for unpaid taxes the company accumulated over more than a decade (it was later overturned, then appealed, and now the case is with the European Court of Justice). The EU fined Google $5 billion, a record sum in an antitrust violation, for abusing its power in the mobile phone market to cement the dominance of its software on the Android platform. She also later opened investigations into Facebook.

Vestager was feared in Silicon Valley and for good reason. Next she looked into Amazon. In 2015, the European Commission launched an inquiry into the e-commerce sector in Europe, sending questionnaires to thousands of sellers, e-commerce companies, and brands. The responses provided a number of threads for the commission to explore. They included sellers complaining that they initially had a hit product on Amazon, but then Amazon went to their manufacturer and sourced the same item itself, selling it for less than the third-party seller (replicating a pattern US sellers were all too familiar with). The results of the inquiry spurred the commission to pursue a more formal case.

In September 2018, European Union antitrust authorities opened up a preliminary investigation into how Amazon treated third-party sellers in Europe. Amazon's European operations were massive, with Prime memberships available in many countries throughout the continent at the time. Europe had more than 30 million Prime subscribers in 2017, according to internal documents. The problems that US sellers, shoppers, and competitors complained about had been exported abroad. Not to mention that Amazon had also become a major employer and e-commerce player inside the Euro zone.

The probe's focus was to find out if Amazon was using data from merchants on its platform and customer purchases in ways that gave the company an unfair competitive advantage. Was it, for instance, algorithmically identifying hit items from third-party sellers to order from their suppliers and sell on its own? The European Commission later began investigating Amazon Prime and how the company determined which seller to feature in its "Buy Box," an important placement on Amazon's shopping pages that features a product to add to your cart. (In the US, nearly 98 percent of Amazon orders are made through the Buy Box.)

Germany represented Amazon's largest market outside the US, making up nearly one-third of Amazon's international sales in 2017. Around the same time that the EU announced its investigation, German's antitrust agency, the Bundeskartellamt, began probing whether the e-commerce giant was preventing fair competition in Germany. "Because of the many complaints we have received we will examine whether Amazon is abusing its market position to the detriment of sellers active on its marketplace," the Bundeskartellamt's president said in its press release, adding that it was looking into practices such as withholding payments, blocking seller accounts without explanation, and using seller data.

The momentum would only build from there. In 2019, Italy's competition regulator began investigating whether Amazon gave an advantage to sellers that used Amazon's own logistics network, or FBA, over other logistics operators. In 2020, the Competition Commission of India investigated whether Amazon had violated local competition law. (India's Competition Commission found Amazon in violation;

Amazon is contesting it.) In 2022, Britain's competition watchdog, the Competition and Markets Authority (CMA), opened up an investigation into whether Amazon was abusing its power and "whether Amazon is using third-party data to give an unfair boost to its own retail business and whether it favours sellers who use its logistics and delivery services — both of which could weaken competition," the regulator said. Amazon offered to make changes to its UK Marketplace to address the concerns, which the CMA accepted.

Amazon was impacting foreign markets in all sorts of ways. In 2018, Amazon posted $66 billion in international revenue (not including AWS), and its sales in those countries impacted local competition. Throughout much of the world, bookstores had been the canary in the coal mine. But even some who had managed to scrape by in the face of Amazon's onslaught found themselves unable to hold on.

––––––––––

On a warm night in July 2005, children lined up at a train station in Shropshire, UK, at eleven thirty p.m., way past their bedtimes. They carried wands and were dressed as wizards. The air was abuzz with the sounds of kids in capes excitedly waiting to board a steam train for a memorable night. In a mere half hour, *Harry Potter and the Half-Blood Prince*, the sixth book in the popular Harry Potter franchise, would officially launch. Anna Dreda, the owner of a cherished bookstore in Much Wenlock, a town in the county of Shropshire, wanted to create the perfect experience for her regular customers and their kids. Just two years earlier, Dreda had bought Wenlock Books from its owner. For fourteen years, she had worked at the store, but her childhood dream was to be a bookstore owner. After reading a book called *A City of Bells* at the age of twelve about a man who has just fought in a war and returned to life in a Cathedral town where he opens a bookshop, Dreda knew that one day she'd have a bookstore of her own.

Now in charge of the place she once worked, owning a three-story bookstore in the town's small High Street, she had finally done it. "I remember to this day, the very first time I put the key in the front door of the shop with it being my shop, my heart just expanded in my body.

It was my dream come true," she says. Wenlock Books occupied a fifteenth-century building complete with wormy old beams and wonky floors. The medieval shop in the medieval town was charming and was cherished by local residents. She hosted story time with moms and their children every week; even toddlers would perk up to listen. Each Christmas Eve, in the evening, she would invite the town for a completely candlelit reading of *The Night Before Christmas*. Book clubs gathered around the big round wooden table on the first floor for discussion while sipping sherry and helping themselves to freshly baked cakes, which were available to customers free of charge.

That night in July, she stood around in excitement. She had chartered the old steam train for the children to ride through the valley of the River Severn to a local hamlet. While the ride itself was about thirty minutes long, Dreda would make it magical: she asked local drama students to dress up as wizards and had magicians on the train performing tricks. The train was abuzz with the merriment and laughter of children and their families. More than 300 people showed up.

When the children arrived at the tiny, decorated train station, Dreda had someone there with owls, as if they were being welcomed to a real-life Hogwarts. Then, the kids were handed their copies of the book.

The train ride back was quiet; the children were all reading. "It was just magical," Dreda recalled. One child who attended the release party was so affected by it all that he grew up to become a book publisher.

Early on, Dreda stocked her shop with bestsellers, children's books, poetry, and whatever else she felt her customers would like. She threw a poetry festival and other community events. She lived on only £1,500 a month, all made through proceeds from her store, but it was worth it. "I never was going to make a lot of money. It was a labor of love," she said.

But in subsequent years, Dreda had to reduce her monthly allowance. First, she lowered it to just £1,000. Then to £750. Customer behaviors were starting to change, with many coming into the store and leisurely browsing the shelves, only to take photos of the books that interested them, but leaving empty-handed. Dreda knew they were buying them on Amazon, whose prices she simply couldn't beat. "Amazon was selling books for just the cost of postage," she said. Some would come to the register with a book and ask if she could match Amazon's price. She couldn't.

She reduced her inventory to cut costs but didn't want her shelves to look bare. So, she began stocking books face forward, making them more visible, and also creatively using the shelf space, which would otherwise have been packed by books with only their spines visible. But as she kept cutting costs, the shelves emptied out. She hammered wood planks on the top ones to cover what wasn't there.

"Gradually, even friends and people who lived in the town were saying to me, 'I can't afford not to buy my books on Amazon,'" Dreda recalls. She held on for a few years without taking any pay, with her partner supporting her, but eventually, by early May 2019, she made the difficult decision to close the store. She described that period as a "month-long surgery without anesthetic." In addition to her own grief, each day customers came into the shop in tears, knowing the store was closing, and she had to console them. Since 1995, the number of independent bookstore owners in the UK has dwindled from 1,894 to 1,072, according to the Booksellers Association.

"People had so many memories attached to the bookshop, and they realized what they were losing," she said, adding that you can buy a book on Amazon, but that the retailer would never be able to replicate the experiences a local bookstore and bookseller provide.

While foreign antitrust regulators seemed to clearly understand the threat that Amazon posed to their partners and competitors, the US lagged behind at policing its own tech companies. But that would soon change.

Rohit Chopra, a progressive commissioner for the Federal Trade Commission, reached out to Khan, whom he had met before. Chopra, too, was in favor of antitrust reform. In 2018, he offered her a role as his summer adviser at the FTC. Khan spent a ton of time at the agency library, where she pored through tomes, studying how the FTC historically pursued antitrust cases. Importantly, during this stint, she learned that many of the tools at the FTC's disposal had been little used or abandoned by contemporary agency regulators.

Khan and the commissioner jointly wrote a law review article for the *University of Chicago Law Review*. "The Case for 'Unfair Methods of Competition' Rulemaking" argued that the FTC had a powerful tool in its arsenal that it wasn't adequately using. In essence, Chopra and Khan believed that the FTC had broader rule-making authority than what it had traditionally been relying on, and they made the case for the agency to use it. When joining the FTC, Chopra had a mission to resuscitate the dormant rulemaking authority of the agency. It turned out that he and Khan were kindred spirits in this regard.

The summer stint at the FTC for Khan would be indelible. Her learnings about FTC rulemaking, as well as the lessons she gathered from the library flipping through historic cases, shaped her views about the agency and its remit.

CHAPTER 10

Watering Flowers in Rotten Soil

DURING A PRIVATE S-TEAM meeting in 2018, Jeff Bezos complained to his top lieutenants about the bad press Amazon was getting. The media was hammering Amazon for how it treated its warehouse workers, blaming the company for empty storefronts on Main Street, and politicians openly criticized the Seattle company for a range of issues from its tax rate to its facial recognition technology and everything in between.

"There were alarm signals being sent from Huseman's team, so there was definitely awareness from that," said someone briefed on the meeting with Bezos.

The writing was on the wall: the tide was turning on the company known for smiles on its boxes. Bezos was displeased.

He felt that Amazon was misunderstood and not doing enough to tell its own story. He was frustrated that Amazon wasn't getting the word out "about all of the great things Amazon was doing for the business community." The company had revamped public relations and public policy three years earlier, but its treatment in the press had only gotten worse. The company was roped into the broader techlash, Khan's article raised existential questions about Amazon's power, and its reputation was taking a beating among everyday people. In 2018, Amazon's ranking in the Reputation Institute's annual RepTrak ranking showed that "Amazon's reputation fell in all of the categories measured by the survey, but it was hit especially hard with regards to citizenship — essentially, how it gives back to its community — and how it treats its workers."

In the meeting, the S-Team began brainstorming a new narrative for the company. Amazon needed to rehabilitate its image, and fast, the team decided.

Doug Herrington, Amazon's senior vice president of its consumer business in North America, took the idea and brought it to Nick Denissen, then a vice president on Amazon's Marketplace side.

They conducted a poll of Amazon's public perception about its impact on small businesses among both informed groups — politicians, media, industry watchers — and uninformed groups, like shoppers. The main question was, is Amazon good for business? The responses were surprising for management. More than half of respondents replied that Amazon was bad for business. The results irked Bezos and Amazon's head of Seller Services at the time, Sebastian Gunningham. They made it the group's goal to improve it within one year.

In 2015, Gunningham's group created an initiative called "Amazon Stories" to spotlight success stories from small sellers on Amazon. The idea was to improve Amazon's image as a supporter of small businesses and deflect attention away from the businesses shutting down all over the world that couldn't compete with the retailer. Every other week, Gunningham and his team had a check-in meeting with Bezos to review the copy. Bezos personally edited some of the posts and was very invested in the initiative, but it fell flat, failing to gain traction.

Each year, Amazon's S-Team zeroes in on the most important of the company's goals and gives just a dozen or so the distinction of a "flagship" goal, emphasizing its importance. It's these goals that get regularly checked at Bezos's level. The pressure was on to improve Amazon's public image, and soon it became a flagship goal.

Denissen and Herrington brainstormed ideas to help highlight

Amazon's work for small businesses. Their first idea was to create a dedicated Prime Day just for small businesses, but that was shot down.

Instead, Amazon started to find ways to highlight some of its small business success stories in advertisements and on Capitol Hill. It emphasized a part of its website called Amazon Handmade, which was similar to Etsy, where merchants like a Montana-based woodworker sold his homemade cheese boards and a stay-at-home mom embroidered hand-knit sweaters for customers. But a person involved with the effort said that the business was a flop, with customers instead flocking to cheaper alternatives mass produced in China that were available on Marketplace. "That's a super nice story but doesn't move the needle," said a member of the small business team.

They used Amazon's top real estate — its home page — to feature some small sellers that would never have had a chance of landing on Amazon.com, where most slots are reserved for blockbuster items that drive tons of high-margin sales. It was unheard of for items like those from small sellers to get a spin on the home page.

In addition, Amazon developed advertising campaigns that would highlight these small sellers. In a meeting with a creative agency and some Amazon executives, Bezos examined the storyboard for a small business in Michigan that sold artisan soaps and candles on Amazon. He personally signed off on the creative, which would then be advertised on television.

In 2018, the commercial for the Little Flower Soap Co. ran on televisions nationally. In it, a shop owner closes her boutique for the night, changing the sign from "Open" to "Open on Amazon 24 Hours." The camera then pans out to show white delivery vans emblazoned with the shop's logo and filled with its products traveling around the world to get to Amazon's customers. It ends with a voice-over saying: "Half of everything sold on Amazon comes from small and medium businesses just like mine," while a laptop screen shows the shop owner's orders on Amazon ticking up. The screen then fills with other small seller logos that eventually merge into the Amazon logo, the simple orange smile. The key takeaway: Amazon is a large company made up of small businesses, said a person who worked on the advertisement.

Amazon wanted to push the narrative of it being a major benefactor of small business, but the reality on the ground was more stark: it was also the catalyst for countless small businesses around the country to shutter at the same time.

————

The convenience of Amazon came at a grave cost for Main Street. Between 2007 and 2017, the number of small retailers fell by 65,000 in the US, according to a report by the Institute for Local Self-Reliance. "About 40 percent of the nation's small apparel, toy, and sporting goods makers disappeared, along with about one-third of small book publishers," the report found.

Kathy McCauslin-Cadieux was one of them. The sixty-eight-year-old former boutique owner, who had run her business for twenty-nine years, greeting her loyal customers with "How can I spoil you?" and a hug, would struggle.

McCauslin-Cadieux started her business in her basement, designing jewelry and clothing with her young son and daughter beside her, infusing them with the energy of entrepreneurship. She never took a business or marketing class, but would hit the jewelry shows and craft fairs each week, selling her designs. The business took off to the point that she opened her first store, and customers followed.

Her success, at its height, was remarkable, with three boutiques and over $1.5 million dollars in gross annual sales. She employed twenty-five women who delighted in helping their customers pick out designer blazers, dresses, and accessories. "I loved making the women who came in feel beautiful," she said.

In addition to the many repeat "ladies" (as she refers to them), her stores benefited from the foot traffic that came in from neighboring shops. "I loved all of it. I was always part of the community. It was just a gift from God."

By 2013, things started to change. Foot traffic began to fall off, and the customers she loved began visiting less. In her boutiques, she started hearing about Amazon more. Every year after 2013, her stores grossed less and less money.

Customers came into the store, looked at items, and then left without purchasing anything. They would order those same items from Amazon.

The breaking point for McCauslin-Cadieux was in 2017. She and an employee spent three hours helping a customer with mother-of-the-bride dresses. They helped her pick out the right fits and silhouettes and treated her to glasses of prosecco. The woman fell in love with one of the dresses. "She felt so beautiful, but then she said, 'I'm going to go online and see if Amazon has it,'" McCauslin-Cadieux recalled.

"After that, I said, 'I'm done. I've had it.'" A few weeks later, McCauslin-Cadieux gathered her employees for a meeting. She was closing her stores after the holiday season. They all hugged and cried.

"Amazon took away my passion," McCauslin-Cadieux said. "I was just done with Amazon. My heart aches every day for my friends who are still in retail. I see how hard they're working, and I know what the story is. I'm so thankful that I don't have the stress of what's going on now."

————

Between 2012 and 2017, Toys "R" Us's sales dwindled from nearly $14 billion to $11.5 billion. Between one-half and two-thirds of the company's earnings went to pay interest from Toys "R" Us's 2005 leveraged buyout. Competition reached a fever pitch in the toy category, with Amazon and Walmart fighting each other for the lowest prices in a race to the bottom.

In the years since its aborted deal with Amazon for its online operation, Toys "R" Us tried to do it itself, but had a hard time breaking meaningfully above 10 percent of its revenues through its website. The logistics alone would prove an impossible hurdle to overcome. Every time it felt it was catching up to Amazon's delivery speeds, the goalposts would move, with Amazon speeding up.

While Amazon was investing heavily in its e-commerce capabilities, Toys "R" Us was cash strapped, recalls Dave Brandon, the CEO of Toys "R" Us from 2015 to 2018. Years earlier, former CEO Jerry Storch raised the alarm about the uneven playing field Amazon had to then New Jersey governor Chris Christie. In the ensuing years, things had gotten significantly worse for the toy retailer. And because Amazon didn't have the same business model or profit pressure, the Seattle company repeatedly undercut the market on toy prices, Brandon recalls, using toys as a loss leader, getting customers to buy them on Amazon and fill their carts with other categories. A loss leader is something Amazon could afford but others couldn't: selling some products at a loss in order to attract customers to other offerings. No one else had the profit center from a cloud computing operation to prop them up.

Brandon voiced these concerns in Washington policy circles. "Amazon doesn't have a profit motive. They're selling at a loss," he would tell them. "They're crushing bricks and mortar retailers; they're doing it purposefully to create a monopoly. Most of us in the bricks and mortar business have been left defenseless because nobody can compete with that."

Bill Simon, Walmart's US CEO from 2010 to 2014, had similar concerns. "I think their approach to business by using the profits of something that's completely unrelated, like web services, to drive people out of retail to build market share is why I think they should be broken up," Simon told me in a recent interview. "I have people who say, 'Well, Walmart put a lot of people out of business, too.' My answer is we did it honest. We did it in retail. We didn't do it by owning an oil company and taking the profits from the oil business and investing it in retail to underprice people," explained Simon.

On September 18, 2017, Toys "R" Us filed for bankruptcy. Between the pressure of Amazon's prices and logistics, and Walmart's decision to go head-to-head with Amazon, Toys "R" Us couldn't compete, said Brandon.

The company known for Geoffrey the Giraffe and raising "Toys "R" Us kids" closed more than 700 stores in the US. More than 30,000 employees lost their jobs.

———

Part of Carney's plan was to skip past the sad sacks of Main Street by bringing Amazon's sellers to life. Thriving sellers meant job creation in the US, and jobs were the quickest way to sway politicians.

Starting in 2015—Amazon's first Prime Day—the company began flying in sellers (on coach, of course) to DC to parade around Capitol Hill. With each subsequent year, its use of sellers as a front for Amazon's PR strategy became bigger, with sellers attending events like the National Governors Association. It didn't matter that Chinese sellers made up 46 percent of Amazon's top sellers on its US Marketplace, according to estimates from Marketplace Pulse.

The sellers were escorted to meetings in DC with their local congressmen and senators. Amazon officials tagged along and watered those flowers. During meetings, Amazon handlers and lobbyists would brief the sellers on suggested dos and don'ts. With Trump's staff, for example, don't bring up China, they suggested. In meetings with the NAFTA team, which oversaw North American trade, it would be great to share how important Mexico is for their businesses.

Bobby Djavaheri, the president of Yedi Houseware Appliances, was one such seller picked to represent Amazon on Capitol Hill. Djavaheri was the model seller to present to lawmakers. His company sold kitchen appliances such as sous vides, air fryers, and pressure cookers on the site and brought in millions of dollars annually from Amazon. Djavaheri's company is based in Los Angeles and employs between ten and fifteen people, depending on the season. He was an American-born success story, the son of Iranian immigrants who fled the country before the revolution, and used his Amazon earnings to employ other Americans. He was the type of feel-good example that showed how Amazon's platform created ancillary jobs throughout the economy.

In April 2019, Djavaheri flew to Washington, DC, for three days of meetings. Over lunch and a moderated panel where Djavaheri and other sellers were given the questions ahead of time, Djavaheri told Representatives Pete Aguilar of California and Brett Guthrie of Kentucky about his experience growing sales on Amazon and creating jobs to fulfill such orders. Amazon also set up meetings for each of the sellers with their local representatives.

Amazon orchestrated every detail. In an email to sellers, a member of the press team wrote, "I will also be in attendance to help you prepare talking points and answers to questions." Public relations and public policy executives coordinated calls weeks before the event to prepare sellers on what to say.

When I asked what sellers got out of the days-long events, one Amazon seller couldn't answer. He felt like he had been tricked into doing Amazon's bidding.

In 2018, Amazon published its first US "Small Business Impact Report" dedicated to burnishing Amazon's image. "We recently took a deeper look at how Amazon is impacting small businesses, and the results are exciting to see. Among the highlights: More than a million US-based small and medium-sized businesses are selling on Amazon; Amazon estimates that small and medium-sized businesses selling on Amazon have created more than 900,000 jobs worldwide; More than 20,000 small and medium-sized businesses worldwide on Amazon surpassed $1 million in sales in 2017," said Jeff Wilke in his inaugural opening note.

The rest of the report goes on to tout some statistics that Amazon would cling to for years to come in its external messaging both to customers and on Capitol Hill: half of the items sold on Amazon come from its Marketplace side of the business, which includes many small businesses. These sellers employ a workforce of hundreds of thousands of employees that they can keep on their payrolls because of their Amazon sales. In other words, Amazon is good for America, and helps Americans prosper.

————

But the full picture of Amazon's impact on the economy and its seller base is far more complicated.

Amazon repeatedly cites the number of jobs it creates both at its company and the companies that sell on its platform. But other researchers have explored Amazon's effects on the retail sector and concluded that it has led to job loss in the US.

A report conducted by the American Booksellers Association with Civic Economics estimates that in 2018, Amazon led to a net loss of 700,000 retail jobs in the US. An analysis by the Institute for Local Self-Reliance found that in 2015, Amazon had displaced enough sales at stores to force the elimination of about 295,000 retail jobs. If you offset the number of employees Amazon had in the US at the time, that meant Amazon led a net loss of about 149,000 jobs. Retail jobs in particular are important to the US economy, supporting more than one in four US jobs, according to the National Retail Federation. It's an essential line of work for millions of Americans who don't have the credentials to enter a white-collar profession. But this is still an incomplete picture. There have yet to be decisive studies on Amazon's true impact on the broader economy as it has grown and expanded into numerous industries.

"Amazon has created more jobs in the past decade than any U.S. company, and we have invested more than $530 billion in the U.S. over the last decade," an Amazon spokesperson said in response. "Beyond our own workforce, Amazon's investments have supported nearly 1.6 million indirect jobs."

When it comes to the millions of small- and medium-sized sellers that Amazon frequently touts, a large percentage report being unhappy with their relationship with Amazon, feeling stuck on a hamster wheel.

Their gripes run the gamut. For one, the amount of fees Amazon charges sellers to use its platform has exploded in recent years, shrinking seller profits and forcing them to raise their prices in order to cover their costs to sell on Amazon.com.

In 2023, Amazon took 45 percent of each third-party sale on Amazon, according to research from the anti-monopoly group the Institute for Local Self-Reliance. So, for every $100 in sales from a third-party merchant, Amazon collected $45 in fees. That's up from a 19 percent "take" from Amazon in 2014, the Institute for Local Self-Reliance found.

The fees Amazon sellers pay range from a commission (often 15 percent) to Amazon on each product, a shipping fee for inclusion in Amazon's Fulfillment by Amazon (FBA) program, and advertising costs. Sellers say that they feel they have no choice but to enroll in FBA so that they can be eligible for Amazon Prime shipping, and that advertising is necessary in order to succeed on the platform.

According to a Marketplace Pulse report, using Amazon's FBA

(logistics) program to fulfill and ship orders is all but required in order for sellers to be successful. "Fulfillment by Amazon (FBA) fees have steadily increased. Amazon has raised fulfillment fees every year and introduced increases in storage fees. Selling on Amazon is tied to using FBA, so it's rare for sellers to be successful without using it," the report states. An Amazon spokesman said that selling on Amazon is "a win-win for our selling partners." In 2022, Amazon said that independent sellers in Amazon's US store sold an average of 7,800 items per minute.

Sellers have complained about feeling forced to use FBA, and some politicians have openly wondered whether Amazon's Prime and FBA programs ran afoul of competition law by tying its businesses together. While difficult to legally enforce, regulators have long examined whether a dominant company is limiting customer choice by forcing buyers that want one product or service (in this case the ability to be on Prime), to buy another (like using Amazon logistics) as well. Representative Pramila Jayapal, a Democrat who represents Amazon's Seattle-area home district, says that Amazon is using tying tactics for its Prime program in order to benefit its logistics arm. She said she has heard from sellers who have complained that Amazon compelled them to use its fulfillment service by making it harder to sell goods on its retail platform. In particular, access to Amazon's coveted Buy Box—which determines which seller of an item is featured for a sale—and getting good placement in search results are contingent upon a seller's participation in the fulfillment program, she said.

Amazon said that being featured in the Buy Box is not contingent on participation in FBA.

Prime presents a conundrum for third-party sellers. The program, where 200 million members worldwide pay a fee to get unlimited fast shipping and other perks like video streaming, is so popular with customers that many sellers feel like they can't afford not to enroll in Amazon's logistics program so that they can be a part of it. Having a Prime badge triples a seller's sales on Amazon. But the logistics program comes with its own costs.

Jerry Kavesh, who sells apparel and footwear on Amazon, learned this the hard way. Kavesh pulled some inventory from FBA because he couldn't afford the fees associated with it. Once he opted out of FBA, he noticed a slowdown in sales for those items compared to the ones he kept in the fulfillment program.

"There's a ramification for not using FBA," he said. "It impacts your searchability and impacts your Buy Box opportunities, because FBA trumps everything when it comes to the Buy Box."

Sellers say that success on Amazon is also predicated on buying advertising from the company.

Because of the explosion in fees, sellers complain that their margins have become so small that they've been forced to raise the prices of their items that they sell on Amazon in order to offset them. That results in higher prices for customers.

Joe, an eighty-one-year-old inventor in Gainesville, Florida, began selling golf cart accessories on Amazon in 2008. (Joe asked for his last name to be withheld.) "It was phenomenal," he says of those early years on Amazon. Joe was able to sell high volumes of items and had high margins at the time.

More recently, his experience has changed. He says he has to spend heavily on advertisements in order to get sales. Every month he spends between $3,000 and $5,000 just on advertisements on the site, he says. With Amazon's fees rising, he's seen his average margin shrink from about 50 percent in the earlier years to around just 12 percent today. As such, he's had to raise his prices to offset Amazon's fees, he said. "I've raised my prices probably 30 percent over the last five years in order to offset the fees," he said.

Brenton Taussig took over the family business, Consolidated Plastics, from his father in 2018. Taussig knew he wanted to run the company from the time he was just ten years old. He knew all of the workers, some of whom still work for him today, and took pride in selling items like entryway mats to schools and businesses.

A decade ago, Taussig and his brother began selling the Stow, Ohio–based company's products on Amazon.com. Today, Amazon accounts for half of the company's sales.

Despite making $10 million a year in revenues on Amazon, the fees have become onerous for Taussig. He pays Amazon $1.5 million each year in commissions and another $1.5 million on advertisements on the website he says. After all the other costs of doing business—shipping items, paying his employees, cost of goods—his Amazon revenues become just $30,000 in total profits for the year after taxes, he says.

"I talk to my wife probably once a month and say, 'What am I doing here?' I'm beating my head against the wall. It's almost like a charity case," he says of selling on Amazon.

The fees from Amazon have led him to increase his prices. Last year, Amazon upped its commission for Taussig's goods from 12 percent to 15 percent without warning. To offset that fee hike, Taussig raised the price of his three-pack of buckets with lids—one of his best sellers—from $65 to $72, he says. The same dynamic plays out with his single buckets, which cost Taussig $3.90 from his manufacturer. After all the fees and costs to do business, he sells them for $30 each on Amazon.

Amazon benefits from the perception that it has the lowest prices because of its early years where it did undercut the market, and because of select loss leading categories where it still does. But in more recent years, sellers say the economics have drastically changed. Behind the scenes, third-party sellers have had to grapple with the rising costs of doing business on Amazon. For many, it has meant hiking up their prices. And because for years Amazon contractually required that sellers list their goods on Amazon at their lowest price, sellers also say they've had to hike their prices at other retailers, such as Walmart.com or Target.com, creating higher prices across retail.

As all of the seeds Bezos planted earlier became enormous businesses, they became inextricably part of doing business on Amazon.com. They fed their own flywheel. More sellers on Amazon means more selection on Amazon.com. More selection on Amazon means more shoppers. Because of the volume of shoppers, sellers feel like they need to sell on Amazon.com, but in order to show up in search results amid loads of other sellers, merchants feel like they have to buy advertising from Amazon. Because of the power of the Prime program, sellers feel like they have to use Amazon's logistics services to get a Prime badge. Amazon collects fees each step of the way.

"My business on my website shrinks at about 4 percent a year. My Amazon business grows at about 6 percent to 8 percent a year with no increase in profitability, but the top line grows," explains Taussig. "So yeah, I'm in a hard spot. Five years ago, if I knew where I was today, if asked whether I would get on Amazon, I'd say absolutely not. But once you're in the ecosystem, it's hard to step away."

Taussig refuses to shop on Amazon himself because of the company's economics for sellers. Instead, he tries to buy directly from manufacturers of products he's buying.

Taussig's wife is pregnant, and a friend recently asked him if he'd leave the business to his child one day. "I really don't think that eighteen years from now that my business will be around," he said.

In addition to hefty fees, sellers have to deal with other concerns: Amazon burying their items in search results if they offered a lower price elsewhere, being subject to competing sellers leaving fake bad reviews that torpedo their sales, counterfeit sellers hawking fake products, and legitimate sellers' accounts being suspended without notice. These are worrisome details for a company that publicly takes credit as a booster of small business.

Billy Carmen, an Amazon seller in Ukiah, California, worries about the level of information Amazon has about his supply chain. The sixty-four-year-old maker of patio products said Amazon has requested sensitive information and invoices detailing his manufacturer's name, address, and contact information, among other details. Many other sellers have also said Amazon has suspended their seller accounts until they provide such information.

"That's a big fear that they will take our manufacturing information and create it themselves, but they demand the information saying if we don't give them the info they'll turn our account off," Carmen said. Amazon accounts for 70 percent of his sales. "It's literally like being held as a prisoner with Amazon, and because of that there's no place else companies like us can go to sell our products. Amazon uses that against us," he said.

Carmen in 2020 sent Amazon invoices from his manufacturer because his account was under threat of suspension for counterfeit claims, even though he created the original product in question. How could he counterfeit something he made? He hadn't seen any Amazon-branded imitations on the site. Amazon said that seller information collected during an IP infringement investigation is not shared with the retail or private brands teams.

For sellers like Carmen, there's no way for them to push back against behavior they find unethical. "It's really, really hard to defend ourselves. The dilemma is it is like the mafia. A brand like us won't survive anywhere else without Amazon, and Amazon knows that."

———————

Amazon's size and power even pulls in brands that have no interest in selling on the site. New York–based Adore Me launched in 2012 as a direct-to-consumer maker of women's lingerie.

Adore Me's designs and business model of selling straight to its customers rather than incurring the fees of selling through other retailers made it profitable. Because of its success, starting in 2016 Amazon consistently reached out to the company to sell on its site. Founder and CEO Morgan Hermand-Waiche repeatedly rejected Amazon's advances.

But in 2019, the company began noticing blatant knockoffs of its brand on Amazon.com. One was named Adome, which looked very similar to Adore Me on the site. It stole photographs of products from Adore Me's website for its images and made cheap knockoffs of Adore Me's products, hoping to capitalize on the company's success, Hermand-Waiche says.

Hermand-Waiche said there were more than a dozen brands on Amazon's website using its images or making cheap counterfeits of its products. Adore Me repeatedly contacted Amazon for help removing the counterfeiters, which were damaging his brand with their cheap quality, but never got a helpful response.

"These counterfeits generate revenue for Amazon, so it empowers Amazon while diminishing the power of our brand. It is detrimental to us," Hermand-Waiche said in an interview. For months, customers bought what they thought was his brand, only to receive cheaply made replicas.

Despite being resistant to joining Amazon, which would cause his margins to decline and result in him losing control of the customer relationship and experience, the CEO says he felt held hostage by the situation.

"What do we do? Do we go on Amazon and then it reduces our margins, it empowers Amazon with our brand presence, and it also gives them the third-party data that gives them the power to then copy Adore Me like they do for every single product?" he recalls thinking. "Or, we do not go on Amazon, keep our integrity, but we have to accept the fact that they are not fighting counterfeits and we have to live with the fact that millions of people will see a product there and believe it is ours when it is not. It is one shitty situation versus another shitty situation. Which evil do you take?"

In summer 2020, Hermand-Waiche made the decision to begin selling his products on Amazon's site. He saw few other options. Suing the giant would have been too costly, he said.

The CEO thinks Amazon is too big. "This is not an Adore Me matter. It affects the American economy. Hundreds of thousands of jobs are on the line. And so at the end of the day, something's gotta be done," he said. In response, Amazon said it has a "zero-tolerance policy for counterfeit products" and continuously monitors its store. Amazon's Marketplace is still flooded with Adore Me knock offs, said Hermand-Waiche.

But for all its issues, there are sellers who rely on Amazon and make a good living on its site. Tahmi DeSchepper left a job in telecommunications consulting to begin making jewelry full time in 2002. On weekends, DeSchepper and her husband would pack up the car with her wares and drive between six and fifteen hours to showcase her designs at fine arts festivals. She estimates she'd attended thirty shows each year.

In 2015, DeSchepper joined Amazon.com to try to reach a bigger audience without being on the road for so many hours. While she had some hiccups learning how to list her products effectively, by 2017, she was up and running. She enrolled in Amazon's delivery program, Fulfillment by Amazon. "It's been a rocket ship ever since," she said.

Amazon now accounts for 98 percent of her sales. Her last full-time year on the road was in 2016. Her sales now are more than five times her 2016 sales, she says. For DeSchepper, who lives in Fairfield, Iowa, being on Amazon means she can reach so many more customers than she could have prior to joining the platform.

When Amazon is presented with seller complaints, it often says that there are many places where they could choose to sell as an alternative. Sellers disagree.

I asked Joe, the golf cart accessory maker, why he continues to sell on Amazon despite the worsening economics for his business on the platform.

"Amazon's the only place to sell, I think. I might as well close up shop if I relied on the other retailers. Amazon's the only one where you sell anything," he said.

———

For all its rhetoric around boosting small business, giving them a platform as sellers, Amazon also wouldn't blanch at copying some, especially if they were too successful, like it did with Fortem. Fortem is a small, Brooklyn-based company with four employees. Its founders have street smarts and a gift for understanding the arbitrage of retailing.

In 2016, in their mid-twenties, Yuriy Petriv and Oleg Maslakov began manufacturing car accessories that they designed in China. Their first product, and their bestseller, is a popular car trunk organizer that straps into people's trunks and holds different items in place. They tweaked and went through many different iterations of the product to get it just right. Nearly 100 percent of Fortem's sales are through Amazon.com.

Petriv and Maslakov got the alchemy right. They launched fifteen different car accessories on Amazon that sell thousands of items every month. As with many sellers, they paid Amazon a percentage of each item sold, paid fees for storing and shipping each item, and paid thousands of dollars each month to advertise their products on the platform.

Petriv and Maslakov's success caught the attention of employees on Amazon's private label team. In early 2019, an employee working on developing new products for Amazon Basics pulled up a detailed report of Fortem's metrics for the car trunk organizers.

The report detailed that Fortem had sold 33,000 units of the organizer during the twelve months covered in the report. It had twenty-five columns with detailed information about Fortem's financials, sales, and expenses. The report showed the product's average selling price during the preceding twelve months was about $25, that Fortem had sold more than $800,000 worth in the period specified, and that each item generated nearly $4 in profit for Amazon. The report also detailed how much Fortem spent on advertising per unit and the cost to ship each trunk organizer.

In other words, this was a treasure trove of data for Amazon's private label employees, who were judged on the number of successful items they brought to market in a given year. Instead of having to dedicate the expensive research and development dollars to engineer the right products and take a risk that they wouldn't sell, they had a road map to make hits, and quickly.

Fortem launched its trunk organizer on Amazon's Marketplace in March 2016, and it eventually became the number one seller in the category on the site.

After the Amazon private label employee pulled Fortem's data, Amazon Basics started to develop their own version of the product. By October 2019, Amazon launched three trunk organizers similar to Fortem's under its Amazon Basics private label brand.

The founders had no idea what was being done to their company and product. They would eventually learn about it from me.

————

Amazon had for years been weirdly cagey about giving specifics about its private label division. It would only categorize private label as small, saying it made up less than 1 percent of its retail sales. (Amazon doesn't include sales from the Whole Foods 365 brand, Amazon Fresh brand, or its devices business when calculating their private brand revenues.)

In 2019, I took over the Amazon beat at the *Journal,* and the business seemed like an area where the company could potentially abuse its power. It was able to own the platform and compete on the platform with a wildly unfair information advantage — access to data that simply no one else could have. It was the textbook definition of an uneven playing field.

Private label brands were as old as retail itself. When CVS or Kroger creates its private label brand of toothpaste, of course it uses store data to figure out what to make. The difference is, CVS or Kroger buy their toothpaste directly from Colgate. It owns that Colgate inventory, prices it, sells it to their customers, and discounts it as needed. The data CVS or Kroger use is their own data since they own the inventory and control the pricing and discounts themselves.

Plus, when a retailer creates a store brand, it's typically for commoditized products to compete in generic categories such as paper towels made by the likes of Procter & Gamble, rather than copycat versions of items created by smaller entrepreneurs.

What Amazon was doing was entirely different. It didn't buy the inventory of third-party sellers. It didn't set the prices, buy the advertising, or have a traditional retail relationship with its third-party sellers. Instead, its model was for these sellers to create their own stores on Amazon and have complete control over how many items to stock and sell and how to price them. These third-party sellers were essentially paying rent to Amazon to exist in its virtual mall. When a private label employee accessed data from third-party sellers, it was akin to breaking into the seller's store after the virtual mall closed and taking all their data.

Amazon employees in the private label division received yearly ethics training where they were told that accessing individual third-party seller data was forbidden. But in practice, there were not adequate firewalls to prevent them from accessing the data, dozens of these employees told me. Many were readily able to pull the reports themselves.

Pulling data on competitors, even individual sellers, was "standard operating procedure" when making products such as electronics, suitcases, sporting goods, or other lines, said the person who shared the Fortem documentation. Such reports were pulled before Amazon's private label team decided to enter a product line, the person said. The practice went on for years without any negative repercussions. Amazon's spokesman said the company has never fired a private brand employee for using individual seller data to create a product, saying that Amazon has never found any instances of employees using the seller data in this way.

In 2015 and 2018, Amazon conducted two internal audits of its private brands business to investigate whether seller data was being accessed in ways that violated internal rules. "We cannot comment on the audits, which were conducted at the request and under the supervision of counsel and are therefore clearly privileged," an Amazon spokesperson said. "But it is important to distinguish between access and use. We are not aware of any instances in which Amazon employees actually used non-public, seller-specific data to develop Private Brands products," the spokesperson continued. The spokesman declined to answer questions about whether its audits found that private label employees could access such data. Amazon's response was interesting. Employees and managers have admitted to me over the years that the use was rampant.

The data held the information needed for these teams to move fast and bring hits to market. Moving fast and bringing hits to market was the blueprint for keeping your job at Amazon and possibly being in line for a promotion. For many employees, the data was too valuable to ignore.

————

Amazon's private label team was under intense pressure to grow sales. Some of the managers were told they were expected to grow their categories into $1 billion brands.

In 2015, Amazon was working on a new private label food brand called Wickedly Prime. In typical Amazon fashion, the team had written a six-pager with the goal of what Wickedly Prime would be prior to getting approval from senior leaders. The report said that it aimed to replicate the top 200 items sold at Trader Joe's, a quirky grocery store with a cultlike following.

Amazon's private brands team took this mandate seriously. Trader Joe's secrets are well guarded. The grocer doesn't allow online shopping, so there is less known about the company's top sellers than those of retailers that have reviews and online shopping available. Much of what Trader Joe's sells it makes itself, with interesting concoctions that fly off shelves, such as cinnamon bun spread and rosemary croissant croutons. It was difficult for Amazon to figure out exactly which 200 items to copy because of this secretiveness, but they were determined to find out.

The team made an important hire by bringing on a category lead from Trader Joe's. When interviewing for the role at Amazon, the Trader Joe's executive wasn't told specifically what she'd be working on. It wasn't until she started and, during her first week, walked into a conference room at headquarters that had kraft paper covering the windows and door to ensure privacy that she started piecing things together. The mysterious conference room was filled with boxes of Trader Joe's food piled high on shelves. Amazon had sent a team member to Trader Joe's to buy up its products — mostly in the snack food section — for Amazon to study for its own brand. It alarmed the employee, who was hired to help create product assortment for Wickedly Prime.

For six months, the employee's manager hounded her for information about Trader Joe's bestselling products. She tried to deflect, but the pressure kept ratcheting up. Finally, the manager demanded that the employee email any documents she had retained from her time at Trader Joe's to another colleague on the team. She emailed over an Excel spreadsheet that detailed Trader Joe's top-selling items nationally over the course of a week. It contained the number of units sold per item over that time period.

But the manager didn't stop with the sales data. He also demanded that she share Trader Joe's margins for each product. When she refused, her manager angrily screamed at her, "You just have to give us the data!" a person who witnessed the exchange said. The employee, who had been pressured for months, burst into tears but did not share the margins data.

Nonetheless, the team disseminated her sales document and started to think about how to incorporate it, but another team member became uncomfortable with the ethics of using Trader Joe's proprietary data and reported it to legal. Soon enough, the handful of the employees who had accessed the data were fired. Amazon responded to the behavior appropriately, but employees on the team say the use of the data was emblematic of the type of pressure they were under.

"We do not condone the misuse of proprietary confidential information, and thoroughly investigate any reports of employees doing so and take action, which may include termination," an Amazon spokesperson said in response to the Wickedly Prime situation.

Just months later, that pressure would ratchet up even more. In 2017, Bezos had a meeting with some senior leaders in the private brands division. Target's and Walmart's private brands businesses were significant percentages of their overall sales, the CEO said. "What percentage of sales was Amazon's private brands?" he asked. The team cowered. Its figures were nowhere near those retail giants. Private brands at Amazon accounted for just around 1 percent of retail sales, they told Bezos.

Bezos said that figure wasn't acceptable. He wanted private brands to grow to be 10 percent of Amazon's retail revenue within five years, he said. Those on the private brands team knew this was impossible, but they would have to try. It had come directly from Bezos.

"So, we created a plan that was really exponential, because the thing you have to understand about private brands is that there's only so many batteries you can sell," a private brands executive at Amazon said to me. "In order to get to a much higher level of revenue you need to launch a number of products each year and they need to be hits."

While there was internal training every year for the team about the appropriate and inappropriate use of third-party data, and a supposed firewall between the private label and third-party teams, employees on the team described lax protocols that were easy to circumvent. In order to give themselves a leg up in going to market with private label products that would succeed, they regularly helped themselves to troves of third-party seller data that detailed what products were hits and other granular details like the costs and margins for each item, multiple people who worked on Amazon private label brands told me.

If they couldn't pull the data themselves, they would simply ask a business analyst with broader systems access to pull reports for them on third-party sellers. One of the people involved called this process "going over the fence." The use of such data became so commonplace at Amazon over the years that employees openly discussed using the data in meetings, and one private label employee was even instructed by her boss to pull the data as part of developing Amazon's own vitamins.

And while Amazon's top leaders, such as Bezos or his S-Team, did not instruct teams to use the data in such a way, employees say there were not proper protocols in place to prevent employees from pulling the data. What's more, Amazon's uber-competitive culture, where every year the bottom 6 percent of employees were cut from an already all-star pool of Ivy League talent, meant that accessing that data to gain an edge was an unspoken incentive to stay ahead.

Numerous research studies have shown that incentives in the workplace tend to backfire. A *Harvard Business Review* article called "Why Incentive Plans Cannot Work" states: "Punishment and rewards are two sides of the same coin. Rewards have a punitive effect because they, like outright punishment, are manipulative. 'Do this and you'll get that' is not really very different from 'Do this or here's what will happen to you.' In the case of incentives, the reward itself may be highly desired; but by making that bonus contingent on certain behaviors, managers manipulate their subordinates, and that experience of being controlled is likely to assume a punitive quality over time." The article goes on to say: "The surest way to destroy cooperation and, therefore, organizational excellence, is to force people to compete for rewards or recognition or to rank them against each other," adding that this environment causes employees to view other colleagues as obstacles to their own success.

At Amazon, the reality that the bottom performers would be let go every year was constantly on everyone's minds, and in many instances led to bad behavior to get an edge over someone else. One former S-Team member recounted that Amazon's rigorous promotion process also could cause bad behavior. "I think the people who make most of those bad decisions are more people who are thirsty for promotion," the S-Team member said. "I think people really optimize for optics at times around the promotion process. I think it's a bit of a side issue with the way you make promotions very rigorous and very document heavy where you got to go through layers. Then everybody thinks you've got to produce a flagship thing to get promoted."

Even Amazon's most-senior leaders were paranoid about their performance. Some say that Bezos believed that employees were expendable, which shaped the company's culture. "You always knew that no matter what level you were, that you're only as good as what you did yesterday," Dave Clark, who was CEO of Amazon's consumer business and an S-Team member before leaving the company after twenty-three years, told me.

In some ways, it reminded me of the Wells Fargo scandal in which the company's bankers opened up millions of deposit and credit card accounts without customers' knowledge. Was Wells Fargo's CEO pushing its bankers to open the fraudulent accounts? No, but the employees were fired if they didn't hit unrealistic goals that were based on the volume of accounts they opened. And for more than a decade, no one stopped the behavior. (Once the scandal was brought to light, Wells Fargo fired 5,300 employees and paid billions in fines.) A culture of unattainable goals, the risk of losing their jobs, and turning a blind eye to bad behavior created a perfect storm for rampant misconduct.

———

Once the data was pulled, sources say Amazon had a sophisticated process in place to copy the brands. An Amazon employee in Seattle working in a certain category would peruse the documents and pick which of the third-party seller's products not only sold the best but also had margins and pricing that Amazon could compete with if it were to create its own product. In essence, Amazon would want to identify products it could make and price for less than the third-party seller all while delivering a higher margin to itself than what that seller brought in for Amazon. The bar was typically a margin improvement of 5 percent, but in some categories it was as high as 10 percent.

Then an employee based in Seattle would flag the third-party product, internally called a "reference ASIN," to Amazon's team in Shenzhen, China. The Shenzhen team, which was in charge of managing Amazon's manufacturing relationships, would order the product to its offices for inspection. Then it would bring it to Chinese manufacturers in Shenzhen that specialized in that product category. The factories would come back with quotes to manufacture the product for Amazon, and if a factory could deliver similar quality and higher margins than what Amazon derived from its own third-party sellers, they would place the order, Shenzhen Amazon employees told me.

For Amazon, the process took the guesswork and design risk out of creating its own products. "They don't want to spend any R&D money on any product and go through the process of redesigning anything," recalled a Shenzhen private label employee. He said they would make tiny tweaks to Amazon's version to look just different enough or to lower the cost but otherwise they made no major changes. Within as little as eight months, its copycat could be available on Amazon.com for purchase.

While the Seattle private label team had aggressive targets to meet, so did their Shenzhen counterparts. They were under pressure to launch 2,000 to 3,000 new items each year, according to people who worked on that team.

I asked a Shenzhen employee if Amazon was concerned about the antitrust implications of using the data. "If someone went into Amazon and took their computers and checked their email inbox, it wouldn't be difficult for them to find the truth. It's not even a secret," he replied.

"We draw a clear line against using non-public, seller specific data to compete with sellers," an Amazon spokesperson said in response. "Public allegations of policy violations have been based on misunderstandings and not on credible evidence."

Fortem was far from being the only victim of Amazon's practices. In many cases, like Fortem, the victims were often small, enterprising businesses, the very types Carney's team had gone to great lengths to depict Amazon as a champion of.

One of those sellers is Travis Killian, who, with six other employees in Austin, Texas, makes and sells seat cushions for office chairs, pillows for people suffering from sciatica, travel umbrellas, and other products. Killian founded Upper Echelon Products in 2015, and the majority of its sales come from Amazon. One of its office chair seat cushions is a bestseller on the website.

Amazon private label employees also took a peek at Upper Echelon's office chair seat cushion, pulling a year's worth of their data, when researching development of an Amazon-branded seat cushion. The data showed that, during that period, Killian had sold more than 111,000 units of his seat cushion, creating $3.5 million in revenues. The report included his marketing spend per unit and other sensitive information. An Amazon employee pulled the data in early 2019. In September 2020, Amazon Basics launched its own version.

In 2020, I shared the data with Killian to see how closely it matched his own from that time. He called it a perfect match. "It's not a comfortable feeling knowing that they have people internally specifically looking at us to compete with us," he told me at the time. "Go ahead and make a seat cushion, but don't steal data from us and use it against us. That's not really cool."

Amazon said there were more than two dozen sellers of the Upper Echelon seat cushion during the period, but would not say how many units those sellers sold. Killian said if that were the case, he isn't sure how the private label data on his seller account the Amazon employees used matched his internal sales data so perfectly.

When victims of Amazon's private label spying find out about it, their reactions are similar. At first they are outraged. Then they become afraid.

Their anger is warranted: the costs of simply using Amazon as a sales channel are steep as it is. Amazon's success is built on the backs of these sellers who pay Amazon a commission for every unit sold, many of whom feel they have no choice but to pay Amazon to advertise their products in search and store and ship their products for them through its Fulfillment by Amazon program.

Amazon presents a catch-22 for third-party sellers who feel like they can't afford not to sell on the website, even if they're exploited. They often beg not to be included in news reports for fear of poking the beast and facing retaliatory consequences, like having their accounts shut down. When Congress would interview them for testimony related to later investigations, they would ask for anonymity out of fear of retribution. One member of Congress compared Amazon to the mafia because of the power it has over small businesses.

When sellers learn that Amazon is not only taking a giant cut of their profits but also spying on them, they are often stunned by the greed. "How much more do they want from me?" is a popular refrain.

Unfortunately, the problem is that Amazon is indeed a "they," and different groups within Amazon battle each other for policies that will help boost their own groups' revenues and metrics. This often comes at the expense of other groups and even the customer. Leadership principles are often weaponized or wholly disregarded to justify decisions that benefit certain business units.

Amazon's search team has often played the thankless role of upholding Amazon's "customer obsession" principle despite bullying from nearly every corner of Amazon's empire to do the opposite of it.

The search team, called A9 (with "A" in reference to the word "algorithms" and "9" for the nine other letters that make up the word), is composed of engineers who were purists and acted as standard-bearers of Amazon's main guiding principle.

Its engineers are sequestered away from Seattle to A9's own offices in Silicon Valley. For years A9 had its own CEO and operated independently from headquarters. (Funnily enough, Amazon set up A9 as its own corporate entity so that it could hire engineers in California without having to charge retail sales tax in the state.)

Amazon is a giant search engine for products. In fact, it's the largest, with over half of all online shopping searches in the US starting on Amazon.com, not Google or other search engines.

A9 controls the all-important search and ranking functions on Amazon's site. Like other technology giants, Amazon keeps its algorithm a closely guarded secret, even internally, for competitive reasons and to prevent sellers from gaming the system.

With millions of items for sale, sorting them instantaneously to give the customer relevant items to their search is A9's North Star. Nothing topped relevance because, at the end of the day, giving the customer what they want was the very definition of being customer obsessed.

Some of the factors in Amazon's algorithm include good ratings, sales volume, price, availability, and low returns, and for years the whole purpose of the algorithm was customer satisfaction. Providing a customer with a relevant item at a great price point was a win for everyone involved, right? As it turned out, not exactly.

Amazon's size and disparate arms meant groups within Amazon compete fiercely with each other. For example, employees working on Amazon's third-party side of the business wanted their sellers to succeed over Amazon's business where it buys products directly from manufacturers and resells them. Employees working for Amazon's private label team creating Amazon-branded products wanted their items added to customer baskets more often than those of the third-party and first-party businesses. Employees working on Amazon's advertising side of the business wanted as much space as possible in the search results for advertisements from sellers, not relevant items to the search term, because they made money for each ad sold. Each group was trying to hit its own internal numbers, and that meant vying for sales from other parts of Amazon's business. And looming in the back of every Amazonian's mind at all times was Amazon's cutthroat management system.

As the keyholders of what showed up in Amazon search, A9 faced a deluge of demands. One very pushy group inside Amazon was its private label team. Under intense pressure to boost their sales, this group of executives lobbied A9 hard and frequently to change its algorithm.

One of the biggest pushers of the change was Doug Herrington, a high riser at Amazon who had been involved in the Diapers.com acquisition years earlier. Herrington had a résumé dotted with all the right names: Princeton University undergrad, summa cum laude; Harvard Business School. He was a partner at the consulting firm Booz Allen Hamilton for a decade. In between, he worked elsewhere before eventually landing at Amazon.

Herrington and his team of retail executives for years asked A9 to give its items a boost in search, according to A9 engineers. They resisted. Giving preferential treatment to its own brands wasn't necessarily customer focused. The private label team found the nerdy purists annoying and complained that it was Amazon's store after all; why couldn't they give themselves an edge? After all, CVS placed its brand of cough syrup next to national brands like Robitussin. They argued that this was no different, sources said.

The private label team experimented with other ways to game the system and drive sales of its own products. It briefly tested a pop-up screen on its app that aimed to divert the sale of a competitor product to Amazon's version. When a customer on the app clicked on Energizer batteries, a screen would take over the page touting Amazon's own brand of lower-priced batteries.

But it always came back to the algorithm and search. The private label team wanted profits added as a criterion for the search algorithm. This would help surface their own line of products — which were required to have higher margins than the competition — in search. The higher they were in search, the more items they would sell.

So not only would they steal ideas from the likes of Fortem's two entrepreneurs; they would then bury them, too.

"We fought tooth and nail with those guys, because of course they wanted preferential treatment in search," said a former A9 senior executive.

"Every single team selling something at Amazon approached search to improve the ranking of their products," said one of the A9 engineers.

A9 was able to resist for so long because the group's leaders were also purists, but a restructuring at Amazon would take place that would change the ability of A9 to fight back on behalf of customers.

———

Back in 2015, A9 had been brought under the fold of Amazon's retail side of the business. But in 2018, a change in leadership meant that A9 now reported to Herrington. Pressure on the search team mounted and the dam finally broke.

The change in leadership coincided with another event at Amazon that would cause a frenzy internally. Bezos directed his S-Team to shore up profitability across retail. (And while it is true that in the early years after AWS launched, its profits helped offset low retail prices and margins on Amazon, what's not known publicly — even to shareholders — is how profitable Amazon's businesses outside of cloud computing have become. In 2018, for instance, Amazon's non-AWS businesses had around $17 billion in profits globally. But in Amazon's annual report, it said its North American, non-AWS business had $7.3 billion in profits and its international business lost $2.1 billion, bringing it to a cumulative $5.1 billion in profits. Why? The internal reports show that Amazon invested $5 billion in its devices units that year, which came out of those profits, and more than $3 billion in content for Amazon Studios, which also came out of those profits. As it relates to the profits, advertising contributed more than $6 billion in profits in 2018. Pushing sellers to buy more and more expensive ad placements, ratcheting up other seller fees, and other internal decisions paid off for the company. Amazon said: "Amazon reinvests capital in our businesses based on our desire to build new and improve existing customer experiences — it has not been our approach to direct profits from one business to influence another's results.")

In order to help with the profitability push, A9 was ordered to do something it found entirely contradictory to the leadership principles it abided by: change the search algorithm.

While most consumers question little about the bits of code that determine what they see, hear, and buy, algorithms are anything but neutral. They are created by humans who can optimize the algorithm in a way that creates an intended result. So, while shopping on Amazon, a customer might assume the search results that they see are most relevant, but changes to an algorithm could prioritize results beyond relevance.

Travel-booking website Orbitz in 2012 tested an algorithm that showed customers using Apple products more expensive hotels in its search rankings for a given city than customers entering the site through PCs. The tests came as a result of learning that Apple customers tended to spend more on hotel rooms than PC users, and data about Mac users' disposable income also supported that.

While the customer using an Apple device assumed that their results for a hotel in Malibu for a set of dates would be exactly the same as someone searching for those dates in Malibu on their Dell computer, the results were vastly different. Orbitz stopped showing Mac users higher-priced hotels after the *Wall Street Journal* revealed the practice in 2012.

The fact that readers were outraged by Orbitz manipulating its search algorithm is telling. Shoppers presuppose that algorithms are fair and neutral. Because of that naivete, algorithms have become an area where companies can hide a lot of sins without customers — or even regulators — finding out.

At first, Amazon executives pushed to add profits to the algorithm itself, so that in addition to showing items that sold well and had high ratings, it would prioritize products that delivered higher profits to Amazon. Given that Amazon's private label line was designed to have higher margins than the items it competes with on the site, this could give it a boost in search and further drive sales. Other sellers with products that delivered a big profit to Amazon also stood to benefit from the change.

But being so blatant about their desired outcome, even behind the scenes, could have proven problematic.

Sitting in a conference room in Seattle discussing the proposed change, Amazon's lawyers interjected. In 2017, Google had been slapped with a $2.7 billion fine from the EU's Margrethe Vestager, who found that Google used its search engine to stack the deck in favor of its comparison-shopping service. Facing greater scrutiny from regulators in Europe and at home, Amazon didn't want to be exposed.

The team looked at other ways to account for profitability without adding it directly to the algorithm. They turned to the metrics Amazon uses to test the algorithm's success in reaching certain business objectives.

When engineers test new variables they add to the algorithm, Amazon gauges the results against a handful of metrics. Among these metrics was whether sales went up, indicating that customers found what they were looking for. Positive results for the metrics they had historically used correlated with high customer satisfaction and helped determine the ranking of listings a search presented to the customer.

Now, engineers would need to consider another metric: improving profitability. Variables added to the algorithm would essentially become proxies for profit: the variables would correlate with improved profitability for Amazon, but it might not be apparent to an outside observer.

A9 engineers were aghast at the work they were being asked to do. Not only did it require months of importing data on profit for items sold on Amazon, but it felt like a major distraction. The project they were working on didn't benefit the customer. They felt conflicted.

"This was definitely not a popular project. The search engine should look for relevant items, not for more profitable items," an engineer at A9 who was reluctantly involved told me at the time.

An Amazon spokeswoman denied that Amazon changed the criteria it uses to rank search results to include profitability.

The A9 engineers were stalwart defenders of relevance. To add insult to injury, around the same time, Amazon removed the "relevance" drop-down on its home page to sort search results. Instead, it said "featured." Relevance was no longer king in Amazon search.

But the extent to which the small business and consumer climate of much of America was shaped by the internal incentives and motivations of a relatively small collection of Amazonians would never make Amazon's PR offensive.

CHAPTER 11

Amazon Proofing

IT WASN'T JUST SMALL players having their lunch eaten, either. For years, retail giants dreaded Amazon and its every move. They had underestimated the tech company for more than a decade. Apparel retailers in particular, a clubby crew of executives that often graduated from Bloomingdale's famed management program, where they learned to manage inventory, strategy plan, and curate merchandise, looked down at Amazon with derision.

Sure, Amazon could hawk gadgets and gizmos, but consumers would never deign to buy their clothes there, they believed.

And yet they were under siege well before they realized it. All the way back in January 2006, America's most influential retail CEOs entered the stately hall of Manhattan's Harmonie Club. Wearing cock-tail attire, they sipped on flutes of champagne and ate passed canapés while catching up on the chaos of the holiday season.

Every year, CEOs of some of the world's largest retailers, who deter-mine what we wear and how we wear it, descended upon the social club for a meeting of the minds.

The salon was run by Gilbert Harrison, a legendary retail invest-ment banker who headed up deal making firm Financo, and attracted the retail elite. Mickey Drexler, who made J.Crew into the iconic preppy American brand, rubbed elbows with the CEO of Macy's, wrap-dress doyenne Diane von Furstenberg, Martha Stewart, and other retail royalty. This year, Sean Combs, better known as P. Diddy, made the rounds wearing a pin-striped suit while chatting about his clothing line.

Over dinner and cocktails, the CEOs discussed trends on the horizon. A hallmark of the event was a lively panel moderated by Harrison. The focus was about branding and marketing, with no mention of e-commerce on the invitation.

The guest list remained largely the same year to year. But in 2006, guests were surprised to find a balding, nerdy new man among them. It was a young Jeff Bezos. He even dressed up for the occasion, ditching his usual uniform of khakis and a polo shirt for a dark suit.

David Jaffe, the former chair and CEO of Ascena Retail Group, the owner of Dress Barn, Lane Bryant, and other retail brands, remembers seeing Bezos at the bar. Jaffe's mother had started the Dress Barn enterprise in the 1960s and with her husband had grown it into a bit of an empire. Jaffe was now at the helm and prided himself on offering working women affordable fashion.

"What are you doing here?" he asked. Bezos's answer made him raise his eyebrows. "Your margin is my opportunity," the young CEO responded. (An Amazon spokesman disputed that Bezos said this.)

It was the only time Bezos attended the event. Earlier in the year, reports surfaced that Amazon was expanding more aggressively outside of books and hard goods and into clothing, Harrison recalls. "I think he was there to learn and to hear what was going on in the industry." Bezos was on that year's panel, alongside Steve Madden, Sean Combs, Bloomingdale's top executive, and a few others.

Amazon's market value was just $19 billion at the time. "People were intrigued by Amazon, but I don't think they totally bought into it," says Harrison.

That would soon change. Weeks after the event, Amazon announced a deal to buy luxury apparel website Shopbop. It would soon move more aggressively into capturing market share in the clothing space. The guest list of attendees from that year now reads like a bankruptcy docket. The CEOs of Linens 'n Things, Filene's Basement, Neiman Marcus, and Modell's were in attendance and listening to an unassuming tech CEO wax retail. They had no idea that the man on stage with the goofy laugh would soon be eating their lunch.

———————

The retailers were too quick to dismiss Amazon, and the rest of corporate America watched the ensuing bloodbath. For the better part of the last decade, the retail story was layoffs, restructurings, store closures, and bankruptcies, in no small part because of Amazon.

Mike Edwards, who was the CEO of bookstore chain Borders Group through its 2011 bankruptcy, remembers being dismissed by other executives when he'd warn them about Amazon's power. "When I got to Staples and was on the executive committee, I said, 'We're next, trust me,'" he recalls. "They looked at me like, 'Oh c'mon, Mike, you're too worked up over Borders.'" But the CEO of office-supply retailer Staples at the time did heed Edwards's warning and hired consulting firm McKinsey to come in and teach the company everything it knew about Amazon. Staples also poached a number of Amazon employees to help them better insulate their business from Amazon's potential to eat into their market share.

It wasn't long before companies outside of retail began to fear Amazon's every move, too. As Amazon diligently spread its tentacles from industry to industry, it sent shockwaves through the corner offices of corporate giants globally. It seemed that Amazon's reach was limitless.

By the mid-2010s there were few boardrooms in America where Amazon's competitive threat wasn't a topic of conversation. A new term began popping up as CEOs and their management teams evaluated what would happen to their spaces if Amazon made a serious move: "Amazon proofing."

There was good reason for publicly traded companies to want to insulate themselves from Amazon. Their investors were worried about their prospects and what battling Amazon meant for their future earnings and business. In 2017, the name "Amazon" was invoked on more corporate earnings calls than President Trump, with one out of ten conference calls mentioning the company. As it continued entering industries, watching Amazon decimate rivals had become a pastime on Wall Street, with one firm even keeping a "Death by Amazon" index.

Often, the mere mention of a rumor about Amazon considering expanding into an industry would cause the stock prices of all incumbents in that space to tank.

The situation played out the same way each time. In 2018, a report suggested that Amazon was looking to buy a movie theater chain. On the rumor, AMC's and Cinemark's stock prices briefly fell. In 2017, meal kit maker Blue Apron's stock price hit an intraday low when it was revealed that Amazon had registered for a trademark related to meal prep kits. The stock market had little confidence in companies going head-to-head with Amazon.

Amazon's name got bandied about in nearly every corner of corporate America because it is one of the only companies operating in nearly every corner of corporate America. That, paired with its meteoric stock price, has made it the phantom bidder du jour for the last decade.

In the instances when Amazon did actually pull the trigger and enter the space, the consequences were more severe. Its acquisition of Whole Foods in 2017 clobbered grocery giants. Kroger's stock fell 8 percent on the day of the deal announcement. SuperValu's stock fell 14 percent. Nearly $22 billion of American grocery chains' market value was erased the day the announcement was made.

Naturally, Amazon's own investors cheered the deal. Amazon's market value rose $15.6 billion when it announced the deal, covering the cost of the acquisition on paper. Wall Street had made a very vocal bet that the sector would not withstand Amazon's entry and that the Seattle giant would disrupt a $750 billion sector as old as time.

Amazon-proofing plans became essential strategic elements for corporate America writ large.

———

On December 3, 2017, CVS Health made the boldest bet in the company's fifty-four-year history by acquiring health insurer Aetna for $69 billion.

The deal caused many to scratch their heads. What was a drugstore chain known for selling candy, greeting cards, and prescriptions doing by buying one of the country's biggest insurance companies?

Looming in the background of one of the year's biggest deals was Amazon. For years, Amazon's name was invoked at CVS board meetings. "I think you ignored Amazon at your own peril," said David Dorman, who was chairman of the board of CVS from 2011 to 2022. The Seattle-based retailer had become a go-to spot for customers to buy cosmetics, cotton balls, and tampons, striking a dent in CVS's retail earnings.

Earlier in 2017, the tech giant caused health companies to collectively shudder when it filed to obtain licenses in several states to be a wholesale drug distributor. CVS for years had been feeling the effects of Amazon on its brick-and-mortar storefronts, where people bought impulse items and sundries, but now it looked as if Amazon might be coming for the lucrative back of the store, where it filled prescriptions. The prescriptions business is a bit like a casino. As people walk to the back of the store to get their medicine each month, passing aisles as they go, they fill their carts with things they didn't know they needed. You walk in for medicine and leave with not just your medicine, but perhaps also items for your bathroom and kitchen.

Amazon proofing his business had long been a priority for CVS's then CEO Larry Merlo and his management team. Wall Street analysts peppered Merlo with questions during earnings calls, asking what the company was doing if Amazon entered the healthcare space. Healthcare represented nearly 18 percent of gross annual domestic production in the US. It seemed an inevitability that Amazon would be drawn to the space given the size of the market.

Merlo began sussing out his options in 2015. If the pharmacist-turned-CEO was going to keep CVS relevant, the company needed to pivot. Merlo and his board of directors put together a list of potential merger partners. Years earlier, CVS bought Caremark, a pharmacy benefit manager, giving it a foothold in the healthcare space. He thought it made sense to double down on healthcare and turned his focus to insurance companies such as Aetna and Anthem. "We decided we weren't just going to be defined by retail pharmacy," recalls Dorman.

As Merlo was evaluating the idea of a combination with one of the main insurance players, the industry consolidated around him. In quick succession, Aetna announced a $34 billion deal to buy Humana on July 3, 2015, while Anthem agreed to buy Cigna for $48 billion that same month. These blockbuster deals would reshape the healthcare space and limit Merlo's options. Jumping the deals — or putting in a competing bid for a company that just announced a merger — is a pretty hostile move. So, for the time being, Merlo put this particular merger plan on hold.

Even still, CVS's management was obsessively on the lookout for any signs that Amazon would enter healthcare in a meaningful way. In 2017, dangerous warning shots were fired as rumors swirled about Amazon making some serious moves in the sector. CVS's board heard a rumor that Amazon had been holding early talks to buy Express Scripts, a giant pharmacy benefits manager with a market value topping $37 billion in 2017, Dorman recalled.

CVS and its bankers pounced into action, renewing interest in acquisition targets, such as Aetna and Anthem, that could help the company fend off Amazon. CVS also thought about selling itself. In early 2017, it reached out to UnitedHealth, one of the biggest health-care companies in the country, about a potential deal. The talks were preliminary and never got very far. UnitedHealth was already doing well, and the idea of acquiring a retailer with 10,000 stores concerned its management team.

"It was a bit of a wake-up call for Larry [Merlo] to realize that the retail business is a bit of an albatross around his neck," said a person involved in the talks. "Fundamentally, people were still viewing Larry as a retailer, not a healthcare company, and I think that gave him even more conviction to do something in managed care."

In February, Aetna's proposed acquisition of Humana fell apart after the Justice Department blocked it. CVS took notice. Aetna would have been too big to swallow had it closed the merger, but with the deal having fallen through, it was now just the right size to buy.

"Literally the day after we gave up on the transaction Larry called me and said, 'Should we talk?'" said Mark Bertolini, then Aetna's CEO. The two had known each other for years. In March, Merlo met with

Bertolini for dinner. While breaking bread, they discussed a range of options from commercial partnerships to a joint venture or even a merger.

Bertolini recalls that, at the time, CVS's front of the store, where it sold retail goods, was under pressure because of the likes of Amazon, and Merlo was interested in looking for new profit streams to diversify.

After the two CEOs met for dinner, CVS had determined it would diversify into the insurance or managed care space. It was interested in Aetna, but Aetna was having simultaneous discussions with Walmart and Walgreens.

For months CVS scanned the landscape and did its due diligence. In May, a CNBC article said that Amazon was hiring a new manager to develop a pharmacy strategy, which included this chilling detail: "Each year, Amazon holds an annual meeting to discuss whether it should break into the pharmacy market."

In June, when Amazon bought Whole Foods, the stocks of CVS and rival Walgreens dipped, which irked CVS's management team. Every time the slightest whispers of Amazon entering the space began circulating, it dented the company's stock.

For months Aetna played CVS, Walmart, and Walgreens off each other. Aetna was the belle of the ball, with lots of leverage on all these suitors, especially as Amazon made its healthcare intentions more explicit. At a September board meeting, CVS's board members reviewed a deck from its bankers at Barclays showing potential acquisition options in the managed care space.

The presentation contained several slides on the competitive threat posed by Amazon. One slide showed what might happen to CVS's business if it chose to do nothing and Amazon kept expanding into the space. It wasn't pretty. "The board had already concluded that doing nothing was a riskier strategy because you couldn't really completely underwrite what Amazon may or may not do," Dorman, the CVS chairman, said.

The board and its advisers discussed the pros and cons of each acquisition target and decided to formally make a bid for Aetna.

On October 11, 2017, Bertolini opened a letter from Merlo. It contained an offer of $195 per share to buy the company he had run for the past seven years. It was good timing. Later that month, news broke that Amazon gained approval to become a wholesale distributor from a number of state pharmaceutical boards.

For weeks CVS and Aetna hammered out the contours of a potential deal. The offer of $195 per share was dismissed as too low, and CVS came back with a higher offer. On December 3, they announced a deal for $207 per share, or $69 billion.

It was a bold deal, and investors thought it an iffy one. When regulators approved the deal, CVS's stock fell more than 7 percent, shaving $6 billion off of its market value. In 2023, Bertolini reflected on the success of the deal. He pointed out that the combined companies' market value is way less than the combined market values of each company before the deal. "I don't think CVS is going to get done what I thought could get done to change the industry," he said.

CHAPTER 12

Less Friction, More Sellers, More Sales (Even Counterfeits)

WHILE THE PUBLIC COMPANIES set about deploying their Amazon-proofing plans to insulate themselves, startups that felt that Amazon was encroaching on their business — or stealing their ideas — often had no recourse. It was a yearslong pattern at Amazon, with the claims of improper behavior only getting louder as its various divisions, from the Alexa Fund to private label to Marketplace, grew in size and leverage.

———

Four years after he'd been wined, dined, and ditched by Amazon, in late 2016, Leor Grebler, the inventor of Echo forerunner Ubi, was at Amazon's giant cloud confab in Las Vegas. Engineers, CEOs, and AWS partners from around the world flocked to the Strip to hear AWS royalty present in a giant auditorium alongside special guests like movie star Robert Downey Jr.

The event is a lesson in contrasts. Disheveled engineers, many of whom are more comfortable with coding language than conversations, flock to Sin City, a flashy town made for gamblers and bottle-service VIPs.

After his Ubi device business had been decimated by Amazon's Echo, Grebler had to pivot. He pitched 200 companies and venture capitalists up and down Sand Hill Road, a well-known area full of Silicon Valley VC funds, for potential investment opportunities, but was turned down.

So, he took his expertise in voice technology and created a software company to help others master these skills. Given Amazon's dominance in the space, he had no choice but to partner with Alexa, even though he was still angry. "We had to swallow that down," he said. That's what brought him to the big Amazon confab at the Venetian Resort in Las Vegas.

After a long day of panels and keynotes, Grebler and a client walked into the conference happy hour to mingle. The event, called Pub Crawl, hosted conference attendees at different swanky bars and lounges across the glitzy Venetian and Palazzo Hotels. They wore jeans and T-shirts and sipped on craft beer and glasses of wine while servers roamed the room with hors d'oeuvres. Bouncing from happy hour to happy hour left some guests buzzed.

At one of the bars, Grebler's client spotted a high-ranking Amazon executive he knew. He walked over to introduce Grebler. As Grebler looked at the executive, it dawned on him: it was Al Lindsay, who three years earlier had visited him in Toronto for a demonstration of his Ubi device.

Lindsay was boisterous. "Oh, I remember who you are now," he exclaimed. "I bet you thought we stole your product," Grebler recalls him saying. For some reason, Lindsay assumed that Grebler was now an Amazon employee and confided in him. He told him that his team at Amazon had considered cutting Grebler's Ubi device off of a text-to-speech engine called Ivona, which was part of the technology for the Ubi. Amazon had acquired the technology after their meetings and had discussed disabling Ubi from it, Lindsay confessed. It turned out to be a moot point because once the Echo launched, Ubi couldn't compete and shut down.

Grebler just stood there in disbelief as the Amazon executive had the gall to say all of this to him. Grebler had in good faith once trusted the company to help him. Lindsay, when reached for comment, said he remembers being introduced to Grebler in Las Vegas but doesn't remember the exchange.

————

Meanwhile, in March 2016, Jason Johnson walked through the towering orange doors and into the art deco halls of the Parker Palm Springs hotel in Palm Springs, California. The CEO of August Home was delighted to be a personal guest of Amazon's leadership team at the exclusive event. Dubbed Mars, the event was invite only, and the guest list consisted of a who's who of innovators, scientists, and tech founders. It even included astronauts. Bezos presided over the three-day event, mingling with guests at demonstrations, talks, and cocktail parties. At the latter, robots served drinks.

In 2011, the idea for August Home came to Johnson while he was at a wedding in Hawaii. A friend was crashing at his place and got herself locked out. With no way to get back inside, he had to call another friend to jump his neighbor's fence and climb through his doggy door in order to get in. Johnson knew there had to be a better way to allow friends and housekeepers into a home without using keys, and he set about figuring out a solution.

He launched the company in 2012 with the goal to develop a smart lock that grants visitors access to homes by generating a specific set of numbers to enter into a keypad for a designated amount of time. In 2014, his first smart lock launched. As home-sharing companies such as Airbnb took off, homeowners turned to the locks to let their guests enter their homes. August Home was off to the races.

The San Francisco–based company was in the midst of launching a skill that would allow customers to use Alexa to lock their doors and had worked deeply with Amazon's development team to integrate the products. It was this innovation that would get Johnson invited to Mars 2016, where "attendees from academia, start-ups, and Fortune 100 companies gather to learn, share, and further imagine," the event's website boasts. While the attendees were there to learn, so was Amazon's founder, who spent the event mingling with a group of 150 of the world's most intelligent people. That year, Hollywood director Ron Howard and bestselling author Dan Brown were alongside guests on the hotel's grounds.

Though notoriously frugal, Amazon does cover the entire bill for the three-day luxe confab. Guest accommodations at the five-star hotel are taken care of. (The hotel typically charges guests over $500 per night.) All of the lavish meals, alcohol, and events are covered by Amazon.

Inside their brightly colored, Jonathan Adler–designed rooms, guests were greeted with luxe swag, which was placed next to their four-post canopy beds when they arrived. Canada Goose down jackets (retail: $750) for stargazing at night in the chilly desert were provided. Amazon Echo speakers were gifted to all attendees.

Bezos and his leadership team were extremely accessible during the conference. One morning, Johnson was invited with a dozen other attendees to go on a trek with the billionaire. They piled into Cadillac Escalades and drove off into the desert wilderness for a survival training session based on the popular show *Running Wild with Bear Grylls*. The group learned how to survive in the woods, made their own stretchers, and ate earthworms together. To his credit, even Bezos plopped an earthworm into his mouth.

When it was over, Bezos turned to his fellow adventurers and bid his farewell. An Escalade pulled up and the billionaire drove back to the resort. The guests, meanwhile, were confused as to how they would get back. Some speculated that perhaps they'd have to use their new-found survival skills to navigate back on their own. Then guards started to yell, telling them to get low; the booming sound of helicopters above was startling. Their rides had arrived. (Bezos, who had been in a helicopter crash years earlier, was not taking risks with helicopters during this period.)

After cleaning up at the hotel, Johnson headed to the outdoor reception that evening, where he bumped into Bezos again. Having spent the better part of the day with him already, they struck up a conversation. Johnson brought up the idea for a collaboration between August Home and Amazon. He discussed a product called the August

Access Platform. The smart lock would grant access to delivery people to drop a package inside a person's home and record the entire encounter. Bezos's eyes lit up, Johnson recalls.

"He immediately walked me over to Jeff Wilke, and he says 'Jeff, you need to talk to Jason. He's got a brilliant idea on how to solve some of the issues of delivery,'" Johnson recalls. "I told him, and Wilke got it and he said, 'Let's set up a meeting.'"

Following the Mars conference, Johnson and his team flew to Seattle to start drafting plans for its Amazon collaboration. The conference room was filled with Amazon executives from different parts of its business, including devices head Dave Limp, and people on the logistics and shipping side. Johnson was a little uncomfortable that product engineers accompanied Limp to the meeting. "I wondered if the people that make electronics are trying to understand my system to make their own."

In the session, Johnson and the Amazon executives outlined what the product could look like and how both companies could benefit from it. August would provide the hardware, and Amazon's customers would benefit from their packages arriving safely in their homes. It was a win-win.

For months, the teams worked on creating the product. But then the Amazon lead on the project began becoming evasive, Johnson recalls.

The next year, Johnson was invited back to the Mars conference. He wanted some answers about where they stood. "I was a little thrown. I don't quite understand where our relationship is heading," he recalls.

At one of the events, he struck up a conversation with Limp, whom he'd gotten to know over that past year. "I said 'Hey, are you going to compete with me and make smart locks?'" Johnson recalls. Limp responded that Amazon had looked into it, and that it was a pretty complex process. "It's much better for people like you and Yale and other smart lock companies," Limp responded. The conversation was unnerving. "I took very clear note that he knew the names of other smart lock companies," Johnson recalls. When he asked Limp for the status of the project, Limp deflected to someone else on his team.

In November 2017, Amazon launched exactly what Johnson had

pitched, with one change: August's products were not used. He was furious.

"That whole thing was my idea. I personally delivered it to Bezos," he said. Johnson confronted a leader in Amazon's group that worked on it. The person admitted that they used his idea, Johnson says. Even worse, they partnered with August competitors Yale and Kwikset on the finished product. They named it Amazon Key.

———————

Another disconcerting pattern were decisions the company made under the guise of customer obsession. In the name of becoming a retailer with unlimited selection in order to speed up its flywheel, Amazon Marketplace contains counterfeiters and purveyors of dangerous products and other merchandise that would be banned from general retailers.

It's these scenarios where Amazon's customer obsession argument breaks down. Amazon makes the same level of profits from a third-party seller of a genuine item as it does from a counterfeit product, so the company's coffers are padded either way. But there is no denying that receiving a dangerous or fake product from Amazon is not in the best interest of the customer, yet it happens all the time.

The linchpin to Amazon's unlimited selection, which sped up its growth, was recruiting sellers aggressively—including from China—and having an automated process sellers use to register on its platform. The latter enables them to start selling goods sometimes as quickly as within hours, people involved with those efforts said. Amazon has relied heavily on software to screen vendors with minimal human intervention. Internal warnings or efforts to add screening measures or other checks to the system were frequently blunted or rejected by executives who prioritized the growth of third-party sellers and the benefits it brought by expanding customer choice, boosting sales, and helping profit margins.

"Telling someone at Amazon that you have an idea that will reduce growth is suicide," said a former category manager who worked for Amazon's Marketplace. "I've never seen Amazon's Marketplace move in any direction other than more sellers, less friction, more money."

The risks from fraudulent sellers on Amazon can be serious for both legitimate brands and would-be customers. In many cases, items on Amazon's unregulated bazaar can also be dangerous to unwitting customers.

Christian Fletcher bought what he thought was a TacMed Solutions tourniquet—a device that is used to stop the flow of blood from an arterial vein in an emergency to prevent someone from bleeding out. He purchased the product on Amazon for hikes in the Sierra Nevada.

After the tourniquet arrived, Fletcher compared the instructions and features on the product with pictures on TacMed's site, the company that made the actual product, and realized it was fake. He sent the fake to TacMed, which confirmed it wasn't theirs. "If you use it and it doesn't work," Fletcher said, "you're dead."

TacMed founder Ross Johnson says Amazon customers have contacted him about counterfeit tourniquets, which break easily. "If the only one you have breaks or doesn't work," he said, "that's a fatality."

The Pasadena Police Department in Texas has ten tourniquets it uses for training that are counterfeit versions of another US brand, said Detective Jason Mitchell, who trains officers on health and safety. He ordered them from Amazon for a low price, knowing they were fake, and says it isn't uncommon for them to malfunction. "Every class I teach, I say, 'If you go to Amazon and buy one of these tourniquets, it could be Chinese junk,'" he said.

Part of the issue is that in a company with as many competing interests as Amazon, leadership principles are often weaponized to further individual or team-specific goals. When teams fighting for their way both invoked "customer obsession" in their arguments, the team whose idea padded Amazon's bottom line often won out.

In late 2017, managers overseeing clothing sales on Amazon met with a senior executive to discuss a problem with some listings. Earlier in the year, Amazon had made it easier for vendors around the world to sell apparel on its platform, which was part of Bezos's push to expand third-party sales. That had led to a surge of merchants hawking counterfeit or unsafe products, said a number of managers who were at the meeting. Among problematic items were baby clothes that weren't flame resistant or smelled like petroleum, employees said.

Alarmed at the quality of the products being listed, managers overseeing baby wear had taken it upon themselves to change the automatic sign-up process to include higher barriers for those selling in their category—known as adding "friction." This created higher hurdles for sellers to jump over before selling their products to unsuspecting parents all over the world. The senior executive at the meeting, Dharmesh Mehta, told them that it wasn't their job to police the site and that Amazon had teams dedicated to responding to product issues, attendees said.

"So we lifted this friction, and we saw huge jumps in sales," said the former manager. Among listings that proliferated were children's pajamas and hoodies with drawstrings near the neck, which Amazon hadn't allowed before.

The US Consumer Product Safety Commission has banned such children's clothing with drawstrings as a strangulation hazard. An agency spokeswoman said that "if a retailer sells items sizes 2T to 12 in the US with drawstrings in the hood and neck area that retailer is breaking the law."

The baby product team argued that customers obsessed about safe and trustworthy products for their toddlers. Mehta won out.

Amazon's spokesperson disputed the anecdote and said that it is "inaccurate and lacked context."

The meeting with Mehta fell into a pattern: executives at the online retail giant frequently put higher priority on expanding selection over maintaining product quality and safety.

In 2019, I flagged twenty sellers of children's clothing with drawstrings around the neck to Amazon. They were removed once I flagged them. Mehta, who had told his team that it wasn't their job to make the website safer for parents shopping for their children, was later elevated to vice president of customer trust and partner support.

In 2019, the *Wall Street Journal* conducted an extensive investigation into Amazon's Marketplace. It found more than 4,000 items for sale that were declared unsafe by federal agencies, banned by federal regulators, or otherwise deceptively labeled. At least 2,000 listings for toys and medications lacked warnings about health risks to children, the *Journal* found. When sending ten children's products for safety testing, the *Journal* was told that "four failed tests based on federal safety standards, according to the testing company, including one with lead levels that exceeded federal limits." In the case of the product with lead — a xylophone — it could be dangerous for a child to put parts of it in their mouth. According to the CDC: "No safe blood lead level in children has been identified. Even low levels of lead in blood have been shown to affect a child's intelligence, ability to pay attention, and academic achievement." In a comment at the time, an Amazon spokeswoman told the *Journal*, "Safety is a top priority at Amazon." (Amazon has said it isn't liable for what third-party sellers list, saying in court cases that it doesn't sell the products listed.)

The rampant counterfeit issue and the fact that there are few regulations for selling on Amazon's website have deterred even a number of former Amazon employees I've spoken to from shopping on the very website that they helped to build. "I don't buy any consumable products on Amazon anymore unless it's direct from the brand," said an employee who worked in Amazon's consumables segment until 2015.

Most Amazon.com shoppers don't know that much of what's sold on Amazon — 60 percent — comes from third-party sellers. And while legitimate sellers and companies make up the ranks of that group, there are also bad actors, counterfeiters, and shoddy brands bypassing safety and regulatory standards. Some of what those sellers are distributing on Amazon would never make its way to the shelves of other retailers. That sort of free-for-all with low barriers to entry also harms legitimate brands, since customers are more likely to blame the name brand, as in the case of Adome and the actual Adore Me, than Amazon, which they see as simply the best place to buy anything.

Consider what happened to the makers of the popular game Settlers of Catan. After years of flagging to Amazon, who failed to respond, about the rampant counterfeiting they witnessed on their product from third-party sellers, in 2018, the game makers took more extreme measures.

In 2016, the company noticed that hundreds of thousands of counterfeit Catan games were flooding Amazon's third-party marketplace, costing the game maker millions of dollars in sales and one- and two-star reviews that affected its brand reputation, said Pete Fenlon, CEO of Catan Studio.

Over the course of two years, Fenlon and his employees investigated the problem and tried to get Amazon to help. Amazon was Catan's largest account, representing more than 20 percent of its sales, he said. In addition to lost sales, Fenlon worried that the counterfeit products could harm customers. Catan rigorously tests the paints and finishes it uses on its board games to ensure that they aren't toxic if a child were to put something in their mouth, he said.

"We tried to present that case to the Amazon buyers and the company as a whole, and the problem we encountered was Amazon's culture," said Fenlon. "We had trouble getting a hold on who to talk to, and when we'd talk to someone, there was a culture of denial and a lack of accountability."

Frustrated by Amazon's lack of response, Fenlon and his team started building a case. They compiled a timeline of their counterfeit problem on Amazon, the numbers of counterfeits of Catan being seized at the border destined for Amazon warehouses, and other troubling information. In the spring of 2018, they compiled all of the information into binders, along with a letter detailing the problem, and hoped that Amazon would take responsibility to police their site to protect brands and customers. The documents were mailed to the offices of dozens of Amazon's top executives globally, including Bezos, Fenlon said.

"We were very, very concerned about society in general and didn't want to just settle," said Fenlon. "We wanted to make sure somebody somewhere of consequence woke up and said, 'Oh my God, this is a problem we should have attacked yesterday.'"

The binders did reach senior leaders, who took action. Catan heard back from Amazon within a month of receiving the documentation to try to work together on stemming the counterfeiting problem. Amazon's spokesperson said that Catan's concerns have been resolved.

Amazon relies on a mix of algorithms and humans to detect bad sellers on its site. Amazon says that in 2022, it spent $1.2 billion on brand protection efforts to combat the problem.

But because of the sheer size of its platform, it's impossible to detect every problematic seller. The children's clothing with drawstrings around the neck, which are banned by other retailers and illegal to sell according to the US Consumer Product Safety Commission, for instance, are back for sale on Amazon's website.

CHAPTER 13

In the Arena

AS THE EARLY SIGNS of the techlash began to take hold, Bezos methodically inserted himself more deliberately into Washington, DC. In late 2016, as the political ground shifted beneath his feet, he had anonymously bought the former Textile Museum in Washington's elite Kalorama neighborhood for $23 million in cash, $1 million above the asking price. The historic manse dates back to 1908, and the architect that designed the West Building of the National Gallery of Art and the Jefferson Memorial was commissioned to build a part of it. It's a stately, imposing building with a columned entryway and red brick exteriors.

Kalorama is one of DC's most exclusive zip codes, and the Textile Museum was just blocks away from the DC homes of the Obamas and Ivanka Trump and Jared Kushner. The neighborhood is also dotted with embassies and the homes of influential lobbyists and advisers. It's a who's who of Washington politics, ensuring run-ins with the country's top decision makers.

Bezos immediately went to work on an ambitious renovation. Inside, work began on a giant parlor, which would serve to host some of Washington's most influential figures for salons and cocktail parties. Other renovations included twenty-five bathrooms, eleven bedrooms, a whiskey cellar, and a walk-in wine room. The renovation plans show the house divided in half. One side would be reserved for Bezos and guests; the other half would have all of the necessary accoutrements for entertaining: a catering kitchen, furniture storage, a coat room, and changing rooms for staff. The nearly 1,500-square-foot ballroom was the pièce de résistance. It featured a limestone fireplace, floor-to-ceiling columns, and a bar. It wasn't just a simple pied-à-terre for the technology billionaire.

This was a change for the man who for decades had blissfully ignored politics and kept his focus on growing Amazon. Now, the CEO found himself owning the country's most important political newspaper and DC's largest home. It was a giant departure from his comfort zone.

"I think Bezos doesn't see a viable threat to Amazon other than government intervention, and you can see that in how much attention he's paid to Washington, DC, in recent years," Stacy Mitchell of the Institute for Local Self-Reliance said.

In line with such thinking, in 2018, at the request of board member Jamie Gorelick, Bezos became a member of the Business Council in DC. The group is a powerful voice in the capital for American business interests. An Amazon spokesperson said that Bezos had always spent time taking meetings with politicians on behalf of Amazon in DC. But it wasn't until nearly seven years into the most tech-friendly president in modern history's tenure that Bezos even met Obama, through an introduction from Carney after an event. Bezos's team in DC, S-Team members, and board members say that it wasn't until his final years as CEO (in 2021, Andy Jassy would succeed him as CEO, with Bezos becoming executive chairman), when scrutiny of the company intensified, that Bezos made a concerted effort. They describe the founder as being uninterested in engaging in these sorts of activities until much later, when the pressure was mounting.

And as Bezos redirected some energy from Seattle to DC, the company followed. In 2019, Amazon decided to place its coveted second headquarters in northern Virginia (the location was heavily sought after, as 238 cities vied for the privilege of hosting a new Amazon headquarters and all the jobs that would come along with it). Northern Virginia is in Washington's backyard, and the proximity of the new headquarters ensured that Washington power players would do business with Amazon interests more regularly, make more money intersecting with Amazon, have their children attend schools with the children of employees, and, more broadly, have the chance to move in the same social circles. The company would be top of mind and wallet in the District. It could devour the capital, just as it had everything else.

––––––––

Any goodwill earned by Bezos at the Trump Tower meeting before Trump took office was short lived. Once in office, Trump targeted Bezos, Amazon, and the *Washington Post*.

In late 2017, a detailed white paper reached President Trump's aides titled, "The Cost of Amazon's Dominance." At the top it read, "Confidential & Protected From Disclosure Pursuant to all Federal Statutes."

The authors argued that the government needed to intervene, given Amazon's singular power. "If the government waits to intervene and is not forward-looking, it will be too late; there will be no competitive alternatives," the report said. Then it dove into Amazon's expansive reach across industries.

As President Trump's staff read through the report, which criticized the consumer welfare standard of the antitrust framework and rehashed arguments Lina Khan made in her paper, it resonated with them. The report was particularly critical of their boss's nemesis, Jeff Bezos, with pages dedicated to how the billionaire had been made rich through anticompetitive behavior.

One page shows Bezos's vast conglomerate under the header "The Bezos Empire is Reminiscent of the Standard Oil Octopus." Others were titled "Anticompetitive Levers Have Made Bezos the Wealthiest Man in the World" and "Anticompetitive Levers Have Allowed Bezos to Amass Outsized Influence." It detailed Amazon's impact on job losses, Main Street destruction, and wages. It ended with a big claim: "USPS Postal Rates Effectively Subsidize Amazon."

How did this report reach the Oval Office, and who put it together? It originated at the hedge fund of a friend of Trump's.

Nelson Peltz, the billionaire CEO of Trian Fund Management, was a titan of industry in his own right. In his seventies at the time, Peltz occupied rarefied air on Wall Street. His activist hedge fund, which took stakes in companies and pushed them to change their strategies, break up, and oust their CEOs, was one of the most powerful firms in operation. CEOs dreaded Peltz taking a position in their stocks. He was so powerful that his name was often uttered in the same breath as that of legendary activist investor Carl Icahn.

Peltz was an expert on corporate America. He studiously investigated companies' balance sheets and earnings reports to identify their weaknesses. As a result, he waged proxy fights with some of America's biggest companies, such as Procter & Gamble, DuPont, and H.J. Heinz (famous for their eponymously named ketchup). He and his associates sat on the boards of directors of numerous public companies, which gave them an insider's view into the state of the world's top companies and what threatened them the most.

That's what made the Amazon white paper all the more remarkable. Peltz's management team didn't write it because he wanted to take a stake in Amazon's stock and force them to make changes, like he did with other companies. They wrote it, initially for their own analysis, because they identified Amazon as one of the biggest threats to modern business. Trian was concerned about the chokehold Amazon had on retail, its negotiating power with vendors, and its effect on prices. And Peltz wasn't alone. Trump's other billionaire friends were telling the president that Amazon had to be stopped. His real estate buddies told him of the damage Amazon was causing to their businesses, like the decline of the once all-powerful mall, which supported so many different corporate interests. In fact, at a lunch months earlier between Peltz, Trump's then lawyer Jay Sekulow, and Trump, the president asked the men to look into Amazon and called the company "a problem," Sekulow recalled to me.

The final pages of Trian's report—the ones that looked at Amazon exploiting the United States Postal Service—especially stuck with Trump's inner circle. If Amazon's low rates were contributing to the demise of the struggling USPS, Trump strongly wanted Amazon to pay more per package it shipped through the agency. It's unclear whether the president had planned on investigating Amazon's use of the Postal

Service prior to the report landing in the White House, but in a series of tweets in March 2018, Trump made his opinion clear. "While we are on the subject, it is reported that the U.S. Post Office will lose $1.50 on average for each package it delivers for Amazon. That amounts to Billions of Dollars. The Failing N.Y. Times reports that 'the size of the company's lobbying staff has ballooned,' and that does not include the Fake Washington Post, which is used as a 'lobbyist' and should so REGISTER. If the P.O. 'increased its parcel rates, Amazon's shipping costs would rise by $2.6 Billion.' This Post Office scam must stop. Amazon must pay real costs (and taxes) now!" he tweeted.

In April, Trump commissioned a task force to investigate the Postal Service's finances. It was led by treasury secretary Steven Mnuchin. "The USPS is on an unsustainable financial path and must be restructured to prevent a taxpayer-funded bailout," the president's executive order stated.

The creation of this task force — and the potential for recommendations that would hurt Amazon's business, such as the USPS raising its prices for Amazon — sent Amazon into a tizzy. "Internally there was panic," said a senior member of Amazon's public policy team. "We crunched the numbers. That would have crippled Amazon if he raised the rate even a very small amount."

Amazon joined a lobbying group called the Package Coalition. "We spent so much time on this, and we really had to fight them," recalls another Amazon executive involved in the effort. "It was terrible, and we were genuinely worried about it. It would have had very serious consequences had it been changed. It was really high stakes for the company."

Behind the scenes, Trump was trying to find any way he could to deliver a blow to his nemesis Bezos. During the Postal Service review, the president even personally pressured the US postmaster general to double the rate the USPS charges Amazon, the *Washington Post* revealed.

Mnuchin's White House task force report did make recommendations for the Postal Service to get back on more sustainable financial footing, but didn't deliver the blow to Amazon that Trump wanted. The report actually found that USPS's delivery of Amazon packages was profitable for the agency, contradicting much of Trump's rhetoric. Amazon's concerns, on this issue at least, were abated. Nonetheless, Trump wouldn't let Mnuchin forget it. Years later, Trump would randomly bring up Mnuchin's inability to stick it to Amazon. In 2020, during meetings dealing with COVID-19, he'd sometimes dismiss the secretary by saying, "You still didn't fix the Amazon situation!" recall people in such meetings.

Still, Trump remained "obsessed" with Amazon and Bezos, according to an *Axios* report at the time. The president had threatened changing Amazon's tax treatment to better help "mom-and-pop retailers," which were being decimated by Amazon, though his fickle nature made his intentions always somewhat unclear. Was he really out to help the USPS or small businesses, or were they excuses for his larger hatred of Bezos? Regardless, he would continue battering the company.

"He's wondered aloud if there may be any way to go after Amazon with antitrust or competition law," a source told *Axios*. When a $10 billion, decade-long Department of Defense cloud contract became available that Amazon was a frontrunner for, Trump intervened to prevent the company's chances, Amazon alleged. In 2018, Trump personally called his secretary of defense, James Mattis, who was involved in procuring the cloud contract, and told him to "screw" Amazon, according to Guy Snodgrass, who worked for Mattis at the time.

In the end, Microsoft won the lucrative cloud contract, and Amazon cried foul. The company protested the decision, writing "improper pressure from President Donald J. Trump, who launched repeated public and behind-the-scenes attacks to steer the JEDI Contract away from AWS to harm his perceived political enemy-Jeffrey P. Bezos, founder and CEO of AWS's parent company, Amazon.com, Inc. ("Amazon"), and owner of the Washington Post." (In the end, the contract was pulled, and later reconfigured.)

Amazon was a constant bête noire for Trump. The scene would play out time and time again in the Oval Office. Members of Trump's Cabinet discussed serious issues, such as trade policy or the economy, and the president would weigh in with a rant about Jeff Bezos. Cabinet sources recount that once Trump began a rant, Larry Kudlow, head of the National Economic Council, and Steve Mnuchin would often make eye contact and roll their eyes as if to suggest "here we go again."

"Our argument was that Amazon is a fabulous company. It's a fabulous service. Consumers love it. So why are we wasting our time on this?" recalls one Cabinet member. That would be met with a narrow-eyed glare from the president. "Of all the things on our radar screen — inflation, interest rates, growth, jobs, wages — Amazon was not one of them," the person said. The people Trump surrounded himself with were less concerned about Amazon and more concerned about social media companies potentially censoring Republicans. Yet the president seemed focused on Amazon.

Trump's animus toward Bezos seemed to be based on many factors: the *Washington Post*'s coverage of his White House, Amazon's effect on competition, and, on a personal level, even jealousy. A close Trump aide said Bezos's wealth was the impetus for a lot of this animosity. "You gotta understand, Bezos is worth a couple hundred billion dollars. And, you know, Trump's been through six bankruptcies."

Another close aide said, "It all stems from Donald's jealousy over Bezos's financial success. Donald measures everything in terms of money. Any chance he would get to knock Bezos, he would. Now couple that with Bezos's acquisition of the *Washington Post*, which was critical of Donald, and it's like a tsunami meets an earthquake." Trump's trade czar, Peter Navarro, had a different take. "I don't see this as a vendetta against Amazon," he said. "I see this as President Trump clearly understanding the threat that Amazon posed economically because of the nature of its business model, which at its core, is profiting because of Communist China. And politically, because Bezos was using his ill-gotten gains to defeat the president."

For Ballard Partners, the constant attacks from Trump made Amazon the busiest client they had as they navigated the company's tense relationship with the White House.

And beyond Trump's personal issues with Bezos, regulators were starting to pay close attention to the tech giant because of its size and business practices. They wondered if Amazon was monopolistic and dug into the sprawling company's power.

They had plenty to analyze. Here's a quick snapshot of Amazon's reach as of 2023:

- More than 200 million people globally pay for Amazon Prime accounts, using the membership to shop on Amazon and stream television, movies, music, and video games. Years of their purchasing data, from what they buy to what they add to their carts and later delete, is stored and used by Amazon employees. They use it to drive more sales across seemingly disparate and unconnected categories, businesses, and services.

- More than 500 million Alexa-enabled devices sit in people's bedrooms, living rooms, and even bathrooms across the globe, answering commands and gobbling up incalculable data from all those homes. These devices know your favorite podcasts, what time you set your alarm for each morning, how many times your child asks it to play "Baby Shark," and what's on your grocery list. They can control your smart home devices such as your front door lock and garage door opener.

- Meanwhile, AWS is the largest cloud computing company in the world. Millions of companies, government agencies (including the CIA), and even Amazon competitors feel that they have no choice but to store their businesses' data on the company's cloud. Netflix, Apple, and NBCUniversal — to name but a few — compete fiercely with Amazon, yet use and pay for AWS.

- In the world's retail infrastructure, the company has amassed an army of merchants who sell their wares to Amazon shoppers. These third-party sellers, which rank in the millions, are the backbone of the nearly limitless selection of goods on its Marketplace. Amazon collects all the fees required of sellers to operate on the site. On top of those fees, it also collects massive amounts of seller data. It then competes with them using its private label division to sell Amazon-branded goods on the same platform.

———

For years, with little interference, Amazon had built itself into a conglomerate that became an 800-pound gorilla in several industries, gobbling up competitors and putting them out of business. That was about to change. In June 2019, a flurry of regulatory activity aimed at Amazon and its technology brethren converted the growing monopoly concerns into potential action. The top antitrust agencies in the US — the Federal Trade Commission and the Department of Justice — split between themselves the responsibility of probing the country's most dominant technology companies as part of preliminary probes into their business practices. The FTC received oversight of Facebook and Amazon. The Justice Department got Google and Apple. At that point, the FTC started its Amazon investigation into the company's business practices under FTC chairman Joseph Simons (he would be succeeded in the role by Lina Khan in 2021).

The same month, the House Judiciary Committee, which focuses on addressing the legality of a wide range of matters pertaining to civil or criminal conduct, announced an investigation into the same four technology companies. The aim of the bipartisan committee was to learn more about the companies' business practices and determine whether the existing antitrust laws and their enforcement had kept up with technological innovation.

Months before, whispers of an impending investigation started to circulate throughout K Street, DC's infamous lobbying hub. Amazon's lobbyists tried to get ahead of the investigation, and began calling the office of Representative David Cicilline, a Democrat from Rhode Island, to set up meetings with Amazon's general counsel and other executives. Cicilline was an important person to lobby, as he was a member of the House Judiciary Committee and the head of its antitrust subcommittee.

In those meetings, Amazon had a highly coordinated message, say people who attended. Amazon's main message was that they were good for small business, and in discussions with Cicilline they touted entrepreneurs from his district who benefited from selling on Amazon.

Amazon's team of executives and outside lobbyists were trying to make that same point with other committee members. With some members, they pointed out how many constituents Amazon employs in their district or dangled the notion of opening up future warehouses in their cities, the people said. Soon, op-eds written by small business owners materialized in their local newspapers saying how detrimental punitive action taken toward Amazon could be for local entrepreneurs. Even before the investigation was formally announced in July, Amazon's lobbying machine was running at full steam.

In July, the Justice Department announced that it was opening a broad antitrust review into whether technology companies, including Amazon, were unlawfully stifling competition. Led by then Attorney General William Barr, the review focused on examining platforms that dominate online retail, social media, and search engines.

Antitrust trouble for Amazon had already been brewing for years in Europe, which has historically taken a much more aggressive stance on tech companies than the US. But now pressure was mounting for Amazon at home.

———

While the regulators readied their arrows, the effects were being felt internally as well. On a whiteboard in Amazon general counsel David Zapolsky's office was a list of banned words. Employees were not to say "market share" or "platform" or "ecosystem" in emails, documents, or other forms of communication, as these terms could signal anticompetitive practices to regulators. Each year, the list of banned words got longer. Amazon's S-Team and its dealmaking teams also began discussing sensitive matters, such as antitrust and M&A, over the Signal app instead of email. Signal is an encrypted messaging app, and unlike email, its texts are not recoverable by regulators once they've been deleted by users.

Dozens of employees told me that managers instructed them to mark all manner of communications "privileged and confidential" even when not seeking legal advice so that certain practices couldn't become known by regulators.

Some of Amazon's own employees, many of whom had joined the company during the good old days when technology companies were celebrated for the ease, convenience, and (presumed positive) disruption they provided, had grown skeptical. Was eking out bigger profits and gaining market share at the expense of their competitors worth the repercussions it had throughout the world, they wondered?

Many of these employees had become incredibly wealthy precisely because of Amazon's dominance and subsequent stock price run, but now their consciences gnawed at them. Just as it became unfashionable during the financial crisis to work at an investment bank, with employees avoiding wearing items embroidered with their employer's logo, Amazon workers began feeling similarly sensitive about their association to a company under public scrutiny.

Tim Bray had joined Amazon's cloud computing business in 2014 when "we were just a group of merry men making the world a better place," he jokes. He refers to the early days as times when technology CEOs graced the covers of glossy magazines in glamour shots. Bray rose the ranks at AWS and became a distinguished engineer at the company, but some of Amazon's behaviors started to concern him. He also grew wary of its size and power. He now thinks Amazon should be broken up. "It's highly injurious to a free market when you have parties who are using fountains of profits from one area of business to invade other areas of business. So yeah, I would like to take an antitrust ax to Amazon," he told me. After more than five years at Amazon, Bray left in 2020.

Some of Amazon's earliest employees have conflicting views about their former employer. Paul Davis, employee number 2, who programmed Amazon's website alongside employee number 1, Shel Kaphan, and Bezos, also believes the company should be broken up.

"I think it's a problem that the retail side of it and the third-party marketplace [have] become intertwined in a way that I think is unhealthy for everyone except Amazon," he told me in an interview.

Davis is confident the company is using third-party seller data in a way to advantage Amazon over those sellers. "I just have no doubt that that's happening. I mean, the company can issue a lot of the denials that it wants, but it's inconceivable to me that Amazon would not have done that. It's just too hard to resist." His solution? Breaking up Amazon into third-party and first-party platforms.

Still, even Davis has a hard time not shopping on Amazon, even though he's tried. He still has his Prime account. Employee number 8, Tod Nelson, feels similarly. "I am so grateful for all Amazon's given me and my experience there. But I think Amazon's bad for the world right now," he said. "They have all the leverage."

"Yes, they have a dominant position. So, is that antitrust? I don't know," said Peri Hartman, who joined Amazon in 1997 and created Amazon's famous one-click shopping feature. "The fact that they have a dominant position has a two-sided effect. One is it means it's hard for competitors to take a significant amount of the market. But on the other hand, it means that you have a very easy way to find products that you're looking for."

Hartman still shops on Amazon.

CHAPTER 14

Congress Calls on Amazon

ON JULY 16, 2019, top executives from Amazon, Apple, Facebook, and Google filed into room 2141 on Capitol Hill for a hearing conducted by members of Congress. The previous month, the long-established but typically quiet House Judiciary Committee's antitrust subcommittee had taken on its most ambitious antitrust investigation in decades. Then chaired by Congressman David Cicilline, a Rhode Island Democrat known for being outspoken and pugnacious at times, it opened an investigation into the potential abuses of Big Tech and whether Amazon, Apple, Facebook, and Google were powerful monopolies that needed to be checked.

Cicilline was reluctant to helm the antitrust subcommittee when it was first offered to him in 2017. At the time, antitrust was not the most exciting area of concern for any ambitious politician.

It's not hyperbole to say the antitrust subcommittee was not where the action was; it just didn't feel like the job any congressperson would want to have. In fact, at the time, it was typically the last subcommittee to be filled. Antitrust was wonky, and people just didn't understand it. To be the face of it? Cicilline wasn't so sure. What's more, he was unfamiliar with the issues involved.

"The truth is, I didn't know anything about antitrust," Cicilline later told me. He decided to meet with New York's Jerry Nadler, a

Democrat, who was chairman of the House Judiciary Committee, for advice. "You know, sometimes you should just take an assignment because you're going to learn a new subject and stretch your mind," Nadler told Cicilline.

So, Cicilline took the role and spent the next two years in the weeds learning about antitrust law. The topic was dense and hard to follow, but he immersed himself in public policy circles to learn everything he could.

The subcommittee included members across the political spectrum, from Democratic progressives to Trump diehards and everyone in between. Antitrust, of all things, seemed to be one of the few areas where Democrats and Republicans could find common ground.

"It's funny, Ken Buck and I don't agree on very much, and in fact, almost nothing but antitrust," said Cicilline about his Republican counterpart on the subcommittee, Congressman Ken Buck of Colorado.

Prior to launching their investigation, some members on the subcommittee viewed Amazon and its brethren purely as American success stories. These companies helped families FaceTime with Grandma across the country and delivered packages to your door within two days. They were centers for innovation and emblematic of the American dream.

"All these folks, they started in their garage. They take a risk. They go and they raise capital and they are successful and they build on that. And I looked at those companies and I thought, 'You know, this is what America is all about,'" Buck said, summarizing his thoughts about Amazon and other Big Tech companies.

In fact, Buck was skeptical about whether a formal investigation into the companies was even necessary. "I was a real believer that the marketplace will take care of this," he recalls. But then his mind changed: once the committee started digging into the issues, he was blown away by what he learned. So much so that he promptly canceled his Amazon Prime account and began placing orders on Walmart.com in silent protest. He even found himself texting photos of Amazon delivery vans fueling up in long lines at his local gas station to Cicilline, complaining that he couldn't escape the "long arm of Amazon."

Aside from their work on the subcommittee, the two representatives had vastly different political views. After the events of January 6, 2021, when Cicilline urged Vice President Mike Pence to use the Twenty-Fifth Amendment, which allows for the removal of the president, Buck thought the idea was crazy, he said. But in an effort to tame Amazon and its peers, they had become staunch allies.

The antitrust subcommittee also had a very prominent backer in the shadows. In a meeting with some subcommittee members, including Jim Jordan (R., Ohio), who joined the subcommittee in early 2020, Trump's trade czar, Peter Navarro, relayed an important message. "The White House supports this investigation," he said. "We have an epidemic of counterfeiting and piracy, and the president wants to stop the flow of fraudulent or counterfeit products from China that are being sold in very high amounts on Amazon," he told the group.

Cicilline, too, came to appreciate how important their job had become. "Shortly after taking this role, the big Cambridge Analytica breach was revealed, and a lot of information about what was happening online and the focus really became the role of these technology platforms in not only our economy, but in our democracy," he told *The Hill*. "The more I've learned about it over these years, the more urgent I believe action is. The more damaging, I think, allowing these technology companies that have monopoly power to continue to operate unchecked from any regulation and continue to grow their power and their market share is."

As executives from the big four tech firms filed into room 2141, Nate Sutton, a top lawyer at Amazon, was nervous, despite previously spending more than nine years as a trial attorney working on antitrust at the Department of Justice. He was prepared: Amazon executives and lawyers had hammered him with questions, covering all that could come up. Nonetheless, being grilled by Congress was uncomfortable, no matter how ready you felt. What's more, the room itself was imposing, with high ceilings and stately brown wood furniture against a wood-paneled wall.

At the hearing, Cicilline would run the show. His expertise had grown, and that had included relying heavily on Lina Khan's guidance, who at the time worked as a lawyer on the subcommittee. She was seated behind him.

Sutton, alongside representatives for Apple, Facebook, and Google, raised his right hand, swearing to tell the truth under the penalty of perjury. Then the proceedings began.

Sutton's prepared opening statements were strong. He made the case that Amazon operated in a very competitive market and touted what a big employer they were in the US. He spoke about how Amazon benefited the economy in myriad ways. "Amazon continues to represent less than 1% of the nearly $25 trillion global retail market, and less than 4% of US retail," read his written opening remarks, citing an oft-repeated line that Amazon used in such settings.

Then the questions began.

The committee pelted Sutton from all sides about Amazon's treatment of its third-party sellers, whether its advertising arm was pay to play, details about its market share of its cloud computing arm, and how it developed its private label brands. Cicilline probed the lawyer on Amazon's private label business like an attack dog.

"Mr. Sutton, doesn't that create a conflict of interest?" Cicilline asked, homing in on Amazon running its Marketplace and creating products for its brands that compete against sellers.

"Thank you for the question. Respectfully, we disagree," said Sutton. "We partner very closely with our third-party sellers. We rely on them to provide broad selection and prices to our customers, and we've been very proud of our investments to help them grow to be a majority of our store and growing twice as fast."

The Rhode Island congressman interrupted him. "That's a different question. What I'm saying is you're selling your own products on a platform that you control and they're competing with products in the Marketplace from other sellers, right?" As the lawyer started to answer, saying that private label products are common in retail, the congressman cut in again: "But the difference is Amazon is a $1 trillion company that runs an online platform with real-time data on millions of purchases and billions in commerce and can manipulate algorithms on its platform and favor its own product. That is not the same as a local retailer who might have a CVS brand and a national brand. It's quite different. So I want to drill down a little bit on the question that Ms. Jayapal asked you. You said, 'We do not use seller data to compete with other sellers online.' You do collect enormous data about what products are popular, what's selling, where they're selling. You're saying you don't use that in any way to promote Amazon products? I remind you, sir: You're under oath."

At the end of the tense exchange, Sutton stated: "We do not use their individual data when we're making decisions to launch private brands."

I watched this exchange at my desk in New York, stunned. Earlier that year, I had begun covering Amazon full-time and, as part of my reporting, I had heard from members of Amazon's private label team who regularly spied on third-party sellers to create private label products. Had Sutton just lied under oath?

————

While that hearing ended in July 2019, behind the scenes, I was trying to figure out the truth. For the *Wall Street Journal*, I had set out to find exactly how Amazon used the massive troves of data from its third-party sellers in its private label division, and before the hearing, an Amazon source confirmed my suspicions: they regularly used the individual data from these sellers to make their own copycat versions and crush the original sellers.

I flew to Seattle and filled my calendar with meetings with former and current Amazon employees who worked on the private label team to learn more. While at the bar of an upscale oyster restaurant in Seattle's Capitol Hill neighborhood, a source gave me the mother lode. Yes, the source regularly used this data when formulating new products for private label bosses. All of the source's colleagues did. Better yet, the source had documents that colleagues had used to make such products and would email them to me.

Weeks later, now back in New York, I received the first zip file containing the documents. The files were a paper trail showing how Amazon copied its third-party sellers.

One set showed Fortem's sales data for the company's car trunk organizer. The report had twenty-five fields detailing the most sensitive information on the organizer, from how many units it sold, the cost to ship and advertise them, and Amazon's margin on each product. It was a road map to reverse-engineer Fortem's bestseller. And then Amazon did it.

So, in March 2020, right before New York City shut down because of COVID-19, I met with Yuriy Petriv and Oleg Maslakov at a restaurant in Lower Manhattan. Neither of the founders knew the purpose of the meeting but agreed to meet that morning. When they arrived, I slid the documents from Amazon across the table to them. They were stunned.

The data for the time period that the Amazon employee pulled was an exact match for their own figures during the period of time. Petriv logged into their seller account on his mobile phone while sitting at the table and compared the two. The 33,000 units sold in the Amazon data matched the 33,000 units sold in Fortem's data. The amount of advertising spent matched in both documents. All twenty-five fields were identical.

Amazon said that there was one other seller of Fortem's trunk organizer during the period of the data the *Journal* reviewed, saying that didn't make the data "individual" third-party seller data since there was another seller. It wouldn't comment on how many days that seller was active or how many sales it made. I reached the other seller of the Fortem trunk organizer, who said for the period of time, he sold only seventeen units of the item. Fortem accounted for 99.95 percent of the total sales on Amazon for the trunk organizer during the period the documents cover, the data indicated.

"They are using their infrastructure to enter a market unfairly and push out individual sellers. Nobody has the resources they have," said Petriv, shaking his head in disbelief.

Then, Petriv and Maslakov did something else that almost every victim of Amazon immediately does. They panicked. As wrong as Amazon's behavior can be, their sellers and partners live in fear of being blacklisted by the giant. Given that, being in the news would, naturally, make anyone scared.

Maslakov became nervous about being mentioned in the *Wall Street Journal* piece. "What if they decide to retaliate against us somehow?" he asked, in an accent that revealed both his Eastern European and old-school Brooklyn roots. Petriv wondered aloud if Amazon would drastically cut its price of its own version of the trunk organizer to try to put them out of business. "We wouldn't be able to stop them, and they've already been very abusive," he said. At the end of the day, Maslakov and Petriv relied on Amazon for their paycheck, even if they had a love-hate relationship with the platform.

Petriv started to get angry about Amazon's spying. "I kind of want to give a big middle finger to Amazon," he said. He coaxed Maslakov, who was on the fence, to cooperate with me.

My original source remembered being rocked the first time they saw the third-party reports in a private label meeting. They weren't supposed to use data from different Amazon units in that way. "Where did you get those reports?" the source asked in a meeting where they were being referenced. Their boss turned around and looked at them in disbelief. "You just ask the business analysts for them," the boss said.

Then, in late April 2020, nine months after the original congressional hearing, and in the midst of the COVID-19 pandemic, we published my investigation on the *Journal*'s front page.

———

David Cicilline was furious the morning of April 23. The chair of the antitrust subcommittee read the *Wall Street Journal* story in disbelief. He felt that Amazon's lawyer Nate Sutton had lied to him and his colleagues under oath. He fumed.

The fifty-eight-year-old congressman did not suffer fools. He came from a family of fighters. His father was a lawyer who defended Rhode Island mafia members in the 1970s and '80s, at the height of the mafia wars. His son went a similar but different route, graduating from Brown University, then Georgetown Law School, before eventually running for office.

Cicilline is not a Luddite. He drives a Tesla, wears an Apple Watch, and frequently tweets. He even has an Amazon Prime account.

Cicilline was used to fighting Goliaths. In 2002, the openly gay politician went head-to-head with Rhode Island royalty, challenging the incumbent mayor, Vincent "Buddy" Cianci Jr. The controversial figure had run Providence for more than 20 years and was inseparable from Rhode Island's political identity. Cicilline ultimately won the 2002 mayoral race because Cianci was convicted of racketeering conspiracy and sentenced to five years in prison. In 2010, Cicilline won the congressional seat vacated by Patrick Kennedy, of the famed Kennedy dynasty, who had held the seat for eight consecutive terms.

A perfect mix of an everyman with elite credentials, the Brown and Georgetown Law alum enjoyed oversized Dunkin' Donuts iced coffees and, early in his career, wore budget suits from Men's Wearhouse. His roots were humble. Cicilline worked odd jobs as a waiter, nurse's assistant, and law clerk to pay his tuition. "I was a hustler. I used to pick people's flowers in their yards and sell them door to door," he said. Cicilline was interested in politics from an early age. In junior high, he attended town council and school committee meetings.

On the morning the *Wall Street Journal* story ran, Cicilline and House Judiciary Committee chairman Jerry Nadler looked for options on how to address what Sutton had potentially done. The committee had two main options. First, they could try to hold Amazon's lawyer accountable for lying under oath by prosecuting him for perjury (something some members did consider, but then dismissed because it would have slowed the momentum of the investigation). The second, which they ended up pursuing, was to use this as an opening to have Jeff Bezos testify. "Any suggestion that an Amazon executive lied to Congress is false," Amazon said in response.

Behind the scenes, after the initial hearing in 2019, the group had been trying for months to get the four CEOs to testify before Congress. While none were keen to appear, Amazon put up the biggest fight, according to the subcommittee.

In early 2020, Cicilline did manage to schedule calls with all of the technology titans about the antitrust committee's investigation, specifically to hear from the CEOs themselves. Apple's Tim Cook had a productive phone call with the congressman. Google's CEO, Sundar Pichai, also held a call. Facebook went a step further, with Zuckerberg taking a personal meeting with Cicilline and Nadler at the latter's Capitol Hill office. Amazon, meanwhile, set up a call with Jay Carney. While the other company CEOs interacted with Cicilline, clearly Bezos stood apart.

Instead, Carney was the CEO's emissary in Washington, DC, on the investigation. The problem was that many of the people he interacted with found him unlikeable. To make matters worse, while Cook, Pichai, and Zuckerberg were deferential in their meetings with Cicilline, Carney came across as arrogant. He told the congressman that Bezos would not be able to testify to Congress like the other tech CEOs, but Amazon could offer up an executive. "He fucked up," said a person familiar with the call. "The smart thing to have done would have been to say that 'we are in the middle of handling the pandemic, but we will find someone internally to participate.'"

As Amazon was angering members of Congress, it was simultaneously hiring a state senator from Washington in a way that may have violated ethics guidelines. In 2017, Guy Palumbo won his state senate seat and served for two years. In February 2019, Amazon privately offered the Democratic state senator of Washington a senior role as a director of public policy. Palumbo had worked at Amazon from 1999 until 2004 and was personal friends with Andy Jassy, who was CEO of AWS at the time he was being rehired.

Palumbo did not sign his employment contract in February, but there was an understanding between Palumbo and Amazon that he would be joining. An email I viewed from Huseman to a staff member in February states that Palumbo would be joining the team and shares that the staff member will report to another member of the team who would report directly to Palumbo. Amazon and the senator would keep it a secret for months. In the meantime, Palumbo worked on a bill he had sponsored in Washington state that would have benefited Amazon greatly. The bill would require state agencies to use cloud computing for new information technology investments. Emails between Palumbo and Amazon officials I viewed showed him working with Amazon and its lobbyists to help try to get the bill passed in the months between accepting the offer from Amazon and officially resigning from the state senate.

For more than three months, the state senator worked on trying to pass the bill (it ultimately failed to pass). In late May, Palumbo and Amazon orchestrated an announcement that he would be leaving his senate seat. But before doing so, Amazon and the senator met to "pull" his government emails to evaluate which emails that mention Amazon might cause public scrutiny about the senator's close ties if the emails were found in public record requests, according to an email I was given that discussed Amazon's strategy. In Amazon's confidential media plan, they say: "As a state senator, Guy has been a vocal advocate for Amazon and tech generally."

In Amazon's rollout plan for the announcement, they advised Palumbo to strategically announce that he was leaving his role on the Friday of a three-day holiday weekend, which was by design: it would mean reporters may miss it and not look too deeply into what was actually going on. Amazon's talking points for the announcement also instructed the team to say that the offer was made after the session, when it had actually been understood since February that Palumbo would join Amazon. In its media notes, it instructs PR to answer the question "When did Amazon know it was going to hire Sen. Palumbo? Shouldn't he have recused himself?" The answer: "The offer came together after session," according to a copy of the media plan. That would imply that he received the offer in late May, not in mid-February. Another question that Amazon prepared, according to its media plan, was "Why did Amazon buy off a sitting State Senator?" The media plan shows Amazon's self-awareness of the impropriety and the consequences of exposure, for both the senator and the company. So, instead, Amazon tried to bury the coverage and only release news of the hiring to preselected news outlets considered "friendly" to "set the tone for future coverage and get ahead of exposé." Amazon general counsel David Zapolsky, Jay Carney, and Brian Huseman signed off on this plan. As of this writing, Palumbo is still employed by Amazon.

While Palumbo did contact Washington state's ethics department on an informal basis in February about whether he could entertain job offers while employed as a senator, he did not disclose that he was in talks with Amazon and that he was working on legislation that would benefit Amazon, according to people familiar with the matter. The ethics committee told Palumbo that it was acceptable to interview for jobs. When he asked a follow-up question about whether he could accept a job offer and work as a state senator until after session, he was told that could be an ethical violation. Palumbo declined to provide further details about the employer or scope of the work, people involved said. He asked if he could get an official opinion in writing, and was told he would have to provide further details in order to receive a formal opinion. So he dropped it. Washington's legislature didn't find out that Senator Palumbo was going to work at Amazon until a few days before the announcement, according to internal Amazon emails. When I described the details of the hiring, people in that office said it could have violated ethics law.

An Amazon spokesman said: "The claims the author is making are false. Guy was not offered any role and thus could not have accepted the role before the senate session ended, and the communication about his hiring was accurate and truthful." The spokesperson said that the communications I viewed from February about Palumbo joining Amazon later in the year "were intended to ensure that no inappropriate contact occurred in the event the company did eventually extend Mr. Palumbo a job offer."

While Sutton was defending the company's private brands practices, that very team was at that moment ripping off a beloved American brand.

In September 2019, an executive from workwear apparel maker Carhartt walked the floor of the Chinese factory that assembles their clothes, inspecting the products. As he did so, he also came across, in another part of the same factory, a production line making what appeared to be Carhartt's bestselling bib overalls and workwear pants. But that area was not designated for Carhartt.

The executive was confused. The product on the competing line was the exact same material as the family-owned business from Dearborn, Michigan — the same colors and even the exact same zippers and trims. He asked the factory who had commissioned the line and learned it was for Amazon Essentials.

The findings set off a chain reaction within Carhartt and Amazon.

Just as the Seattle-based giant exploited third-party sellers on its website by making fast follows of their bestselling items, it frequently alienated national brands that sell on the first-party side of the business, which means they sell their products directly to Amazon in bulk and Amazon then resells them to customers.

For years, Carhartt had been an important seller on Amazon. The industrial-wear company was founded in Detroit in 1889 and has catered to workers for much of its history, making durable pants and jackets sported by construction workers, electrical workers, and people in the agricultural sector. More recently, some of its items had become trendy in the streetwear space, but, for the most part, it was closely associated with blue-collar work attire.

Over the years, Carhartt worked with Amazon but always kept Amazon's portion of its overall sales at a smaller percentage than Amazon wanted. The company was wary of relying too heavily on Amazon only to have the retail giant demand harsher terms, such as higher margins or higher advertising spend.

In many ways, Carhartt was, by design, very different from Amazon. "We reported to Main Street, not Wall Street," said Harry McPherson, a retired Carhartt executive who worked at the company until 2018. He said that as a result, the company was very involved in improving the surrounding community near its headquarters, and that the internal culture was one where employees cared for each other.

A year before the Carhartt executive found the Amazon knockoffs, Amazon's private label management targeted Carhartt for its design team to copy, people involved said. A brand manager at Amazon provided the private label team with the top-selling items in the work-wear space. Using that list, the private label managers zeroed in on the items from Carhartt to replicate for Amazon's own brand: Amazon Essentials. Using this list that identifies every best seller on Amazon by vendor and style, Amazon private label employees then "go after" those vendors, a person who worked on the team said. The strategy was a core part of Amazon's private label business, with upper management, including S-Team member Herrington, made aware of how the team developed practices using such data in 2018, one of the people said.

Using the data, Amazon Essentials decided to create near-exact versions of Carhartt's bestselling hooded jacket, bib overall, and workwear pants. Amazon found the same factory Carhartt uses for the pieces and began producing some of them in the summer of 2019.

Once the Carhartt executive found the look-alike products, the company contacted Amazon about the dupes, the people said. Amazon immediately stopped its production of the look-alikes and began an internal investigation into its private label design practice. This led to the company doing a "Correction of Errors," a lengthy process where employees deconstruct a mistake they made, measure the impact of the mistake, and come up with solutions to ensure it doesn't happen again. In order to salvage the Carhartt dupes, Amazon added new features to them to differentiate from Carhartt's own designs so that they could sell them, the people said.

As a result of the investigation, Amazon private label managers stopped identifying just one item for Amazon to use as inspiration for Amazon Essentials, which would be easier to spot as a replica, when designing its goods. Instead, they would choose three items for Amazon Essentials to use as a reference point, with the goal of combining aspects from all three for their versions to avoid these kinds of flare-ups going forward.

While the new policy helped Amazon avoid the appearance of copying brands on its sites, in practice, it didn't change much, said one of the people. It wouldn't stop copying; it would just get better at figuring out how to do it.

———————

Brands that Amazon wanted to sell on its site but had turned them down also faced similar consequences. In 2016, Allbirds launched its first sneaker, the Wool Runner. The lightweight, eco-friendly shoe with a distinct design became an instant success for the company. "It put us on the map," said Joey Zwillinger, CEO of Allbirds, in an interview.

Three years of research and development went into creating the Wool Runner. The company developed a proprietary fabric at an Italian mill. It worked with a Brazilian chemical company to create a sustainable sole that was carbon negative. Dozens of people, from an Italian last maker who molded the shape of the shoe, to their lead designer in New Zealand who created the striking design, worked on it.

Amazon consistently contacted Allbirds to sell on its site, said Zwillinger. The startup always declined. Eventually, the Allbirds team noticed an interesting phenomenon on Google's search engine. When typing in "Wool Runner," the top results that appeared were knockoffs of the shoe sold by third-party sellers on Amazon's site, he said. It seemed as if Amazon was buying advertisements on Google to siphon demand for the hit product to its own site, he said. The company was effectively profiting from the demand for the Wool Runner by hijacking the search term and then directing shoppers to counterfeit versions of the shoe.

"To see a company with the deep pockets of Amazon try to siphon off demand and give it to copycats is really frustrating," said Zwillinger.

After years of trying to get Allbirds to sell on its website, in 2019 Amazon launched a shoe that looks nearly identical to the Wool Runner called Galen. Amazon's version sold for less than half of what the Wool Runner sells for and isn't eco-friendly (one of the things that makes Allbirds distinct and appealing to its customers). In reviews for Amazon's version of the Wool Runner, customers reference Allbirds.

"Over 50 percent of product searches originate on Amazon.com's search bar. They obviously have a huge amount of information, and I have to imagine that a lot of people type 'Allbirds' into Amazon's search bar," said Zwillinger. He thinks that search data guided Amazon's decision to make a copycat version of his hit product, which he says looks "eerily similar" to his shoe.

He has no doubt that Amazon's Galen version of his shoe has cannibalized his business, but to what extent he isn't sure. "You can't help but look at a trillion-dollar company putting their muscle and their pockets and their machinations of their algorithms and reviewers and private label machine all behind something that you've put your career against," Zwillinger told me in an interview in 2020.

"If you're sitting there and at your fingertips you know what everyone in America is searching for, tempting would be an understatement to say what you might want to do with that data," he said about Amazon. "You might consider taking that data and using it to make something that siphons off that demand as quickly and effectively as possible."

In November 2023, in a sudden reversal, Allbirds began selling on Amazon. Allbirds saw a survey that more than 50 percent of its core demographic shopped on Amazon.com as their first-choice retailer for back-to-school needs, said Zwillinger. He says the rationale was this: "The reality we are facing is that consumers are shopping there because of the perceived convenience of Prime, so let's not ignore that." In the interim, Amazon has stopped making its Galen sneaker.

———

Back in DC, the committee might have finally found their opening to get Bezos to testify in light of potential perjury. On the morning of April 23, Nadler and Cicilline issued a joint statement addressing Amazon's truthfulness. "This is yet another example of the sworn testimony of Amazon's witness being directly contradicted by investigative reporting," Cicilline said in the statement. "At best, Amazon's witness appears to have misrepresented key aspects of Amazon's business practices while omitting important details in response to pointed questioning. At worst, the witness Amazon sent to speak on its behalf may have lied to Congress."

The momentum had truly turned against Amazon. During the Democratic presidential debates, in the lead-up to the 2020 presidential election, Amazon was repeatedly name-checked by candidates vying for the nomination.

Bernie Sanders attacked the company for not paying its fair share of taxes. Andrew Yang attacked it for ruining Main Street. "Raise your hand in the crowd if you've seen stores closing where you live," Yang said. "It's not just you. Amazon is closing 30 percent of America's stores and malls and paying zero in taxes while doing it." Elizabeth Warren went for the jugular. "Look, you get to be the umpire in the baseball game or you get to have a team, but you don't get to do both at the same time," said Warren, attacking Amazon's private label business and hinting that the company should be broken up.

Not even Joe Biden, the eventual nominee, was all that friendly to Amazon. Despite Jay Carney being a close associate while Biden was vice president, he would not do his former press chief any favors with respect to his current employer.

Amazon general counsel David Zapolsky, a top donor to the Biden campaign who had given more than $250,000 to different funds supporting his presidential run, hosted a fundraiser for the candidate, where Biden then surprisingly railed about Amazon's size and power.

At a $2,800-per-head fundraiser at Zapolsky's home, Biden acknowledged his surroundings. "I'm in the House of Amazon here," he said. The presidential candidate then criticized Amazon's effects on the economy. "Seriously, think of the change that is taking place and why people are frightened. Nothing bad—you've done good things. But 200,000 salespeople are out of work because people are shopping online now." Amazon's logistics head Dave Clark—a moderate Republican—attended the fundraiser and was annoyed by the comments, as were other Amazon executives.

A week after the *Wall Street Journal* story about Amazon's private label employees using seller data to create Amazon branded products ran, Congress issued a bold request. It released a letter, directed at Bezos: "In light of our ongoing investigation, recent public reporting, and Amazon's prior testimony before the Committee, we expect you, as Chief Executive Officer of Amazon, to testify before the Committee."

Bezos could evade Congress for only so long.

PART III

Showdown

CHAPTER 15

The World Shuts Down and Amazon Comes Out a Winner

WHILE BEZOS MANAGED TO evade Congress for as long as he did, his Kalorama mansion was making its social debut among some of the District's power players. He wouldn't testify before Congress until July, but he would begin 2020 with quite a show. On January 25, a tuxedo-clad Jeff Bezos invited some of the world's most powerful people to his Washington, DC, mansion.

The guest list ranged from members of President Trump's inner circle, including his daughter Ivanka Trump, her husband, Jared Kushner, and senior adviser Kellyanne Conway, to Microsoft cofounder Bill Gates. Former Republican speaker of the house Paul Ryan, Senator Mitt Romney, and Federal Reserve chairman Jerome Powell were all invited. It was a who's who of Washington, tech, and finance's most powerful people in one place, and Bezos was the man of the hour presiding over the affair.

Earlier in the evening, members of Washington's elite attended a private gala thrown by the Alfalfa Club (Bezos was among them). On the last Saturday of every January, this group of just 200 attendees assembles for its annual banquet of filet mignon and lobster at the Capital Hilton hotel.

In DC, where members-only clubs are rampant, Alfalfa Club membership is particularly difficult to get. The club was founded in 1913 to celebrate the birthday of General Robert E. Lee. Members have included Neil Armstrong, Madeleine Albright, and Katharine Graham. Membership is capped: in order to get an invite, another member has to pass away.

The 2020 event's keynote speaker was Republican Utah senator Mitt Romney, who brought Hollywood actor Ben Stiller as his guest. "Everyone's worried about artificial intelligence and robots taking over the world. That's not true or I would be president now," Romney said in his opening remarks.

Following the gala, most guests made their way over to DC hot spot Cafe Milano in Georgetown for an after-party. But in 2020, the hottest after-party in town was the invite to Bezos's mansion.

Bezos had whittled down the list, which was already a who's who, to an even smaller group, heightening the exclusivity of the party. His staff set up a tent and heat lamps on the back deck that opens up to his lawn so guests could sip cocktails alfresco. Bezos had been more present in DC for a few years, as he promised he would be. That included meetings at the paper he bought and his work as part of the Business Roundtable, an association made up of the CEOs of some of America's top companies. But tonight he was playing host. The "Amazon embassy," as some called it, was now open for business.

Alfalfa Club members sporting gold medallions with red, white, and blue striped ribbons walked into the front entrance of Bezos's ornate red brick home where they were struck by the beautiful interiors.

The fact that Jared and Ivanka showed up was a feat in and of itself. Earlier in the week, the President had unleashed a missive on Twitter: "Two stone cold losers from Amazon WP. Almost every story is a made up lie, just like corrupt pol Shifty Schiff, who fraudulently made up my call with Ukraine. Fiction!" He was referring, with his usual mockish tone, to two *Washington Post* reporters who had a book coming out just days later titled *A Very Stable Genius: Donald J. Trump's Testing of America* and Democratic congressman Adam Schiff, who led the first impeachment of the sitting president.

During the party, Lauren Sánchez, Bezos's new girlfriend, sought personal advice from another guest: Trump senior aide Kellyanne Conway. Bezos got together with Sánchez during the end of his twenty-five-year marriage to MacKenzie Scott, from whom he was now divorced.

"You've had a lot thrown at you. How do you handle it?" asked Sánchez, who had become the focus of tabloid fodder. Among the stories: Sánchez's brother leaked details of their affair to the *National Enquirer* and, of course, the divorce itself, which made headlines around the world.

"Please, have you looked in the mirror? People are jealous of you," Conway exclaimed. "I would say they're jealous because you're dating him." She pointed to Bezos. "But honestly, even before you were dating him, have you taken a look in the mirror? You're gorgeous!"

As Sánchez blushed, Conway told Bezos's girlfriend, who frequently chronicles her workouts on Instagram, that if she ever wanted to chat some more, Conway could even join her for a slow jog around the neighborhood. It was a gesture of goodwill, knowing how seriously Sánchez took exercise.

The year before, Conway offered some unsolicited personal advice to Bezos at the Gridiron Club dinner, another yearly Washington banquet. Bezos was fresh off of the affair scandal at the time. "Don't let the fuckers bring you down," Conway told him.

Despite President Trump's ire toward Bezos and Amazon, some of his closest associates, and even his family, didn't seem to hold Bezos or his company in anything but high regard.

But not all. Earlier that night, at the Alfalfa Club, Bezos promised something he didn't follow through on that would create an enemy of a member of Trump's team. Peter Navarro, Trump's trade czar, had already been annoyed by the proliferation of counterfeit and dangerous products from China flooding into America. These ran the gamut: from fake versions of American brands to fake pills marketed as brand names like cholesterol medicine Lipitor and erectile dysfunction drug Viagra. Amazon was the largest e-commerce platform in the US. Since nearly 40 percent of all online sales came from Amazon and its marketplace was open to international sellers, Navarro had identified the company as a big conduit for illegal and dangerous goods. He'd been trying to nail down a meeting with Bezos for months; he wanted to share his team's findings and figure out a way for them to agree to reduce or remove this problem entirely. His requests had gone unanswered. Navarro's boss was also interested in solving the issue. "He told me to get these guys, you know, get to the problem," Navarro says of Trump.

At the Alfalfa Club dinner, Navarro spotted Bezos and walked over to him. Bezos was mid-conversation, but Navarro introduced himself anyway. The trade czar had just received a report from the Customs and Border Protection agency. Navarro had instructed the agency to aggressively search overseas shipments coming into the US and see what was in them. The investigation revealed that one in ten packages the team opened contained either counterfeit goods or items that could be a public health issue, Navarro told me in an interview. "I told him about it and was just trying to appeal to his better angels."

When he approached Bezos that night, the CEO responded with a smile. "I'd love to meet with you about it," he said. He gave Carney's number to Navarro to arrange the meeting. The next day, Navarro called Carney to schedule. But Carney told him Bezos wouldn't meet. Instead, Carney could do the meeting. Navarro was incensed and complained about it in an interview with the *Washington Post*. In response, Bezos posted a snarky Instagram post. It was an image with an all-white background with "Business Question" written in big black font, accompanied by the caption:

> Let's say you're at a big cocktail party and someone you don't know comes up to you while you're talking to your dad and girlfriend and asks for a meeting. Let's say this person is the kind of person who actually uses the word "minions" to describe the people who work for you.
>
> How do you respond:
>
> A) Yes, I'll definitely meet with you.
> B) No, I won't meet with you.

C) Tell you what. Call so and so and they'll work something out.

D) Quietly resolve to become a shut-in.

E) Something else (fill in the blank)

A Seinfeld "Serenity Now!" button (second pic) for whoever comes up with the best answer.

————————

I later asked Navarro why he thinks Bezos wouldn't meet with him. "There's two theories to that. One is that he's a sociopath. He doesn't give a shit about the American people or the American public and he just wants to make money. And two: he knows he's got a very serious problem and if he tries to solve it, it's going to cost him profits," he replied, adding that he is "disgusted" by Bezos and Carney. (Navarro was later found guilty of two counts of contempt of Congress for not complying with a subpoena related to the January 6 attack on the Capitol.)

Needless to say, Navarro was not at the afterparty, but other members of the Trump White House were. This was all part of a necessary — and calculated — charm offensive. The company was under siege in DC, and Bezos was doing his part to right the ship his way.

His prior apathy toward DC and politics wasn't evident that night in January. It's harder to inflict pain on a company when you are being charmed by the CEO, and that was on full display. Bezos held court at the bar, catching up with Bill Gates — once in the antitrust hot seat himself at Microsoft — and Warren Buffett. He roamed the room mingling with the Kushners, JPMorgan CEO Jamie Dimon, and former secretary of defense James Mattis.

Bezos had spent twenty-five years creating an empire, and he planned on keeping it that way. And the timing couldn't be better. The world was about to shut down — many of the guests who worked in the administration would scramble to respond, and people globally, not to mention businesses, would be completely shaken by it. But Amazon, built so studiously, so expansively, and already such a dominant force, would take full advantage — and benefit handsomely.

―――――――

If people thought that Amazon might be a monopoly before COVID-19 hit, the ensuing crisis left no doubts as to the company's power. Consumers flocked to Amazon during the height of the lockdowns to stock up on daily necessities. They ordered Clorox wipes on Amazon.com, groceries through Whole Foods. Spent hours streaming videos on Amazon Prime. Companies relied on AWS while their employees worked from home.

Only one company could provide nearly all the needs for Americans — not to mention the needs of people around the world — who were scared and stocking up as they sheltered in place and watched the news of what was happening in real time.

It also made clear just how diminished American retail as a whole had become, in no small part because of Amazon's dominance. How many alternatives were out there by 2020? The COVID-19 crisis laid bare the shrinking number of options for daily goods. People couldn't find enough toilet paper, paper towels, and cleaning products as they hunkered down at home.

Even President Trump had to turn to Amazon in the throes of the pandemic's worst days because critical supplies couldn't be found elsewhere. In April, the White House ordered the Federal Emergency Management Agency (FEMA) to spend nearly $13 million on thermometers from Amazon.

―――――――

State after state announced lockdown mandates, which meant people had to stay at home. As a result, office buildings remained empty and foot traffic in downtown areas diminished. Much of physical retail was forced to shut down because they weren't deemed essential services. And even if it was an essential business, like a grocery store, and remained open, many shoppers wouldn't risk going in person for fear of catching the virus. So, naturally, they turned to the internet to shop. A large swath of smaller shops and mom and pops didn't have e-commerce capabilities, so the retailers with online arms, such as Walmart, Target, and Amazon, benefited the most from this shift in consumer habits.

While the rest of the world suffered, Amazon benefited mightily. Unemployment claims rose to historic levels across the country as Bezos added more than $74 billion to his net worth during the first few months of the pandemic, with his net worth reaching $189 billion in July 2020. Meanwhile, according to the US Bureau of Labor, "total civilian employment...fell by 21 million from the fourth quarter of 2019 to the second quarter of 2020, while the unemployment rate more than tripled, from 3.6 percent to 13.0 percent."

It was truly a tale of the haves and have nots. During the first year of the pandemic, approximately 200,000 more businesses closed in the US than in normal years. Storied retailers such as Neiman Marcus, JCPenney, Lord & Taylor, and J.Crew couldn't stay afloat during this time and filed for bankruptcy protection. Lord & Taylor had survived nearly 200 years of changing consumer tastes, wars, and past pandemics, but COVID-19 did them in. The pain was felt globally. In the UK, department store Debenhams announced it would shutter. Arcadia Group, which owned Topshop and Miss Selfridge, filed for administration and began selling off its brands. Amazon had already eliminated lots of retail competition over the years, but the pandemic cemented it as a de facto retailer of choice.

Amazon's stock price rose nearly 50 percent to a record market cap of $1.5 trillion during the first half of 2020. The S&P index, which tracks the 500 largest publicly listed companies in the US, fell by 4 percent during the same period.

Another contrast: whereas other companies were downsizing, in hiring freezes, or outright closing, Amazon was one of the few major companies on a hiring spree to fulfill the onslaught of orders. During the first two years of the pandemic, the company hired hundreds of thousands of workers in its warehouses to do the grueling work of packing and shipping boxes to consumers. The company would double its already massive logistics network of warehouses, sorting stations, and other essential infrastructure in less than two years.

While Bezos's pockets were being padded, some warehouse workers, already being pushed to their limits, contracted the virus on the job. Some would die. Amazon wouldn't disclose the number of warehouse workers who have died from COVID-19. An informal group of Amazon warehouse workers got together early in the pandemic to share information across its network and discovered at least ten deaths by September 2020, but that figure may be low. One of the organizers says they've heard of many more unconfirmed deaths.

Times were desperate, the economy was in free fall, and people of all kinds, from the overqualified white-collar worker to someone who ran their own small business, found themselves having to make choices they would otherwise never consider. Having their own work lives displaced, they turned to Amazon, which was on a hiring spree to fill warehouse positions. It meant risking their lives; they may have been entirely overqualified for a labor-intensive job, never having worked in one before. But what choice did they have? They needed to make money; they needed to feed their families and pay rent.

Preschool teachers, business owners, executive chefs, and entrepreneurs applied for warehouse jobs paying $17 an hour. They applied not because they dreamed of working long hours on their feet, packing boxes, but because they needed the money. Amazon was, for many whose lives were upended by the pandemic, an opportunity to get a job, since it was one of the few companies capable of offering thousands of jobs in the midst of the pandemic. As others hunkered down at home, these new hires became frontline workers, joining what became the "essential" class of jobs that the rest of the country depended upon. But unlike nurses or doctors or even transportation workers, these were reluctant heroes, doing what was required to make a living during a period of extreme upheaval.

In the pandemic's early days, fifty-year-old Ginette Zuras-Hummel was one of them. She was vastly overqualified but saw no other option. She owned her own business, Integrity Billing & Consulting, in Wilsonville, Oregon, which she had to temporarily close as infections spread. Her clients were chiropractors, massage therapists, and acupuncturists who had to halt operations because of social-distancing measures. As a result, Zuras-Hummel's monthly revenue went from about $12,000 to less than $2,500—a sum too small to cover the rent for her home and office space. Zuras-Hummel applied for a Small Business Administration disaster loan for her business, but was told she had 36 million people ahead of her. "I'll be out of business by then," she said at the time. She needed another option.

So, in April 2020, Zuras-Hummel was hired as a picker at Amazon's Whole Foods grocery stores. During orientation, she found people from all walks of life and many in similar situations. She made fast friends with a former Intel employee who had just been laid off from her $100,000-a-year job at the start of the pandemic.

From April to June, Zuras-Hummel spent thirty hours a week packing customer orders for oat milk and organic steak. Social distancing was tough because of all of the other new pickers at Whole Foods, as well as the shoppers who did come into the store. "It gave me a lot of anxiety," she said.

In June, she quit to refocus all her energy on her own business. But in the little time she spent working for Amazon, she said she saw firsthand how well the company did during the pandemic. "They made a fortune during that time. They cornered the world."

During the lockdowns, few witnessed the pain of store closures more acutely than mall owners. For years, these CEOs dealt with the likes of Amazon putting its tenants and anchor stores out of business. It forced them to scramble to fill vacancies, figure out how to bring back foot traffic as shopping habits moved online, and diversify their tenant base away from retail. When pandemic lockdowns set in, the problems became insurmountable for many. Mall operators CBL Properties and Washington Prime Group filed for bankruptcy during the pandemic.

On November 1, 2020, Pennsylvania Real Estate Investment Trust, better known as PREIT, filed for bankruptcy protection. Months of shutdowns left the Philadelphia-based mall operator with tenants unable to pay their rent, and PREIT defaulted on its debt obligations. PREIT operated twenty malls and was founded in 1960, originally focused on apartments and office buildings. But in 2003, it bought a mall operator in order to pivot to the retail sector. At the time, malls had a higher multiple on Wall Street than apartments or office buildings, and the company was looking to capitalize. At its height, PREIT owned seventy malls.

Much had changed in the decades since malls served as vital community hubs in towns. In addition to being meeting places, malls were also good for the towns and states for the financial benefits the malls paid, like taxes, and how they drove residents to spend on local businesses. But the internet age brought changes, and malls didn't hold the kind of power they once did, including the communal ethos it inspired. The COVID-19 pandemic would only exacerbate that trend.

Joe Coradino, the CEO of PREIT, remembers the industry rationalizing away the threat of Amazon during the early days. "They would say, 'Oh, people will continue to shop because of the communal nature of it,'" he recalls. "I think if you were really honest with yourself you had to say, 'God, this is going to have an impact, and we need to think through how to act.'"

During a talk in 2014 with the company's summer interns, who were mostly college students, Coradino asked them to guess what percentage of retail was e-commerce. Coradino, who has been in the real estate industry for decades, remembers being taken aback by their answers. At the time, less than 10 percent of shopping was done online. The students gave their guesses, saying 70 percent. It was an "aha" moment. "The fact they thought that meant they lived that," he said. If some of his core customers — college students — were likely buying 70 percent of their items online, it didn't bode well for mall retailers.

Online shopping did eat into mall sales, and as time wore on, Coradino started experiencing his anchor tenants file for bankruptcy or close hundreds of their stores. He began preemptively selling his lower-performing malls to avoid getting stuck with big vacancies. He put twenty of them up for sale in 2012, when he became CEO. And while he had to react to other, smaller tenants closing shop over the years — bookstores, toy stores, among others — the risk of empty anchors was a much bigger problem since they were harder to fill.

Anchor tenants were having a hard time, with many of them unable to compete with Amazon. Sears filed for bankruptcy in 2018. JCPenney became a shell of itself and eventually filed as well. The phenomenon became so pronounced that it was dubbed the "retail apocalypse" by media pundits.

Coradino was enjoying a day at the Jersey Shore in August 2016 when his phone rang. He was given bad news. Macy's, a major mall anchor tenant, had announced that it was closing 100 stores. He had six malls with a Macy's, and with them gone, something would have to take its place in each location. "That was a big deal," he said, calling it an "oh shit moment."

"Part of the reason for the department stores closing stores was the online threat with Amazon," said Coradino. Between 2016 and 2021, America's largest department store chains cut around 40 percent of their stores, according to a *Washington Post* analysis. During the same period, Amazon's market capitalization rose from $299 billion to $1.7 trillion. Since 2000, tenant vacancies at malls have steadily increased, from 5 percent in 2000 to more than 11 percent in 2022, according to data from Moody's.

What's more, the loss of department stores led to massive job losses. Between 2001 and 2017, department store employment shrunk by a third. Half a million of those jobs disappeared — roughly eighteen times more than were lost in coal mining during that period.

Cafaro's mall in Monroe, Michigan, is emblematic of the problem. The mall used to count Target, JCPenney, and Sears as anchors. When they were around, on a good weekend, hundreds of thousands of people would visit the mall. Since then, "every single anchor has left," says Cafaro. Now, the mall has several hundred visitors on weekends. Cafaro has been able to weather the storm by keeping its debt levels low and pivoting its malls to different tenants. Many mall operators have not been as lucky.

In 2016, PREIT sported a $1.7 billion market value. By late 2019, before the company had to deal with the impact of COVID-19, its market value had dwindled to $410 million. In the interim, instead of growing, PREIT had to shed many malls in order to try to remain solvent.

When the pandemic began, mall operators initially thought the lockdown orders would last a few weeks. But weeks extended into months, and their tenants defaulted on their rents. While his malls were closed, Coradino looked out his window to see boxes piled high on a neighbor's porch. Every day, new shipments of online orders would arrive. "It looked like they had a cardboard factory," he jokes. It's likely that many of those boxes had smiles on them.

That neighbor wasn't alone. More and more shoppers turned to online shopping, accelerating an already difficult trend for the retailers who held a mall presence or otherwise had stand-alone stores in cities around the country.

On November 1, 2020, PREIT filed for bankruptcy in order to financially restructure itself. It later reemerged, and its remaining malls focus less on apparel and more on dining and entertainment. It even installed Amazon lockers, where customers can pick up their Amazon packages, to try to recapture foot traffic and incremental spending. But unlike the early aughts, when Wall Street put a high valuation on mall retailers, that faith is now gone. For much of 2023, PREIT traded as a penny stock with a market value below $2 million. On December 11, 2023, PREIT filed for bankruptcy again.

———

Winston Churchill is credited with saying, "Never let a good crisis go to waste," and Amazon's top leaders took that advice to heart during the pandemic. The S-Team saw its role in delivering to Americans as an opportunity to recast itself as a hero and mend some bridges in Washington.

During the pandemic, "essential" workers, who are not usually celebrated for what they contribute to society, suddenly became national heroes. Oft-ignored grocery store clerks, delivery personnel, and the people shipping the world their packages at the risk of contagion were now garnering public attention. Amazon had a lot of those very people on its payroll. In addition to that, its role in hiring hundreds of thousands of people was helping with the unemployment crisis gripping the country. "We were hiring a ton of people when most companies were firing a ton of people. There's no doubt that we had a measurable impact on the unemployment rate," said an S-Team member.

This could ingratiate the company to the president for once, they reasoned. Bezos held phone calls with top White House officials, such as Kushner, about how Amazon could help the administration in its COVID-19 efforts. It worked. The president gave a speech and, for once, Amazon was mentioned in a positive light.

Amazon saw this as an opportunity to spin their size and scale as actually a good thing. "I'm hopeful that this creates a little more balanced view of these companies and why scale and omnipresence are actually helpful. It may temper the demonization from Trump," said a board member in an interview at the time.

For a while, it seemed to do just that.

———

In mid-March 2020, President Trump held a conference call with the nation's largest grocery chains. The CEOs of Walmart, Kroger, Target, and Costco, among others, discussed making sure the food supply chain was in a position to handle the demand and hoarding happening nationwide. Trump also asked for a commitment that grocery stores would stay open. Dave Clark, then Amazon's senior vice president of worldwide operations and who oversaw Whole Foods, was also on the call. Clark took the meeting from inside his wife's closet at their Dallas home. His two small children were home from school because of lockdowns, and it was the only quiet place in his house with cell phone service. He had yet to set up a proper home office. "I got off that call and told my wife, 'Okay, we're going to be in quarantine for a year.' It was very clear that this was big, and it was bigger than maybe you just really kind of got. There really wasn't an answer," recalls Clark.

Later that day, Trump stood on a podium surrounded by the rest of his Coronavirus Task Force, wearing a blue tie and American flag pin, and addressed the nation. "I just had a phone call with very impressive people — the biggest in the world, in the world of stores and groceries and all. And I'll give you the names." He led with Amazon's Dave Clark.

Amazon was thrilled. Later in the week, Bezos sent a company-wide email to rally his troops. "Your efforts are being noticed at the highest levels of government, and President Trump earlier this week thanked this team profusely," he wrote.

The White House briefly put aside its gripes with Big Tech and instead asked that they help the administration deal with the pandemic. It tapped Google, Apple, and Amazon for different roles. In a sense, this was unavoidable. These companies had grown too big and too powerful; even their critics, besieged by a crisis, had no choice but to partner with them.

For Amazon, the goodwill was short-lived. Amazon even got in its own way.

A warehouse worker in Staten Island, New York, had become very vocal that he and his colleagues did not have enough masks, gloves, and other protective gear to prevent them from contracting the virus during shifts. That worker was Chris Smalls, and in March 2020, he staged a walkout at his warehouse. Shortly thereafter, he was fired. Amazon denied that Smalls was fired for staging the walkout. They claimed it was due to a social-distancing violation when he was supposed to be quarantining. But Amazon has a history of firing workers who publicly criticize the company or engage in walkouts.

Smalls, who is Black, was vocal about Amazon's mistreatment of its warehouse staff. His complaints got picked up by national media. It became an optics problem for Amazon, which was trying to generate good press from the work it was doing to deliver necessities to Americans. The headlines being hijacked by Smalls and his effort to shine a light on unsafe work conditions in the middle of a pandemic rankled executives. As Smalls said in a statement: "Amazon would rather fire workers than face up to its total failure to do what it should to keep us, our families, and our communities safe."

In an S-Team meeting that Bezos attended, senior leaders discussed the narrative being formed around COVID-19 safety conditions for warehouse workers. Amazon's general counsel David Zapolsky suggested picking apart Smalls. "He's not smart, or articulate, and to the extent the press wants to focus on us versus him, we will be in a much stronger PR position than simply explaining for the umpteenth time how we're trying to protect workers," he wrote in notes from the meeting.

The plan was to discredit Smalls and then make him "the face of the entire union/organizing movement," according to leaked documents *Vice News* obtained. While at least some of Amazon's warehouse workers were dying and many more were falling ill from COVID-19, Zapolsky and the rest of the S-Team were looking for ways to spin the story and attack Smalls, who would later go on to launch a union effort that would garner even more headlines, in order to tarnish the warehouse storyline once and for all. (Interestingly, Carney personally identified as pro-union.)

The notes were a rare look inside the public relations machine that Amazon created to contend with public scrutiny. Zapolsky's notes indicate that there was "general agreement" among major S-Team members on the strategy. Rather than empathize with its employees, who were the backbone of Amazon's pandemic efforts, and address their fear of becoming sick at work, Amazon executives thought it best to distract from that narrative and demonize Smalls. It didn't work.

Once *Vice*'s story ran, the public viewed Zapolsky's comments as racist. "Amazon's attempt to smear Chris Smalls, one of their own warehouse workers, as 'not smart or articulate' is a racist & classist PR campaign," Representative Alexandria Ocasio-Cortez tweeted. Amazon denied the accusations of racism, saying that Zapolsky didn't even know Smalls's race at the time of his comments.

Zapolsky issued a statement with a pseudo-apology for his remarks without directly apologizing to Smalls. In fact, the apology included some of the same spin from the original notes that still placed blame on Smalls.

Later that same month, Bezos's public spat with Navarro took on a new dimension. The US trade representative's office put Amazon's web domains in Canada, France, Germany, India, and the UK on its "notorious markets" list of platforms that are believed to facilitate counterfeiting. Amazon viewed it as retaliation from Navarro. "This purely political act is another example of the administration using the U.S. government to advance a personal vendetta against Amazon," an Amazon spokeswoman said at the time. "Amazon makes significant investments in proactive technologies and processes to detect and stop bad actors and potentially counterfeit products from being sold in our stores." Navarro had a different take, saying: "This is an action clearly justified by the behavior of the worst counterfeit-enabler in the world, Amazon. The Amazon brain trust would rather fight this out in the media through their swamp-creature spin doctors than clean up their marketplace in the urgent ways necessary to protect and defend the American people from fraud and often physical harm from dangerous counterfeit products." (Amazon would be removed from the "notorious markets" list after Trump left office, but there are still rampant and legitimate claims about counterfeiting on its websites.)

———

Unable to leave home, Americans were bored and escaped into the world of Joe Exotic and big cat zoos by streaming Netflix's *Tiger King* and other shows (the number of hours people spent streaming content skyrocketed during the pandemic). Many people also decided to invest in their homes, focusing on upgrades that they otherwise may not have had time to do before. They bought devices to make their TVs smart and improve their home entertainment setups and purchased new security devices, like doorbell cameras.

For once, the company that had perfected the art of logistics was ill-equipped to fulfill the volume of orders coming in. Demand was that intense. Amazon found itself in an enviable position: it had so much business coming in, it even had to turn much of it away. For the first time in its history, during March 2020 Amazon moved to a model where it would prioritize "essential" items, like cleaning supplies, face masks, pantry items, and work-from-home accessories that customers needed to simply survive the lockdowns. Whole categories of "nonessential" items would be prohibited from being shipped to its warehouses in the US and Europe during this period in order for them to ensure that the essential goods could get out the door in Amazonian fashion.

It even turned off many of the bells and whistles it created over the course of its history to incentivize customers to add items to their carts. That was how much Amazon meant to everyday consumers.

But Amazon's prioritization of "essential items" revealed a curious pattern. Roku, the biggest maker of streaming devices in the US at the time, could no longer sell its streaming devices on Amazon's site. But

Amazon's Fire TV was selling rapidly. Ring doorbells, an Amazon brand, were still available for sale, but competitor Arlo had massive delays, as they weren't deemed "essential." The focus on "essential" goods, it appeared, wasn't simply products that were actually essential, like toilet paper, but included Amazon's own devices that were, objectively, nonessential, but made "essential" on their website.

Despite already making money hand over fist during the pandemic's early days, Amazon also managed to give its own brands a leg up over competitors on its website.

This was problematic for rival device makers. Customers tend to buy a product, and if they're satisfied, stick with the brand and buy whatever else is part of its suite of offerings. So, if during the pandemic shoppers purchased an Arlo doorbell, they would be more inclined to continue buying other Arlo smart security devices for the rest of their homes. The same went for customers who bought Amazon's device brands.

Amazon, when questioned by Congress why its own devices were able to ship during the pandemic while others weren't, chalked it up to a "mistake." Amazon became aware that shipments of certain Amazon devices that did not fall into the priority categories had been inadvertently included in the list of products with faster delivery promises. "This was unintentional," the company said in written responses to Congress.

Amazon corrected what they called a mistake on March 29, meaning that for more than a week, its own products shipped to customers and got embedded into their homes, while its main rivals did not.

Nonetheless, every Fire TV device bought because it was the only option on Amazon had lasting effects. Every time a customer bought a movie on that Fire TV, for instance, Amazon got a cut. For every Ring doorbell bought because it was the only option, Amazon had the chance to sell its monthly security plan.

And even as the pandemic brought companies to their knees from lost demand, Amazon was extracting its pound of flesh from partners. The company in recent years had become so large and so powerful that in order to have the privilege of becoming an Amazon supplier, it often demanded a piece of your business and future profits in the form of warrants. Warrants allow for companies or individuals to buy stakes in companies at potentially steep discounts compared to market value.

In April 2020, ChargePoint, one of the country's largest electric vehicle charging station networks, saw its sales begin to drop. Many of ChargePoint's clients were large companies installing their charging stations in the parking lots of corporate campuses. With people no longer reporting to the office, orders for the company's charging stations and software declined, and the company started struggling financially. Its CEO, Pasquale Romano, was forced to lay off 5 percent of its workforce while he figured out ChargePoint's next move. At the time, the privately held company was valued at around $1 billion.

On an early April conference call, Romano acknowledged that the company was struggling, but pointed to a major win. He told employees that ChargePoint had just landed a several-million-dollar deal to provide Amazon with charging stations for its European fleet of delivery vans. It was a much-needed lifeline for the company, which was also in the process of trying to secure additional equity financing.

In a June 30 email to his staff, Romano changed his tune: the Amazon deal was off. In an email with the subject line "Amazon," he wrote:

> Some of you may have been involved in requests with Amazon. We're proud of some of the commercial business we've had increasing engagement with them. We were recently awarded the charging business for most of their European delivery van pilots. Everyone involved was very excited to be included. We view Amazon business with caution because of their history of eventually vertically integrating out strategic suppliers. We'd rather be in a position to have their business and contend with the challenges than to not have it at all. It represents a learning opportunity for ChargePoint. Sounds great, right?
>
> So why walk away from a deal that seems so great? You read that correctly, we walked away. During contract negotiations, there were some terms that were highly irregular. For

confidentiality reasons I can't get into specifics. They had nothing to do with the price of our solutions nor the other parameters in a deal like this. The pricing was appropriate, support terms are stringent...Here's the lesson: regardless of how enticing a customer Amazon is, there's a point at which the deal becomes a bad deal. I believe that our counter proposal in hindsight was even more generous than we should have accepted. But in the frenzy of an early market you see the scramble for customers clouding business judgment all the time...We can't allow ourselves to place too large a premium on those elements and get ourselves into something we regret later. It's hard to evaluate this. We have to be disciplined to benefit ourselves in the long run.

The details that ChargePoint's CEO couldn't share with his team were tactics that showed a common move Amazon's muscle used during negotiations. ChargePoint was in the very late stages of signing the deal with Amazon's electric vehicle team when Amazon's corporate development team swooped in with different terms. They said Amazon was ready to go through with the negotiated contract (it took months to hammer out), but added that it wanted warrants for 15 percent of the company's shares on an "as diluted basis" in exchange, ChargePoint executives said. In effect, it meant ChargePoint would have had to give Amazon warrants for between 18 to 20 percent of its shares (and would potentially make Amazon a one-fifth owner of the company). If the company was acquired, those warrants would have automatically vested as part of Amazon's terms. ChargePoint's CEO couldn't accept the terms and said no. As a result, Amazon backed out of the deal.

ChargePoint later went public and at one point reached nearly $11 billion in market value.

ChargePoint's decision to refuse Amazon's terms is not one that many companies, finding themselves in similar situations, have the stomach to make. In fact, over the last decade, Amazon has made demanding warrants a routine business maneuver when finding vendors and suppliers for its various arms. Amazon would not disclose how many companies it has extracted warrants from. But sources have confirmed that Amazon has gotten warrants under market value from more than 100 private companies as well as a number of public company stakes. In the last few years in particular, the company has aggressively pushed the practice, Amazon executives said.

When Amazon began the practice a decade ago, there was no precedent to regularly add warrants to their deal negotiations. The team sleuthed through financial documents from the 2008 recession and found lending statements related to bank bailouts that came with warrants attached to them, an Amazon executive said. It was a revelation for the dealmaking team.

What Amazon's executives discovered was that some investors do often ask for warrants as part of risky deals. In these cases, they include them when they invest in companies that need to shore up their finances or need a bailout, such as when Berkshire Hathaway CEO Warren Buffett took warrants in companies he helped prop up during the financial crisis, like General Electric. But most companies don't make obtaining warrants a regular part of their commercial agreements, Amazon executives said.

So while it wasn't common practice, Amazon would adopt it. Internal documents spell out the company's formal program in place for obtaining warrants:

> Managers are expected to identify warrant opportunities and secure warrants as part of their day-to-day contract negotiations whenever we expect to have a material impact on a company and will create value beyond what's captured in the commercial relationship. Our impact may be material if any one (or combination) of the following is met:
>
> - Our relationship is expected to generate 10% or more of the company's revenue or profits (either through the scale of our direct business relationship or through new opportunities we create for the company); or

- The company can reference Amazon or its affiliates as customers through PR, marketing or other association; or
- We meaningfully contribute to a company's overall value (e.g., by validating technology, improving scalability, transferring core competencies, improving market segment positions, launching a new product or service, sharing data).

Since the program was adopted, a large portion of vendor or supplier deals Amazon struck would meet one of the three criteria laid out in its internal guidelines. In fact, the guidelines were so aggressive that if Amazon decided *not* to demand warrants in companies that hit the thresholds, they needed permission from Amazon's CEO or CFO in order to move forward on the deal. "Entering into an agreement that meets any of the criteria above and does <u>not</u> include warrants will require the below approvals: For transactions with spending, revenue or proceeds projected to be greater than US$10 million in value: Amazon.com Inc. CEO or CFO approval," the document says.

In its supplier deals that include warrants, Amazon throws its weight around to exact lucrative terms, knowing many companies won't refuse, according to former Amazon executives who worked on the deals. Amazon is required to report the dollar amount of warrants it has the option to buy on its balance sheet, and it amounts to $2 billion.

Amazon's first major warrants deal with a publicly traded vendor was in 2016. Amazon was seeking a cargo plane partner to help build out its massive logistics network. Executives reasoned that the company's potential partners were all smaller, lesser-known companies with stagnant growth, and that a major contract from Amazon would invigorate their stocks. According to a person who worked on the deal, Amazon wanted some of that potential upside.

It proposed a deal, with warrants, to Ohio-based Air Transport Services Group (ATSG). The aircraft-leasing company initially pushed back on the warrant stipulation. Its team flew to Seattle and had "intense, protracted negotiations" where Amazon got ATSG to agree to the structure. "It took a lot of convincing," one of the people in the meeting said.

As a result of the arrangement, Amazon currently owns around 19.5 percent of ATSG, making it the biggest shareholder.

Amazon executives knew it would need to lease many more planes to handle explosive growth in its delivery operation, and the success of striking a warrant deal with ATSG emboldened them to demand similar terms from other companies.

In talks with Atlas Air Worldwide Holdings, Amazon broached a ten-year leasing deal with similar terms. This time, Amazon demanded warrants that would amount to up to 20 percent of Atlas's equity over five years—with an option for 10 percent more later—depending on how much business it gave Atlas. Amazon also wanted the right to elect a director to Atlas's board, after meeting certain milestones.

People involved on both sides said that warrants were a condition of the Atlas partnership. "There was definitely a sense that if it wasn't agreed to there wouldn't be a deal," said one of the Atlas people. Atlas executives didn't want to pass up the revenue opportunity from Amazon and viewed giving up the warrants as the price of doing business.

When it announced the deal in May 2016, Atlas lauded the deal, including the equity arrangement. Its share price soared 27 percent that day. Such jumps have been common when Amazon has done warrant deals with publicly traded suppliers.

The strike price for the Atlas warrants was $37.50, slightly below where the shares were trading before the deal was announced. Amazon later exercised warrants for 9 percent of Atlas's stock and sold the shares, according to an Atlas spokeswoman. Amazon wouldn't comment on how much it made on its sale of Atlas stock.

Atlas has never done a similar deal, an Atlas spokeswoman said. Amazon did not elect a board member to the company's board, but the fact that the option was a condition of the deal speaks to the Charge-Point CEO's concerns about "eventually vertically integrating out suppliers." Amazon had strategically replaced its former partners over the years, eventually learning the mechanics of their businesses and bringing them in-house to be run by Amazon. And once Amazon mastered their craft and moved the capability in-house, it left its partners with a big void in their revenues from Amazon, which was often one of their biggest clients. By having access to a board seat, Amazon could sop up even more information about how a company operated and learn more about its sector. It would give them access to future road maps, long-term business plans, and competitive threats. That way if Amazon decided to flip the switch from customer to operator, it had all of the data at its fingertips to act.

And while Amazon extracted such conditions, it was smart about covering its tracks so as not to run afoul of regulators. Former Amazon executives said they avoided doing anything during supplier negotiations, such as putting its ultimatums in writing, that would leave a paper trail.

The breadth of the warrant deals spans Amazon's entire conglomerate structure, from warrant deals with call center operators to grocers and natural gas providers, and, according to former executives, most companies complied with the terms. In interviews, they also acknowledged that they found the deals to be unfair and one-sided, saying the companies weren't in a position to refuse and that most of the upside went to Amazon.

––––––––––

By 2020, Amazon was one the largest mega-conglomerates ever to exist, and the strength of each disparate business meant that many of its customers worked with not just one tentacle of the Amazon octopus, but with several. When sitting across the table from Amazon, other companies felt the full power of Amazon's ability to push its terms and services on them, or threaten punitive action.

Amazon had perfected a tactic of leveraging dominance in one business to compel partners to accept terms from another. These tactics went beyond typical product bundling and tough negotiating, in part because the company has threatened punitive action on vital services it offers, such as its retail platform. So, if you're a device maker that doesn't want to accept certain terms that Amazon's Alexa team is pushing, you might find yourself in a position where Amazon threatens to pull your ability to sell on Amazon.com, like it threatened smart thermostat maker Ecobee.

Partners often agree to Amazon's demands because of its power in a range of market sectors. In the spring of 2020, AT&T's WarnerMedia found itself in this exact spot. The company launched HBO Max, a new premium streaming service meant to compete with Netflix and other streaming behemoths during the early days of the COVID-19 pandemic, trying to capitalize on the binge watching going on at home.

But when HBO Max launched, it was conspicuously absent from Amazon's Fire TV. The reason was because, behind the scenes, the two companies were locked in a monthslong battle where WarnerMedia executives tried to resist Amazon's attempts to strong-arm the company into other agreements across Amazon's properties. The two companies had partnered together for years. HBO existed as a channel on Amazon Prime Video. As part of that deal, Amazon retained a cut of subscription fees customers paid to HBO each month, and Amazon owned the customer data.

When WarnerMedia was launching HBO Max, it no longer wanted to be a channel on Prime Video, which is part of the company's Prime platform. It just wanted to be able to distribute its app through Fire TV, which is a different Amazon unit within its devices business. Amazon told the company that it couldn't distribute through Fire TV without also remaining on Prime Video, according to several people involved in the discussions. In essence, Amazon was tying WarnerMedia's ability to use Amazon's Fire TV distribution to the condition that it also work with Prime Video.

Relationships between programmers and Amazon's Prime Video have often been tense. Amazon sells subscriptions to other entertainment companies' channels in return for a significant cut of that revenue as well as a slice of advertising inventory if the platform has commercials.

WarnerMedia's then CEO Jason Kilar, a former senior executive at Amazon who worked closely with Bezos during the company's early days, instructed his team not to back down. They wouldn't capitulate, and launched Max in May 2020 anyway. It was a risky move. The company had around 5 million subscribers via Amazon Prime Video that would have trouble accessing its new streaming platform.

In August, the two sides began negotiating again. Kilar and Jassy had come up together at Amazon and knew each other well. Warner-Media was a big customer of AWS. Kilar told Jassy that if the two sides couldn't reach an amicable deal, WarnerMedia would have to reconsider its cloud partnership.

In response, Amazon told WarnerMedia that HBO Max could distribute through Fire TV if it kept the channel on Prime for several months, spent a certain amount of advertising dollars on Amazon's properties, and kept its lucrative cloud computing contracts with AWS. Over the next few months, the two sides worked in earnest toward a deal.

But in November, Amazon called WarnerMedia and threw a curveball. The deal would be off unless WarnerMedia and its parent company AT&T agreed to spend an additional $1 billion on its cloud computing contract. The WarnerMedia executives were stunned. They couldn't justify that cost on AWS, which it was already spending a lot to use. But Amazon's power was on full display. In the end, they agreed to spend an additional $100 million with AWS, which was a costly deal, but it's emblematic of the devil's bargain partners make given Amazon's reach.

Executives from WarnerMedia complained about Amazon's behavior during the negotiations to the House antitrust subcommittee investigating Amazon's business practices, said people familiar with the probe. It also answered questions from other regulators.

As the pandemic raged on through the summer, Congress would finally get its chance to interview the man they had been seeking.

CHAPTER 16

Bezos (Finally) Goes to Washington

IT WAS JULY 2020, and Bezos was headed for the hot seat. This hearing would finally enable Congress to question all four of the Big Tech CEOs — of Google, Facebook, Apple, and Amazon — at the same time.

Behind the scenes, Amazon executives had been dead set for months on preventing the billionaire from appearing before Congress. In a meeting with top lawyers at Amazon, associate general counsel Andrew DeVore adamantly told attendees that "Jeff would testify over my dead body." That managed to be true for a very long time.

Internally, Amazon executives feared the optics. They had visions of the tobacco CEOs appearing before Congress in the 1990s, right hands in the air, shoulder to shoulder, coming across poorly. They didn't want history to repeat itself. They also worried the hearing could become a spectacle, with Bezos being pummeled with questions about his wealth and work conditions for warehouse workers.

Interestingly, while Seattle executives fought tooth and nail to keep Bezos from testifying, many Amazon executives in the DC office felt like the company was creating unnecessary tension with the committee. The DC team had employees who had worked on Capitol Hill before joining Amazon. They couldn't understand why Amazon was being so difficult about Bezos testifying. They also knew that Congress could subpoena Bezos, which would mean he would lose all leverage and be forced to appear, and that would look even worse. When Amazon's senior leaders heard more murmurs that Congress may use its subpoena power, they made the recommendation that Bezos testify.

It was yet another example of what had been a years-long disconnect between Seattle's directives and DC's. Executives in Amazon's DC office had an intimate knowledge of how things were done in Washington. They had held posts at the Department of Justice, the FTC, and other government offices on Capitol Hill. As stereotypically swampy as DC could be, they knew things were done by building relationships, not through scorched-earth tactics. The disconnect would reach its peak during this time.

The Seattle team didn't have much interest in building bridges in DC, and one senior public policy employee said they didn't have any understanding of how Washington worked. "It was DC 101," the person said.

It didn't help that Bezos had recently told his top lieutenants to "punch back" to criticism from DC and the press. While Bezos was spending more time in the capital between his *Washington Post* and Blue Origin ventures, the company's instincts were to aggressively battle detractors, a strategy its own DC team found confounding. It became emblematic of Amazon's confrontational relationship with both the media and legislators. The aggressive, often arrogant persona derived from the company's approach to public relations and how it did business often bled over into its public policy efforts.

Their approach was markedly different from their tech peers. Other technology CEOs were kissing rings on the Hill. Congressional staffers joked that Mark Zuckerberg could practically give a tour of Congress because he appeared in meetings so often.

Microsoft's Brad Smith was considered the gold standard on how to manage government relations. Smith, an attorney who was Microsoft's vice chair and president overseeing regulatory, legal, and corporate affairs, frequently visited DC to meet with top officials. He was very effective at getting his boss, Microsoft CEO Satya Nadella, invited to prestigious White House events and roundtables. Smith regularly had meetings at the White House during Trump's presidency and was adept at keeping the regulatory attention off of Microsoft, which was no easy feat as the broader techlash enveloped DC.

Both of the teams Carney headed — public relations and public policy — by contrast, found Carney to be enigmatic. The executive was routinely absent from making big decisions in both of his organizations and seemed to take very little interest in antitrust, even though it was one of the biggest obstacles facing Amazon, members of his team said.

He was absent at times, but no one really understood why. In Seattle, executives often just assumed that he was busy in DC on public policy issues. Meanwhile, his DC team assumed its boss wasn't around because he was busy working on public relations with the Seattle team. Because Carney maintained residences in both Seattle and Washington, DC, his teams just assumed that he was perhaps at the other location; if he wasn't in DC, he must be in Seattle, and vice versa. Over the years, many have told me they "have no idea what Jay Carney does." (His defenders note that Carney spent a lot of time personally advising Bezos, much of which would not be visible to his teams.)

And while executives at the other three Big Tech companies made inroads with congresspeople and other lawmakers who were determining legislation that focused on reining them in, Carney was not. Congressional staffers and their bosses involved in the investigation found the executive to be abrasive and not forthcoming with detailed responses when asked specific questions. Amazon quickly developed the worst reputation among the four companies the subcommittee was investigating.

"Amazon had the biggest middle-finger-to-Congress approach that I've ever seen with any company I've ever dealt with," said Garrett Ventry, former chief of staff to Representative Ken Buck, who worked closely on the congressional investigation.

I once asked Cicilline why he thought Amazon was adamant about not having Bezos appear before Congress. He responded, "Because of the power that they have in the marketplace, and because they have been allowed to behave with really no significant regulation or account-ability, they have developed an extraordinary sense of arrogance. So I think they're very unaccustomed to not answering questions from any-body about anything." He went on. "I also think in part because some of their behaviors were some of the most pernicious behavior we saw in the investigation, so I think they have good reason not to want to share their business practices or documents or testimony, because I think it would have established even more clearly what we were able to estab-lish during the course of the investigation which was that they were engaging in very anticompetitive, monopolistic behavior that was hurt-ing consumers and small businesses and innovation and generating them profits never seen in the history of the world."

As the hearing approached, the subcommittee went into overdrive, scheduling hours-long Microsoft Teams conference calls to prepare. They collected tens of millions of pages of emails and documents from the four companies, which took up 97 percent of the committee's server, and pored over them for evidence to present at the hearing.

Amazon also jumped into action. Its lobbyists littered Capitol Hill with Amazon's one-pager of talking points. They leaned especially on Democratic members of the committee, trying to get them to break from Cicilline's agenda, recalls one of the members. But the Democrats would not be moved; they would present a united front at the hearing.

Bezos prep started in May, with his team compiling briefing books for the CEO. In late June, over conference calls, they explained the pro-cess to him, worked on testimony, and played videos of other CEOs testifying before Congress as examples of what to do and what not to do. The videos included Mark Zuckerberg's awkward congressional hearing 2018, videos of Apple CEO Tim Cook, and even bank CEOs.

Two weeks before the hearing, Bezos holed up in the Seattle head-quarters with a handful of executives that included Jay Carney, David Zapolsky, public relations executive Drew Herdener, Brian Huseman, and lawyer Karen Dunn from law firm Paul, Weiss, Rifkind, Wharton & Garrison LLP. A few public policy employees from the DC office flew in.

Nearly every day thereafter, the team assembled in a conference room at Amazon's Day 1 building from midmorning until the early evening for intense prep sessions. This included mock trials.

Vaccines hadn't yet been released, so they took measures to not get each other, or Bezos, sick. The DC team wore masks and stayed in Airbnbs instead of hotels. Inside the conference room, everyone except Bezos initially wore masks, but the muffled sound and the inability to see facial expressions was making the prep challenging. So they ditched them. Instead, maintenance installed large panes of Plexiglas in the room in between each seat so that they could maintain precautions but forgo the masks.

Earlier in her career, Dunn had co-led debate prep for Barack Obama as part of his reelection campaign. She could be feisty. After a particularly cringeworthy debate against Mitt Romney in 2012, Dunn offered some not-so-subtle advice to Obama: "You need to punch him in the face!" In 2016, she co-led debate prep for Hillary Clinton, who was facing an unpredictable Donald Trump in the lead-up to the election.

Debate prep zeroes in on intuiting which questions and criticisms will be raised and crafting canned answers to deftly navigate them. It's also, for the preppers, a way to get under their client's skin, determine how they respond to questions that rankle them, and cause them to lose their cool, all to assess how best to teach them to handle all possible scenarios. Dunn went particularly hard at Bezos during prep, trying to rattle him. People involved said that, to his credit, Bezos never blew up during the mock questioning, even though he was hit with tough questions: on taxes, his wealth, and even George Floyd, whose murder by a police officer in 2020 sparked a nationwide reckoning and a summer of protests in which Floyd became a symbol of the systemic treatment of Black Americans by law enforcement.

Interestingly, Bezos was prepared to admit at the hearing that he paid too little in taxes. His meager tax bill was something that the billionaire was repeatedly criticized for, and the team expected the hearing to focus on it. In Bezos's view, tax reform was misguided. Raising income taxes wouldn't affect CEOs like him, whose salaries figured little in their wealth. Instead, capital gains taxes needed to be raised in order to fairly force Bezos and other billionaires like him to pay their fair share. (Congress ultimately didn't ask Bezos any questions about his personal wealth, much to the prep team's disappointment.)

The team also pelted him with questions about Amazon's private brand business, which they believed would be another big focus, and gave him scripted answers. They told him to reference Amazon's internal policy of not using individual third-party seller data. Bezos insisted on adding a caveat, according to people involved in the prep. He wanted to add "we have a policy, but I can't say it's never been violated." People involved in the prep said he was insistent on that clause so that he wouldn't perjure himself. (An Amazon spokesman said, "It is not advisable for a senior leader at a company the size of Amazon to unequivocally state a policy has never been broken.")

Unsurprisingly, Bezos — who instituted a culture of writing six-page memos at his company, and who would scrupulously edit or rewrite public statements himself in the early years — wrote his own opening statement. It began about his unwed seventeen-year-old mother pregnant with him while in high school. It would show his humble beginnings and paint him as someone who would go on to fulfill the American dream. The public policy team didn't expect the personal anecdotes, but thought it was a good idea: it would humanize him as an entrepreneur with an against-all-odds background making it in America, a savvy businessman who innovated his way to the top. People involved with the prep said the main goals were for Bezos to answer the questions truthfully and to come across as humble and respectful.

Typically before a big hearing, the CEOs do a requisite friendly phone call to thank each member for their time and for being open to hearing their point of view. Both Tim Cook and Mark Zuckerberg called members a week before the hearing. It's a way for CEOs to ingratiate themselves to committee members ahead of what will likely be a tense affair. Yet, Bezos was conspicuously silent. Then, all of a sudden, the day before the hearing, representatives for Bezos called the members to say they could chat with the billionaire. Many turned him down.

Democratic representative Pramila Jayapal's district includes Seattle. Since being elected to Congress in 2016, she has offered many times to meet with Bezos, though the invites have gone unanswered. His employees make up a large chunk of her constituents, and his business has direct effects on Seattle and its surrounding areas. Jayapal also sits on the antitrust subcommittee.

"The day before the hearing, I got a call that he wanted to talk to me," Jayapal recalled. She declined because the invite was so transparent. "I just said, 'I'd be happy to set up a time with you after the hearing.'"

Amazon noted that because the hearing date was changed, they were unsure of when the hearing would be rescheduled, and because of the pandemic, normal routines of dropping into a committee members' office before a hearing were disrupted.

For the hearing, the antitrust subcommittee had requested that each of the CEOs testify separately, but Bezos's camp vehemently rejected that idea. They wanted him to testify alongside Zuckerberg, Pichai, and Cook because they were convinced that in that setting, most of the questions would be directed at Facebook and Google.

But Amazon's team was wrong. The reason for the hearing "was largely about Amazon. All of the other CEOs had testified before," said one member of the antitrust subcommittee. Bezos would not be spared.

———

The hearing was originally set for July 27, but then an unforeseen tragedy took place: ten days prior, Representative John Lewis, the legendary civil rights activist and long-standing congressman from Georgia, died. As a matter of respect, with Lewis lying in state in the Capitol rotunda, the subcommittee asked if it could reschedule the hearing. Three of the CEOs agreed without question. Facebook even rescheduled its earnings announcement to accommodate the new date.

Meanwhile, Bezos was the only CEO to refuse, with his team saying he could meet only on the original date but at a different time if need be, said some of the people involved with the investigation. Committee members viewed this as arrogant. Some were even outraged by it. "I don't think people in his orbit understood that what he was saying was essentially 'I am more important than John Lewis's memorial,'" said a congressional aide who worked on the committee. Cicilline even pulled a power move to make Amazon comply. While Carney was in a meeting with Huseman and other public policy officials, his phone rang. It was the speaker of the House, Nancy Pelosi. She wanted to talk about the new hearing date and make him and, by extension, his boss come to their senses.

After that call, Amazon relented. The hearing was rescheduled for July 29, and Bezos would accommodate. An Amazon spokesperson denied that the company was difficult about rescheduling.

The afternoon of the hearing, members of the antitrust subcommittee filed back into room 2141 on Capitol Hill. This time, things looked different. The members wore face masks and sat apart to abide by social-distancing measures.

Some of the congresspeople even flew into DC for the hearing. The CEOs, meanwhile, opted not to fly in via their private jets for the meeting because of the pandemic. Instead, they joined via a Webex teleconference line. The year's most highly anticipated and dramatic inquisition would essentially be like a giant Zoom call, complete with technical difficulties. The room had an Orwellian feel to it, recounted one of the attendees. Beamed in on a giant screen up high were some of the world's richest and most powerful men.

"Many of the practices used by these companies have harmful economic effects. They discourage entrepreneurship, destroy jobs, hike costs, and degrade quality. Simply put, they have too much power," Cicilline said in his opening statement. Lina Khan sat to his right, wearing a navy blue mask and powder blue blazer. "As gatekeepers of the digital economy, these platforms enjoy the power to pick winners and losers, to shake down small businesses, and enrich themselves while choking off competitors. Their ability to dictate terms, call the shots, upend entire sectors, and inspire fear represent the powers of a private government. Our founders would not bow before a king, nor should we bow before the emperors of the online economy."

Each CEO then gave his opening statement. Wearing a dark suit and tie, Bezos began by going to impressive lengths to portray himself, the world's richest man at the time, as an everyman. His personal story is undeniably compelling and heartfelt — his seventeen-year-old, unwed pregnant mother taking him to her classes at night; his adopted father coming over from Cuba as a teenager without knowing English. His roots were humble, though his empire had made him worth, at the time, around $189 billion, which naturally placed him in elite company, as far away from an everyman as possible.

He then hit all of the Jay Carney–approved talking points. Amazon is a giant employer in this country, creating more jobs in the US than any other company over the last decade. "The retail market we participate in is extraordinarily large and competitive. Amazon accounts for less than 1 percent of the $25 trillion global retail market and less than 4 percent of US retail," he recited, a well-worn figure Amazon had rolled out in recent years to combat the narrative forming about its size. Amazon declined repeated requests to answer questions about how it derives the 4 percent figure. In 2021, Amazon sold more than $325 billion worth of retail goods in the U.S., according to sources, a staggering amount of product.

Once the questions began, something strange occurred — for the entire first hour of questioning, not a single question was directed at Bezos. It turned out that the world's richest technology baron was having technology problems. Cicilline called a recess so that someone could fix the connection.

After the recess, with his Webex connection now working, Bezos was available to finally answer. Despite missing an hour of the hearing, he would end up receiving fifty-nine questions, just two short of what Google's CEO fielded. Tim Cook of Apple was the big winner: only thirty-five questions were directed at him.

In a particularly tense exchange, Representative Jayapal interrogated

Bezos on whether his private label team uses third-party seller information to make products.

"Mr. Bezos, in July 2019, your employee Nate Sutton told me under oath in this committee that Amazon does not, quote, 'use any specific seller data when creating its own private brand product,'" she said. "So let me ask you, Mr. Bezos, does Amazon ever access and use third-party seller data when making business decisions? And just a yes or no will suffice, sir."

Bezos stuttered and offered a brief introduction before saying: "I can't answer that question yes or no. What I can tell you is we have a policy against using seller-specific data to aid our private label business. But I can't guarantee you that that policy has never been violated," Bezos responded, prefacing his prepped answer as he said he would.

Jayapal then referenced the 2020 *Wall Street Journal* story I reported, which had driven Cicilline to question whether Sutton had perjured himself back in 2019, and asked if Bezos denied the findings in the report.

"I'm familiar with the *Wall Street Journal* article that you're talking about, and we continue to look into that very carefully. I'm not yet satisfied that we've gotten to the bottom of it, and we're going to keep looking at it."

"I'll take that as you're not denying that," said Jayapal. "I will tell you, a former Amazon employee in third-party sales and recruitment told this committee, quote, 'There's a rule, but there's nobody enforcing or spot checking. They just say, "Don't help yourself to the data." It's a candy shop. Everyone can have access to anything they want.'"

Subcommittee members were shocked that Bezos and his team didn't have a more definitive answer, especially given what the article detailed. Amazon knew Bezos would be probed on its private brand practices. But the internal investigation was not yet finished.

For the next two hours, Bezos was barraged with questions on private label practices, counterfeits on the site, how his company treats its sellers, and whether it steals technology from entrepreneurs via its Alexa Fund.

Bezos would, at times, appear contrite after learning about the ways his company treats sellers. After a congresswoman played an audio clip of a seller who was blocked from selling on the site without reason, he said, "It does not at all to me seem like the right way to treat her, and I am surprised by that."

More often than not, he didn't seem familiar with the way Amazon operates, at least in the ways the committee was framing his company's practices. When a congresswoman asked Bezos how much money he was willing to lose to bring competitor Diapers.com to its knees, he responded with: "I—I don't know the answer—the direct answer to your question." In many instances, he said he was unfamiliar with what the representatives were referencing and offered to circle back with answers once he knew.

Congressman Joe Neguse (D., Colorado) brought up whether Amazon was stifling innovation through its dealmaking and venture capital arm. In order to illustrate, Neguse referenced an anecdote from our recent *Wall Street Journal* story.

"I read that article, but I didn't remember that piece of it. I—I apologize for that. I don't know the specifics of that situation, and I would be happy to get back to your office with more information about that," Bezos said in response.

Suddenly, the man who had all the data and the wherewithal to build Amazon the way he did was speechless. (Nearly a century ago, when John Rockefeller met with the commission of the Ohio Supreme Court to address Standard Oil's business practices, he also was short on answers. One newspaper headline after the inquisition read "Rockefeller Imitates a Clam" and went on to say "The virtue of forgetting, which is one of the most valuable virtues that a monopolist can have under cross-examination, is possessed by Mr. Rockefeller in its highest degree.")

"Jeff was under oath, and needed to be 100% sure of his answers. Amazon comprises disparate businesses, each with its own customers and operational complexities," said an Amazon spokesman, adding that Bezos answered the lawmakers' questions to the best of his ability, with the company following up with answers that he couldn't give during the hearing.

The congressional committee viewed the hearing as a win. The committee proved that they knew these companies intimately, had done their research, and were holding them accountable for transgressions they deemed essential to the inquiry.

But Bezos's team viewed the hearing as a win as well. Back in Seattle, after the testimony, Bezos thanked the team for all their hard work in preparing him. Many on the team had worked eighty-hour weeks leading up to the hearing. As he and some senior leaders on the prep team headed to another meeting, others went to an outdoor patio at Amazon's offices for some beers and to decompress while some went for dinner in a parking lot of a Seattle restaurant. They could finally relax for a bit after what felt like a marathon of work. For the most part, the team viewed Bezos as getting through the hours of questioning "with no major flesh wounds," said a person involved in the prep. But, they acknowledged, it was also clear that while Bezos got through this round, the scrutiny was just beginning. Hearings, testimony, and probes into Amazon's business were likely to become the new normal.

———

Around the same time as the CEO hearing, Amazon was also receiving inquiries from the Federal Trade Commission, then still under the Trump administration, which was in the process of investigating the company. The agency requested loads of information, including internal documents, emails, and business plans.

An executive on the Marketplace side of the business was asked for his documents and business plans, which included notes written in the margins of printouts. The executive was in the midst of leaving Amazon for a new job, so left a pile of the documents on the desk in his office for the legal team to pass on to the FTC. Strangely, the documents went missing. Amazon said that the executive left in the midst of the COVID-19 pandemic and that his office had been given to someone else. When they went to his office to collect the documents, "we learned that the space had already been cleaned and emptied out for a new employee — who was not involved in the FTC investigation. As a result, we were not able to collect these materials," an Amazon spokesman said. I called Amazon in March 2022 asking for comment about the missing documents. It was only at that point that Amazon alerted the FTC about the missing documents, even though they went missing in August 2020. "The WSJ story had no impact on Amazon's decision whether to disclose to the FTC the inadvertent disposal of a limited number of hard-copy documents," Amazon said.

As the summer wore on, Amazon's public policy team cozied up to presidential candidate Joe Biden's campaign. In August, Carney participated in a panel as part of the Democratic Party convention that addressed job creation in rural America.

On the virtual conference call, Carney sat in front of a framed Joe Biden poster and touted Amazon's role as a major employer. "We have added 600,000 jobs in the US in the last ten years, the most of any company anywhere," he said. While true, the vast majority of those jobs were warehouse roles, but Carney didn't elaborate.

He also corrected the moderator. Amazon isn't the biggest retailer in the country, Walmart is, he said, repeating the well-worn 4 percent of US retail statistic that Amazon touts.

Yet, inside Amazon's legal department, paranoia arose around how much longer Amazon could deflect to Walmart on questions of size and scale. Amazon typically would cast Walmart as the bigger player when it came to the size of its retail sales, but an internal memo from 2021 prepared by Amazon's legal team indicated that Amazon would soon catch up. "Since the early days of antitrust populism against Amazon, we have leaned into a simple message to put concerns about Amazon's size and its related economic power in the retail industry into perspective: Amazon's retail sales are smaller than Walmart's," the memo reads. "With Amazon's continued growth, however, total sales through Amazon will be approaching Walmart's," it continues, before providing talking points to downplay Amazon's growth. One reads: "Nothing is forever. Argue that historically, there has always been churn in the position of the largest retailer, and the business models they were employing E.g., Walmart with its superstores overtook Sears as the largest retailer in 1991, while Sears, which had initially employed a mail order model, took the position of largest retailer in the 1960s."

Over the next few months, Amazon's employees and PACs would funnel money into Biden's campaign. Employees from Amazon made up the fifth-largest source of donations to the Biden campaign, after only Alphabet employees and Microsoft employees, donating more than $2.3 million to the campaign.

On October 6, 2020, Congress unleashed a scathing report that was the culmination of its sixteen-month investigation into Big Tech. It said that each of the four technology companies had monopoly power in certain areas. The 449-page report presented its findings on each company and made recommendations on how to totally reshape the way technology companies operate. In short, it called for legislation that, at its most extreme, could break them up, or, at the very least, make them operate more fairly.

The report attacked Amazon's copycat tendencies, its "bullying" of third-party sellers, practices related to Fulfillment by Amazon, its advertising businesses, and a litany of other anticompetitive behaviors it found in interviews and by poring over 24,299 internal emails and documents from Amazon.

The subcommittee had determined that Amazon had amassed "monopoly power" over sellers on its site. The report had more pages dedicated to Amazon than any of the other companies.

"To put it simply, companies that once were scrappy, underdog startups that challenged the status quo have become the kinds of monopolies we last saw in the era of oil barons and railroad tycoons," the report proclaimed.

One of its major recommendations was to prevent these giant technology companies from making products that compete with sellers on their platforms. The consequences of such legislation would be most deleterious for Amazon. If lawmakers were to adopt the suggestion, it could cause Amazon to exit business lines, such as its private label and devices businesses. Other measures were aimed at stopping self-preferencing.

After it released the report that Tuesday afternoon, Cicilline and other committee members went to work on drafting legislation to address their recommendations.

––––––––––

That same month, Brian Huseman called a meeting for his public policy team. The executive wanted to explain where he viewed the team's efforts. He called it Public Policy 3.0, or the third stage of Amazon's public policy efforts. Public Policy 1.0 was the townhouse stage, he told attendees, where Amazon bootstrapped its public policy work with very little staff and just a handful of issues. Public Policy 2.0 was building up the team and making strategic hires. They were now at Public Policy 3.0. They had the staff, and they had the resources; it was now time to take their efforts to the next level, he said. As part of this, Amazon's team would become proactive, not reactive, when it came to imminent legislation that involved them or curtailed their businesses. As part of their efforts, they were to be "hyperlocal," building relationships from the ground up across the country.

It seemed like Amazon's public policy shop had hit its stride. It was flush with resources and had the employees to execute Huseman's vision of going to the next level. And it was just in time for a showdown on the horizon. The end of 2020 saw a spate of actions that tightened the screws on Big Tech. In October 2020, the Department of Justice sued Google for violating antitrust laws related to its search distribution contracts. In December, the FTC filed a lawsuit against Facebook for illegal monopolization. The antimonopoly momentum was finally building in significant ways in the US, a backlash that was reminiscent of governmental actions that followed the Gilded Age.

CHAPTER 17

"Too Much Toxicity to Make It Worthwhile"

THROUGHOUT 2020, AMAZON FACED the prospect of another four years of a Trump White House, which had been challenging for Amazon and its founder, to say the least.

But Carney felt confident that Biden would become president. In the months leading up to the election, the Amazon executive's Twitter account was filled with tweets lauding his former boss. In one, Carney donned a blue surgical mask while holding a "Biden Harris" sign. In another, he stands next to a sign for the Biden Environmental Training Center in Delaware, donning cargo shorts and sunglasses. Still, as the last election had proven to Amazon's public policy team, a Trump win could not be ruled out, and the race appeared pretty close because of late-counted mail-in ballots, creating a tense situation for most Americans, including Amazon's top ranks.

On November 7, 2020, after days of counting ballots, Biden was declared the winner. Carney celebrated the news: "Very excited by the fact that I'm going to need a new mousepad! #46, @JoeBiden!" he tweeted, with a photo of a white mouse pad with a crest saying "Vice President of the United States" with Biden's signature underneath. He changed his Twitter header to a photo of himself with Biden's arm draped around his neck, the two of them grinning, at a press event years earlier.

This was the moment Carney had been waiting for. He was hired the year before the 2016 election, with the hopes of being an effective political operator. But Trump's shocking win left him on the outs with a Republican administration for four years. But finally the Democrats were back in office. Even more important, *his* Democrats were in office.

As Biden built out his team, Carney looked more and more well positioned. Ron Klain, whom Carney had worked closely with while in the Obama White House when Klain served as Vice President Biden's chief of staff, was named President Biden's chief of staff. (Notably, Klain had also advocated for Carney to get the press secretary job under President Obama.) Others Carney knew well would get jobs: Antony Blinken, whom Carney performed with in a DC-area jam band, was named secretary of state, and Jen Psaki, a friend from the Obama years, was appointed as White House press secretary.

After four years of being sidelined as Amazon took big meetings with the Trump White House and influential Republican decision makers, Carney looked like he'd finally have the influence in DC the company had hired him to wield.

But as it turns out, Carney had overestimated the reception of his former colleagues as the emissary for Amazon. Times had changed; it wouldn't be a warm welcome.

———

One morning in February 2021, chief of staff Ron Klain's phone lit up with a text from Carney. The text was a complaint. Days earlier, President Biden and his staff welcomed the chief executives of JPMorgan Chase, Lowe's, Gap, and Walmart to the White House to talk about a proposed stimulus package meant to revive the economy amid the pandemic. It particularly stung that the White House invited the CEO of Walmart, one of Amazon's fiercest competitors. Carney pleaded with his former colleague to consider Amazon for future events. He expressed his frustration at the slight and reminded Klain that Amazon is the country's second-largest employer and had hired hundreds of thousands of people to handle demand during the first waves of COVID-19. Despite their long history of working together, there would be no special treatment or favoritism. In fact, some days it felt like the opposite to Amazon.

The text was one in a series of frustrated messages from Carney, which were often angry in tone, said White House aides. Some even referred to the texts as "firebombs."

In December, Carney shot off another message to Klain. It was in response to a *Politico* article, which claimed that Walmart had become a "key ally" of the Biden administration. The report referenced yet another meeting between the president and Walmart CEO Doug McMillon. It got under Carney's skin. The article wasn't wrong, as the White House was in pretty frequent communication with the Walmart CEO and his executives about inflation. Given the volume of business Walmart did in grocery and retail, the company was a good proxy for the broader economy and could share details of where they were experiencing price hikes from vendors with the administration. (Around this time, inflation was beginning to tick up from rising gas prices and food costs.) Carney questioned Klain on the relationship. Carney remembered the not-so-distant history of Walmart being considered a public enemy of the Democratic Party. (In 2016, liberals ranked Walmart as the top company on the Fortune 500 list that was the "worst for America.") Five years later, it seemed like the company was being welcomed with open arms by the Biden administration. To add to the frustration, Carney learned that White House officials worried that inviting Bezos to presidential roundtables and other events would rankle Progressive politicians, such as Amazon critics like Senator Elizabeth Warren and Senator Bernie Sanders. As one person put it: Amazon and Bezos "had too much toxicity to make it worthwhile."

Knowing politics, Carney understood the optics, but he pushed ahead. He tried making the case that, criticism notwithstanding, Amazon had been raising wages; in fact, it paid more per hour than Walmart. Sure, Amazon was anti-union, but it's not as if Walmart had unionized its workforce. And again, what about all the jobs Amazon had provided when the country was in need? The arguments fell on deaf ears.

Amazon had hired Carney with the understanding that he would get their senior leadership team a seat at the table with the president, influencing policy and making connections on Capitol Hill. Yet it wasn't working. Then there were times where Carney refused to use his connections. When the DC staff asked Carney to call Secretary of State Blinken about a matter, Carney, who often spoke about being close to him, told his team: "I can't do that; he's a friend." The administration had changed, but the executive's efforts felt fruitless to many in Amazon's public policy office.

"Initially, people thought Jay would be an asset," said a senior Amazon public policy official. "As far as engaging with the administration, that obviously didn't really pan out. Inside of Amazon, there were sort of whispers like, 'He has no juice with the administration.'"

———

Amazon's boilerplate statement when answering questions about antitrust investigations was "All large organizations attract the attention of regulators, and we welcome that scrutiny." But in reality, Bezos encouraged a combative stance. In March 2021, arrows were being slung from all directions; yet rather than being diplomatic, like most corporations that set up meetings with legislators to explain their policy positions or engaged in a public relations campaign to change public sentiment, Amazon took a different approach.

For months, Bezos had felt like Washington, DC, was piling on Amazon. Politicians were openly attacking the company as its workers in Alabama sought to unionize, siding with the workers and characterizing Amazon as heartless. And like the other attacks, they came from both sides of the aisle. In mid-March, Republican senator Marco Rubio surprisingly backed the warehouse workers' unionization efforts in an op-ed for *USA Today*. "Here's my standard: When the conflict is between working Americans and a company whose leadership has decided to wage culture war against working-class values, the choice is easy—I support the workers. And that's why I stand with those at Amazon's Bessemer warehouse today," he wrote. "Uniquely malicious corporate behavior like Amazon's justifies a more adversarial approach to labor relations. It is no fault of Amazon's workers if they feel the only option available to protect themselves against bad faith is to form a union," the senator continued. "But Amazon should understand that waging a war on small businesses and working-class values has burned bridges with former allies."

In Bezos and the S-Team's view, there wasn't another company in American history that had received such hostility from lawmakers. Yes, politicians at varying times had attacked industries like Big Pharma and Big Tobacco, but the vitriol directed purely at Amazon was unprecedented, they felt. The treatment was even different from what the rest of Big Tech was experiencing, they argued. While Facebook had become a political pariah as well, they felt Amazon's treatment was even worse.

And the blows kept landing. On March 22, President Biden announced that he would nominate Lina Khan as a commissioner of the Federal Trade Commission. There are five commissioners at the agency, including the chair. For Amazon, it was as if Biden had hand-picked the candidate it was most fearful of having at the FTC. (Behind the scenes, Senator Elizabeth Warren and other progressives were pushing the administration to name Khan.)

On March 24, Amazon's retail CEO Dave Clark openly attacked Bernie Sanders on Twitter. The Vermont senator had long condemned the company for its treatment of warehouse workers and was planning a visit to Amazon's Alabama warehouse, where workers were nearing a historic vote to unionize.

Clark's tweets were the product of meetings among some of Amazon's top leaders, including Jeff Bezos. On these conference calls, Bezos, Clark, Carney, Andy Jassy, and public-relations executives Drew Herdener and Ty Rogers discussed how Washington had it wrong, in their opinion, and how leaders were unfairly targeting Amazon. Bezos and Clark were known for being the most pugnacious of the group, so Clark started devising a tweet focused on Sanders. (Clark had a reputation as a pot stirrer on Twitter. After then CEO of FedEx Fred Smith called the notion of Amazon disrupting FedEx's logistics business "fantastical," Clark cheekily tweeted: "Ho!Ho!Ho! Have a Fantastical Holiday everyone!!!," with a photo of an Amazon Prime branded jet.)

Bezos had a theory that nobody paid attention to you on Twitter unless you had an edge. He felt that there was limited upside to tweeting out the facts politely. Nobody would read or engage with them. Rather than simply rebut criticism or correct the record, he urged his leadership team to deliver biting tweets that could garner attention.

On the call, Clark read a version of the Bernie tweet he eventually sent. Everyone weighed in, tweaking words here and there to make their point. There was a lot of testosterone flying, people involved said, but no one pushed back on the tone. One person involved said there was no way to make Sanders dislike Amazon any less than he already did, so they weren't worried about offending the senator.

When drafts began circulating that read as unprofessional, Huseman and a DC public relations executive flagged them. They argued that, while it was fine to push back against inaccuracies, it wasn't acceptable to personally attack legislators. Soon, the two of them found themselves removed from the email chain, and Clark's tweet went live.

"I welcome @SenSanders to Birmingham and appreciate his push for a progressive workplace. I often say we are the Bernie Sanders of employers, but that's not quite right because we actually deliver a progressive workplace for our constituents: a $15 minimum wage, health care from day one, career progression, and a safe and inclusive work environment. So if you want to hear about $15 an hour and health care, Senator Sanders will be speaking downtown. But if you would like to make at least $15 an hour and have good health care, Amazon is hiring," Clark tweeted.

At the time, many elected officials were siding with the workers seeking a union and casting Amazon management as dismissive of their demands. In general, the S-Team was very sensitive to this type of negative coverage of the company. "The way the government was weighing in on this—particularly on some of these labor issues that they didn't know anything about—just didn't feel right," said an S-Team member. Bezos in particular was aggressive in wanting to defend the company and fight back. "For a month or so he'd been an 'every blade of grass' guy. He'd say, 'we can't let anything factually inaccurate stay. We have to go push back.' He went on a tear," the person said.

Indeed, the hours spent by one of the world's richest men and his very powerful team of executives on how best to troll a sitting senator on Twitter reveals how important this seemingly absurd task was for them.

The tweet immediately created a backlash, with the president of the Retail, Wholesale and Department Store Union calling the tweets "arrogant and tone deaf." Sanders responded to the tweet, saying "All I want to know is why the richest man in the world, Jeff Bezos, is spending millions trying to prevent workers from organizing a union so they can negotiate for better wages, benefits and working conditions."

Members of Amazon's executive team were proud of themselves. They thought they had landed their blow. They did, though by going nuclear and waging a war on legislators so deliberately, they managed to destroy relationships on the Hill — already a delicate dance. It even pissed off Amazon's employees. What's more, the public was dumbfounded and made their feelings known online.

Later that day, Congressman Mark Pocan of Wisconsin chimed in, responding to Clark's tweet by saying: "Paying workers $15/hr doesn't make you a 'progressive workplace' when you union-bust & make workers urinate in water bottles." The latter was referencing scathing reports where several Amazon drivers describe urinating in bottles as to not waste time finding a bathroom, which could slow down their delivery times.

Years earlier, Amazon had hosted Pocan for a tour of its Kenosha, Wisconsin, warehouse, and the visit stuck with him. He recalls being impressed by the technology and innovation on display, while also taken aback by the backbreaking physical labor the warehouse workers had to endure.

"I made the comment to the person I went to the warehouse with that we should take a video of one of the pickers and show that at every high school in America. Every student would want to get a high-skilled job or college degree," he said. Since then, when Pocan read reports of

Amazon workers saying they were under so much pressure to make their numbers that they didn't have time for actual bathroom breaks, he believed them.

This time, in response to the backlash, Amazon tweeted from its corporate account, @AmazonNews: "You don't really believe the peeing in bottles thing, do you? If that were true, nobody would work for us. The truth is that we have over a million incredible employees around the world who are proud of what they do, and have great wages and health care from day one. We hope you can enact policies that get other employers to offer what we already do." The company's social media team wrote this tweet, not the executive group, though they were emulating the aggressive tone set by Clark.

Amazon got pummeled in the replies, with some users speculating that the account was hacked. Others called the company arrogant, and lambasted Amazon for disputing accounts from its own warehouse workforce. The tweet was so shocking that reporters wrote about it, making it a news story in and of itself. Pocan also responded to their corporate account's tweet: "And yes, I do believe your workers. You don't?"

Amazon's public policy team in DC was horrified. Neither tweet was run by them, and what's worse, Huseman had recently made major inroads with Pocan, who was co-chair of the congressional LGBTQ+ Equality Caucus. Huseman had had dinner with the congressman and his husband at an Equality PAC event and had developed a good rapport.

What's more, Amazon was coming under more and more scrutiny for its power. Making enemies of sitting congresspeople and senators who might vote on bills that would affect the company seemed confounding.

"It was such an aggressive tone with someone who is a policymaker," Pocan recalled. "It was a huge public relations failure."

Despite the blowback online, and despite the fact that Amazon's tweets drew even more attention to its treatment of warehouse workers, Bezos and his deputies did not pivot. They next turned their ire toward Senator Elizabeth Warren.

The Massachusetts senator had long expressed her view that

Amazon was too big and needed to be broken up. On March 25, she tweeted that Amazon didn't pay its fair share in taxes and that she would be introducing a bill to address that. Amazon responded from its corporate account in a string of tweets starting with: "You make the tax laws @SenWarren; we just follow them. If you don't like the laws you've created, by all means, change them. Here are the facts: Amazon has paid billions of dollars in corporate taxes over the past few years alone."

Warren responded: "I didn't write the loopholes you exploit, @amazon—your armies of lawyers and lobbyists did. But you bet I'll fight to make you pay your fair share. And fight your union-busting. And fight to break up Big Tech so you're not powerful enough to heckle senators with snotty tweets."

Amazon's corporate account replied: "This is extraordinary and revealing. One of the most powerful politicians in the United States just said she's going to break up an American company so that they can't criticize her anymore." Bezos and his deputies had their hands all over the language.

Again, the company was skewered online. People equated them to Standard Oil. Some said that even though they shopped on Amazon, they were turned off by their petty social media behavior. Even the blue-check accounts weighed in, with one verified user responding: "Look how completely unethical you have to be to work for the @amazonnews social media team. Utterly without morals, just pure trash."

After a week of blowback, Amazon issued an apology about the "pee" tweet, as it was called internally. Not only was it insensitive; it was also inaccurate. In a blog post, the company backpedaled to assuage the situation.

> This was an own-goal, we're unhappy about it, and we owe an apology to Representative Pocan. First, the tweet was incorrect. It did not contemplate our large driver population and instead wrongly focused only on our fulfillment centers. A typical Amazon fulfillment center has dozens of restrooms, and employees are able to step away from their workstation at any

time. If any employee in a fulfillment center has a different experience, we encourage them to speak to their manager and we'll work to fix it.

Second, our process was flawed. The tweet did not receive proper scrutiny. We need to hold ourselves to an extremely high accuracy bar at all times, and that is especially so when we are criticizing the comments of others.

Third, we know that drivers can and do have trouble finding restrooms because of traffic or sometimes rural routes, and this has been especially the case during Covid when many public restrooms have been closed.

Yet, Amazon didn't apologize for the prior tweets as being too aggressive and unprofessional, only that it had bad information. The apology included: "We will continue to speak out when misrepresented, but we will also work hard to always be accurate."

One of the executives in the meetings to formulate the Sanders and Warren tweets says that if not for the corporate account's "pee" tweet, the whole exchange would have been a win. "I think if I could go back and unwind that whole cycle I would, but mostly because of the pee in the bottle tweet," he said.

Huseman texted Pocan to apologize: "Congressman Pocan, this is Brian Huseman from Amazon. (We've met at Equality Caucus Events.) I wanted to make you aware of this blog post apologizing to you for the company's recent Twitter comments. I also want to personally apologize to you on behalf of the company. I know it's Easter Weekend but I can speak at any time or schedule something formally with your office. Thank you. Brian."

Pocan didn't respond. Amazon had blown up the relationship.

As a result of the "pee" tweet, Amazon social media instituted a rule that any acerbic response directed at a legislator had to be approved by a senior member of the team before being released.

Bezos also began acting differently after the exchange. He stopped pushing Amazon's executives to post cutting messages on Twitter, according to some S-Team members. Just before officially retiring as

CEO in July 2021, he introduced two new leadership principles that contrasted deeply with the culture as it had existed: "Strive to be Earth's Best Employer" and "Success and Scale Bring Broad Responsibility." Internally, many found the new leadership principles to be ironic. For one, Bezos had a view that employees were expendable, says a former S-Team member. And its combative engagement with regulators investigating the company's power and size didn't convey that Amazon took the responsibility of its size seriously. A person in the original tweet drafting meetings said the new leadership principles seemed like a reaction to the social media fiasco. An Amazon spokesperson says the new leadership principles were unrelated to the tweets.

———————

Just before Bezos stepped down, the Biden administration dealt Amazon possibly its deadliest blow. On June 15, 2021, Amazon's public policy team was watching an antitrust hearing a Senate Judiciary subcommittee was conducting on smart home technology. They had prepped an Amazon lawyer from the Alexa team to testify for the hearing. Over the course of the questioning, Senator Amy Klobuchar leaked a bit of news. "Lina Khan was just named the chair of the FTC. An interesting development from an antitrust standpoint."

A collective "What the fuck?" was let out by some of Amazon's top policy and legal executives. Emails and texts started flying back and forth. "Did Senator Klobuchar just say that Lina would chair the whole agency?" they asked.

Amazon officials quickly worked the phones, contacting their sources. Had the senator misspoken? No, she had not. The antitrust wunderkind, whose rise was tied to identifying Amazon as a monopoly, would head the agency regulating it. "This was an 'oh shit' moment," said one Amazon public policy official. And it wasn't just Amazon that was shocked; it even came as a big surprise for many top officials at the FTC.

Months earlier, Amazon's top brass had gotten bent out of shape by the fact that Khan would have any role at the FTC. Now she would be in charge?

The appointment set off warnings inside Amazon's DC office and even its Seattle headquarters. Over the years, as Amazon got bigger and bigger, the company had clung to the consumer welfare standard. "Largely, we've thought about it mostly the same way the whole time, which is: if we stay consumer focused, that's going to address most of this. Most of antitrust is really about the protection of the consumer, and if we stay focused on that, we'll be fine," Dave Clark told me in an interview. "I think we certainly pay more attention to it, largely because you have to. It's an in-your-face conversation on a regular basis," he said. (Clark, an S-Team member, left Amazon in 2022 after twenty-three years at the company.)

If there was any hope that an incoming Biden administration would be friendlier to Amazon than the previous administration, all of that was now dashed. The appointment of Khan left nothing in doubt.

With this and other appointments, the president legitimized what Borkians derisively called the "hipster antitrust movement." The movement demanded a dramatically different interpretation of antitrust laws, as they were being applied, which had the potential of turning Khan's arguments into policies that would take direct aim at Amazon's business model. Biden later named Jonathan Kanter, another prominent Big Tech critic, as assistant attorney general for the Department of Justice's Antitrust Division. Earlier in the year, he appointed law professor Tim Wu, whose 2018 book, *The Curse of Bigness*, explained how we were living through the "new gilded age," to the National Economic Council as a special assistant to President Biden for technology and competition policy. In progressive antitrust circles, coffee mugs emblazoned with "Wu & Khan & Kanter" became a coveted item. The movement was going mainstream.

This new generation represented modern-day trust busters who were in favor of antitrust law interpretations that thrived under Louis Brandeis, a former associate justice of the Supreme Court, who was appointed by Woodrow Wilson in 1916. He was well known for going after monopolies while on the bench and previously as a lawyer. In 1914, both the Clayton Antitrust Act and the Federal Trade Commission Act were passed by Congress, which were designed to combat monopolistic business practices. Brandeis was instrumental to such work. Another term for the "hipster antitrust" movement that more accurately described them was the "New Brandeis Movement."

And Khan's views were shared by the administration. Speaking just weeks later before signing an executive order that focused on stricter antitrust enforcement, Biden made his own feelings on the issue clear. Speaking from the podium, he said:

> Between them, the two [President] Roosevelts established an American tradition — an antitrust tradition. It is how we ensure that our economy isn't about people working for capitalism; it's about capitalism working for people.
>
> But, over time, we've lost the fundamental American idea that true capitalism depends on fair and open competition. Forty years ago, we chose the wrong path, in my view, following the misguided philosophy of people like Robert Bork, and pulled back on enforcing laws to promote competition.
>
> We're now 40 years into the experiment of letting giant corporations accumulate more and more power. And where — what have we gotten from it? Less growth, weakened investment, fewer small businesses. Too many Americans who feel left behind. Too many people who are poorer than their parents.
>
> I believe the experiment failed. We have to get back to an economy that grows from the bottom up and the middle out.

Shortly after Khan became chair, Amazon filed a twenty-five-page motion seeking that Khan recuse herself from any antitrust investigations that involved the company, their reasoning being her past history of criticizing Amazon. "Chair Khan has made numerous and highly detailed public pronouncements regarding Amazon, including on market definition, specific conduct and theories of harm, and the purpose, effects, and legality of such conduct. Indeed, she has on numerous occasions argued that Amazon is guilty of antitrust violations and should be broken up," the complaint said.

———

In June 2021, the House introduced five proposed bills that, if passed, would curb the power of Big Tech. One of the proposed bills could even force a breakup of companies such as Amazon, as it stated that a dominant company meeting certain criteria wouldn't be able to compete on any platforms it also operates in if it had the ability to give its own products an advantage. In essence, its passage could require Amazon to effectively shed or divest its devices and private label businesses altogether.

After the House bills were announced, Amazon's policy team catapulted into action to try to swat them down. The company reached out to third-party sellers and helped them craft editorials for local newspapers about Amazon's importance as their selling platform, according to an internal strategy report I obtained. "Between July and October of 2021 we will activate individual sellers to submit opinion pieces to local and regional news outlets expressing opposition to pending federal legislation that would be detrimental to their businesses. We will coordinate the efforts of multiple teams internally so that all seller policy activations July-September are coordinated and aligned on messaging related to the legislation," the internal memo said.

Journalists were bombarded with statements from a group of tech-funded advocacy groups and trade associations such as the Chamber of Progress, NetChoice, and the Connected Commerce Council. Each disputed the merits of the proposed legislation. Amazon is known to fund all three groups. The company, like Big Tech writ large, saw all of these governmental actions as existential threats, and their lobbying machine went into overdrive.

After the House conducted its investigation into Big Tech and held its markup, Senator Amy Klobuchar, a Minnesota Democrat, began working on a companion Senate bill. In January 2022, the Senate Committee on the Judiciary voted to advance the American Innovation and Choice Online Act, a bill aimed at large technology companies that would prevent them from favoring their own products and services on their platforms over those of competitors. It would need a full Senate vote to be passed. (There was also another bill circulating in the Senate that would affect Apple and Google.)

In order for the bills to pass, it was imperative they be voted on before the Christmas recess in 2022. Klobuchar and Chuck Grassley, a Republican senator from Iowa, were sensitive to the timeline and worked to secure votes for the bills. The hope was to bring the bills to vote before the new Congress took office in 2023.

————

On the morning of March 9, US Attorney General Merrick Garland received a letter detailing a rather bold request from some members of the House Judiciary Committee. The members wanted Garland to investigate Amazon and some of its top executives for potential criminal obstruction of Congress.

The letter accused Amazon of refusing to provide information that lawmakers sought as part of an investigation by the body's antitrust subcommittee into Amazon's competitive practices. The letter alleged that the refusal was an attempt to cover up what it calls a lie that the company told lawmakers about its treatment of outside sellers on its platform. (They were referring to Amazon lawyer Nate Sutton's 2019 testimony in which he said, "We do not use any seller data to compete with them.")

Congressional aides were locked in a battle with Amazon's lawyers, lobbyists, and public policy officials. They argued over evidence the subcommittee said Amazon refused to produce. Among the evidence was the internal investigation Amazon conducted into its private brand business after the *Wall Street Journal* story revealed a pattern of using seller data to reverse engineer their own products. In October 2020, Amazon sent a letter to the committee saying that its internal probe determined that its private label team did not misuse third-party seller data. Despite this, Congress wanted to see the actual report, but the company's lawyers rebuffed them, claiming it was privileged information.

"Amazon repeatedly endeavored to thwart the Committee's efforts to uncover the truth about Amazon's business practices," the congressional letter to Garland said. "For this, it must be held accountable."

It was yet another example of Amazon being aggressive in DC and uncooperative with investigators. Regulators investigating the company have recounted issues scheduling meetings or obtaining documents from Amazon, while acknowledging how combative they tend to be. Rather than cooperate, Amazon always made things difficult, they said. It wouldn't even share a report that allegedly cleared them of any wrongdoing. "From the very beginning, Amazon in every way they could stonewalled this investigation," Congressman Cicilline told me. Of all four of the tech companies being investigated, he said Amazon gave them the most trouble.

Previous audits of its private label business were usually conducted in-house, but this time Amazon hired law firm K&L Gates LLP. It did so to ensure that the results of the audit were "legally privileged," meaning that outside agencies couldn't obtain it, people involved in the decision said. "This was stated in meetings clearly. A big issue internally was whether the company could be forced to hand over the investigation," one said. Amazon was also concerned about regulators knowing who to interview inside Amazon on these issues, so ensuring the report was privileged helped make sure that team members involved would be protected from testifying, said two of the people. Even internally, the content of the report was kept secret. Most of the S-Team wasn't allowed to access or read it. The heads of some of the private label teams didn't see the report. Interestingly, once the audit was complete, suddenly ironclad firewalls were put in place, according to a senior private brands executive. "There were steps that were taken to make it systems-wise impossible [to pull the data]. They isolated data into specific clusters and they locked down the data tables and structures."

Months before going to the attorney general, in October 2021, Congress sent a letter to Amazon's new CEO Andy Jassy urging him to provide "exculpatory evidence" to corroborate sworn testimony by Bezos and Amazon lawyer Sutton. Amazon refused to comply.

That November and December, lawyers representing Amazon met with congressional lawyers about the report and other issues over a series of meetings. Some of the congressional staffers attended the meeting optimistic that Amazon would provide the internal report and prove that they hadn't misled Congress. In that event, they would scrap plans to refer Amazon to the DOJ for a criminal referral.

In meetings in Washington, DC, congressional lawyers probed the team of lawyers from Wachtell, Lipton, Rosen & Katz and Covington & Burling LLP about Amazon's private label business. The legal teams hadn't worked on the K&L Gates investigation and weren't privy to the contents of the report, the people said. When the subcommittee asked Amazon to provide it with its report, Wachtell said it was legally privileged. Amazon was declaring that its internal report didn't show evidence of wrongdoing but for some reason wouldn't share it with Congress. They wanted Congress to take them at their word. At this point, the congressional lawyers began exploring involving the attorney general.

An Amazon spokesman said: "We investigate credible allegations and we have found no instances of employees using individual third-party seller data to create private label products." When I asked if the company found instances of private label employees accessing the seller data, the company declined to answer. When I asked why Amazon would refuse to share a report that cleared them of any allegations, including a criminal referral, the company also declined to answer.

Internally, the private brands business was becoming a much bigger headache than some thought it was worth. Top executives discussed the possibility of exiting the business entirely to alleviate regulatory pressure, but eventually shelved the idea, keeping it in their back pocket. Instead, if the FTC decided to file a monopoly lawsuit against Amazon, the executives discussed offering the concession of exiting its private label business to the agency.

––––––

In May, Chris Smalls, the Amazon employee in Staten Island that had galvanized workers to form a union, attended a meeting with Vice President Kamala Harris and labor secretary Marty Walsh. Ironically, Smalls had an easier time getting a meeting at the Biden White House than Bezos did. The meeting also included union organizers from Starbucks and retailer REI. Biden, to Amazon's disappointment, had been known to say that he planned to be "the most pro-union President in American history."

Smalls wore a flashy jacket that said "Eat the Rich" on it with an Amazon Labor Union shirt and Yankees baseball cap. To everyone's surprise, Biden walked in to greet them all. He went over to Smalls with a big grin on his face, giving him a handshake and a hug.

"You're trouble, man," Biden said, with a chuckle.

"Yeah, I am," Smalls replied.

"I like you, you're my kind of trouble," Biden said.

"Good trouble," replied Smalls, referencing civil rights activist John Lewis's famous line.

"I got in a little trouble, you may recall. I was saying I was looking forward to [Amazon] getting organized. But you got it done in one place. Let's not stop," said Biden, who even tweeted a video of the exchange.

Amazon executives were apoplectic. To see the president embrace Smalls was just too much. "It was a kick in the face," said one policy executive. "People said, 'OK we aren't going to have a relationship with this White House,'" recalled another.

Klain was soon on the receiving end of an angry message from Jay Carney. According to White House officials, this was the most fraught of the exchanges between Amazon and the Biden administration.

Bezos was also irked, and criticized the president on Twitter. Just a few days after hosting Smalls, President Biden tweeted, "You want to bring down inflation? Let's make sure the wealthiest corporations pay their fair share." Bezos retweeted the president, saying, "The newly created Disinformation Board should review this tweet, or maybe they need to form a new Non Sequitur Board instead. Raising corp taxes is fine to discuss. Taming inflation is critical to discuss. Mushing them together is just misdirection."

Despite the Twitter meltdown just weeks earlier, after which Bezos seemed to indicate to deputies that the company should be less aggressive on Twitter, here he was taking potshots at the president.

The next day, the president tweeted: "Under my predecessor, the deficit increased every single year. This year, we're on track to cut the deficit by $1.5 trillion — the biggest one-year decline ever. It matters to families, because reducing the deficit is one of the main ways we can ease inflationary pressures." Bezos again responded, tweeting: "In fact, the administration tried hard to inject even more stimulus into an already over-heated, inflationary economy and only Manchin saved them from themselves. Inflation is a regressive tax that most hurts the least affluent. Misdirection doesn't help the country."

Bezos's tweets rankled some members of the S-Team, who found them counterproductive. The White House, meanwhile, viewed them as retaliation for meeting with Smalls. When Klain and Carney finally spoke over the phone, Carney accused the White House of being deliberately disrespectful toward Amazon. White House aides were surprised by his tone. President Biden had made no secret of his pro-union stance, so Amazon shouldn't have been offended by the meeting, they reasoned.

But Amazon's S-Team thought it was unprecedented for a president to take a side in an active labor battle. "Even in the great debates where presidents help negotiate, they typically haven't said who's right or wrong. I think the surprising element was how much [Biden] and the administration leaned into 'Amazon is bad for labor,'" said an S-Team member.

"The economy's doing reasonably well; we're making a lot of progress. I don't understand why this is what Mr. Bezos had to say," Klain said to Carney, referring to the tweets.

"Bezos had been very publicly critical of the president in a way that [Walmart CEO] Doug McMillon wasn't, so it's much easier to have conversations with someone who's not out there kicking the shit out of you. It's hard to pick up the phone and talk to someone and have a candid conversation with him when that's their public posture," a White House official said. It was yet another reminder of how poorly Bezos and his team of executives navigated DC. There was little give and take or diplomacy. And it kept getting worse.

An Amazon executive countered: "Not once did Joe Biden pick up the phone and call Jeff Bezos before he tweeted that. They weren't reaching out to invite Jeff because he had become public enemy number one of Elizabeth Warren and Bernie Sanders." In fact, while CEO, Bezos never received a phone call from Biden or was invited for a meeting with the president while he's been in office.

———

Heading into the summer of 2022, tech lobbying reached a fever pitch. Those in favor of the American Innovation and Choice Online Act wanted it brought for a vote before the August recess. They pressured Senator Chuck Schumer to schedule the vote, assuring the Senate majority leader that they had enough votes for it to pass.

Time was ticking for the bill. Klobuchar and its backers wanted to act swiftly. Beyond the midterms, it was also a frenetic time, as votes were also being scheduled on issues ranging from the war in Ukraine to abortion rights. Rumors circulated that Schumer was committed to a summer vote on the antitrust legislation. In response, the lobbyists worked to beat it down.

Huseman's "Public Policy 3.0" was on full display. Just like Amazon had paraded its third-party seller success stories around Capitol Hill to meet legislators, the company reached back out to try to recruit them to fight the proposed legislation on Amazon's behalf. In a post to sellers, Amazon said that the bill posed a threat to the livelihood of Amazon's third-party sellers and urged them to email their senators. Amazon launched a website dedicated to stopping the legislation from being approved, where it directed sellers to contact their senators in order to urge them to oppose the legislation.

The irony was rich. Amazon's sellers, who often use the term "indentured servitude" to describe their relationship to the company, were now being asked to do Amazon's bidding in its quest to maintain the status quo, where Amazon rakes in billions of dollars off the backs of its sellers. Many of the sellers, meanwhile, rely on Amazon Marketplace for their livelihoods. To that end, some of the proposed legislation could even benefit these sellers by making Amazon a more even playing field, but no matter. Amazon was relentless. Playing into their fears, it told sellers that the bills could result in Amazon's third-party marketplace being shut down.

Legislators involved in the proposed bills say that they don't jeopardize Amazon having a third-party marketplace. Instead, it would prevent Amazon from competing unfairly against third-party sellers by favoring its own brands. In any case, fearful sellers contacted their representatives to urge them not to pass the legislation.

Because of years of building up its team of public policy employees — and lobbyists — under Carney, Amazon was in a position to meet with most senators involved with the bills and share their opinions and research.

In a sign of how worried Amazon was about the legislation, even Jassy personally called a number of senators, including Senator Schumer, to express his reservations and ask them to oppose it. Ironically, as Amazon's top leaders were making the case that the company wasn't too big, internally Jassy was telling his deputies that Amazon could be a $10 trillion company — the world's largest by valuation — over the next decade. It saw about $9 trillion of opportunities it could grow into. Some senior executives were wary. "You can't be a vertically integrated $10 trillion company. Not everyone wants to live in Amazon town," recalls an S-Team member. (But Amazon's team did push ahead, stealing more and more market share from rivals. And yet another one of Bezos's early seeds would grow into a full-fledged behemoth. In 2022, Amazon secretly overtook UPS as the biggest nongovernmental delivery service in the US by parcel volume. In 2020, it had eclipsed FedEx, whose former CEO just years earlier called the notion of Amazon being a major competitor "fantastical." You underestimated Amazon at your own peril. Amazon celebrated the milestone in secrecy, high-fiving each other and then getting back to work. "There's not a lot of perceived value in chest thumping on being the biggest," said a former senior Amazon logistics executive about the milestone in light of FTC scrutiny. "Only bad things come from saying you are the biggest.")

In June, Klobuchar, Grassley, Cicilline, and Buck held a joint press conference to address the need to schedule the vote as soon as possible. The personal appeals and lobbying efforts were not dissuading them.

Instead, Klobuchar and Grassley spoke about the millions of dollars Big Tech was spending on advertisements to shoot down the bill, putting pressure in states where they could potentially get elected officials to back off from voting for them. "We're confronted with these big tech companies, spending tens of millions of dollars on ads, and also on front groups, to spread falsehoods about our bill," Grassley said.

All told, the companies would spend a whopping $100 million just on ad campaigns alone. Many of the ads targeted swing states, such as New Hampshire, with an intent to stop senators such as Maggie Hassan (D., New Hampshire) from supporting the bill. They appeared to work. Weeks earlier, Senator Hassan's chief of staff urged other chiefs to delay a vote ahead of the midterm elections. Senator Hassan was up for reelection, and her chief of staff called the bill controversial. Senator Michael Bennet's (D., Colorado) chief of staff also urged for a delay on the call. Paranoia set in for some of the Democrats who were vying for reelection. It didn't help that Big Tech was also a major donor to Democrats.

Amazon's lobbyists created a false narrative that the bill, if passed, would destroy Amazon Prime. During the press conference, Cicilline tried to correct the record. "First, nothing in this bill prevents any platform from offering the products or services that consumers today enjoy, such as Amazon Prime, Google Maps, or the iPhone," he said.

Yet Amazon clung to the narrative. An advertisement paid for by a trade group backed by Amazon depicted the company as a pandemic-era hero. In the commercial, a narrator says: "Washington politicians have a law that could break Prime's guaranteed two-day free delivery and threaten our fragile economic recovery." It ends with a call to action: "Tell your senators: Don't break our Prime."

An Amazon spokesman called the bill "vaguely worded" and said that it would have mandated that Amazon allow other logistics providers fulfill Prime orders, which would have made it difficult to fulfill its Prime two-day shipping requirements.

Ken Buck was visibly exasperated at the press conference:

I'm not sure why I'm here. We conducted a sixteen-month investigation last Congress. It involved field hearings, it involved testimony from the four CEOs of the monopoly big tech companies.
Now at no point in time did leadership say to us, "We're not
going to move this bill forward, you shouldn't do that." In fact,
just the opposite. We received encouragement. Then we held a
twenty-nine-hour markup in Judiciary Committee. Twenty-
nine hours. Every bill — the six bills that we considered —
passed with a bipartisan majority. And not just a bipartisan
majority, a number of Republicans joined Democrats. Nobody
at that point said to us "Don't do this, because these bills are
never going to hit the floor." In fact, just the opposite. The American people saw it. They liked it. They understand it. They may
not understand antitrust law. I don't understand antitrust law,
but they do understand that there is something wrong when
companies that are this big control speech platforms in a democracy. That's what they get. That's what the threat is here. And yet,
the bills haven't hit the floor. That was a year ago that we held
that twenty-nine-hour markup. There's something wrong with a
system of government that sits on six bills for a year.

To the dismay of Klobuchar and other advocates of the legislation,
Schumer would not schedule the vote before the August recess. People
started to question his lack of urgency.

The majority leader was at ease with the technology giants, fundraising in San Francisco and Seattle. It even leaked that one of his
daughters is a registered lobbyist for Amazon. Another of his daughters
worked for Facebook (now renamed as Meta). The senator was a focus
of a 2018 *New York Times* investigation into Facebook's lobbying efforts.
In the piece, Senator Schumer is described as having contacted a top
Democrat on the Intelligence Committee and warning him to back off
harsh questioning of Facebook in relation to its role in the 2016 presidential election.

Progressives became so incensed by the lack of a vote that they started hounding Schumer around New York and DC. After one of his PAC fundraisers in July, a group of protesters showed up screaming at the senator to schedule the vote. One attendee was dressed up as Mr. Monopoly, donning a fake white mustache and top hat. He carried an oversized check, the type used at a charity event, for the amount of $100 million, written for "Protecting Big Tech." It was signed by the Monopoly man.

A group stationed a television screen replaying an antitrust segment from HBO's *Last Week Tonight with John Oliver* on repeat outside of Schumer's Brooklyn and DC homes. In another stunt, a protester had a giant Prime Day billboard with Chuck Schumer's face in the middle, with Senators Hassan and Bennet flanking him. Under each politician, it had a price that they could be "bought" for. It totaled the amount of money each had accepted from Big Tech. For Schumer, the tally was $487,000.

In the midst of the battle with Washington to preserve Amazon's advantages, Carney resigned from Amazon. In early 2022 former president Obama introduced Carney to Airbnb CEO Brian Chesky, who was looking for someone to head up policy and communications. In late July, Carney announced that he'd be joining Airbnb. The timing wasn't ideal, with Amazon in the middle of a major fight over proposed legislation, but executives say that the writing had been on the wall. Carney became less engaged internally and had spent a couple weeks that summer working from Nantucket, becoming less of a presence in the company's offices, they said. At the end of the summer, when Carney left, there was no going-away party.

———

As the year drew to a close, Klobuchar and Cicilline insisted they had the sixty votes needed to pass the American Innovation and Choice Online Act. But it would not be brought to a vote after all. As a result, for it to have a chance, it would have to be reintroduced all over again.

Big Tech came out victorious. Yet, each side had a different postmortem perspective. It came down to votes. The tech giants said the bill was flawed and there weren't enough votes for passage.

And privately, Senator Schumer wasn't convinced they had the sixty votes. For months, Schumer had asked the sponsors for their list of committed votes, but never received one.

"On this bill, they just weren't unified," said Adam Kovacevich, founder of the Chamber of Progress, a tech-backed lobbying group that lobbied on behalf of Amazon, Google, and others. "You had probably a dozen Democrats saying, 'I don't know about this one. I have concerns about this one.'" Meanwhile, those in favor, including Klobuchar and Cicilline, insist they had the votes.

One thing for certain is that Big Tech's lobbying power and dollars, and Amazon's mobilization of its sellers and customers, made a huge impact on the outcome.

"Big Tech really flooded the zone," said Katie McInnis, who was then the head of public policy at search engine DuckDuckGo, which was in favor of the legislation. "They not only had these ads; these companies were holding briefings for staffers where they were lying to them about how this bill would be affecting their services."

Amazon's mobilization of its massive army of sellers and customers who love Amazon Prime created a groundswell of advocacy against the bill. Amazon had stoked enough fear among both groups for them to believe in the possibility of them being forced to dismantle the Marketplace and Prime. They in turn called and emailed their representatives in droves. In some ways, their ability to mobilize so many customers and sellers illustrated just how big they were. Amazon Prime has more than 200 million members—getting any fraction to contact their representatives would be massive.

Colorado senator Michael Bennet's office was flooded with calls and emails from Amazon sellers and customers. The office received five constituent messages against the bill for every one message in support of it, said a person at the office. Groups funded by Amazon played lots of ads in Colorado.

"It was a feature of their campaign to spread misinformation to make false claims," said Cicilline, referring to how Amazon claimed that the bill would eliminate Prime or its third-party Marketplace. He says that Big Tech's lobbying efforts intensified to a level he had never seen in his decade-plus of service in Congress. (In June 2023, Cicilline left Congress.) "They all claim they don't engage in self-preferencing and advancing their own products and services unfairly. All the bill would do is prohibit that kind of discriminatory conduct that the platforms claimed they weren't doing anyway. They were afraid of it because it's exactly what they're doing."

CHAPTER 18

The FTC Sues Amazon

SINCE TAKING OVER THE top job at the FTC in June 2021, Lina Khan's transition had not been smooth. While Khan had become the face of a movement gaining momentum in the country, as hipster antitrust went mainstream and there was a new skepticism about Big Tech's power, she wasn't welcomed with open arms at the agency she now helmed.

The 106-year-old institution had become notoriously risk averse, bringing forward carefully crafted cases with a high probability of winning. One former employee described the FTC staff as being "obsessed with its track record," adding that "persistent across the agency is a fear of losing and having a sterling record." Another put it less kindly, calling it "the chickenshit club," referring to a quote made by James Comey when he was US Attorney for the Southern District of New York, describing lawyers who chased only cases they could win, not the hard cases Comey believed the department should make a priority. (This was chronicled in Jesse Eisinger's 2017 book by the same name.)

Part of the agency's focus on wins was practical: losses could set bad precedent for future cases and erode the FTC's authority. They took that responsibility seriously, being standard-bearers for both the culture of the FTC and the preservation of the agency's power. There were also opportunity costs. The agency was limited in resources and thus focused on going after "bread and butter" cases that were clear antitrust violations. It had been reluctant to squander those resources too often on cases that didn't fit its standard of what a winning case looked like.

Prior to being named chair, Khan had criticized the FTC's approach. She spoke of the agency being weak and allowing too much consolidation in corporate America. She openly espoused a different interpretation of the antitrust laws from the ones the FTC had been enforcing for the last forty years.

To some within the agency, Khan was viewed as a radical. As one former commissioner described it, prior changes in leadership were a bit like a relay race, where the outgoing chair passed the baton to the incoming one to carry on the agency's mission. But Khan was not interested in maintaining the status quo. "The real sea change that we're seeing now is that Khan came in and said, 'Antitrust has been a disaster. Everybody here has done a terrible job and is asleep at the switch. Everybody previously was ineffective and did nothing,'" says a former FTC commissioner.

Even beyond ideological differences, there were other points of tension. It didn't help that, unlike many of her predecessors, Khan hadn't been an insider, rising up the ranks to claim the top job. Khan was more of an unorthodox choice, less a person who put in their time and more an outsider who came to shake things up. Many prior chairs had served as commissioners or had other roles within the agency before taking the top job. This ensured that the culture and norms would remain consistent even as leadership changed. The FTC could be insular, and many employees felt that Khan — the youngest chairperson in the agency's history — hadn't earned her stripes.

But Khan was no stranger to resistance. After she had graduated law school, Khan sought a job as a law professor and interviewed at Harvard, Yale, and Stanford. But because she threatened the traditional views of antitrust, she was shut out from receiving offers, recalls David Singh Grewal, one of her mentors. In a sign of how the antitrust establishment viewed Khan, the lead antitrust professor at Yale Law School, George Priest, said: "Her ideas are forty years out of date. We've moved on from there." He says he regrets not writing a rebuttal to the paper that launched his own student's career. But resistance from antitrust intellectuals was one thing. Leading a staff of more than one thousand people as the head of the FTC, many of whom shared those establishment views, would be a different kind of challenge itself.

There were also early missteps that baffled staff. At the start, staffers complained that Khan wasn't very visible within the FTC's offices. Instead of meeting with large groups at the agency to introduce herself, she met with small groups, staff say. Her staff also instituted a gag order shortly after Khan began that prevented employees from speaking on panels, at conferences, and making other public appearances. Those types of speaking engagements are a big part of the FTC's mission, and its staff were irked by the moratorium and viewed it as a sign of distrust from the new chair.

At its core, however, was what Khan had said: antitrust enforcement had been too lax. She was going to bring about change by reverting to an interpretation of the laws, not through the established thinking of the past forty years, but through what she argued was their original intent. For her critics, this was radical. But Khan's supporters argued it was actually the opposite: she was an originalist who wanted to enforce the laws the way they had been first intended. She was not willing to maintain the paradigm shift of the 1970s that changed how the government regulated the private sector. That era, in Khan's view, had run its course, even if the establishment ideas still held sway in antitrust circles writ large. She wanted to sue for illegal activities based on dormant legal theories that hadn't been enforced in decades. In Khan's eyes, just because they hadn't been enforced recently, that didn't make the behaviors any less illegal.

Going after tougher cases using dormant legal theories was the opposite of the play-it-safe ethos of the FTC. Critics accused Khan of espousing a new motto: "winning by losing." While Khan of course wanted to win cases, the perception was that she thought that even cases the FTC lost could be beneficial because they would demonstrate her point to Congress: antitrust laws needed to change in order to better regulate modern corporations. In essence, losing would create a track record to show the inadequacy of the current laws.

"They're prepared to lose these cases," said a former senior staffer at the FTC during Khan's tenure. Khan has pushed back against the notion that she's intentionally lost cases. Nonetheless, she did bring forward hard cases that inherently had lower chances of winning.

The FTC's 2022 case to block Meta's acquisition of a virtual-reality startup called Within Unlimited is emblematic of the kind of internal tension the FTC faced under Khan. It revealed how both sides saw which cases to pursue and why. On the one hand, the agency's lawyers and experts advised against suing based on the merits of the case and the agency's chances of winning, *Bloomberg* reported. The FTC was relying on a rarely used legal argument that Meta's acquisition in a nascent space would hinder *future* competition. When the commissioners voted, the two Republican commissioners voted against it. But the agency pushed ahead, later losing its challenge to block the merger with a federal judge declining the FTC's request to issue a court order to halt the deal.

In late 2022, the FTC sought to block Microsoft's $69 billion deal to acquire Activision Blizzard. In its press release, the FTC said that the deal "would enable Microsoft to suppress competitors to its Xbox gaming consoles and its rapidly growing subscription content and cloud-gaming business, and its blockbuster gaming franchises such as Call of Duty."

In July 2023, a federal judge rejected the FTC's attempt to stop Microsoft's deal from closing. "The FTC has not identified a single document which contradicts Microsoft's publicly stated commitment to make Call of Duty available on PlayStation," the federal judge wrote. The decision was a serious blow to the agency. Many antitrust experts and even those inside the agency started questioning whether Khan's agenda would lead to a steady stream of losses.

"They're not winning much of anything. Plus, they've lost agency authority and are at risk of losing much more," says Joshua Wright, a former Republican FTC commissioner. "The stakes of the FTC losing are greater than ever. It's more than just losing the cases — it's the bad precedent and loss of power to carry out the mission in the future."

Speaking to a crowd at the Economic Club of New York later that month, Khan was asked about her record.

"In federal court [we] have lost two merger cases," Khan said, adding that the agency had brought forward between thirteen and twenty cases during that period, with a number of the companies abandoning their acquisitions. While those weren't court victories, the FTC viewed companies dropping their mergers as wins. "We only bring cases that we think we should win, that we can win. Every time we have that type of setback, we look very closely at, you know, where could we have done better? Where do we fall short? And use that to inform our approach going forward."

The tensions between Khan and the FTC staff dented morale. At the end of Khan's first year in office, the FTC engagement and satisfaction score dropped to 64.9, down 24 points from the year prior, in the Best Places to Work in the Federal Government rankings. The FTC usually ranked very high on the list, which was a source of pride for the agency.

The FTC has five commissioners, including a chair, who vote on whether to bring antitrust cases forward. The commission has always been composed of both political parties. Soon after Khan took over, partisan differences would emerge on how best to approach the cases they pursued. The two Republican commissioners often dissented with Khan's opinions. One of the Republican commissioners expressed concern that her agenda to reform antitrust law was an overreach of the agency's powers.

Christine Wilson, a Republican FTC commissioner serving alongside Khan, lambasted Khan's views on antitrust. "I understand that Chair Khan seeks sweeping legal reforms in the antitrust arena — but I disagree with her willingness, in search of that goal, to inflict harm on the agency and deprive the FTC of the talent that has made the agency a Best Place to Work since 2012," she said in a statement to the *Washington Post* after the workplace rankings were published.

Khan inherited an investigation into Amazon that had begun under the Trump administration. As she settled into the role, work picked up on the case. The FTC pelted Amazon with deposition requests — so much so that the company found them excessive. In hours-long meetings with FTC lawyers, Amazon executives answered a broad swath of questions. Many came away from the meetings feeling like the FTC was on a fishing expedition rather than pursuing information about a specific business practice, or what's referred to as a "theory of harm." Nonetheless, Amazon produced millions of pages of documents for the FTC and more than 100 terabytes of data over the course of the investigation.

In these meetings, Amazon's lawyers asked the FTC to share specifics of its case against the company and outline the theories of harm. For the better part of 2022, the agency declined to provide such details.

Eventually, in a virtual meeting in Washington, DC, in late 2022, the FTC explained the scope of its case to Amazon's lawyers. The FTC identified five behaviors: Amazon tying its Fulfillment by Amazon service to its Prime program, the company's use of data and third-party data, Amazon's Prime program locking customers in, self-preferencing, and Amazon's pricing strategy.

Around the same time, Amazon and the European Commission announced a settlement of the various investigations the European Commission was conducting on Amazon's use of third-party seller data, its Prime business, and how sellers are selected to be featured in the Buy Box.

Amazon agreed to a number of concessions to alleviate the European Commission's concerns without facing hefty fines or admitting wrongdoing. It agreed to begin siloing all third-party seller data so that the rest of Amazon couldn't benefit from the insights that data produced, either through its algorithms or from employees accessing the data themselves. For its Prime program, it said it will allow sellers to work with logistics companies outside of Amazon's own logistics operation and remain Prime eligible as long as they could fulfill the speedy shipment requirements. It also agreed to feature a second competing offer in its Buy Box in certain scenarios.

While some grumbled that Amazon got off easy, European Commission officials weighed a full-on, yearslong investigation during which Amazon would likely accumulate even more power in the interim, followed by a lengthy court case, versus the ability to get quick commitments to change the behaviors that they viewed as potentially illegal. They chose the latter.

———

Heading into 2023, with the pending lawsuit on the horizon, Amazon made some changes to its practices that could potentially lessen regulatory concerns.

Roku, which had been blocked from buying advertising placements on Amazon.com for its products, noticed that Amazon was easing up on the practice. That summer, Amazon announced plans to reintroduce Seller Fulfilled Prime, a program for sellers to ship items to customers through other logistics partners and still be eligible to be part of the Prime program as long as they met the speed required for Prime. Amazon had discontinued the program in 2019, only allowing a select number of sellers to fulfill through outside logistics companies. The majority of sellers had to use FBA in order to qualify for Prime. (Initially, Amazon announced there would be a 2 percent fee for sellers to enroll in Seller Fulfilled Prime, but the company swiftly dropped the planned fee after backlash.) "Amazon reopening Seller Fulfilled Prime or doing anything to try and get ahead of the FTC is like a kid hiding all their dirty clothes under their bed and saying their room is clean. The only thing that will put an end to Amazon's illegal behavior is this lawsuit," FTC spokesman Douglas Farrar said.

Inside the company's private brands division, a big shake-up was underway. Instead of adding selection to private brands at a furious pace as it had for much of its history, Amazon was now slashing assortment. Part of the decision was economic: after the boon of the pandemic shifted more dollars to online shopping, Amazon's sales dropped back to reality. The company had built too much capacity during the pandemic that it now didn't need, which hurt profits. And CEO Andy Jassy was pushing divisions to shore up their profitability. Amazon slashed thousands of corporate jobs and cut unprofitable business as it hit one of its worst financial stretches in recent history.

But regulators weighed on the business, too, sources said. Amazon went from forty-five private brands in 2020 to fewer than twenty by 2023. It cut twenty-seven of its thirty clothing brands and decided to focus on a select number of in-house brands that sold well.

What Amazon was moving toward was more in line with tradi-tional retail private-brand strategies of focusing on a few hundred or thousand commoditized products, like house brand paper towels, rather than copying niche products like car trunk organizers from small sellers like Fortem. Focusing on the basics would eliminate much of the criticism Amazon received from launching items too similar to those of its own sellers.

Another reason Amazon's own brands became less profitable was because of damage control it did after the *Wall Street Journal* story about Amazon's use of seller data ran. After that 2020 article, Amazon curbed a yearslong practice in which its own brands were given a boost in the search results on its site in special placements — the kind of edge other sellers could gain only by buying ads. That change caused many of Amazon's brands to be buried in search results, making it harder for items to sell. The cost of warehousing all of that inventory was signifi-cant and made it a target during the cost cutting.

————

On August 15, 2023, Amazon general counsel David Zapolsky sat down at a computer alongside legal colleagues and outside counsel to "meet" with FTC chair Lina Khan and the agency's other commissioners.

It was the final formality before the FTC's lawsuit would be filed, commonly known as a "last rites" meeting. The name refers to the Catholic tradition of giving a dying person confession and communion so that they can be absolved of their sins and attempt to avoid hell.

The point of such meetings is for a company under investigation to appeal to the commissioners with their arguments against a lawsuit. Some companies use the opportunity to offer concessions to the FTC in order to settle and avoid a lengthy legal battle.

Amazon lawyers headed into the meeting a bit frustrated. The FTC hadn't shared with the company what sort of concessions it would find acceptable. It was Amazon's view that Khan was not receptive to any sort of settlement, and that the lawsuit was a train moving full steam ahead.

That day, Amazon's legal team met with the comissioners. The agency was down to just three: Khan and two Democrats. Republican commissioner Christine Wilson, a vocal critic of Khan's agenda, had resigned in protest to Khan's leadership. (Wilson left no doubt as to her feelings about Khan. "Much ink has been spilled about Lina Khan's attempts to remake federal antitrust law as chairman of the Federal Trade Commission. Less has been said about her disregard for the rule of law and due process and the way senior FTC officials enable her. I have failed repeatedly to persuade Ms. Khan and her enablers to do the right thing, and I refuse to give their endeavor any further hint of legitimacy by remaining. Accordingly, I will soon resign as an FTC commissioner," she wrote in an op-ed. "My fundamental concern with her leadership of the commission pertains to her willful disregard of congressionally imposed limits on agency jurisdiction, her defiance of legal precedent, and her abuse of power to achieve desired outcomes," Wilson added.)

During the meetings, Amazon's team invoked the consumer welfare standard repeatedly. Interestingly, since 2021 Amazon had been working with the Antitrust Education Project, a think tank founded by Robert Bork Jr., the son of the late Robert Bork. Amazon helped fund the group, whose mission was to promote the consumer welfare standard. The Antitrust Education Project saw Khan as a threat to Bork's legacy. During the last rites meeting, Amazon claimed that changes to its business model would raise prices for customers.

In the end, Amazon did not offer any concessions. Some FTC staff left with the impression that the tech giant didn't take the lawsuit seriously. The two sides were at an impasse. The lawsuit would be filed.

———

On September 20, 2023, the FTC's Bureau of Consumer Protection unredacted pieces of a separate, smaller lawsuit filed in June against Amazon. This lawsuit alleged that Amazon purposefully signed up consumers to its Prime program without their understanding and made it very hard to cancel their Prime memberships. The FTC also added three Amazon executives to the lawsuit: Neil Lindsay, Russell Grandinetti, and Jamil Ghani. The unredacted bits of the complaint publicly shamed the three executives and painted the executives in a very poor light. It showed that they knew they were tricking people into unwittingly paying for unwanted Prime subscriptions.

In one meeting described in the Bureau of Consumer Protection lawsuit, the head of Amazon Prime at the time, Neil Lindsay, rationalizes the behavior. "In a meeting with Amazon designers, Defendant Lindsay was asked about Amazon's use of dark patterns during the Prime enrollment process," the complaint said. "Lindsay explained that once consumers become Prime members—even unknowingly—they will see what a great program it is and remain members, so Amazon is 'okay' with the situation." (Amazon said the FTC's claims were "unfounded.")

Days later, on September 25, Amazon's legal team was in a state of nervous energy. There hadn't been much communication between the company and the FTC since the virtual meeting, but Amazon started to hear murmurs that the long-anticipated monopoly lawsuit would imminently be filed.

Amazon's team worked to polish its planned response to the bigger case Khan was working to issue. Internally, the team had believed that Khan would make Amazon Prime's bundling a major focus of its lawsuit. Prime bundling regularly came up during the interrogations with the FTC and was one of the areas that the FTC had read to Amazon about the case. The FTC believed that the company's Prime membership, with all of its disparate perks — free shipping, streaming, free food delivery on Grubhub, etc. — created a "moat" around shoppers. Once customers paid for Prime, they stayed within the Amazon ecosystem — shopping with Amazon, watching Amazon content, and all else that came at the expense of Amazon's competitors. In fact, according to internal documents I obtained, in 2017 the average Prime customer in the US spent $2,250 on Amazon. The FTC even found that in 2021, Amazon considered a plan to "decouple" Prime into separate shopping and entertainment benefits but rejected it because it feared that offering the option would make it easier for customers to substitute or turn toward the competition, such as Netflix or Walmart+.

Amazon felt that attacking Prime would be a losing case for the FTC and prepared to fight it publicly. The company and its lobbyists claimed that the reason for the delay between the last rites meeting and the lawsuit being filed was because the FTC was having trouble recruiting state attorneys general to sign on because they were deterred by the popularity of Prime. Amazon's response, much like with Klobuchar and Grassley's American Innovation and Choice Online Act, would be to harness the popularity of Prime and cast the FTC as an enemy seeking to break up the service.

They weren't wrong in their thinking. Amazon had anticipated the signs correctly, but it wouldn't end up mattering in the end.

————

On September 26, 2023, the FTC filed its lawsuit against Amazon, alleging that the company was maintaining an illegal monopoly. The agency was joined by seventeen state attorneys general in its allegations. In a happy coincidence, the case just happened to be filed on the anniversary of the founding of the FTC.

The agency made a bold charge: Amazon was a monopoly, and the power it wielded caused the company to *raise prices* across retail. This was different from what most people expected. Khan had railed against the consumer welfare standard that made consumer prices the be all and end all of whether a company was deemed anticompetitive. Yet, here was the woman who used her pulpit to push the limits of modern antitrust reform filing a suit that some might even call "traditional," focusing on consumer pricing. It wasn't nearly as radical as it could have been, and it even left out elements that Amazon had figured would be central to the case, such as Prime bundling.

Sitting at a desk wearing a dark blush suit with an American flag behind her, Khan explained the case to reporters.

"We set forth a detailed set of allegations laying out how Amazon is a monopoly that is raising prices on American consumers and small businesses and engaging in a concerted strategy to unlawfully exclude rivals and undermine competition," Khan said. "Sellers are effectively paying a 50% Amazon tax that has steadily been increasing over the last decade. And prices are higher for shoppers as a result. In fact, Amazon's one-two punch of seller punishments and high seller fees often forces sellers to use their inflated Amazon prices as a price floor everywhere else. And so as a result, Amazon's conduct causes online shoppers to face artificially high prices, even when they're shopping somewhere other than Amazon."

The case came down to two major claims: Amazon's power over sellers on its platform forced them to use Amazon's other services in order to be successful. The FTC alleged that merchants felt forced to use Amazon's Fulfillment by Amazon program to ship their goods in order to be eligible to be part of Prime, and felt like they had no option but to buy advertising from Amazon in order to show up in search results. Basically, Amazon was pay to play, and success as a seller was predicated on paying Amazon a range of fees for other services from its various tentacles. The cost for these services was substantial.

In fact, the fees had grown so onerous that it was becoming harder and harder for these sellers to preserve their margins. "Amazon now takes one of every $2 that a seller makes," Khan told reporters. And because Amazon's take of revenues rose from 19 percent in 2014 to 45 percent in 2023, according to antimonopoly group the Institute for Local Self-Reliance, sellers had to raise their prices for their goods in order to offset Amazon's fees, raising what customers ultimately paid. That led to the FTC's second claim.

The FTC alleged that Amazon's long-standing practice of penalizing third-party merchants who sell their items for less on competitor websites inflated prices across the internet. For years, Amazon contractually required merchants to guarantee that their goods would have the lowest prices on Amazon. Some of these merchants also sold their goods at other retailers. If they were found in violation of this contract, Amazon would bury their items in search, prevent them from being featured in the Buy Box, or threaten to wholly delist them from the site, the FTC said. This made sellers fearful of marking down their goods even temporarily to participate in sales at rival websites. They couldn't afford to be booted from Amazon.com or retaliated against.

While the company did away with the contracts for this practice in 2019, it was still unofficially being enforced through an algorithm, the complaint alleged. The FTC referenced an internal document written weeks after Amazon dropped its contractual price parity requirement that said that the company planned to use an algorithm to enforce its "expectations and policies," which "ha[d] not changed."

The combination of these two tactics — higher prices from offsetting Amazon's "tax" and Amazon's requirement of having the lowest list price — created a scenario where a seller's Amazon price became their floor price across retailers. And because of Amazon's exploding fees, if a seller raised that price to offset the cost of doing business on Amazon, it also meant that seller's prices were raised on Walmart.com, Target.com and even the seller's own website, the suit alleged. Even if the seller could make a higher profit at a lower price point at other retailers, they had to price their goods at the Amazon price or higher, or face potential punishment. In other words, Amazon was so powerful it dictated the prices as a whole across retail, and it was costing both the merchant and the consumer.

Because Amazon merchants felt forced to use Fulfillment by Amazon, this stunted the growth of rival logistics companies that could have been alternative options for shipping their goods, the FTC alleged. It prevented rivals to Amazon from gaining scale to effectively compete against the giant.

In making its case, the FTC used Amazon's own words against the company. It liberally quoted from internal emails from some of Amazon's top executives to show the company doing the very things the agency alleged. This showed intent and awareness of the actions the agency claimed were anticompetitive.

For instance, in internal communications, Amazon executives admit that its requirement to offer the lowest price on Amazon has a "punitive aspect" for sellers and acknowledge that sellers "live in constant fear" of Amazon. The company even conducted an internal analysis in 2018 that found that it had increased seller costs to the point that "it has become more difficult over time [for sellers] to be profitable on Amazon," an executive wrote.

Another part of the complaint detailed Amazon's use of an internal algorithm codenamed Project Nessie. The FTC alleged that this secret algorithm worked to test higher prices on goods Amazon sold to improve margins for Amazon and get competitors to raise their prices as well. Given how powerful Amazon had become, the move had a ripple effect, raising prices for consumers across the e-commerce landscape, the FTC claimed. In instances where competitors didn't raise their prices to Amazon's level, the algorithm automatically lowered the price back down. And it was big business: Amazon made more than $1 billion from the algorithm between 2016 and 2018, the complaint alleged. The lawsuit described Amazon as essentially acting as a price-fixing cartel, with other members of the cartel unwittingly going along with price hikes. Ultimately, customers paid the price.

Amazon said that the FTC "grossly mischaracterize[d]" the algorithm and that Nessie was used only in situations where prices became so low that things became unsustainable. The company did use Nessie in the way the spokesman described. When Amazon matched a discounted price from a competitor, such as Target.com, and other competitors would follow, lowering their prices, Amazon and the competitors would often remain locked in low-price battle well after Target ended its sale. So, employees used Nessie to exit from the battle and normalize pricing, employees told me. The FTC said this was not the only use for the algorithm, and that Amazon used Nessie to raise prices of items not locked in price battles to improve profits.

Amazon said that they discontinued Nessie in 2019. The FTC's complaint shows Amazon executives considered turning the algorithm back on in 2021 and 2022 as inflation hurt the company's profitability. In January 2022, Doug Herrington, then senior vice president for North America Consumer at Amazon, emailed senior leaders with a suggestion. Maybe they should turn on "[o]ur old friend Nessie, perhaps with some new targeting logic." The email was included in the lawsuit.

In totality, the FTC's case painted a picture of the enormous power Amazon held in e-commerce and how its monopoly power hurt customers not only on its website, but elsewhere. The ramifications of Amazon's power didn't exist in isolation. Rather, they had real consequences for Americans, causing higher prices for customers on a range of goods, even if they weren't buying them from Amazon.com. In essence, the company commanded asymmetric power across retail.

In addition to the FTC's two major arguments, it made the case that as a monopoly, Amazon had degraded its services to customers. It listed a number of behaviors to illustrate this point. One was the sheer number of advertisements that show up in search results on the website. Amazon executives acknowledged that many of the ads were irrelevant to search queries and created "harm to consumers," according to one Amazon executive quoted in the complaint. Nonetheless, in an internal email, Bezos encouraged the practice.

Even though he was the standard-bearer of "customer obsession," Bezos instructed his team to accept higher rates of irrelevant ads in search queries, as the ads were high margin, the FTC said. (Amazon's advertising business has had gross margins around 90 percent, according to internal documents I viewed, so even irrelevant ads are profitable.)

"Mr. Bezos directly ordered his advertising team to continue to increase the number of advertisements on Amazon by allowing more irrelevant advertisements, because the revenue generated by advertisements eclipsed the revenue lost by degrading consumers' shopping experience," the complaint alleges. In one internal document, an Amazon executive flagged the worsening experience for shoppers because of irrelevant ads, circulating a search result for water bottles that showed an advertisement for "buck urine." The case also mentioned the self-preferencing of its private label brands, which wasn't central to the lawsuit, but was a long-standing problem that most sellers had to deal with, and came up in my reporting repeatedly.

And, to top it all off, the FTC described efforts by the company to thwart the investigation. Amazon made "extensive efforts to impede the government's investigation and hide information about its internal operations," the agency argued. Amazon had this reputation in regulatory circles: it was difficult during the House Judiciary antitrust subcommittee's investigation, it had thrown out documents that the FTC requested as part of the investigation, and it intentionally marked emails privileged and confidential to escape scrutiny. It refused to provide the results of an internal investigation to a congressional sub-committee even though it risked a criminal referral.

In recent years, it had begun heavily using encrypted chat messaging apps for sensitive discussions, including those surrounding antitrust and mergers and acquisitions. "Amazon executives systematically and intentionally deleted internal communications using the 'disappearing message' feature of the Signal messaging app. Amazon prejudicially destroyed more than two years' worth of such communications—from June 2019 to at least early 2022—despite Plaintiffs instructing Amazon not to do so," the FTC said.

Amazon posted a lengthy response on its blog, and general counsel Zapolsky said: "The lawsuit filed by the FTC today is wrong on the facts and the law, and we look forward to making that case in court." The company felt that they could justify the behaviors that were being questioned: they had required Amazon's FBA program for Prime inclusion to ensure fast shipping to customers, and they recently reintroduced Seller Fulfilled Prime. They also argued that they featured the lowest prices on Amazon in order to offer customers low prices. But the truth was, inside Amazon, senior executives have long worried about the exact dynamics presented in the case, sources told me.

The FTC was coy about what a proper remedy for the described transgressions would be. Khan evaded questions from reporters about whether the FTC wanted to break Amazon up. But deep within the complaint, for those reading closely enough, was the phrase "structural relief." The agency said that it was seeking "any preliminary or permanent equitable relief, including but not limited to structural relief, necessary to redress and prevent recurrence of Amazon's violations of the law." Structural relief means a breakup or divestiture in antitrust circles, and the FTC was pursuing that as an option. Some antitrust experts suggested that the FTC, for instance, could call for Amazon to spin off its logistics network.

The case was also remarkable for what it didn't include. The FTC's case was incredibly narrow in scope, and what's more, it didn't test newfangled legal theories. This was a pretty standard and narrow case focused on two main tactics. Amazon wouldn't be able to lean on its well-worn arguments about the value of Amazon Prime to rally its customers and garner outrage after all.

It seemed that Khan was a step ahead of the giant. Just a month earlier, Amazon Prime bundling was set to be a major complaint in this FTC lawsuit. The FTC was prepared to make the case that the company's program, with all of its perks and services, trapped customers in the Amazon ecosystem, creating a moat around customers. But the agency decided to scrap this in order to present a more winnable case.

The truth was, the losses did weigh on FTC staff. And the Amazon case, being Khan's white whale, had to be bulletproof. No one liked losing, but losing a case against Amazon would be an embarrassment. The concessions the agency made in what it pursued and it left out of its lawsuit are instructive.

The FTC during the course of its investigation found lots of potentially anticompetitive behavior that it could have included in its lawsuit. But it needed a cohesive argument that would resonate with the courts and ultimately pursued a case it felt it could win.

"The big omission I think in terms of things investigated by Khan and Congress is the store brands," said Adam Kovacevich, founder of the Chamber of Progress, a tech-backed trade group that works with Amazon. Kovacevich says it's possible that Amazon scaling back on private brands caused the FTC not to pursue it.

"I feel like Amazon wanted Lina to bring a novel, difficult case. They were banking on that. They wanted to play into every weird thing about her and [her] pushing the boundaries," said a longtime Khan ally. "So in a way it's genius to come within the accepted boundaries of antitrust enforcement."

Even so, Khan's critics and antitrust pundits had a field day with the lawsuit. They pointed out discrepancies between her original opus and what she ultimately filed. "After a sprawling investigation, the Federal Trade Commission on Tuesday voted 3-0 to sue Amazon in federal court for what amounts to offering low prices and fast service," declared the *Wall Street Journal* op-ed page, which had been one of Khan's harshest critics since she took over the agency.

I asked Khan's allies whether the lawsuit was a tacit admission that

Khan couldn't change the interpretation of antitrust laws. Was this a sign that she'd operate within the Borkian standards of antitrust enforcement? Or just a one-off more traditional case? They defended the chair, saying that the Amazon Khan wrote about in 2017 was building its monopoly by cutting prices to levels competitors couldn't compete with and putting rivals out of business. They said that today's Amazon was now a late-stage monopoly, and without the competition it had already eliminated, it could raise prices on customers and offer degraded services.

"Amazon is taking advantage of its power to squeeze consumers, more so than it was even just a few years ago. That's part of the stage of development of Amazon as the monopolist," explains Stacy Mitchell, who works at the Institute for Local Self-Reliance.

Amazon's march toward dominance in those early years when its prices *did* undercut the market left a graveyard of its competitors in its wake. With fewer competitors, the company could hike prices and offer frustrating experiences (the volume of ads in search results), and yet customers would still return. It could continually raise the price of its Prime program (in 2022, it raised the price of Prime from $119 to $139 a year). Amazon could now charge "monopoly rent" while still trading off of its earlier reputation as having the lowest prices.

Whether this was a winnable case depended on who you asked. The antitrust world had become increasingly partisan since Khan became chair, and antitrust experts had different views of the complaint. For one, in 2021 the District of Columbia sued Amazon for driving up prices by requiring that Amazon have the lowest prices on its platform. In 2022, Amazon was able to have that suit dismissed. While the FTC's complaint made a much stronger argument than the DC lawsuit, it had some similarities. (The dismissal of the DC suit didn't stop California from filing its own lawsuit against Amazon in 2022 alleging that Amazon's contracts with third-party sellers inflate prices, stifle competition, and violate the state's unfair competition laws.)

"I think it's a hard case for them to win," says Bilal Sayyed, former director of the Office of Policy Planning at the Federal Trade Commission. "My thinking is low probability of success."

"The complaint dwells expansively on how the challenged

restrictions had the effect of raising the prices that consumers paid for products sold on the Amazon platform. That theory of harm is a pillar of the 'consumer welfare' framework," said William Kovacic, a former Republican chairman of the FTC. "The FTC is not saying that Amazon's conduct had no other adverse consequences, but the price effect is the injury featured most prominently." He called it "a winnable case, but a difficult case to win."

———

Amazon's S-Team was meeting at the company's Seattle offices the day the lawsuit was filed. As the meeting let out, CEO Andy Jassy pulled general counsel David Zapolsky aside. He asked what Amazon's top legal executive made of the case. Zapolsky thought the FTC case was misguided.

That night, after a full day of media briefings, Khan had dinner with members of the Federalist Society, a conservative group of lawyers that had a prominent role in recommending Supreme Court candidates who ended up on the bench, as well as other judges who fill out the judiciary across the nation.

Khan's invitation to meet in a private room of a DC restaurant and talk about antitrust with the Federalist Society was both interesting and curious. It's important to acknowledge that the lawsuit will ultimately be determined by the courts. Many judges had been shaped by the post-Borkian views of legal precedent. But the fact that one of the most prominent conservative legal groups was hosting the chair as their guest and was interested in listening to her views suggested a glimmer of hope for the FTC.

———

In early November, Amazon held a company-wide meeting. The session takes place at a large auditorium at Amazon's Seattle headquarters a few times a year and is streamed to employees around the world. Usually, different business leaders give updates on their initiatives, from speedier delivery to climate goal progress, and then S-Team members answer audience questions.

As it was taking place just weeks after the company had been sued, the second question Andy Jassy addressed was what Amazon's position on the lawsuit was. He called general counsel Zapolsky up to the stage. Wearing an olive-green sweater over a button-down with blue jeans, a salt-and-pepper-haired Zapolsky stepped up to offer his perspective.

"These theories that the FTC brought, they're not new. They've been kicking around a while. A couple of these theories have already been kicked out of the courts," he said referring to the dismissed DC attorney general's lawsuit.

Zapolsky made no mention of the punitive behavior from Amazon when sellers offer a lower price elsewhere, but instead spun the narrative. "The FTC takes issue with us refusing to show prices that are higher than what our biggest competitors are showing," he told the crowd. "If somebody lists at Amazon and it's at a higher price than what Walmart's selling it at, they can sell it on Amazon. We let customers buy it. But we don't feature it. We don't put it in the front of our shop window. We don't put it in our featured offer box. We think that's absolutely fair. We'd rather lose an individual sale than a customer because a customer loses trust in the way we price."

Zapolsky said he looked forward to presenting Amazon's defense in court. As to how Amazon's employees should think about the lawsuit in the interim, he offered some interesting advice. "Amazon is this heavily scrutinized company, and you read the papers and sometimes it can be a bummer. And when your relatives call and say 'what's this headline we see about the FTC?' you really have to adopt the Tao of Taylor Swift," he told the audience. Then, he recited some lyrics: "Haters gonna hate, you gotta shake it off." The crowd burst into laughter.

Before stepping off the stage, he told the audience: "We like our facts. We think this case is wrong on the law and the facts. We'll see them in court."

Epilogue

ANTITRUST LAWSUITS DO NOT move quickly. It will likely take years for us to know the verdict. Regardless of the outcome, it's worth wondering if the damage has already been done.

Amazon's dominance has not lessened despite numerous regulatory investigations into the company's business practices. The company has only gained more power, forging ahead into more industries. As I was reporting for this book, Amazon acquired 1Life Healthcare, a primary-care practice better known as One Medical. It means that my doctor's office, and all of my corresponding data, labs, and other charts, are now owned by Amazon.

Its power continues to grow. Amazon also did what was once thought impossible — it surpassed both UPS and FedEx to become the biggest delivery business in the US by parcel volume. It is now the largest nongovernmental parcel carrier in the country. But with so much scrutiny on the company, such milestones are no longer glorified as they once were. Instead, executives celebrated quietly and got back to work. Quiet or not, unseating UPS and FedEx speaks to the allegations in the FTC's lawsuit — sellers feel compelled to use Amazon's logistics to be part of Fulfillment by Amazon, routing ever more parcels through Amazon's own warehouses.

Amazon's market value took a dip after the pandemic as the explosive pace of online growth slowed, and it furiously laid off workers and adjusted its businesses to meet the demand dips. But the company has since stabilized. It's again worth more than $1.5 trillion.

Consider how difficult it would be to avoid the conglomerate for a week if you tried. If you call a Lyft or stream on Netflix, you are within their ecosystem. Both companies use Amazon Web Services. If you buy a Peloton bike, there's a good chance that Amazon will deliver it. Going to watch the new James Bond film? Amazon now owns MGM, which has a giant film catalog, including the Bond films. Three-fourths of people who use a robotic vacuum cleaner in North America use the iRobot Roomba. Amazon agreed to buy iRobot in 2022, creating concerns that the company would soon have detailed data about the insides of customers' homes, since it "maps" spaces through its technology. It was yet another incursion that began with Alexa. (In this case, scrutiny from the European Commission caused Amazon to abandon the acquisition in early 2024.) Amazon has indeed become the daily habit that its founder envisioned.

———

Many of the main architects of Amazon's dominance have left the company in recent years. Dave Limp, Jay Carney, Jeff Blackburn, Dave Clark, and Jeff Wilke have all left to pursue other ventures. Even Jeff Bezos is now executive chairman, as Jassy runs the company as CEO. These days, the billionaire seems to spend more time on his $500 million megayacht than on Amazon's day-to-day operations. He even announced that he is permanently leaving Seattle—a city synonymous with Amazon—to relocate to Miami. Even so, the culture Bezos created persists. A drive to win—and survive—trumps all else. Its unforgiving nature, talent review, and promotion system remain in place. Employees, regardless of how brilliant, still feel as if they're auditioning for their job daily, and feeling expendable continues to be a problem. The culture continues to cultivate patterns of behavior that enable bad actors who want to gain an edge, or cut corners, in order to stay employed. Jassy's edict that Amazon could one day be worth $10 trillion is proof enough that the company still lives by its founder's mentality that "your margin is my opportunity."

As Amazon finds more opportunities and continues to grow, the future hangs in the balance. It's already done so much to reshape our daily lives and upend the economy; it's transformed Main Street and how we behave. Where we go from here is anyone's guess, but it's impossible to ignore what Amazon has achieved in industry after industry, and what that means for the rest of us.

By now, the jig is up. Companies can no longer underestimate Amazon's size and power. It is an 800-pound deterrent to would-be competitors. Every industry it enters it can transform, become a market leader, and scare off others from attempting to enter the space. The rate of new business formation in the US has fallen by nearly 50 percent since the 1970s, as large businesses like Amazon make it harder for entrepreneurs to find success in certain markets.

Even if the FTC wins its lawsuit and if it were to break up Amazon, the pieces themselves are market leaders in their own right. And that's assuming the FTC manages to break them up. Consider what happened after the breakup of Standard Oil. The individual companies spun out actually *increased in value*. The sum may be worth more than the whole, or the whole may continue to grow. While it's impossible to forecast the future, the impact of Amazon on our daily life — and on this century — has already been substantial. They may be in a war now, but they've also arguably won a larger war.

Acknowledgments

ANYONE WHO WRITES A book knows it takes a village. As a first-time author, I learned that adage holds true, and this undertaking would not have been possible without the numerous people who helped edit, produce, and guide this book.

I am eternally grateful for my killer editor, the indefatigable Pronoy Sarkar, who was in the trenches with me on this project from start to finish. He is a dream editor who improves everything he touches. Many thanks to the team at Little, Brown, including Lena Little, Anna Brill, Michael Noon, Maria Espinosa, and Lucy Kim. I was lucky to work with Eric Lupfer, my tireless agent, who also was a great sounding board, first read, and constant source of great ideas when we first set out to shape this narrative.

My immense gratitude to my amazing *Wall Street Journal* colleagues and editors who helped report some of the stories that made up the backbone of this book and deftly edited them. They include Jason Dean, Brad Olson, Scott Austin, Matthew Rose, Mitch Pacelle, Steve Yoder, Cara Lombardo, Patience Haggin, Joe Flint, Shane Shifflett, Sebastian Herrera, Jim Oberman, and Brent Kendall. Thank you to Matt Murray and Jamie Heller, who were extremely supportive when I told them that I wanted to dig into the black box that is Amazon while living across the country in New York.

I had the most thoughtful and helpful first readers of this book. In addition to my husband, they included my father-in-law, Kirk Walker,

Emily Glazer (who gave feedback during maternity leave!), David Benoit, and Caroline Walker. I am so thankful for their input and advice along the way.

I am grateful for being connected with Paul Sliker, who has done a masterful job on publicity for this book. Ben Kalin did a truly expert and extremely thorough fact check. All errors are my own.

Friends and colleagues have written brilliant books of their own and were kind enough to lend me their tips about the process. They include Maureen Farrell, Eliot Brown, Rob Copeland, Tom Gryta, Ted Mann, Joann Lublin, Brody Mullins, Liz Hoffman, Zeke Faux, Tripp Mickle, William Cohan, and Melissa Korn.

My sources trusted me with their stories and internal documents at great risk to their own careers. I admire their bravery, and I could not have written this book without their involvement. Other thanks are owed to Doug Melamed, Daniel Francis, Amanda Lewis, Matt Stoller, and Richard White, among many others, for their guidance on certain parts of the book. Special thanks to Miriam Placide.

I am tremendously lucky to have loving and supportive parents, Dianne and Joe, who have always fostered my curiosity. They are my biggest cheerleaders and a source of inspiration. My mother set the most amazing example of how to be a badass working mother, and my father instilled a healthy dose of skepticism in me, which probably helped lead to my career path where I question everything. I am blessed beyond measure to be their daughter.

My son, Beckett, was with me every step of this way. I wrote parts of this book on my couch early in my pregnancy and finished it while he was a toddler old enough to (often) say "Mama writing big, long book" while sneaking off with my antitrust research books. I hope he'll be proud to read this book one day.

Last but certainly not least, there's a good chance that without the support, love, and motivation of my husband, this book would have lived as a Google document on my computer forever. He pushed me to put the book into the world and was my first reader and a constant support system throughout. Thank you, Whit.

Notes

PROLOGUE

xi   **Amazon is the titan:** Lina M. Khan, "Amazon's Antitrust Paradox," *Yale Law Journal* 126, no. 3 (January 2017): 564–907.

xii   **a third of all online shopping:** Sara Lebow, "Amazon Will Capture Nearly 40% of the US Ecommerce Market," Insider Intelligence, March 23, 2022.

xiv   **"The only goal that should guide":** Robert H. Bork, *Antitrust Paradox* (Basic Books, 1980).

xiv   **By the late 1880s:** Daniel Yergin, *The Prize: The Epic Quest for Oil, Money, and Power* (Simon & Schuster, 1991).

xv   **He was also accused of spying:** *Standard Oil Company of New Jersey et al., Appts., v. United States*, https://www.law.cornell.edu/supremecourt/text/221/1.

xv   **Its bribing of rail officials:** Ida M. Tarbell, *The History of the Standard Oil Company*, vol. 2 (Alpha Editions, 2020).

xvi   **trading at a 372 forward price-to-earnings ratio:** Data provided by FactSet, https://factset.com.

xvi   **a 15,189 percent total shareholder return:** Daniel Goleman, "The Best-Performing CEOs in the World," *Harvard Business Review*, November 2014.

CHAPTER 1: WHAT MAIN STREET DIDN'T SEE COMING

4   **the number of malls in America:** "U.S. Marketplace Count and Gross Leasable Area by Type," International Council of Shopping Centers, January 3, 2023.

6   **Fewer than 23 percent of Americans:** Jennifer Cheeseman Day, Alex Janus, and Jessica Davis, "Computer and Internet Use in the United States: 2003," US Census Bureau, Current Population Reports P23-208, October 2005.

8   **The projections for internet:** "Amazon CEO Jeff Bezos on *The David Rubenstein Show*," *The David Rubenstein Show*, YouTube, September 13, 2018.

8   **"Anything growing that fast":** "Amazon CEO Jeff Bezos on *The David Rubenstein Show*."

8 **"Jeff, this is a really good idea"**: "Amazon CEO Jeff Bezos on *The David Rubenstein Show*."

8 **He also told Bezos that D. E. Shaw**: Peter de Jonge, "Riding the Wild, Perilous Waters of Amazon.com," *New York Times Magazine*, March 14, 1999.

8 **"The idea was always that someone"**: De Jonge, "Riding the Wild, Perilous Waters of Amazon.com."

9 **a 70 percent chance**: Brad Stone, *The Everything Store* (Little, Brown and Company, 2013).

9 **Bezos typed the first version**: David Sheff, "The Playboy Interview: Jeff Bezos," *Playboy*, February 1, 2000.

10 **In 1994, only 3 percent of Americans**: "Americans Going Online...Explosive Growth, Uncertain Destinations," Pew Research Center, October 16, 1995.

10 **"one of the iffiest business propositions"**: G. Bruce Knecht, "Wall Street Whiz Finds Niche Selling Books on the Internet," *Wall Street Journal*, May 16, 1996.

11 **a device made of baking pans**: "Jeff Bezos: 'Cleverness Is a Gift, Kindness Is a Choice,' Princeton — 2010," Speakola, May 30, 2010.

11 **he even used a screwdriver**: John Cook, "Jeff Bezos's Mom: 'I Knew Early on That He Was Wired a Little Bit Differently,'" *GeekWire*, May 8, 2011.

11 **being at the beginning of the alphabet ensured**: Sheff, "The Playboy Interview: Jeff Bezos."

12 **Most angel investors committed**: John Cook, "Jeff Bezos Had to Take 60 Meetings to Raise $1 Million for Amazon, Giving Up 20% to Early Investors," *GeekWire*, December 1, 2013.

12 **In November, Bezos called Alberg**: Tom Alberg, *Flywheels: How Cities Are Creating Their Own Futures* (Columbia University Press, 2021).

CHAPTER 2: GROWTH OVER PROFITS

16 **Amazon had $12,438 in sales**: Robert Spector, *Amazon.com: Get Big Fast* (HarperCollins, 2002).

17 **Friends pointed out that *relentless***: Brad Stone, *The Everything Store: Jeff Bezos and the Age of Amazon* (Little, Brown, 2013).

18 **Orders came in from every state**: Spector, *Amazon.com.*

18 **"We had very low expectations"**: Spector, *Amazon.com.*

19 **Amazon started the year with around a dozen employees**: Spector, *Amazon.com.*

20 **"a pretty penny for a firm"**: "Amazon.com High on IPO. So Is Its Valuation," *Wired*, March 26, 1997.

21 **The investors warned of competition**: Kara Swisher, "Amazon.com CFO Sells Investors on the Merits of Losses for Years," *Wall Street Journal*, March 25, 1999.

21 **one of the year's largest IPOs**: "Special Report — Year-End Review of Markets & Finance — *WSJ* Interactive Edition." *Wall Street Journal*, n.d.

22 **"Quattrone told Bezos"**: Ari Levy, "How Jeff Bezos Convinced Frank Quattrone to Add Another $2 to Amazon's IPO Price, Recalls John Doerr," CNBC, May 15, 2017.

22 **Amazon would price at $18**: Ari Levy, "How Jeff Bezos Convinced Frank Quattrone to Add Another $2 to Amazon's IPO Price, Recalls John Doerr," CNBC, May 15, 2017.

23 **"Selection and price are important"**: "Amazon.com Announces New Pricing and Twice as Many Titles," AboutAmazon.com press release, March 17, 1997.

23 **"It was so scary"**: Mathias Döpfner, "Jeff Bezos Interview with Axel Springer CEO on Amazon, Blue Origin, Family," *Business Insider*, April 28, 2018.

24 **One of the responses that stuck**: "Amazon CEO Jeff Bezos on *The David Rubenstein Show*," YouTube, September 13, 2018.

25 **accounting for about 40 percent of the company's inventory**: Amazon 1998 Annual Report.

26 **"Well, Mr. Bezos"**: Doreen Carvajal, "Bookstore Goliaths Fax to the Finish," *New York Times*, November 9, 1998.

26 **He was valued at $1.6 billion**: Hayley C. Cuccinello, "Jeff Bezos through the Ages: The World's Richest Person in Photos," *Forbes*, October 1, 2019.

27 **"We will continue to make investment decisions"**: Jeff Bezos, "2020 Letter to Shareholders," About Amazon, April 15, 2021.

27 **stock price fell by more than 90 percent**: Andrew Davis, "At One Point, Amazon Lost More Than 90% of Its Value. But Long-Term Investors Still Got Rich," CNBC, December 18, 2018.

27 **"Cement," she said**: Swisher, "Amazon.com CFO Sells Investors on the Merits of Losses."

30 **His profile in *Time* encapsulates**: Joshua Cooper Ramo, "Jeffrey Preston Bezos: 1999 Person of the Year," *Time*, December 27, 1999.

30 **"There is no hype here"**: Dawn Kawamoto, "eBay Roars into Public Trading," CNET, January 2, 2002.

31 **Amazon launched an online auction site**: Mark Leibovich, "Amazon to Offer Auctions," *Washington Post*, March 30, 1999.

33 **"You name it, Amazon will sell it"**: Joshua Quittner, "Person of the Year: An Eye on the Future," *Time*, December 27, 1999.

CHAPTER 3: "THE INVASION OF THE MBAS"

35 **He urged attendees to think**: James Marcus, *Amazonia: Five Years at the Epicenter of the Dot.com Juggernaut* (New Press, 2004).

36 **In 1987, they won the state title**: "Jeff Blackburn," Concord-Carlisle High School Athletic Hall of Fame, n.d., http://www.cchshalloffame.org/blackburn.html.

36 **"Ever since I was a little boy"**: "Jeff Blackburn."

39 **"Under the flag of customer obsession"**: James Jacoby, dir., "Amazon Empire: The Rise and Reign of Jeff Bezos," *PBS Frontline*, February 18, 2020.

40   **years of Amazon's use of stack ranking:** Katherine A. Long, "Internal Amazon Documents Shed Light on How Company Pressures Out 6% of Office Workers," *Seattle Times*, June 21, 2021.

46   **Toys "R" Us flagged four thousand toys:** Mylene Mangalindan, "How Amazon's Dream Alliance with Toys 'R' Us Went So Sour," *Wall Street Journal*, January 23, 2006.

47   **"We are at a point in the relationship":** Mangalindan, "How Amazon's Dream Alliance with Toys 'R' Us Went So Sour."

CHAPTER 4: SPREADING ITS TENTACLES

48   **"The first realization we had":** "Fireside Chat with Michael Skok and Andy Jassy: The History of Amazon Web Services." Harvard Innovation Labs. October 21, 2013.

49   **"Look, I know you guys think":** "Fireside Chat with Michael Skok and Andy Jassy."

49   **"What they were building didn't scale":** "Fireside Chat with Michael Skok and Andy Jassy."

50   **"That was a big realization for":** "Amazon Web Services CEO Andy Jassy, Full Interview, Code 2019," Recode, June 10, 2019.

50   **Jassy asked the S-Team to provide:** "Fireside Chat with Michael Skok and Andy Jassy."

50   **At just thirty-five years old:** "Fireside Chat with Michael Skok and Andy Jassy."

51   **"There were lots of times afterward":** Jake Swearingen, "How Amazon Web Services Reinvented the Internet and Became a Cash Cow," *New York Magazine*, November 26, 2018.

52   **In the 1960s, low interest rates:** Nicholas Gilmore, "The Forgotten History of How 1960s Conglomerates Derailed the American Dream," *Saturday Evening Post*, November 1, 2018

53   **acquired more than 350 companies:** "Our History," ITT, n.d., https://www.itt.com/about/history.

53   **It had a bank division, GE Capital:** Thomas Gryta and Ted Mann, "The Long Shadow of GE Capital Looms over GE," *Wall Street Journal*, March 25, 2018.

53   **Jack Welch, the company's late CEO:** Jason Zweig, "GE and the Belief in Management Magic," *Wall Street Journal*, November 13, 2021.

54   **made over seven hundred acquisitions:** Robert Frank and Robin Sidel, "Firms That Lived by the Deal Are Now Sinking by the Dozens," *Wall Street Journal*, June 6, 2002.

55   **"To reverse its years of underperformance":** "Hedge Fund Third Point Pushes UTC to Split into 3 Businesses — Letter," Reuters, May 4, 2018.

55   **Within a year of the breakup:** Daniel Yergin, *The Prize* (Simon & Schuster, 1991).

56   **The heir to Samsung was arrested:** Matt Stevens, "Samsung Heir Elevated to Chairman after Jail Stint," *New York Times*, October 27, 2022.

56 **"We know we are under-owned"**: Thomas Gryta, "'The End of the GE We Knew': Breakup Turns a Page in Modern Business History," *Wall Street Journal*, November 9, 2021.

56 **"The notion of plugging financial services"**: Thomas Gryta and Ted Mann, "GE Powered the American Century—Then It Burned Out," *Wall Street Journal*, December 14, 2018.

62 **data is now ascribed a higher value than oil**: "The World's Most Valuable Resource Is No Longer Oil, but Data," *The Economist*, May 6, 2017.

65 **it spent nearly $850 million**: Nick Wingfield, "Amazon Opens Wallet, Buys Zappos," *Wall Street Journal*, July 23, 2009.

66 **In 2010, Quidsi planned to ship**: "Amazon Scoops Up High-Volume Diaper Company Quidsi," *SFGate*, November 9, 2010.

67 **"Moms are one of the most important"**: "Internal Report Regarding Marketing to Students and Moms" (internally annotated), 2010, internal Amazon document.

68 **Bezos's underlings ordered up**: "Diapers.com—looked at them ever?" February 9, 2009, Amazon internal email, https://democrats-judiciary.house .gov/uploadedfiles/00151722.pdf.

68 **He included a transcript of his**: "Benchmarking—Diapers.com," May 12, 2009, Amazon internal email, https://democrats-judiciary.house.gov/uploadedfiles /00142833.pdf.

68 **"More evidence these guys are our 1 competitor"**: Doug Herrington to Tom Furphy et al., "FW Diapers.com - looked at them ever?," February 9, 2009, https://democrats-judiciary.house.gov/uploadedfiles/00151722.pdf.

69 **"more aggressive 'plan to win'"**: "FW: Soap.com," June 8, 2010, Amazon internal email, https://democrats-judiciary.house.gov/uploadedfiles/00132026.pdf.

69 **Amazon lost $200 million selling diapers**: "Diaper Customer P&L," Amazon.com internal report, n.d., https://democrats-judiciary.house.gov /uploadedfiles/00000001.pdf.

69 **"What Amazon did was against the law"**: Dana Mattioli, "How Amazon Wins: By Steamrolling Rivals and Partners," *Wall Street Journal*, December 22, 2020.

71 **"We had a vision of what we wanted"**: Mark Lore, interview with Tony Gonzalez, *Wide Open with Tony Gonzalez* (podcast), November 11, 2019.

71 **The FTC was in the process**: Brad Stone, *The Everything Store: Jeff Bezos and the Age of Amazon* (Little, Brown, 2013).

75 **the company began working on it in 2012**: Jeff Bezos, *Invent and Wander: The Collected Writings of Jeff Bezos* (Harvard Business Press, 2020).

CHAPTER 5: IN YOUR HOME

77 **it has sold more than 487 million books**: Danny McLoughlin, "Amazon Kindle, E-book, and Kindle Unlimited Statistics," WordsRated, November 10, 2022.

78 **internal Amazon emails show**: Email chain regarding the acquisition of Ring, released by Congress, November 1, 2017.

80 **"They just take money from their monopoly business":** Janko Roettgers, "Sonos CEO says Amazon Is Breaking the Law by Selling Echo Smart Speakers below Cost," *Protocol*, August 5, 2020.

80 **with more than 109,000 customers:** Brad Stone, *Amazon Unbound: Jeff Bezos and the Invention of a Global Empire* (Simon & Schuster, 2021).

80 **many consumers preferred using their Echo speakers:** Sara Perez, "Siri Usage and Engagement Dropped since Last Year, as Alexa and Cortana Grew," *TechCrunch*, July 11, 2017.

80 **the biggest voice-enabled speaker:** Sara Perez, "Amazon to Control 70 Percent of the Voice-Controlled Speaker Market This Year," *TechCrunch*, May 8, 2017.

81 **more than 87 million Echo devices:** Michael Levin and Josh Lowitz, "Amazon Echo—Who Owns How Many?" Consumer Intelligence Research Partners, September 20, 2022.

81 **more than 500 million Alexa-enabled devices:** "Amazon Introduces Four All-New Echo Devices; Sales of Alexa-Enabled Devices Surpass Half a Billion," AboutAmazon.com press release, May 17, 2023.

83 **The company lost more than $5 billion:** Dana Mattioli, Jessica Toonkel, and Sebastian Herrera, "Amazon, in Broad Cost-Cutting Review, Weighs Changes at Alexa and Other Unprofitable Units," *Wall Street Journal*, November 10, 2022.

84 **"There was a cacophony of voices":** Spencer Rascoff, "Sonos' John MacFarlane: Never Be Satisfied," *dot.LA*, July 3, 2018.

84 **sold more than a million Echo devices:** Stone, *Amazon Unbound*.

87 **his great-aunt was the inspiration:** Rob Kuznia, "South Bay's Chet Pipkin May Be the Most Famous Tech Mogul to Come from Hawthorne," *Daily Breeze*, August 8, 2011.

88 **nearly 4,700 Amazon employees had unauthorized access:** Simon Van Dorpe, "Amazon Knew Seller Data Was Used to Boost Company Sales," *Politico*, April 30, 2021.

88 **Amazon's general counsel David Zapolsky was aware:** Van Dorpe, "Amazon Knew Seller Data Was Used."

90 **In late 2017, Amazon was launching an update:** Dana Mattioli and Joe Flint, "How Amazon Strong-Arms Partners Using Its Power across Multiple Businesses," *Wall Street Journal*, April 14, 2021.

91 **The Canadian company said no:** Mattioli and Flint, "How Amazon Strong-Arms Partners Using Its Power across Multiple Businesses."

92 **Seventy percent of shoppers don't scroll:** "FTC Sues Amazon for Illegally Maintaining Monopoly Power," Federal Trade Commission, November 2, 2023, https://www.ftc.gov/system/files/ftc_gov/pdf/1910134amazonecommerce complaintrevisedredactions.pdf.

94 **Roku would submit a list:** Dana Mattioli, Patience Haggin, and Shane Shifflett, "Amazon Restricts How Rival Device Makers Buy Ads on Its Site," *Wall Street Journal*, September 22, 2020.

94 the *Journal's* tests: Mattioli, Haggin, and Shifflett, "Amazon Restricts How Rival Device Makers Buy Ads on Its Site."

95 More than 50 percent of product searches: Brian Connolly, "Is Selling on Amazon FBA Worth It in 2023?" Jungle Scout, September 27, 2023.

95 Emails in 2017 between Amazon's management team: Email from Allen Parker to Brian Olsavsky re: Ring and Blink, October 11, 2017, released by Congress, https://democrats-judiciary.house.gov/uploadedfiles/00214132 .pdf.

95 "To be clear, my view here": Email from Jeff Bezos to Dave Limp re: Ring, December 15, 2017, released by Congress, https://democrats-judiciary.house .gov/uploadedfiles/00173560.pdf.

96 The advertising team apologized: Mattioli, Haggin, and Shifflett, "Amazon Restricts How Rival Device Makers Buy Ads on Its Site."

96 Google said in December: Jack Nicas, "Google Pulls YouTube from Amazon Devices, Saying It Isn't Playing Fair," *Wall Street Journal*, December 5, 2017.

96 "Groupon is blocked": Email chain discussing blocking Groupon and e-commerce competitors, released by Congress, December 20, 2010.

CHAPTER 6: VENTURE CAPITAL OR CORPORATE ESPIONAGE?

99 "So I was turned into a venture investor": Ingrid Lunden and Brian Heater, "Alexa Fund's Paul Bernard Talks OpenAI, What's Catching His Eye, and Remaining Relevant as Amazon Restructures," *TechCrunch*, January 24, 2023.

99 Sequoia Capital turned a roughly $60 million investment: Ryan Lawler, "Sequoia's a Big Winner in Facebook's WhatsApp Acquisition, with Its Stake Worth about $3 Billion," *TechCrunch*, February 19, 2014.

111 Nucleus chose to settle: Dana Mattioli and Cara Lombardo, "Amazon Met with Startups about Investing, Then Launched Competing Products," *Wall Street Journal*, July 23, 2020.

112 "They asked for our customer list": Mattioli and Lombardo, "Amazon Met with Startups about Investing."

112 "We may have been naïve": Mattioli and Lombardo, "Amazon Met with Startups about Investing."

112 Amazon's cloud computing unit launched: Mattioli and Lombardo, "Amazon Met with Startups about Investing."

112 She stopped filling them in: Mattioli and Lombardo, "Amazon Met with Startups about Investing."

113 an Amazon product manager even tweeted: Will Ahmed, "On Competition," LinkedIn post, 2023, https://www.linkedin.com/posts/willahmed_a-story -in-4-parts-activity-7058529344142372864-8tHO.

114 "They are using market forces": Mattioli and Lombardo, "Amazon Met with Startups about Investing, Then Launched Competing Products."

CHAPTER 7: LOOPHOLES, POWER PLAYS, AND A BILLIONAIRE'S MEDIA GAMBLE

118 **He collected antique books:** Jeff Patch, "Amazon.com Lobbyist Has Full Cart of Issues," *Politico*, March 19, 2007.

119 **"I even investigated whether":** William C. Taylor, "Who's Writing the Book on Web Business?" *Fast Company*, October 31, 1996.

120 **A 2011 report by Credit Suisse:** Stu Woo, "Amazon Battles States over Sales Tax," *Wall Street Journal*, August 3, 2011.

120 **Between 1995 and early 2012:** Peter Elkind, "Amazon's (Not So Secret) War on Taxes," *Fortune*, May 23, 2013.

120 **State sales taxes took off:** "State Budgets Basics," Center on Budget and Policy Priorities, revised May 24, 2022.

120 **California, for instance:** Verne G. Kopytoff, "Amazon Takes Sales Tax War to California," *New York Times*, July 13, 2011.

120 **Texas sent Amazon a tax bill:** "Texas Sends Amazon.com a $269 Million Tax Bill," Reuters, October 22, 2010.

121 **up to 9 percent off:** "State and Local Sales Tax Rates, Midyear 2023," Tax Foundation, July 17, 2023.

121 **In the late 1960s, Sears's annual sales:** Suzanne Kapner, "Inside the Decline of Sears, the Amazon of the 20th Century," *Wall Street Journal*, October 31, 2017.

124 **amounting to $22 million:** Greta Cuyler, "Amazon Brings Jobs with New Robbinsville Facility," *Princeton Magazine*, holiday 2014.

124 **"Such deals generally result in lower tax revenues":** Mike Davis, "Robbinsville Entices Amazon Intermediary by Upping PILOT Incentive Plan," NJ.com, November 9, 2012.

124 **Christie said it could add:** "Amazon, Christie Reach Compromise on Sales Tax Collection," *NJBiz*, May 30, 2012.

124 **"Amazon's multi-million dollar investment":** "Amazon to Open Fulfillment Center in Robbinsville, Creating Hundreds of Jobs," AboutAmazon.com press release, January 8, 2013.

125 **The number of people employed:** "New Jersey's Retail Trade Industry Sector," New Jersey Department of Labor and Workforce Development, Office of Research and Information, Winter 2021–2022.

125 **By 2008, Amazon had physical locations:** Elkind, "Amazon's (Not So Secret) War on Taxes."

126 **In some years, that goal:** Shayndi Raice and Dana Mattioli, "Amazon Sought $1 Billion in Incentives on Top of Lures for HQ2," *Wall Street Journal*, January 16, 2020.

129 **print advertising revenue dropped:** Rick Edmonds, "State of the News Media 2013 Shows How Industry Is Responding to 'Continued Erosion' of Resources," Poynter, March 18, 2013.

129 **The industry was shrinking:** Erin Karter, "As Newspapers Close, Struggling Communities Are Hit Hardest by the Decline in Local Journalism," *Northwestern Now*, June 29, 2022.

130 **"The newspaper business is a declining business"**: Alex Shephard, "Warren Buffett Was a Terrible Newspaper Owner," *New Republic*, January 31, 2020.

131 **"If you're interested, I am"**: William Launder, Christopher S. Stewart, and Joann S. Lublin, "Jeff Bezos Buys *Washington Post* for $250 Million," *Wall Street Journal*, August 5, 2013.

131 **"We will need to invent"**: Jeff Bezos, "Jeff Bezos on Post Purchase," *Washington Post*, August 5, 2013.

CHAPTER 8: CRAFTING THE MESSAGE

132 **Amazon slowed the delivery**: David Streitfeld, "Hachette Says Amazon Is Delaying Delivery of Some Books," *New York Times*, May 8, 2014.

133 **Amazon was in a public dispute with**: Polly Mosendz, "Amazon Has Basically No Competition Among Online Booksellers," *Atlantic*, May 30, 2014.

134 **For example, the blowback**: Stephen Foley, "Malcolm Gladwell Criticises Amazon in Hachette Dispute," *Financial Times*, September 18, 2014.

134 **Amazon completely pulled books**: Brad Stone, "Amazon Pulls Macmillan Books over E-Book Price Disagreement," *New York Times*, January 29, 2010.

134 **Amazon PR didn't answer questions**: "Inside Amazon's Warehouse," *Morning Call*, September 18, 2011.

138 **Amazon would spend a record $16.1 million**: "Top Spenders," OpenSecrets.

138 **Amazon went from having little lobbying power**: "Amazon.com Lobbying Spend," OpenSecrets.

140 **"I'm here to celebrate"**: David Bienick, "Amazon Shows Off Massive, New Warehouse on South Coast," WCVB-TV, March 24, 2017.

141 **The *Times* interviewed more than a hundred**: David Streitfeld and Jodi Kantor, "Inside Amazon: Wrestling Big Ideas in a Bruising Workplace," *New York Times*, August 15, 2015.

142 **"Here's what the story didn't tell you"**: Jay Carney, "What the *New York Times* Didn't Tell You," Medium, October 19, 2015.

142 **"If I didn't internally take"**: "1.15: Celestial Navigation (with Jay Carney)," *The West Wing Weekly* (podcast), July 20, 2016.

143 **"Amazon's comms team readily employs"**: Ali Breland, "How Amazon Bullies, Manipulates, and Lies to Reporters," *Mother Jones*, June 25, 2021.

144 **a note in a draft version**: Jeffrey Dastin, Chris Kirkham, and Aditya Kalra, "The Amazon Lobbyists Who Kill U.S. Consumer Privacy Protections," Reuters, November 19, 2021.

147 **Trump claimed that Bezos believed**: "Trump Says Washington Post Owner Bezos Has 'Huge Antitrust Problem,'" Fox News, May 13, 2016.

148 **Bezos took direct aim**: Maya Kosoff, "Jeff Bezos: Peter Thiel Is 'a Contrarian,' and Contrarians 'Are Usually Wrong.'" *Vanity Fair*, October 20, 2016.

148 **Months earlier, Bezos had tweeted**: Jeff Bezos (@JeffBezos), "Finally trashed by @realDonaldTrump. Will still reserve him a seat on the Blue Origin rocket.

#senddonaldtospace http://bit.ly/1OpyW5N," Twitter, December 7, 2015, 6:30 p.m.

151 **When it came time for Bezos:** "Transcript: Trump's Introductory Remarks with Tech Executives." *Wall Street Journal*, December 14, 2016.

153 **Brian Ballard read Trump's:** Brody Mullins and Julie Bykowicz, "Florida Lobbyist Thrives in Trump-Era Washington," *Wall Street Journal*, October 21, 2020.

153 **Ballard's services became so in demand:** Mullins and Bykowicz, "Florida Lobbyist Thrives in Trump-Era Washington."

157 **Bezos's mobile phone rang:** Martin Baron, *Collision of Power: Trump, Bezos, and the Washington Post* (Flatiron Books, 2023).

158 **"When you can't answer something":** Monica Nickelsburg and Todd Bishop, "Q&A: Jay Carney on the Trump White House, Amazon Antitrust Scrutiny, and Working for Bezos," *GeekWire*, October 10, 2019.

158 **Irked his son:** Donald Trump Jr. (@DonaldJTrumpJr), "Hey @amazon So is it your companies [*sic*] official corporate position that the the [*sic*] thousands of Americans who work in the Trump Administration aren't 'patriots' because that's what your top spokesman (and former Obama hack) @JayCarney just said???" Twitter, October 10, 2019, 11:06 a.m.

CHAPTER 9: TECHLASH

160 **"what can only [be] called a religious conversion":** William Kolasky, "Aaron Director and the Origins of the Chicago School of Antitrust, Part II—Aaron Director: The Socrates of Hyde Park," *Antitrust* 35, no. 1 (Fall 2020): 101–106.

161 **Railroad, steel, and other industrial companies:** Alan Axelrod, *The Gilded Age: 1876–1912: Overture to the American Century* (Sterling Publishing, 2017).

161 **the front page of the:** "Making Artificial Ice," *New York Times*, July 3, 1890, https://timesmachine.nytimes.com/timesmachine/1890/07/03/103250764.html?pageNumber=1

161 **"Political evils and business":** "Politicians Becoming Alarmed." *New York Times*, July 4, 1890, https://timesmachine.nytimes.com/timesmachine/1890/07/04/103250892.html?pageNumber=1

162 **In 1850, prior to the Civil War:** "The Idle Rich," *American Experience*, PBS, n.d., https://www.pbs.org/wgbh/americanexperience/features/1900-idle-rich.

162 **"Morgan merged hundreds of steel firms":** Tim Wu, *The Curse of Bigness: Antitrust in the New Gilded Age* (Columbia Global Reports, 2018).

162 **The court sided with the federal government:** "The Northern Securities Case," Theodore Roosevelt Center, n.d., https://www.theodorerooseveltcenter.org/Learn-About-TR/TR-Encyclopedia/Capitalism-and-Labor/The-Northern-Securities-Case.

163 **"Join the empire, or face complete destruction":** Wu, *The Curse of Bigness*.

163 **"And nothing was too small":** Ida M. Tarbell, *The History of the Standard Oil Company*, vol. 2 (Alpha Editions, 2020).

163 **Standard Oil's market share grew:** Wu, *The Curse of Bigness*.

163 **"The company transported more than four-fifths of all oil"**: Daniel Yergin, *The Prize: The Epic Quest for Oil, Money, and Power* (Simon & Schuster, 1993).

164 **"It seems unwise, therefore, to construct rules"**: Robert H. Bork, *Antitrust Paradox: A Policy at War with Itself* (Basic Books, 1980).

165 **"significantly impair[ed] both competition"**: Bork, *The Antitrust Paradox*.

165 **"Business efficiency necessarily benefits consumers"**: Bork, *The Antitrust Paradox*.

166 **"Defendants were convicted not of injuring competition"**: Bork, *The Antitrust Paradox*.

168 **Cincinnati Northern Kentucky International Airport having two-thirds**: Phillip Longman and Lina Khan, "Terminal Sickness," *Washington Monthly*, March 1, 2012.

168 **Within an hour of the announcement**: Ethan Bronner, "Robert H. Bork, Conservative Jurist, Dies at 85," *New York Times*, December 19, 2012.

170 **Her dad worked as a management consultant**: Sheelah Kolhatkar, "Lina Khan's Battle to Rein in Big Tech," *New Yorker*, November 29, 2021.

171 **"I have stated my concerns"**: Donald J. Trump (@realDonaldTrump), "I have stated my concerns with Amazon long before the Election. Unlike others, they pay little or no taxes to state & local governments, use our Postal System as their Delivery Boy (causing tremendous loss to the U.S.), and are putting many thousands of retailers out of business!" Twitter, March 29, 2018, 7:57 a.m.

172 **a Russian fake news campaign**: "Report of the Select Committee on Intelligence, United States Senate, on Russian Active Measures Campaigns and Interference in the 2016 U.S. Election, Volume 2: Russia's Use of Social Media with Additional Views," Report 116-XX, n.d., https://www.intelligence.senate.gov/sites/default/files/documents/Report_Volume2.pdf.

172 **After the election**: National Intelligence Council, "Background to 'Assessing Russian Activities and Intentions in Recent US Elections': The Analytic Process and Cyber Incident Attribution," January 6, 2017, https://www.dni.gov/files/documents/ICA_2017_01.pdf.

172 **as many as 126 million Americans**: Mike Isaac, "Tech Executives Are Contrite about Election Meddling, but Make Few Promises on Capitol Hill," *New York Times*, October 31, 2017.

172 **"The epidemic of malicious fake news"**: Jessica Taylor, "'Lives Are At Risk,' Hillary Clinton Warns over Fake News, 'Pizzagate,'" NPR, December 8, 2016.

172 **"Mark Zuckerberg should pay"**: Jude Dry, "Hillary Clinton: Mark Zuckerberg 'Should Pay a Price' for Facebook Political Ads," *IndieWire*, November 2, 2019.

173 **Years later, Senator Elizabeth Warren**: Craig Timberg, Isaac Stanley, and Tony Romm, "Democratic Debate Underscores the Growing Animosity between the Party and Big Tech," *Washington Post*, October 16, 2019.

173 **"The firm harvested private information"**: Matthew Rosenberg, Nicholas Confessore, and Carole Cadwalladr, "How Trump Consultants Exploited the Facebook Data of Millions," *New York Times*, March 17, 2018.

173 **Chris Hughes, who co-founded Facebook:** Chris Hughes, "It's Time to Break Up Facebook," *New York Times*, May 9, 2019.

174 **"Facebook was a company that was incredibly popular":** Timberg, Stanley, and Romm, "Democratic Debate Underscores the Growing Animosity."

176 **"Microsoft unlawfully required":** "Justice Department Files Antitrust Suit against Microsoft for Unlawfully Monopolizing Computer Software Markets," Department of Justice press release, May 18, 1998.

177 **"Between 1970 and 1999":** Tim Wu, "What the Microsoft Antitrust Case Taught Us," *New York Times*, May 18, 2018.

177 **The EU fined Google:** Matina Stevis, "E.U.'s New Digital Czar: 'Most Powerful Regulator of Big Tech on the Planet,'" *New York Times*, September 10, 2019.

178 **98 percent of Amazon orders:** Amazon (eCommerce): Revised Redacted Complaint, November 2, 2023, https://www.ftc.gov/system/files/ftc_gov/pdf/1910134amazonecommercecomplaintrevisedredactions.pdf.

178 **Germany represented Amazon's largest market:** Jasmine Enberg, "Amazon around the World," Insider Intelligence, November 13, 2018.

178 **"Because of the many complaints":** David Reid, "Amazon Investigated by the German Antitrust Authority," CNBC, November 29, 2018.

178 **In 2022, Britain's competition watchdog:** Yadarisa Shabong, Radhika Anilkumar, Angus MacSwan, and Bernadette Baum, "Amazon Faces UK Probe over Suspected Anti-Competitive Practices," Reuters, July 6, 2022.

CHAPTER 10: WATERING FLOWERS IN ROTTEN SOIL

184 **In 2018, Amazon's ranking:** Dennis Green, "Amazon Reputation Falls in Annual Ranking," *Business Insider*, September 8, 2018.

186 **the number of small retailers fell:** Stacy Mitchell and Ron Knox, "Issue Brief: How Amazon Exploits and Undermines Small Businesses, and Why Breaking It Up Would Revive American Entrepreneurship," Institute for Local Self-Reliance, June 16, 2021.

190 **"We recently took a deeper look":** Jeff Wilke, "Small Businesses Reaching Customers around the World," AboutAmazon.com, May 3, 2018.

190 **net loss of 700,000 retail jobs:** "Prime Numbers: Amazon and American Communities," American Booksellers Association and Civic Economics, February 2019.

191 **If you offset the number:** Stacy Mitchell and Olivia LaVecchia, "Amazon's Stranglehold: How the Company's Tightening Grip Is Stifling Competition, Eroding Jobs, and Threatening Communities," Institute for Local Self-Reliance, November 2016.

191 **supporting more than one in four:** Mark Mathews, "Latest Study Shows Heightened Importance of Retail to the U.S. Economy," National Retail Federation, July 20, 2020.

191 **That's up from a 19 percent "take":** Stacy Mitchell, "Amazon's Monopoly Tollbooth in 2023," Institute for Local Self-Reliance, September 2023.

192 **access to Amazon's coveted Buy Box:** Dana Mattioli and Joe Flint, "How Amazon Strong-Arms Partners Using Its Power across Multiple Businesses," *Wall Street Journal*, April 14, 2021.

192 **Having a Prime badge triples a seller's sales:** Amazon (eCommerce): Revised Redacted Complaint, November 2, 2023, https://www.ftc.gov/system/files /ftc_gov/pdf/1910134amazonecommercecomplaintrevisedredactions.pdf.

193 **"There's a ramification for not using FBA":** Mattioli and Flint, "How Amazon Strong-Arms Partners."

195 **"It's literally like being held as a prisoner":** Dana Mattioli, "How Amazon Wins: By Steamrolling Rivals and Partners," *Wall Street Journal*, December 22, 2020.

198 **Nearly 100 percent of Fortem's sales:** Dana Mattioli, "Amazon Scooped Up Data from Its Own Sellers to Launch Competing Products," *Wall Street Journal*, April 23, 2020.

199 **The report also detailed that:** Mattioli, "Amazon Scooped Up Data."

204 **"going over the fence":** Mattioli, "Amazon Scooped Up Data."

205 **"Punishment and rewards":** Alfie Kohn, "Why Incentive Plans Cannot Work," *Harvard Business Review*, September–October 1993.

205 **Wells Fargo fired 5,300 employees:** "Wells Fargo—A Timeline of Recent Consumer Protection and Corporate Governance Scandals," Congressional Research Service, updated February 27, 2020.

207 **The data showed:** Mattioli, "Amazon Scooped Up Data."

207 **Killian said if that were the case:** Mattioli, "Amazon Scooped Up Data."

208 **pay Amazon a 15 percent commission:** Mitchell, "Amazon's Monopoly Tollbooth in 2023."

209 **over half of all online shopping searches** Sara Lebow, "Shoppers Start Their Product Search on Amazon," Insider Intelligence, August 9, 2022.

210 **When a customer on the app:** Jay Greene, "Amazon Tests Pop-Up Feature Touting Its Lower-Priced Products," *Wall Street Journal*, March 15, 2019.

211 **"We fought tooth and nail":** Dana Mattioli, "Amazon Changed Search Algorithm in Ways That Boost Its Own Products," *Wall Street Journal*, September 16, 2019.

212 **Orbitz stopped showing Mac users:** Dana Mattioli, "On Orbitz, Mac Users Steered to Pricier Hotels," *Wall Street Journal*, June 26, 2012.

213 **Amazon's lawyers interjected:** Mattioli, "Amazon Changed Search Algorithm."

213 **Variables added to the algorithm:** Mattioli, "Amazon Changed Search Algorithm."

213 **"This was definitely not a popular project":** Mattioli, "Amazon Changed Search Algorithm."

CHAPTER 11: AMAZON PROOFING

217 **the name "Amazon" was invoked:** Julie Verhage, Muyao Shen, and Justina Lee, "Executives Are More Worried about Amazon Than Trump Setbacks," Bloomberg, July 31, 2017.

218 **On the rumor, AMC's and Cinemark's stock:** Todd Wagner and Mark Cuban, "Movie Theater Stocks Drop on Report Amazon Is Going to Disrupt Their Industry Next," CNBC, August 16, 2018.

218 **meal kit maker Blue Apron's stock price:** Anita Balakrishnan, "Why Is Blue Apron (APRN) Stock Down? Amazon Files Meal-Kits Trademark," CNBC, July 17, 2017.

218 **Kroger's stock fell 8 percent:** Rani Molla, "Amazon's Whole Foods Buy Removed Nearly $22 Billion in Market Value from Rival Supermarkets," *Vox*, June 18, 2017.

218 **Amazon's market value rose:** Bob Pisani, "After Its Stock Pop, Amazon Will Get Whole Foods Essentially for Free," CNBC, June 16, 2017.

219 **Wall Street analysts peppered Merlo:** Sharon Terlep and Laura Stevens, "The Real Reason CVS Wants to Buy Aetna? Amazon," *Wall Street Journal*, October 27, 2017.

219 **Healthcare represented nearly 18 percent:** "National Health Expenditures 2017 Highlights," Centers for Medicare and Medicaid Service, n.d.

221 **Each year, Amazon holds an annual meeting:** Christina Farr, "Amazon Considering Online Prescriptions," CNBC, May 16, 2017.

222 **On October 11, 2017:** CVS Health Corporation, "S-4, Definitive Merger Proxy," January 4, 2018.

222 **On December 3, they announced:** CVS Health Corporation, "S-4, Definitive Merger Proxy."

222 **CVS's stock fell more than 7 percent:** Glenn Fleishman, "CVS Drops $6 Billion in Value the Day after Its Aetna Merger Was Approved," *Fortune*, October 11, 2018.

CHAPTER 12: LESS FRICTION, MORE SELLERS, MORE SALES (EVEN COUNTERFEITS)

231 **"four failed tests":** Alexandra Berzon, Shane Shifflett, and Justin Scheck, "Amazon Has Ceded Control of Its Site. The Result: Thousands of Banned, Unsafe or Mislabeled Products," *Wall Street Journal*, August 23, 2019.

231 **Amazon has said it isn't:** Alexandra Berzon, "How Amazon Dodges Responsibility for Unsafe Products: The Case of the Hoverboard," *Wall Street Journal*, December 5, 2019.

CHAPTER 13: IN THE ARENA

234 **$23 million in cash:** Beckie Strum, "Amazon CEO Jeff Bezos Buys D.C. House, Once a Museum," *Mansion Global*, January 12, 2017.

234 **Other renovations included twenty-five bathrooms:** Sam Dangremond, "Jeff Bezos Is Renovating the Biggest House in Washington, D.C.," *Town and Country*, April 4, 2019.

235 **It featured a limestone fireplace:** Dangremond, "Jeff Bezos Is Renovating."

235 **238 cities vied for the privilege:** Sara Salinas, "Amazon Narrows the List of Metro Areas for Its New Headquarters to 20," CNBC, January 18, 2018.

238 **"While we are on the subject":** Donald J. Trump (@realDonaldTrump), "While we are on the subject, it is reported that the U.S. Post Office will lose $1.50 on average for each package it delivers for Amazon. That amounts to Billions of Dollars. The Failing N.Y. Times reports that 'the size of the company's lobbying staff has ballooned,' and that…," Twitter, March 31, 2018, 8:45 a.m.

238 **the president even personally pressured:** Damian Paletta and Josh Dawsey, "Trump Personally Pushed Postmaster General to Double Rates on Amazon, Other Firms," *Washington Post*, May 18, 2018.

239 **Trump remained "obsessed" with Amazon and Bezos:** Jonathan Swan, "Trump Hates Amazon, Not Facebook," *Axios*, March 28, 2018.

239 **"He's wondered aloud":** Swan, "Trump Hates Amazon, Not Facebook."

239 **"improper pressure from President Donald J. Trump:** *Amazon Web Services, Inc., v. United States of America* bid protest, filed December 9, 2019.

CHAPTER 14: CONGRESS CALLS ON AMAZON

248 **"Shortly after taking this role":** Rebecca Klar, "David Cicilline Led the Fight against Big Tech. Here's What Comes Next," *The Hill*, March 19, 2023.

250 **"We do not use their individual data":** "Online Platforms and Market Power, Part 2: Innovation and Entrepreneurship," House Judiciary Committee, July 16, 2019, https://www.congress.gov/event/116th-congress/house-event/109793.

252 **His son went a similar but different route:** Jack Brook, "Going Up against Goliath," *Brown Alumni Magazine*, November–December 2020.

253 **He drives a Tesla:** Ashley Gold, "Cicilline Exit Interview: The Antitrust Champion on Leaving Congress," *Axios*, May 15, 2023.

253 **enjoyed oversized Dunkin' Donuts iced coffees:** Zachary Block, "On the Campaign Trail," *Brown Alumni Magazine*, September–October 2002.

253 **"I was a hustler":** Block, "On the Campaign Trail."

260 **"You can't help but look at a trillion-dollar company:"** Dana Mattioli, "How Amazon Wins: By Steamrolling Rivals and Partners," *Wall Street Journal*, December 22, 2020.

261 **"Raise your hand in the crowd":** Stephie G. Plante, "Democratic Debates 2020: Andrew Yang on Universal Basic Income and Saving Malls." *Vox*, August 1, 2019.

261 **Amazon general counsel David Zapolsky…hosted:** Nandita Bose, "Amazon and Big Tech Cozy Up to Biden Camp with Cash and Connections," Reuters, October 1, 2020.

261 **"Seriously, think of the change":** Jim Brunner, "Speaking at the 'House of Amazon,' Joe Biden Gently Raises Company's Role in Middle-Class Job Losses," *Seattle Times*, November 15, 2019.

CHAPTER 15: THE WORLD SHUTS DOWN AND AMAZON COMES OUT A WINNER

266 **"Everyone's worried about artificial intelligence":** Anna Palmer and Jake Sherman, "Politico Playbook: Inside Alfalfa," *Politico*, January 26, 2020.

266 **"Two stone cold losers":** Donald J. Trump (@realDonaldTrump), "Two stone cold losers from Amazon WP. Almost every story is a made up lie, just like corrupt pol Shifty Schiff, who fraudulently made up my call with Ukraine. Fiction!" Twitter, January 20, 2020, 1:48 p.m.

269 **Let's say you're at a big cocktail party:** Jeff Bezos (@JeffBezos), Instagram, February 6, 2020.

270 **In April, the White House ordered:** Justin Rohrlich, "Coronavirus Forces White House to Send Amazon Millions in New Business," *Quartz*, April 29, 2020.

271 **By July, his net worth was $189 billion:** Tom Huddleston Jr., "Jeff Bezos Added $13 Billion to His Net Worth in One Day — and That's a Record," *CNBC*, July 21, 2020.

271 **"total civilian employment":** "Unemployment Rises in 2020, as the Country Battles the COVID-19 Pandemic," Monthly Labor Review, Bureau of Labor Statistics, June 2021.

271 **During the first year of the pandemic:** Ruth Simon, "Covid-19's Toll on U.S. Business? 200,000 Extra Closures in Pandemic's First Year," *Wall Street Journal*, April 16, 2021.

273 **"I'll be out of business by then":** Dana Mattioli, "A Month Ago, They All Had Stable Jobs. Now They Want to Work for Amazon," *Wall Street Journal*, April 9, 2020.

275 **America's largest department store chains cut:** Abha Bhattarai, "Kohl's, Macy's, and Nordstrom Have Reported Steep Sales Drops during the Pandemic. Can They Win Back Shoppers?" *Washington Post*, April 16, 2021.

275 **Half a million of those jobs disappeared:** Paul Krugman, "Why Don't All Jobs Matter?" *New York Times*, April 17, 2017.

278 **"He's not smart, or articulate":** Paul Blest, "Leaked Amazon Memo Details Plan to Smear Fired Warehouse Organizer: 'He's Not Smart or Articulate,'" *Vice*, April 2, 2020.

279 **"Amazon's attempt to smear Chris Smalls":** Alexandria Ocasio-Cortez (@AOC), "Amazon's attempt to smear Chris Smalls, one of their own warehouse workers, as "not smart or articulate" is a racist & classist PR campaign. If execs are as concerned abt worker health & safety as they claim, then they should provide the full paid sick leave ALL workers deserve," Twitter, April 2, 2020, 8:42 p.m.

280 **"This is an action clearly justified":** William Mauldin and Alex Leary, "U.S. Tags Amazon Sites as 'Notorious Markets,'" *Wall Street Journal*, April 29, 2020.

281 **"This was unintentional":** "Questions for the Record for Amazon following the July 29, 2020, Hearing of the Subcommittee on Antitrust, Commercial, and Administrative Law, Committee on the Judiciary," Congress.gov, September 4, 2020, https://www.congress.gov/116/meeting/house/110883/documents/HHRG-116-JU05-20200729-QFR052.pdf.

284 **The team sleuthed through financial documents:** Dana Mattioli, "Amazon Demands One More Thing from Some Vendors: A Piece of Their Company," *Wall Street Journal,* June 29, 2021.

285 **Executives reasoned that the company's potential partners:** Dana Mattioli, "Amazon Demands One More Thing from Some Vendors: A Piece of Their Company," *Wall Street Journal,* June 29, 2021.

285 **"It took a lot of convincing":** Mattioli, "Amazon Demands One More Thing."

286 **"There was definitely a sense":** Mattioli, "Amazon Demands One More Thing."

286 **When it announced the deal in May 2016:** Mattioli, "Amazon Demands One More Thing."

CHAPTER 16: BEZOS (FINALLY) GOES TO WASHINGTON

292 **"Amazon had the biggest middle-finger-to-Congress approach":** Dana Mattioli, "Amazon's Washington Strategy Wins Few New Friends in the Biden Era," *Wall Street Journal,* March 10, 2022.

299 **Only thirty-five questions were directed:** "Lawmakers from Both Sides Take Aim at Big Tech Executives," *New York Times,* July 29, 2020.

300 **"Rockefeller Imitates a Clam":** Ron Chernow, *Titan: The Life of John D. Rockefeller, Sr.* (Vintage, 2004).

303 **donating more than $2.3 million:** OpenSecrets, "Top Contributors, federal election data for Joe Biden, 2020 cycle," March 22, 2021, https://www.opensecrets.org/2020-presidential-race/joe-biden/contributors?id=N00001669&src=c.

303 **"Companies that once were scrappy":** Subcommittee on Antitrust, Commercial, and Administrative Law of the Committee on the Judiciary of the House of Representatives, "Investigation of Competition in Digital Markets," July 2022, https://www.congress.gov/117/cprt/HPRT47833/CPRT-117HPRT47833.pdf.

CHAPTER 17: "TOO MUCH TOXICITY TO MAKE IT WORTHWHILE"

305 **"Very excited by the fact":** Jay Carney (@JayCarney), "Very excited by the fact that I'm going to need a new mousepad! #46, @JoeBiden!" Twitter, November 12, 2020, 6:56 p.m.

307 **liberals ranked Walmart:** Chris Matthews, "Here Are the Fortune 500 Companies Liberals and Conservatives Hate the Most," Yahoo Finance, June 6, 2016.

309 **"When the conflict is between working Americans":** Marco Rubio, "Sen. Marco Rubio: Amazon Should Face Unionization Drive without Republican Support," *USA Today,* March 12, 2021.

310 **"I welcome @SenSanders to Birmingham":** Dave Clark (@DavehClark), "I welcome @SenSanders to Birmingham and appreciate his push for a progressive workplace. I often say we are the Bernie Sanders of employers, but that's not quite right because we actually deliver a progressive workplace for our constituents," Twitter, March 24, 2021 (since deleted).

311 **"All I want to know":** Bernie Sanders (@BernieSanders), "I look forward to meeting with Amazon workers in Alabama on Friday. All I want to know is

why the richest man in the world, Jeff Bezos, is spending millions trying to prevent workers from organizing a union so they can negotiate for better wages, benefits and working conditions," Twitter, March 24, 2021, 9:52 p.m.

311 **"Paying workers $15/hr":** Mark Pocan (@RepMarkPocan), "Paying workers $15/hr doesn't make you a 'progressive workplace' when you union-bust & make workers urinate in water bottles," Twitter, March 24, 2021, 10:29 p.m.

312 **"You don't really believe":** Amazon News (@AmazonNews), "You don't really believe the peeing in bottles thing, do you? If that were true, nobody would work for us. The truth is that we have over a million incredible employees around the world who are proud of what they do, and have great wages and health care from day one," Twitter, March 24, 2021, 10:29 p.m.

313 **"You make the tax laws":** Amazon News (@AmazonNews), "1/3 You make the tax laws @SenWarren; we just follow them. If you don't like the laws you've created, by all means, change them. Here are the facts: Amazon has paid billions of dollars in corporate taxes over the past few years alone," Twitter, March 25, 2021, 8:46 p.m.

313 **"I didn't write the loopholes":** Elizabeth Warren (@SenWarren), "I didn't write the loopholes you exploit, @amazon — your armies of lawyers and lobbyists did. But you bet I'll fight to make you pay your fair share. And fight your union-busting. And fight to break up Big Tech so you're not powerful enough to heckle senators with snotty tweets," Twitter, March 25, 2021, 11:09 p.m.

314 **"This was an own-goal":** "Our Recent Response to Representative Pocan," AboutAmazon.com, April 2, 2021.

317 **"The two [President] Roosevelts":** Joe Biden, "Remarks by President Biden at Signing of an Executive Order Promoting Competition in the American Economy," White House, July 9, 2021.

317 **"Chair Khan has made numerous":** Recusal petition by Amazon.com, June 30, 2021.

320 **Previous audits of its private label business:** Dana Mattioli, "Amazon's Washington Strategy Wins Few New Friends in the Biden Era," *Wall Street Journal*, March 10, 2022.

321 **Instead, if the FTC decided:** Dana Mattioli, "Amazon Has Been Slashing Private-Label Selection amid Weak Sales," *Wall Street Journal*, July 15, 2022.

322 **"I got in a little trouble":** Joe Biden (@JoeBiden), "Chris Smalls is making good trouble and helping inspire a new movement of labor organizing across the country. Let's keep it going," Twitter, May 11, 2022, 12:59 p.m.

322 **"You want to bring down inflation?":** Joe Biden (@JoeBiden), "You want to bring down inflation? Let's make sure the wealthiest corporations pay their fair share," Twitter, May 13, 2022, 6:02 p.m.

322 **"The newly created Disinformation Board":** Jeff Bezos (@JeffBezos), "The newly created Disinformation Board should review this tweet, or maybe they need to form a new Non Sequitur Board instead. Raising corp taxes is fine to discuss. Taming inflation is critical to discuss. Mushing them together is just misdirection," Twitter, May 13, 2022, 10:56 p.m.

323 **The next day, the president tweeted:** Joe Biden (@POTUS), "Under my pre-decessor, the deficit increased every single year. This year, we're on track to cut the deficit by $1.5 trillion—the biggest one-year decline ever. It matters to families, because reducing the deficit is one of the main ways we can ease inflationary pressures," Twitter, May 14, 2022, 3:18 p.m.

325 **"There's not a lot of perceived value":** Dana Mattioli and Esther Fung, "The Biggest Delivery Business in the U.S. Is No Longer UPS or FedEx," *Wall Street Journal*, November 27, 2023.

326 **the companies would spend a whopping $100 million:** Rebecca Klar and Karl Evers-Hillstrom, "How Big Tech fought antitrust reform—and won," *The Hill*, December 23, 2022.

326 **Senator Hassan's chief of staff urged:** Adam Cancryn and Emily Birnbaum, "In Private, Vulnerable Senate Dems Back Off Tech Bill," *Politico*, May 26, 2022.

326 **Senator Michael Bennet's:** Adam Cancryn and Emily Birnbaum, "In Private, Vulnerable Senate Dems Back Off Tech Bill," *Politico*, May 26, 2022.

328 **a 2018 *New York Times* investigation:** Jack Nicas, "Delay, Deny and Deflect: How Facebook's Leaders Fought through Crisis," *New York Times*, November 14, 2018.

328 **It was signed by the Monopoly man:** Steven Nelson, "Schumer Confronted in DC by Anti–Big Tech Protesters Calling for Antitrust Vote," *New York Post*, July 26, 2022.

CHAPTER 18: THE FTC SUES AMAZON

334 **The agency's lawyers and experts advised:** Leah Nylen et al., "FTC's Khan Overruled Staff to Sue Meta over Virtual Reality Deal," Bloomberg, July 29, 2022.

334 **When the commissioners voted:** "FTC Seeks to Block Virtual Reality Giant Meta's Acquisition of Popular App Creator Within," Federal Trade Commission, July 27, 2022.

334 **the deal "would enable Microsoft to suppress competitors":** "FTC Seeks to Block Microsoft Corp.'s Acquisition of Activision Blizzard, Inc.," Federal Trade Commission, December 8, 2022.

335 **"In federal court [we] have lost two merger cases":** "FTC Chair on Consumer Protection and the Marketplace," C-SPAN, July 24, 2023.

335 **At the end of Khan's first year in office:** Cat Zakrzewski, "FTC Plunges in Workplace Rankings during Lina Khan's First Year," *Washington Post*, July 13, 2022.

335 **"I understand that Chair Khan":** Zakrzewski, "FTC Plunges in Workplace Rankings during Lina Khan's First Year."

337 **It cut twenty-seven of its thirty clothing brands:** Dana Mattioli, "Amazon Cuts Dozens of House Brands as It Battles Costs, Regulators," *Wall Street Journal*, August 10, 2023.

338 **That change caused many of Amazon's brands:** Mattioli, "Amazon Cuts Dozens of House Brands as It Battles Costs, Regulators."

339 **"My fundamental concern with her leadership":** Christine Wilson, "Why I'm Resigning as FTC Commissioner," *Wall Street Journal*, February 14, 2023.

344 **And it was big business:** Dana Mattioli, "Amazon Used Secret 'Project Nessie' Algorithm to Raise Prices," *Wall Street Journal*, October 3, 2023.

346 **"any preliminary or permanent equitable relief":** "Amazon, Inc.: Complaint for Relief," Federal Trade Commission, September 26, 2023.

347 **"After a sprawling investigation":** "Lina Khan Has a Weak Case against Amazon," *Wall Street Journal*, September 27, 2023.

EPILOGUE

352 **Three-fourths of people who use a robotic vacuum:** Dan Gallagher, "Amazon's Roomba Deal Has Shades of Fitbit," *Wall Street Journal*, August 5, 2022.

352 **"maps" spaces through its:** https://www.nytimes.com/2017/07/25/technology/roomba-irobot-dataprivacy.html.

353 **The rate of new business formation:** "Fact Sheet: Executive Order on Promoting Competition in the American Economy," White House, July 9, 2021.

Index

About the Author

DANA MATTIOLI has been a reporter for the *Wall Street Journal* since 2006. She has written investigative pieces and front-page stories about Amazon since 2019 and was a finalist for the Pulitzer Prize for Investigative Reporting for her work on Amazon. Her Amazon coverage also received the 2021 Gerald Loeb Award for Beat Reporting. In 2021, she received the WERT Prize, an award from the Women's Economic Round Table that honors excellence in comprehensively reported business journalism, for her Amazon investigations and received a Front Page Award for her Amazon coverage.

Prior to covering Amazon, Dana held one of the *WSJ*'s highest profile beats covering mergers and acquisitions. During her sixteen-year career at the *WSJ*, she has produced a string of investigations and page-one stories on CEOs, boards of directors, technology companies, and retailers. Dana is the recipient of a second Gerald Loeb award for breaking news, the SABEW breaking news award, and two New York Press Club awards and was a finalist for the Larry Birger Young Business Journalist Award. Dana has appeared on CNBC, *Good Morning America*, Fox Business News, and Cheddar. She was the subject of a *Wall Street Journal* advertisement campaign about how the newspaper's highest-profile stories came together.